I0763132

MUSEUM IN TRANSIT

10 Contemporary Artists in the NYC Subway

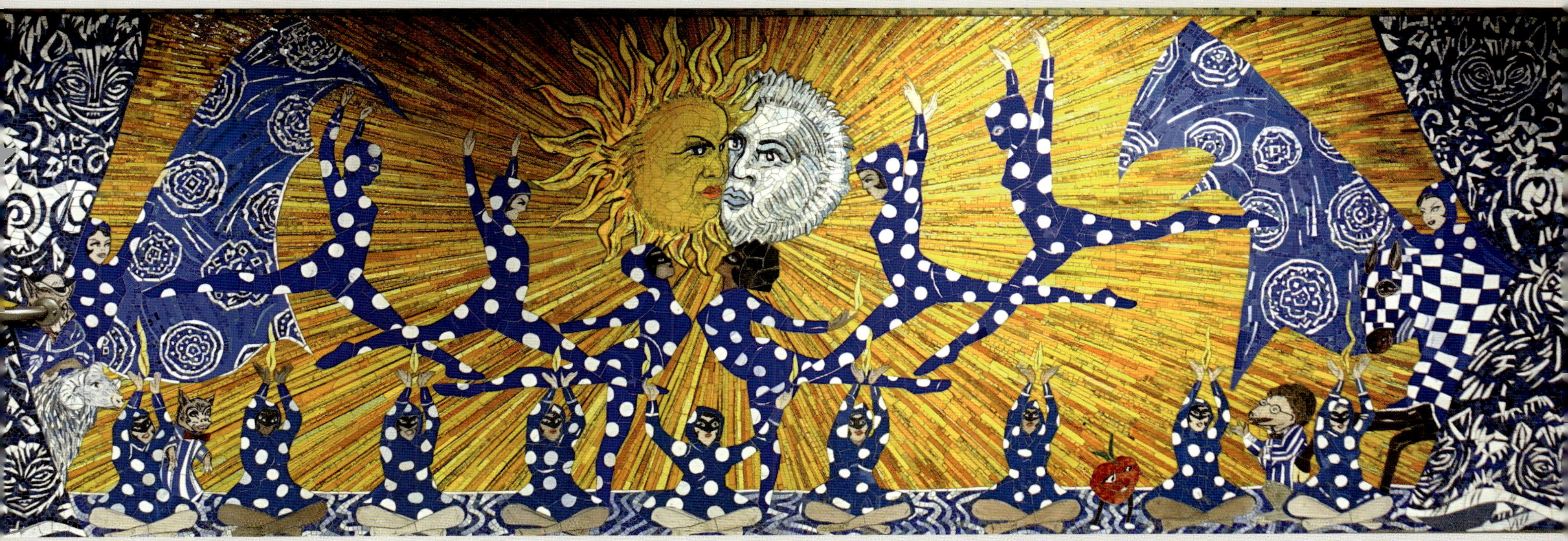

XHINGYU CHEN

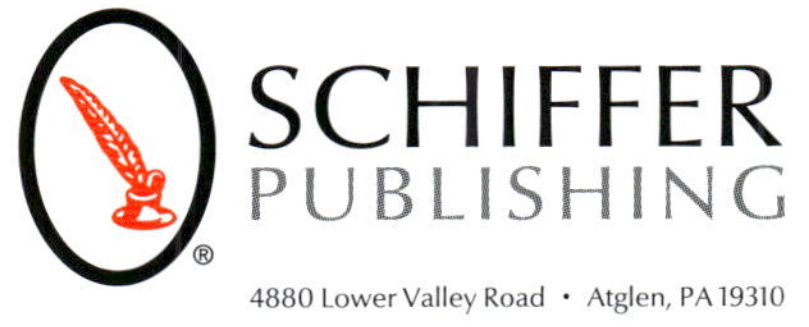

SCHIFFER
PUBLISHING
4880 Lower Valley Road • Atglen, PA 19310

Other Schiffer Books by the Author:
Chinese Artists: New Media, 1990–2010, 978-0-7643-3675-1

Library of Congress Control Number: 2025940095

Edited by Jesse J. Marth
Designed by Alexa Harris
Cover design by Molly Shields
Type set in Greycliff CF / Area

Image Credits
Cover: *People's Instinctive Travels: Homage to the Tribe*, 2019, by Eamon Ore-Giron, Bay Parkway (N Train), photo by Peter Peirce.
Title Page: *No Less Than Everything Comes Together*, 2021, by Marcel Dzama, Bedford Avenue (L Train).
Back Cover: *Revelers*, 2008, by Jane Dickson, Times Square Station.

ISBN: 978-0-7643-7104-2
ePub: 978-1-5073-0663-5

Printed in China
10 9 8 7 6 5 4 3 2 1

Published by Schiffer Publishing, Ltd.
4880 Lower Valley Road
Atglen, PA 19310
Phone: (610) 593-1777; Fax: (610) 593-2002
Email: info@schifferbooks.com
Web: www.schifferbooks.com

FSC
www.fsc.org
MIX
Paper | Supporting responsible forestry
FSC® C104723

Dedicated to my favorite travel and art companions,
Gabriel and Sacha

CONTENTS

INTRODUCTION

When it comes to art and culture, New York City is an embarrassment of riches. It is home to institutions that, like pop stars, go by one name: the Met, MoMA, the Whitney. There are numerous neighborhoods, each spanning multiple city blocks, dedicated to galleries. The city plays host to art fairs, festivals, open studio events, and other cultural events throughout the year. There is not one season for art; the whole city teems with artistic energy every single day. And yet, there is one place that has captured my imagination more than any gallery or museum: the subway.

Growing up in New York City, I was tangentially aware that some stations featured mosaics or sculptures, but I rarely questioned how they got there or who was behind them. That changed when artist Nick Cave's monumental mural for the 6th Ave. corridor in Times Square was unveiled in 2020. The presence of an artist of Cave's stature made me think twice about blithely walking by these artworks on my commute. What other treasures would this world underground reveal? Thus began a journey throughout the NYC subway system that has yielded some truly surprising finds.

There was celebrated performance artist Vito Acconci at Yankee Stadium, modern master Sol Lewitt at Columbus Circle, and legendary graphic designer Milton Glaser (the man behind the iconic "I Love New York" logo) at Astor Place. The journey also opened my eyes to artists I had little to no knowledge of– Korean American artist Ik-joon Kang at Main St / Flushing, pioneering land artist Mary Miss at Union Square, and textile artist Xenobia Bailey at Hudson Yards.

Public art can often be divisive. The "high art" camp will characterize some works, fairly or not, as pedestrian. The other side will lament that artists are too conceptual. Exploring the NYC subway system, I was happy to find that often these commissioned works straddled these opposing camps perfectly. It gave me the idea to investigate some of these artists further, exploring how each artist produced artworks with wide appeal while adhering to their personal vision.

This book is a result of that exploration, a look into the oeuvres of artists whom I admire, with their MTA Arts & Design commissioned work as the springboard. It is by no means a complete catalog of the MTA project; there are over 350 artworks throughout the system and more are added every year. Rather, these artists represent a wide spectrum of voices and disciplines with a keen eye for how their art can have maximum impact in the public sphere. The MTA project made me see artists in a different setting, creating a new way for me to explore these artists. That is what I set out to do with this book: introduce readers to a select group of artists through their public commission and dive deeper into their practice to give a retrospective view into their work. These are celebrated artists who have all exhibited in galleries and museums around the world but anyone can experience their works simply by riding the subway.

ABOUT MTA ARTS & DESIGN

The term "subway art" can cause some confusion for many who are unaware of the source of these permanent commissions. All the artists explored in this book were commissioned by MTA Arts & Design to create artwork for subway stations. MTA Arts & Design was created in 1985 as MTA Arts for Transit & Urban Design during a time when the subway system was undergoing broad improvements and new legislation (Percent for Art) mandated that 1 percent of all city-funded construction projects should include public art. The program harkened back to when the subway was first built 120 years ago; engineers and architects at the time believed that any structures built for public use should also be aesthetically pleasing. This was especially important for the subway, which intimidated would-be riders with its concrete-and-steel tunnels. Beautiful mosaics and soaring arches greeted commuters to ease fears and instill a sense of pride in their city.

The permanent artworks that I focus on are only one small part of a program that includes art for digital displays, photography and poster projects, a poetry program, and a music program where musicians audition to get a coveted performance spot in one of the many high-traffic stations. There are also permanent artworks in nonsubway stations on the Long Island Railroad and Metro North systems. MTA Arts & Design does not cover guerrilla interventions and graffiti art. Since its inception over three decades ago, the program has commissioned over 300 artists to create artwork throughout the system, with many more to come.

THE ARTISTS

Firelei Báez (b. 1981)

163rd ST. / AMSTERDAM AVENUE (C TRAIN)

***Ciguapa Antellana, me llamo sueño de la madrugada (who more sci-fi than us)*, 2018**

Firelei Báez is an artist who creates fantastical worlds informed by the traditions and folklore of her Dominican and Haitian roots. She often references the trauma and violence of a postcolonial world but overlays this political exploration with imagery drawn from the rich cultural traditions of Hispaniola; native flora and fauna, textiles, and elements of folk tales all figure in her paintings, sculptures, and large-scale installations. For *Ciguapa Antellana, me llamo sueño de la madrugada (who is more sci-fi than us)* at 163rd Street in Washington Heights, Báez creates lush landscapes dotted with cultural signifiers: Hand talismans hang from trees, an Afro pick grows out of a bush. They are also inhibited by *ciguapas*, mythical creatures from Dominican folklore that take female form and are covered by thick, long hair. *Ciguapas* are often characterized as wild, malevolent beings that wish to do harm on travelers, but in the artist's hands, they are magical, beautiful forms, as much a part of the jungle landscape as palms and birds of paradise. The title of the work is taken from Dominican American writer Junot Diaz's novel *The Brief Wondrous Life of Oscar Wao*, where *ciguapas* are referenced.

Courtesy of Firelei Báez Studio

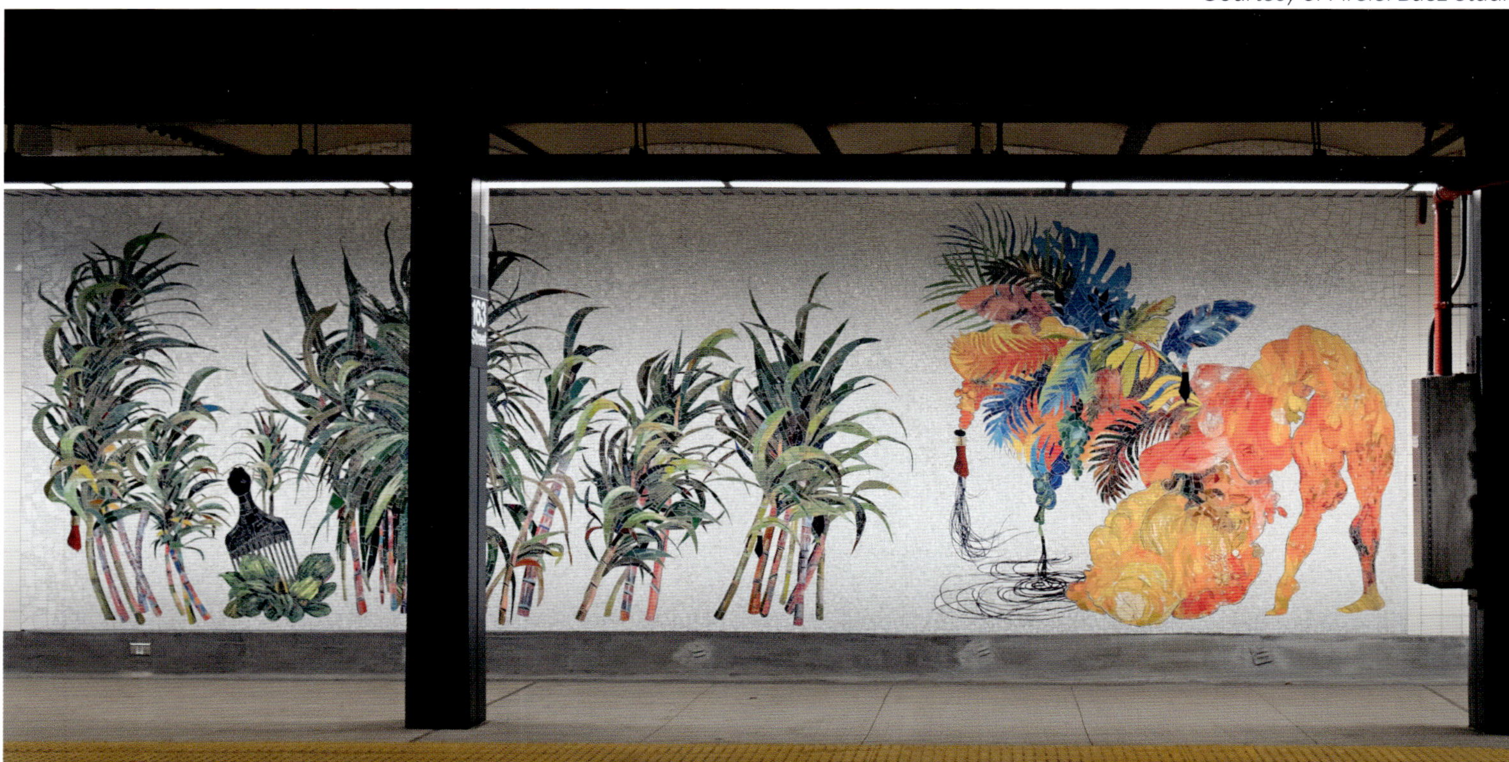

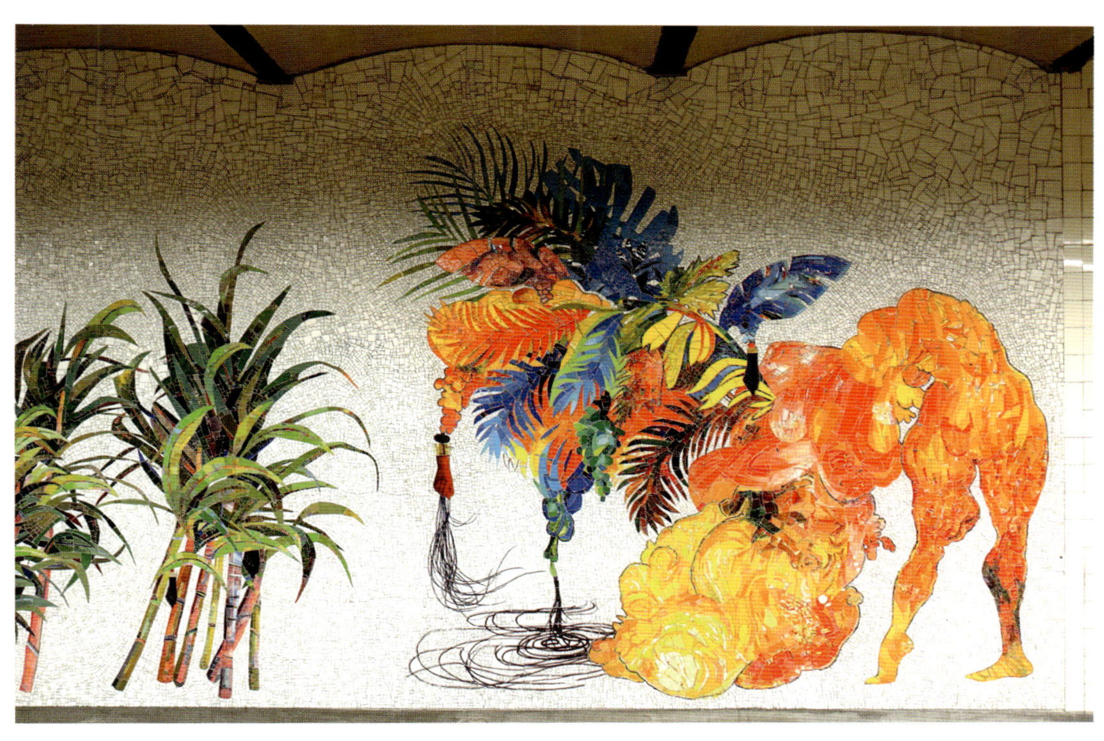

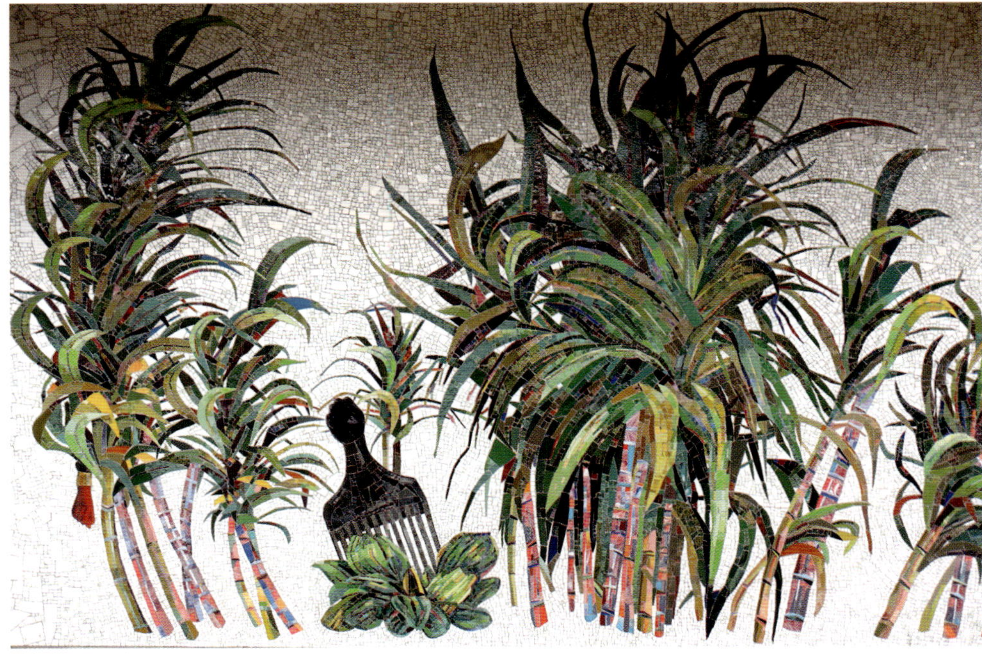

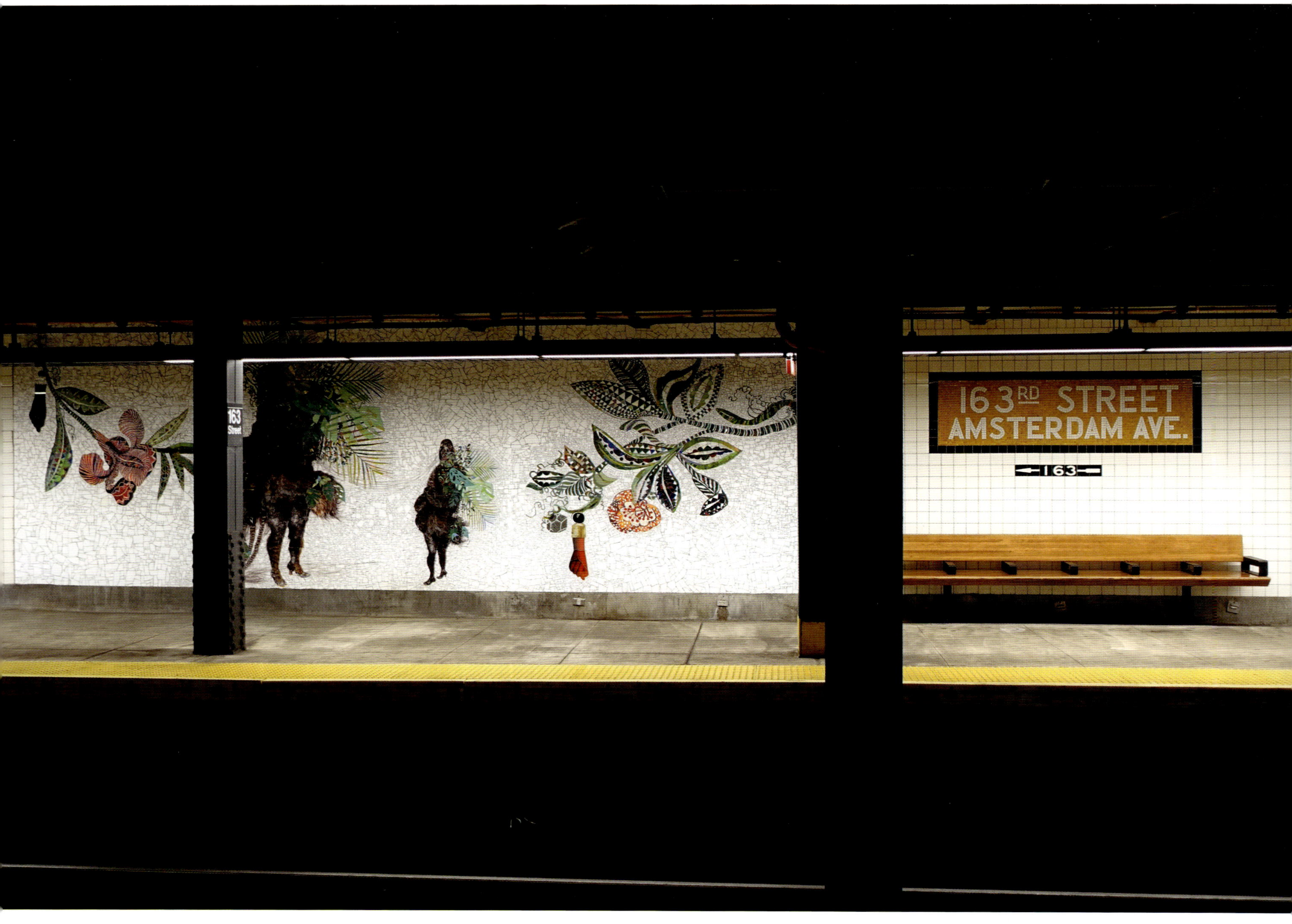
163RD STREET
AMSTERDAM AVE.
163
163
Street

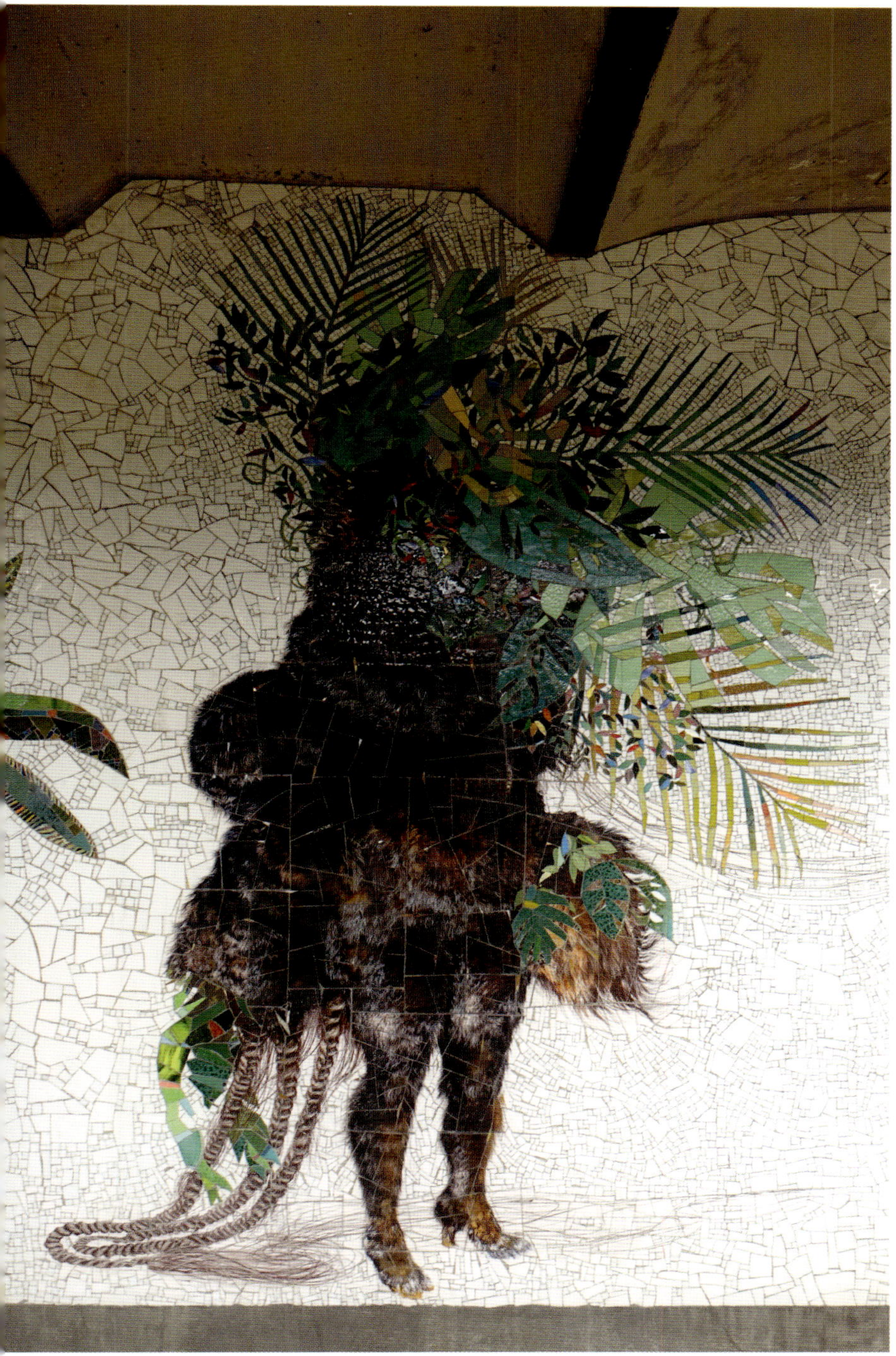

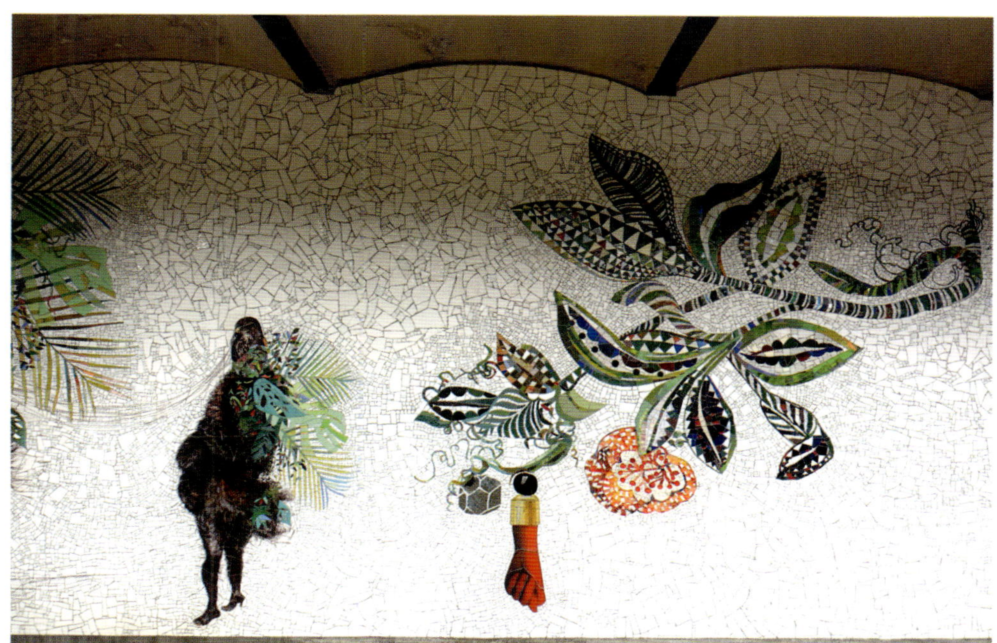

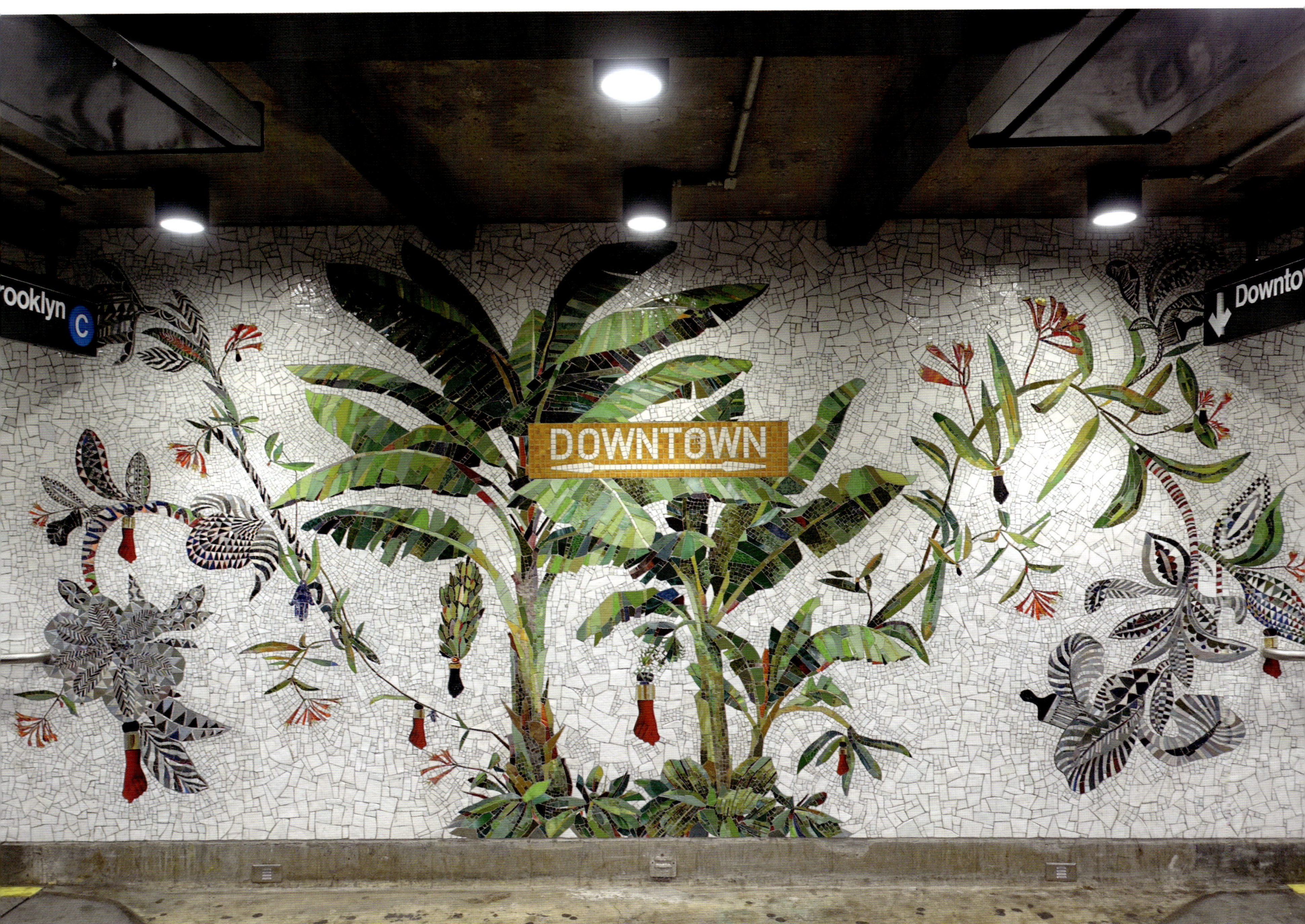
rooklyn C
DOWNTOWN
Downto

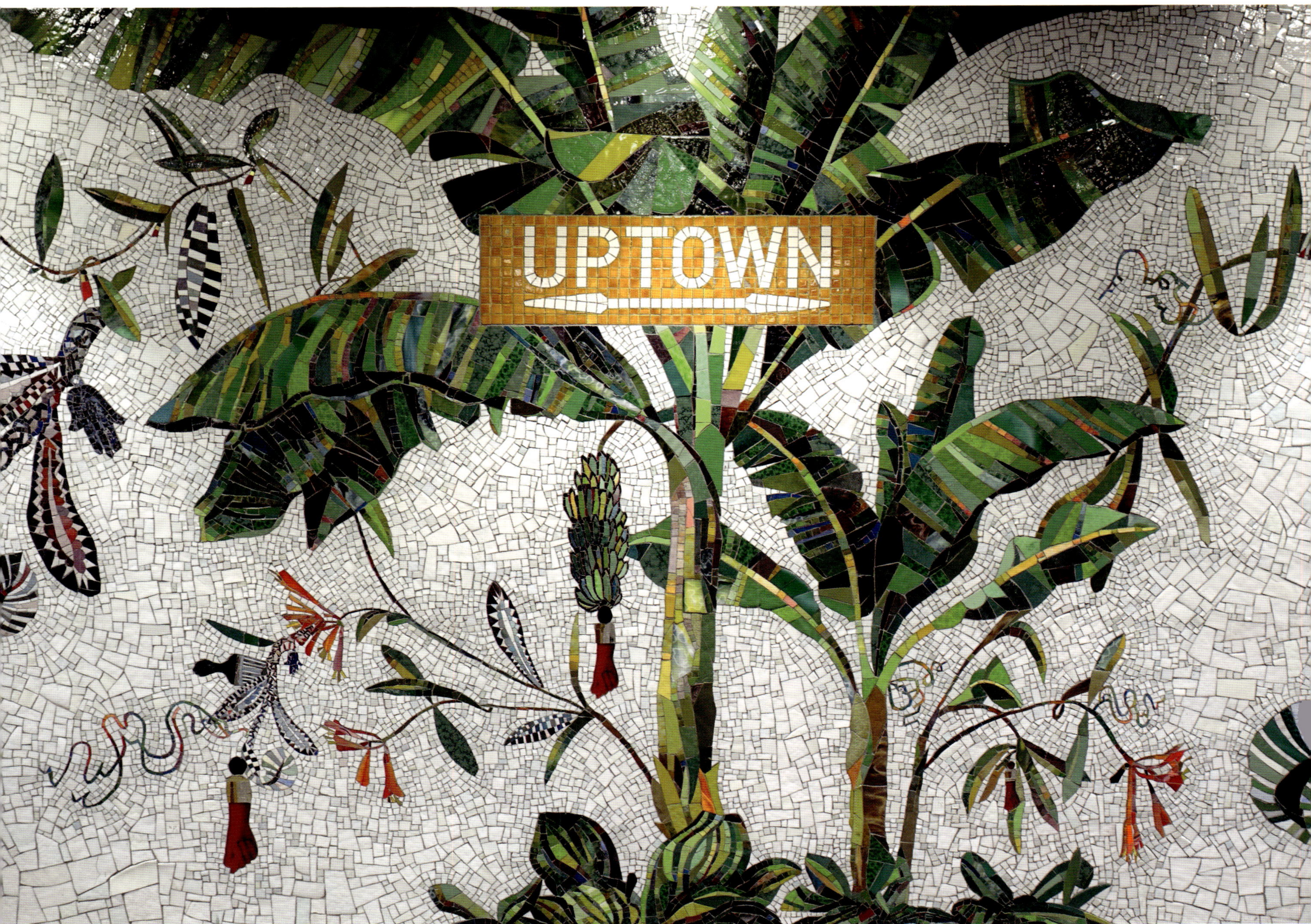
UPTOWN

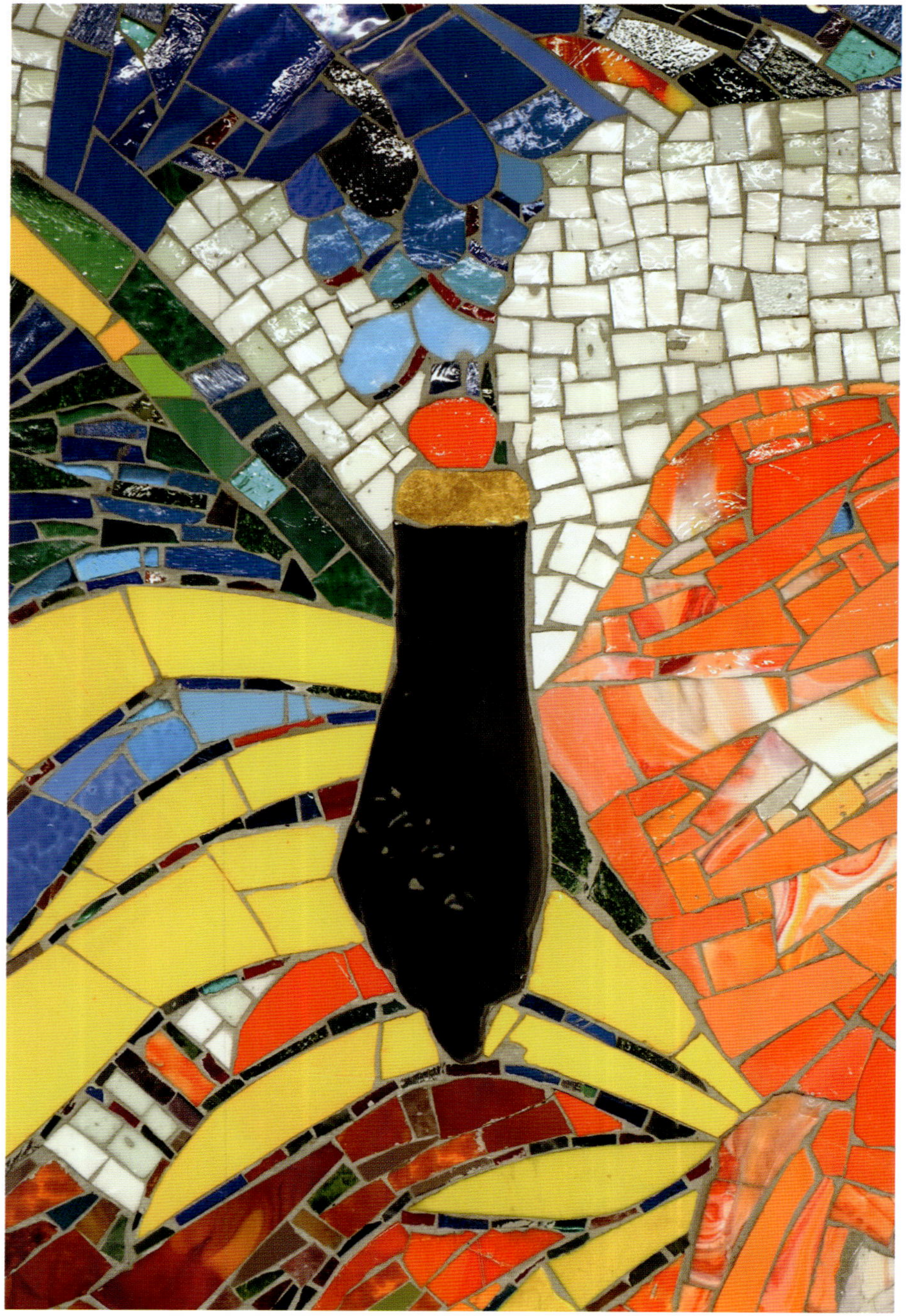

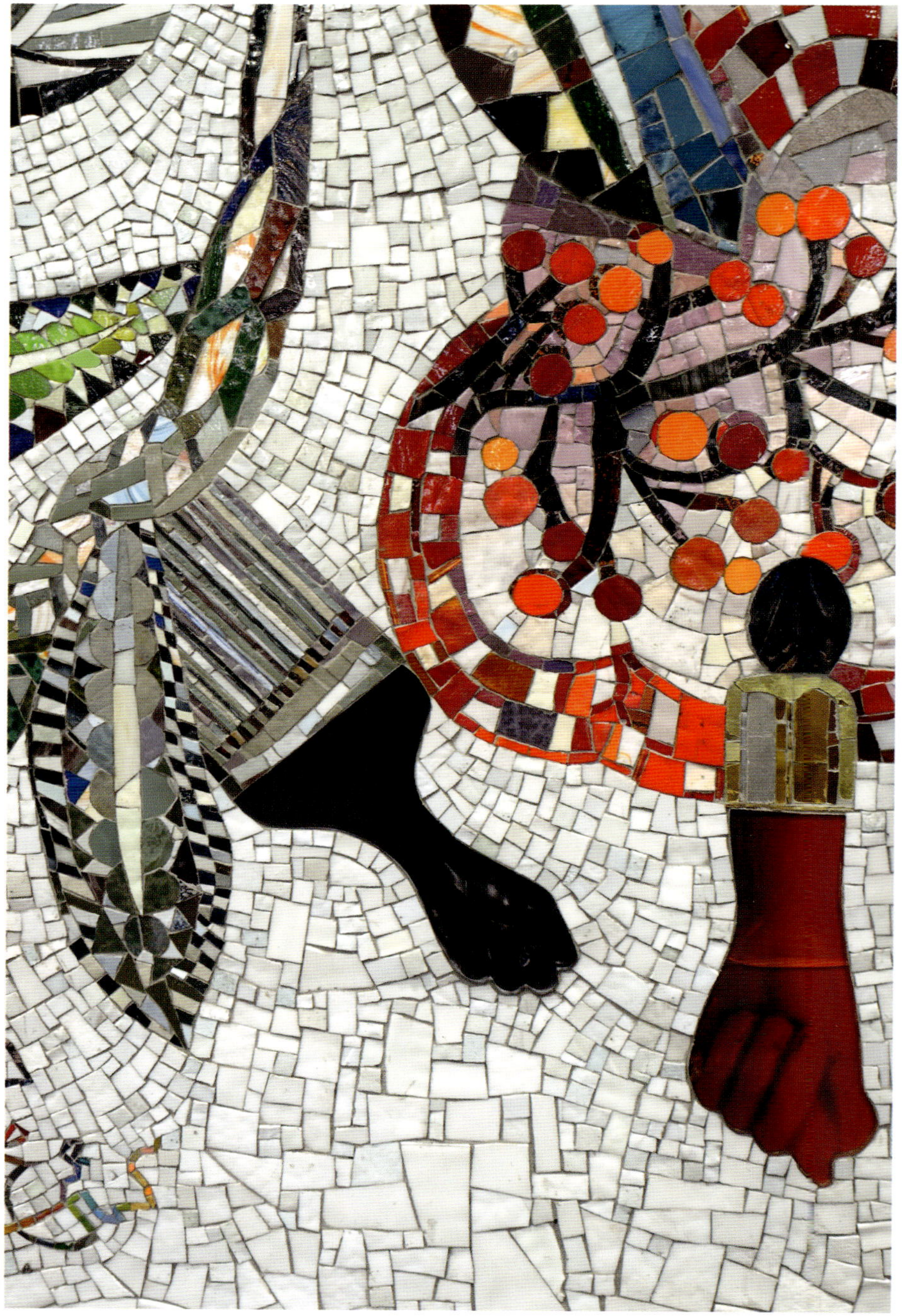

Báez is a student of history, particularly of the African diaspora, and often paints directly on old maps, architectural specs, political pamphlets, and newspapers. These archival sources are never read at face value; in fact, she often subverts the intentions of the source material, bringing to the forefront repressed or forgotten histories. In *Fruta Fina, Fruta Estraña (Lee Monument)*, luscious red fruits are intertwined with twisting ropes of hair; inspired by the Billie Holiday song about the lynchings of Black people, this "strange fruit" is overlaid on design specs for a monument to the Confederate general Robert E. Lee. Her exuberant use of color invites viewers closer before they are confronted with violent realities of the subject matter. Acutely aware of the complex cultural lineages of her own history, Báez mines the rich mythology and folklore of her background for much of the imagery she uses in her work. Those hand talismen that feature in her subway mosaic are called *manos de azabache* and are used to ward off negative energy and the evil eye. The mysterious *ciguapas* make appearances in many of her paintings and drawings, recast in her work as a bold affirmation of feminine power.

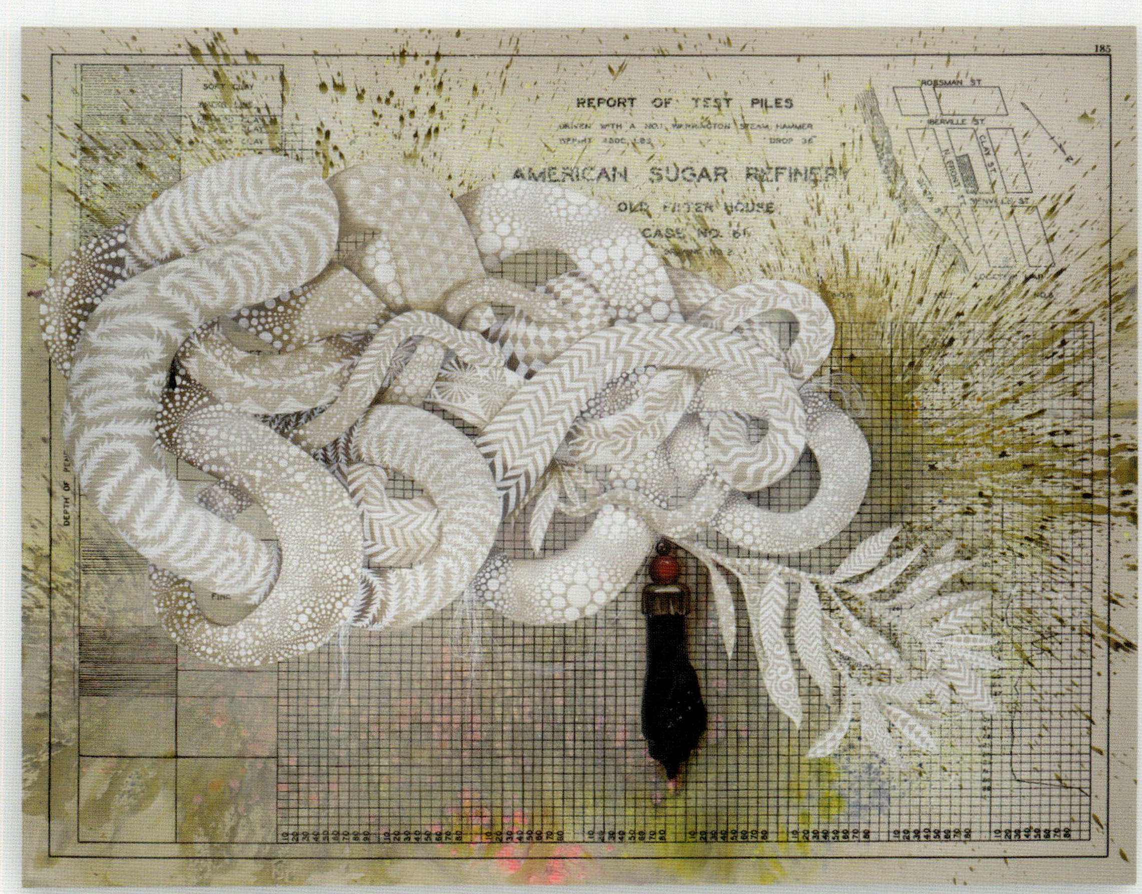

***Tignon for Ayda Weddo (or that which a center can not hold)*, 2019**
Oil and acrylic on printed canvas
Courtesy of Firelei Báez Studio

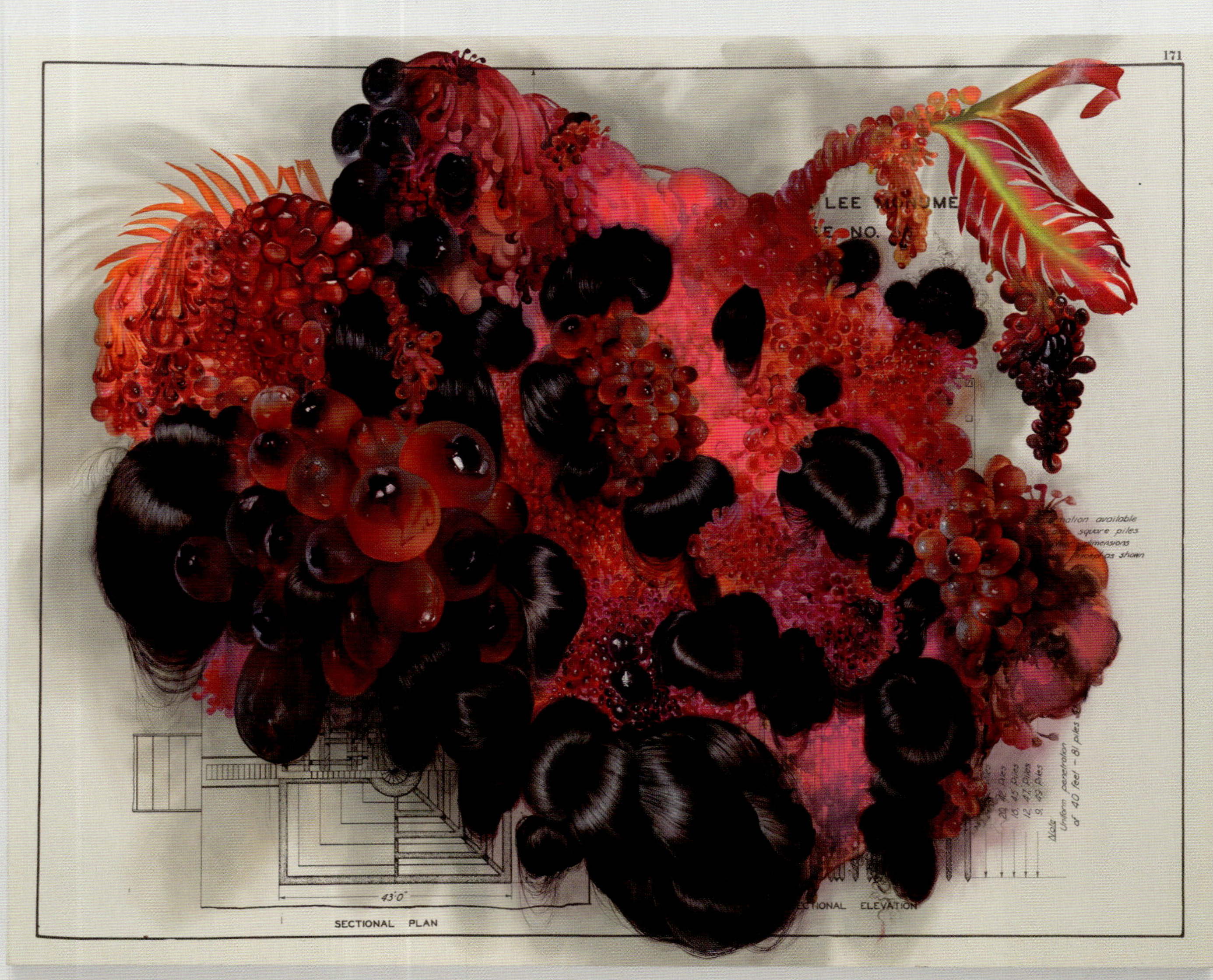

***Fruta Fina, Fruta Estraña (Lee Monument)*, 2022**

Oil and acrylic on archival printed canvas

Courtesy of Firelei Báez Studio

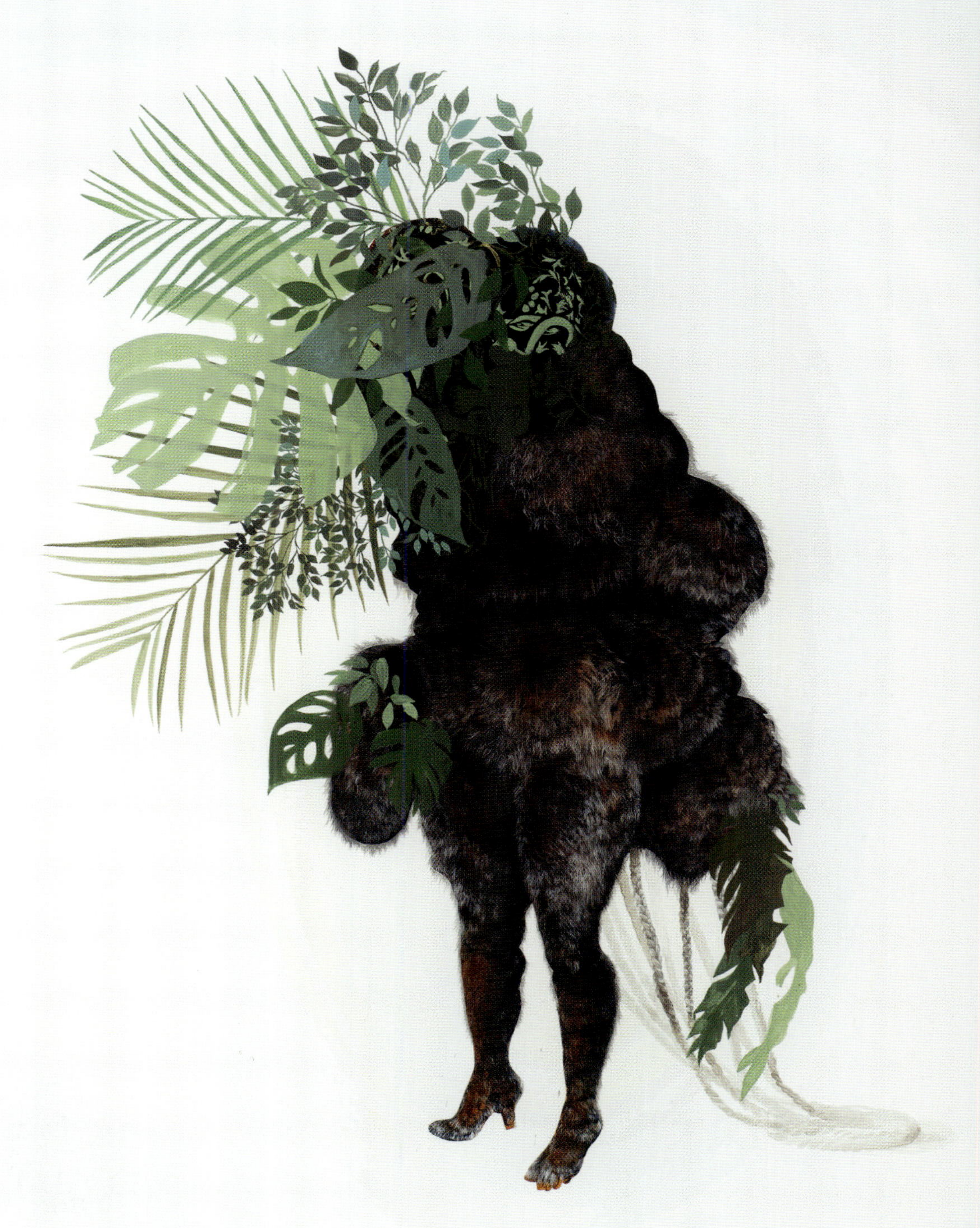

***Ciguapa Pantera (to all the goods and pleasures of this world)*, 2015**
Acrylic and ink on paper
Courtesy of Firelei Báez Studio

Báez was raised by her aunts and grandmother, whom she called her first historian, an upbringing that she says "sparked a curiosity to engage with the nuanced and complex lives of the elders around me." That often meant interrogating the "shared histories between these overlapping groups that shape who we are today, much of which are so often buried, marginalized and interwoven with misconceptions." In *Muzidi Calabi Yau Space (or a matter of navigation)*, made for *Milk of Dreams*, the 59th Venice Biennale, she created an underwater world where victims of the Atlantic slave passage live and thrive in an Eden-like paradise. It was a continued exploration of the Afro-futuristic concept of Drexciya, a myth born from two Detroit-based DJs in the late 1990s, in which they imagined an underwater nation populated by the unborn children of pregnant women thrown off slave ships. The women in the paintings are water breathing, having evolved elaborate gills that recall the ornamental costumes of their ancestral lands. Muzidi are reliquary figures that honor one's ancestors but also protect descendants from misfortune and illness. In these mythical beings of her own creation, she seems to pay homage to the women who raised her, referencing the traumatic history they were born from, while also casting a new light in which to see, and learn from, these women. Throughout her work, she reaches back to stories and symbols, as seen at 163rd St., but never lingers in the past, always proposing a new way of seeing the world.

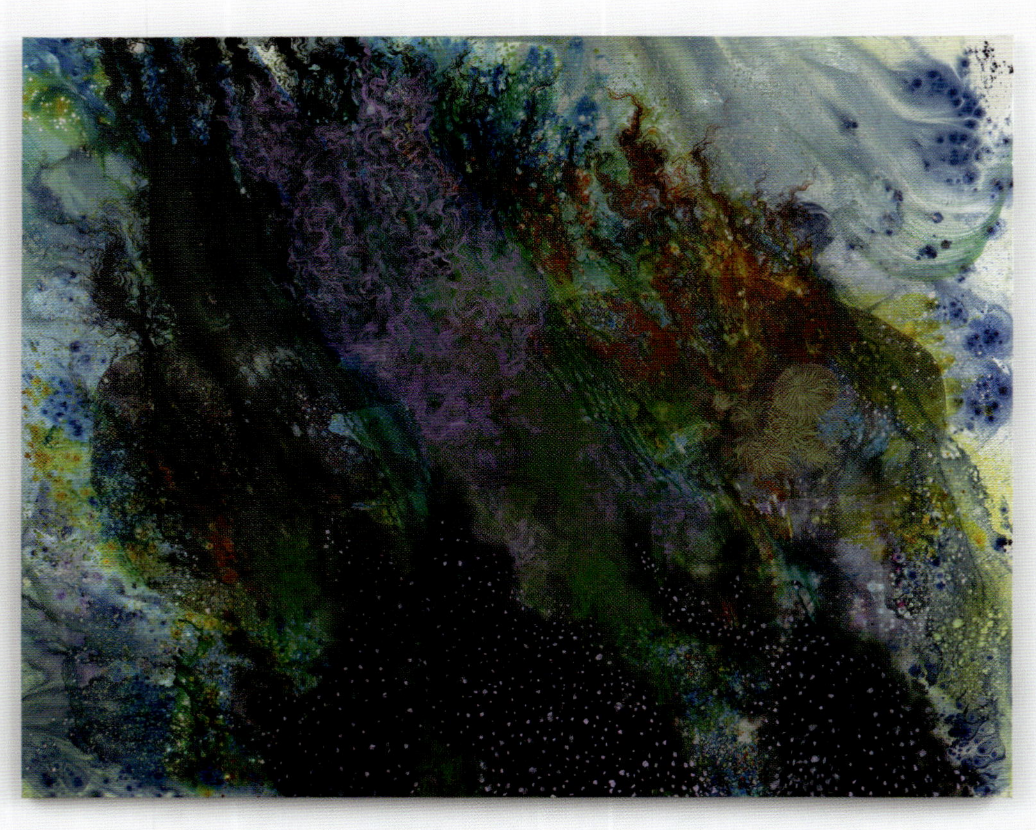

***Untitled (Drexciya)*, 2020**
Oil and acrylic on canvas
Courtesy of Firelei Báez Studio

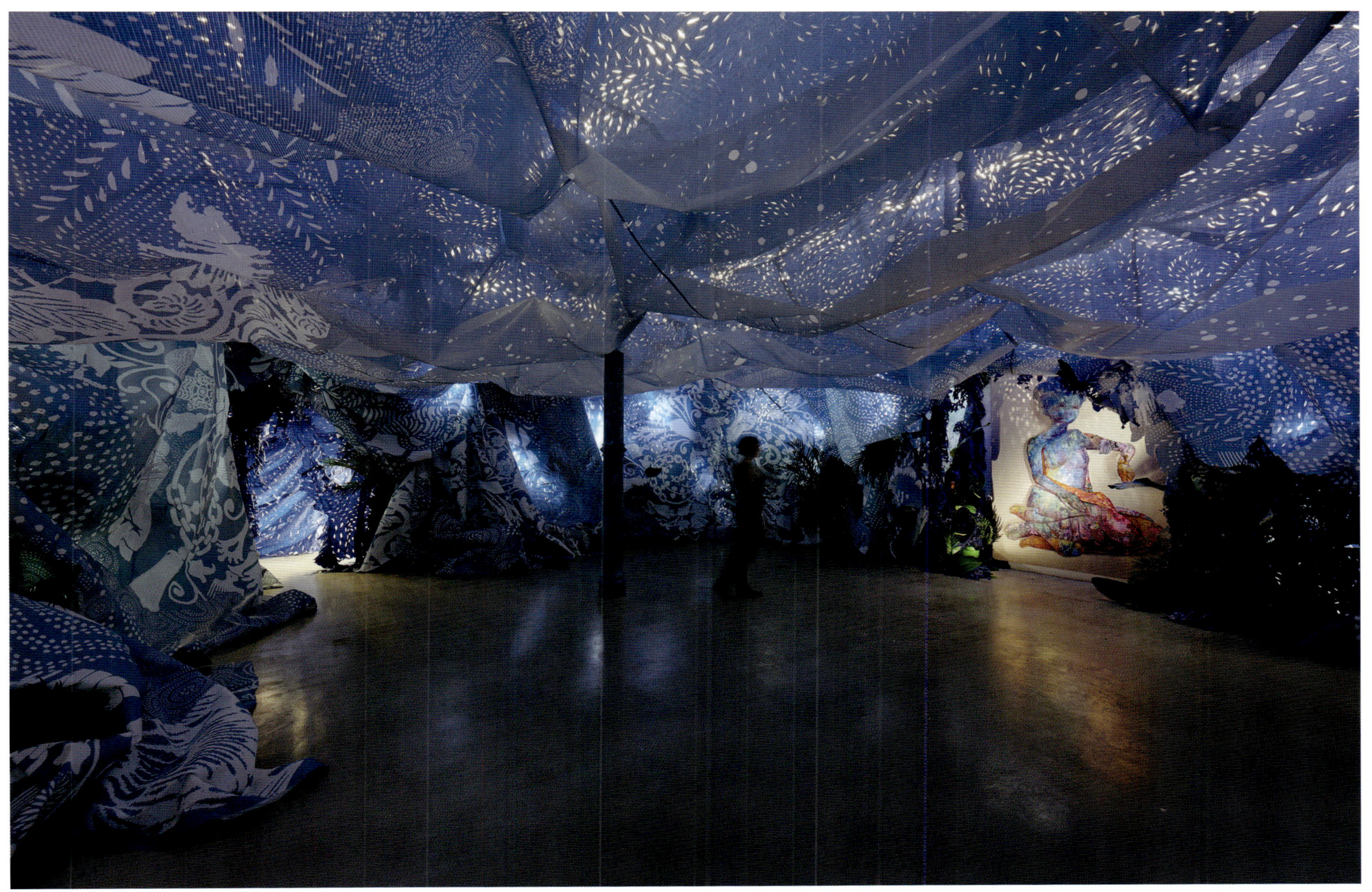

***A Drexcyen chronocommons (To win the war you fought it sideways)*, 2019**
Two paintings, hand-painted wooden frame, perforated tarp, printed mesh, handmade paper over found objects, plants, books, Oman incense, palo santo
Installation view
Courtesy of Firelei Báez Studio

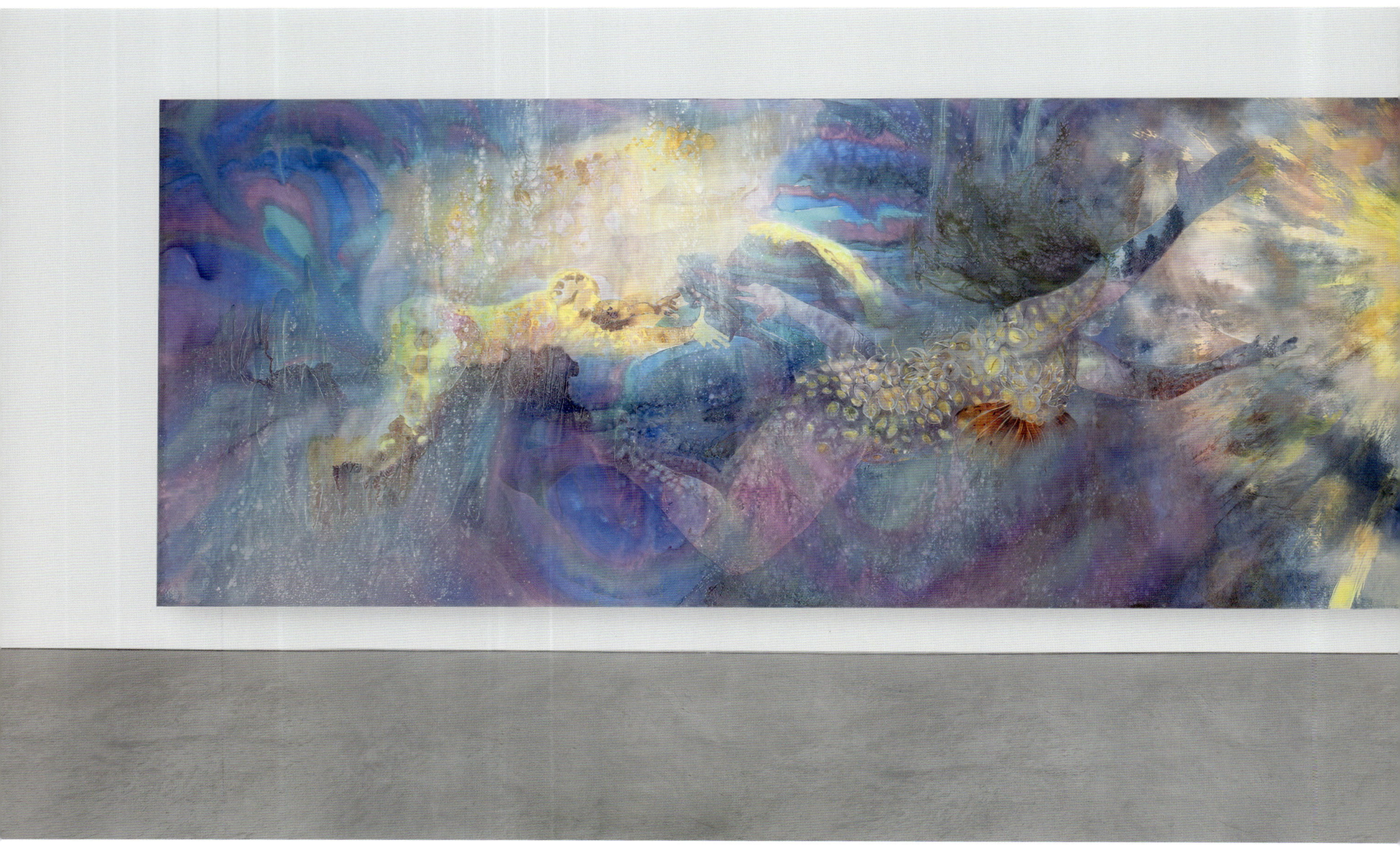

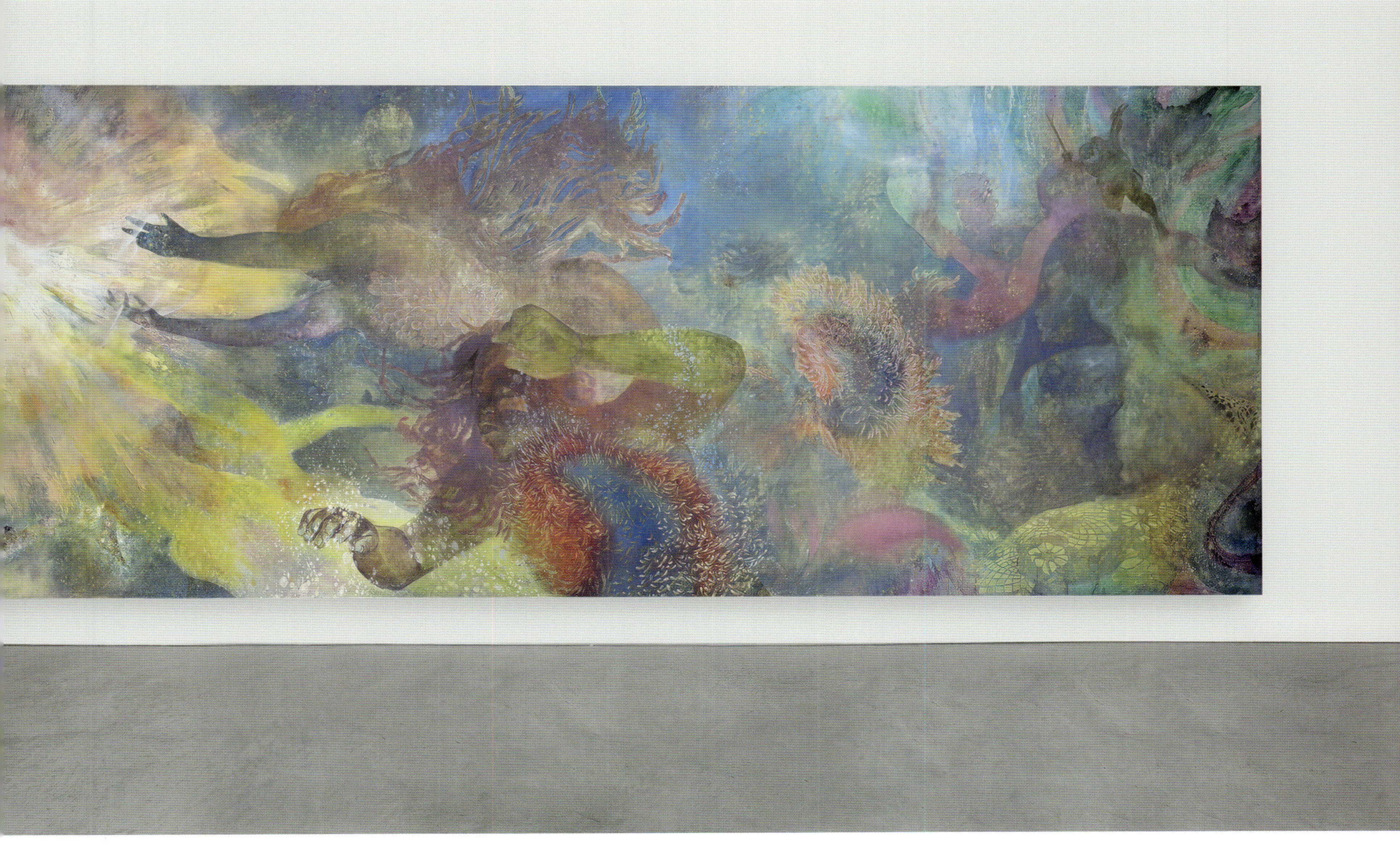

***Muzidi Calabi Yau Space (or a matter of navigation)*, 2022**
Oil and acrylic on canvas (diptych)
Exhibited at the 59th International Art Exhibition of La Biennale di Venezia with accompanying soundtrack composed by Tina Tallon and Rob Walker, Venice, Italy
Courtesy of Firelei Báez Studio

Nick Cave (b. 1959)

TIMES SQUARE STATION

***Each One, Every One, Equal All*, 2021-2022**

At several points in the Times Square station, the walls of the passageways explode with the color and dynamic movements of Nick Cave and his Soundsuits. Part installation, part costume, his Soundsuits are elaborately adorned and festooned with materials from buttons to ceramic objects. They are often worn by dancers in exuberant dance performances, where beads and fringes leap and twirl along with the dancers. In the transit tunnel from Bryant Park to Times Square, his Soundsuits unfurl like a mosaic scroll painting, the figures whirling along with commuters. At the end of the S-train platform and along a wall by the turnstile, his Soundsuits are packed together, all leaping and dancing as one happy, chaotic group; Cave discovered that this particular wall sits right where the New Year's Eve ball is dropped above the station, so all his figures mimic the shape and path of that iconic crystal ball. Serendipitously, he already had videos of Soundsuited dancers jumping on trampolines to draw inspiration from. One wall of the subway platform in particular vibrates with energy, since Cave has added silhouette lines, combining graphic elements to his contemporary rococo figures, framing them within the posts lining this area. It is like seeing the dancers and their kinetic auras all at once.

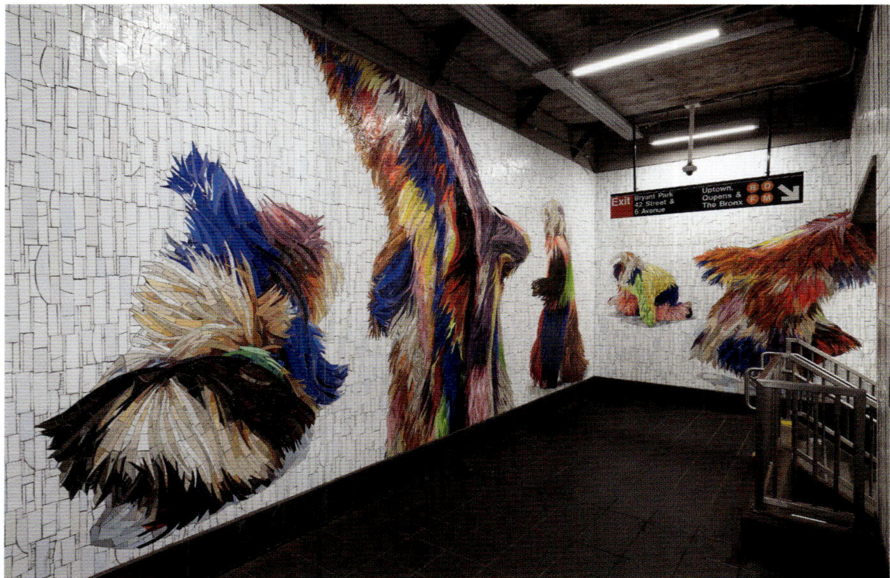

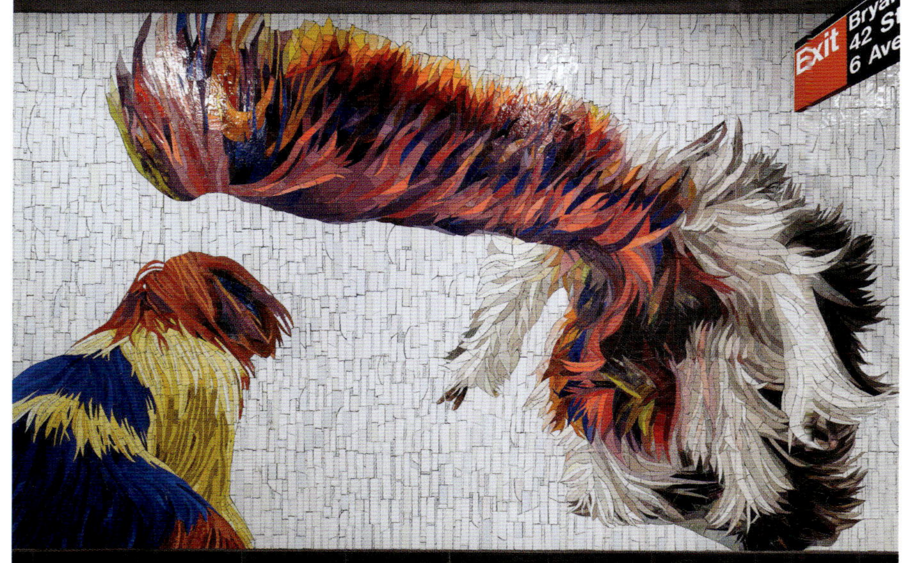

Courtesy of the artist and Jack Shainman Gallery

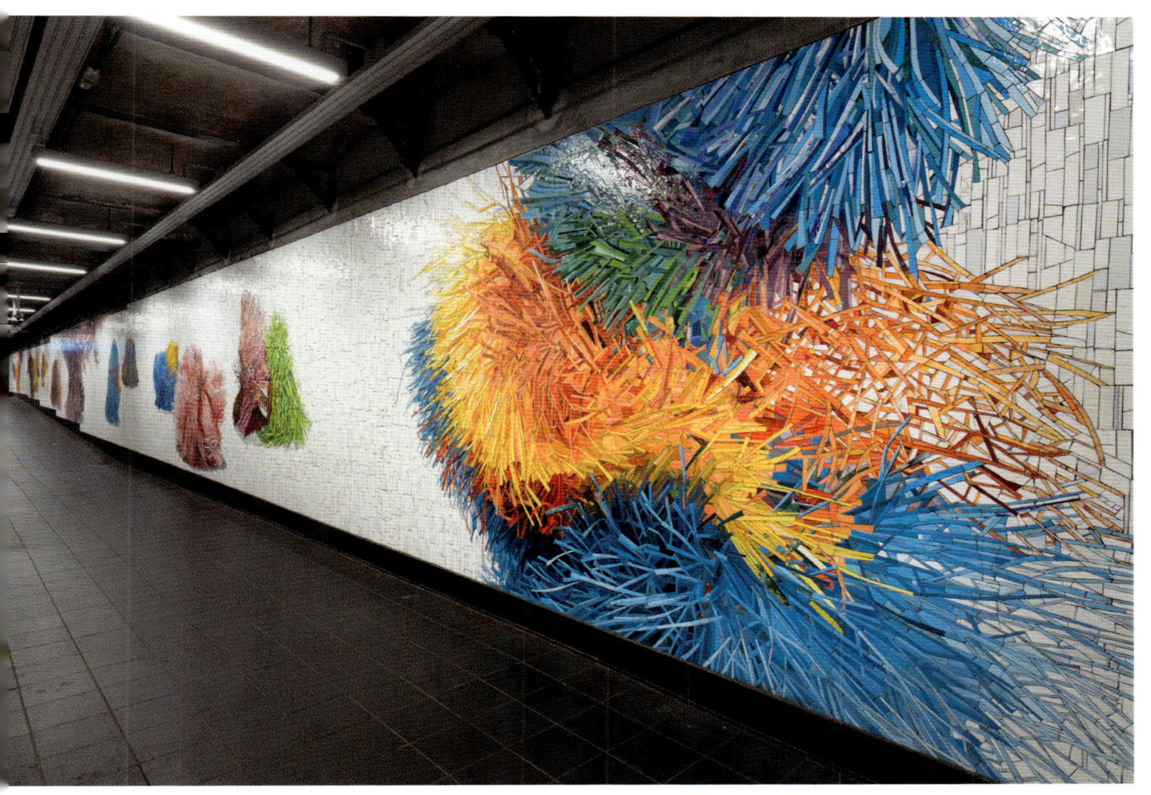

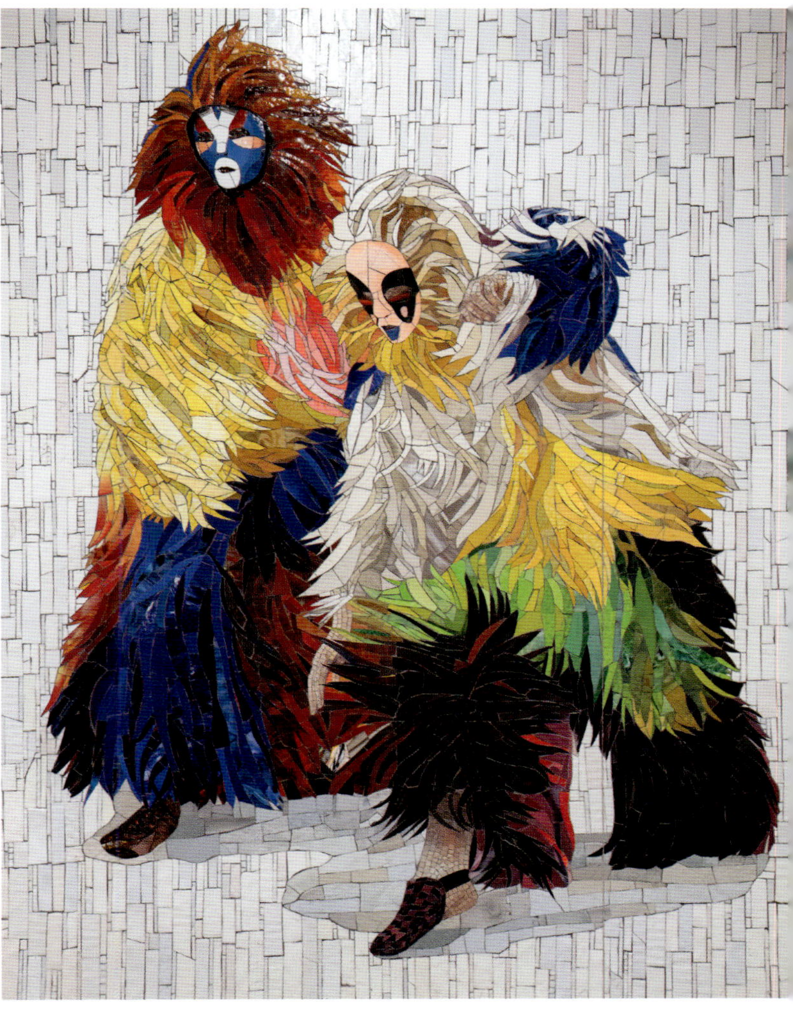

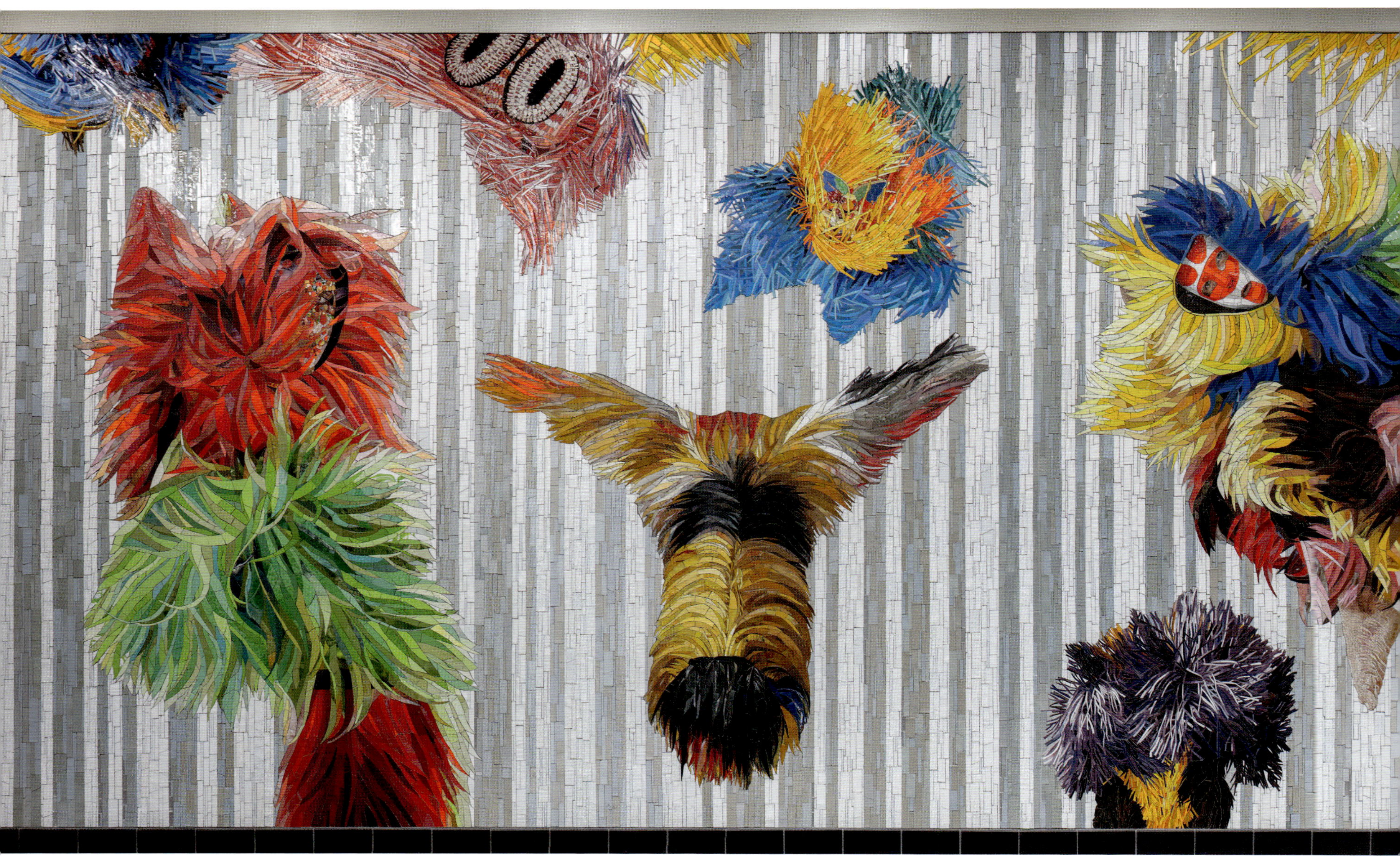

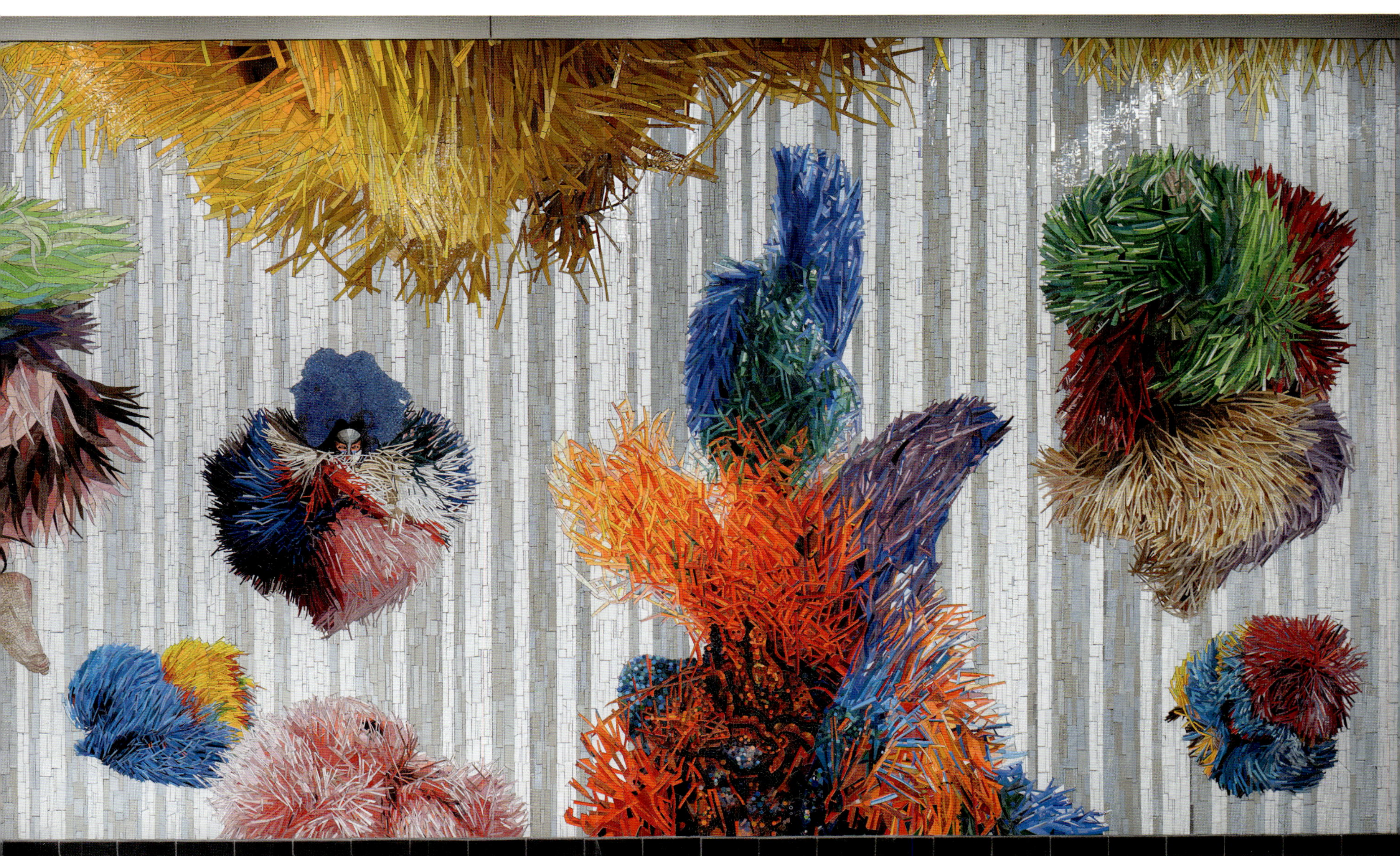

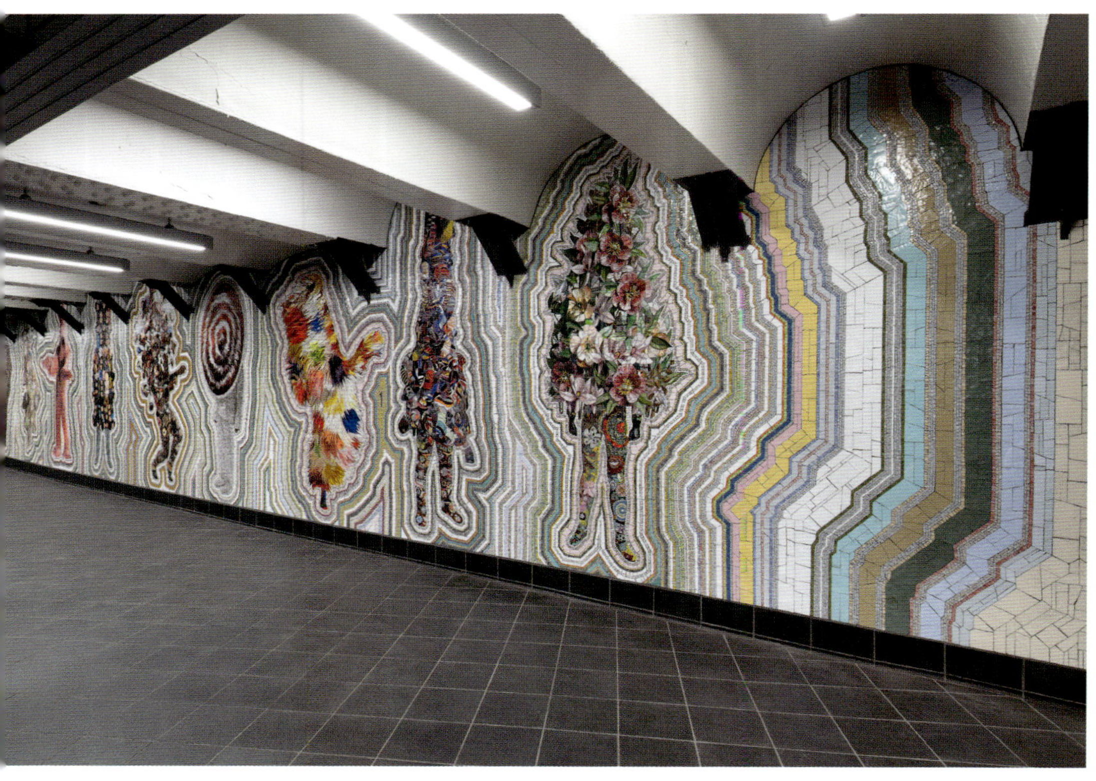

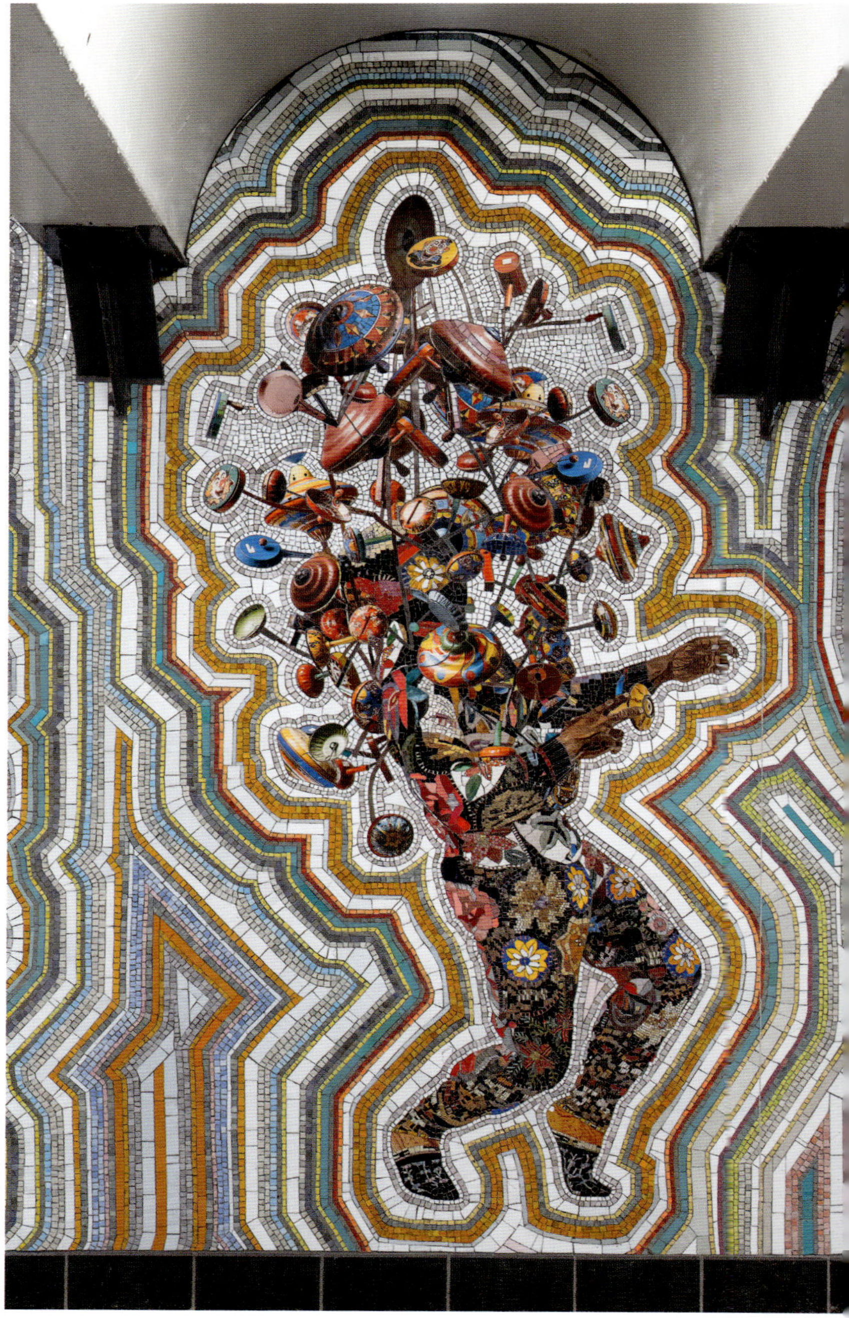

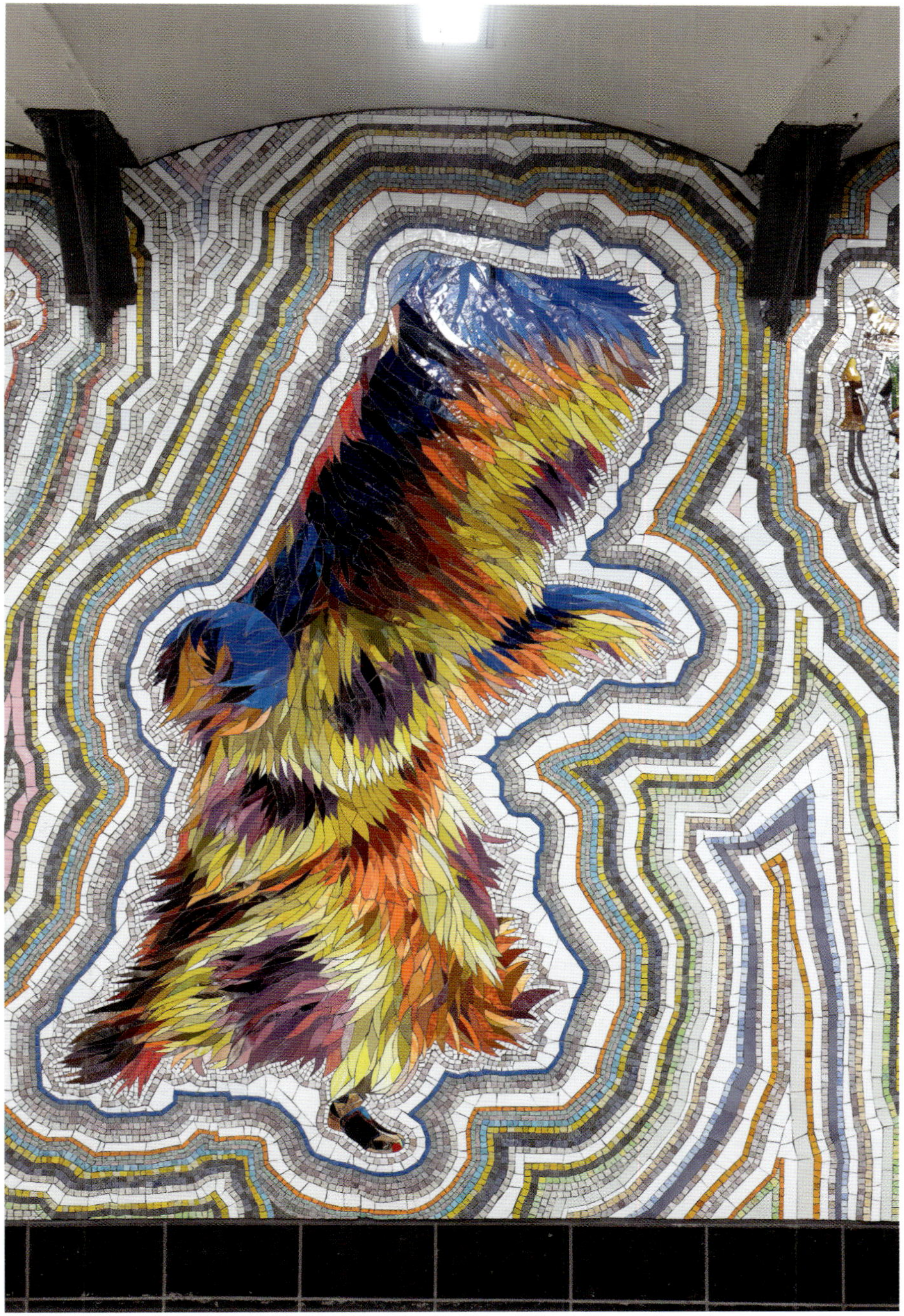

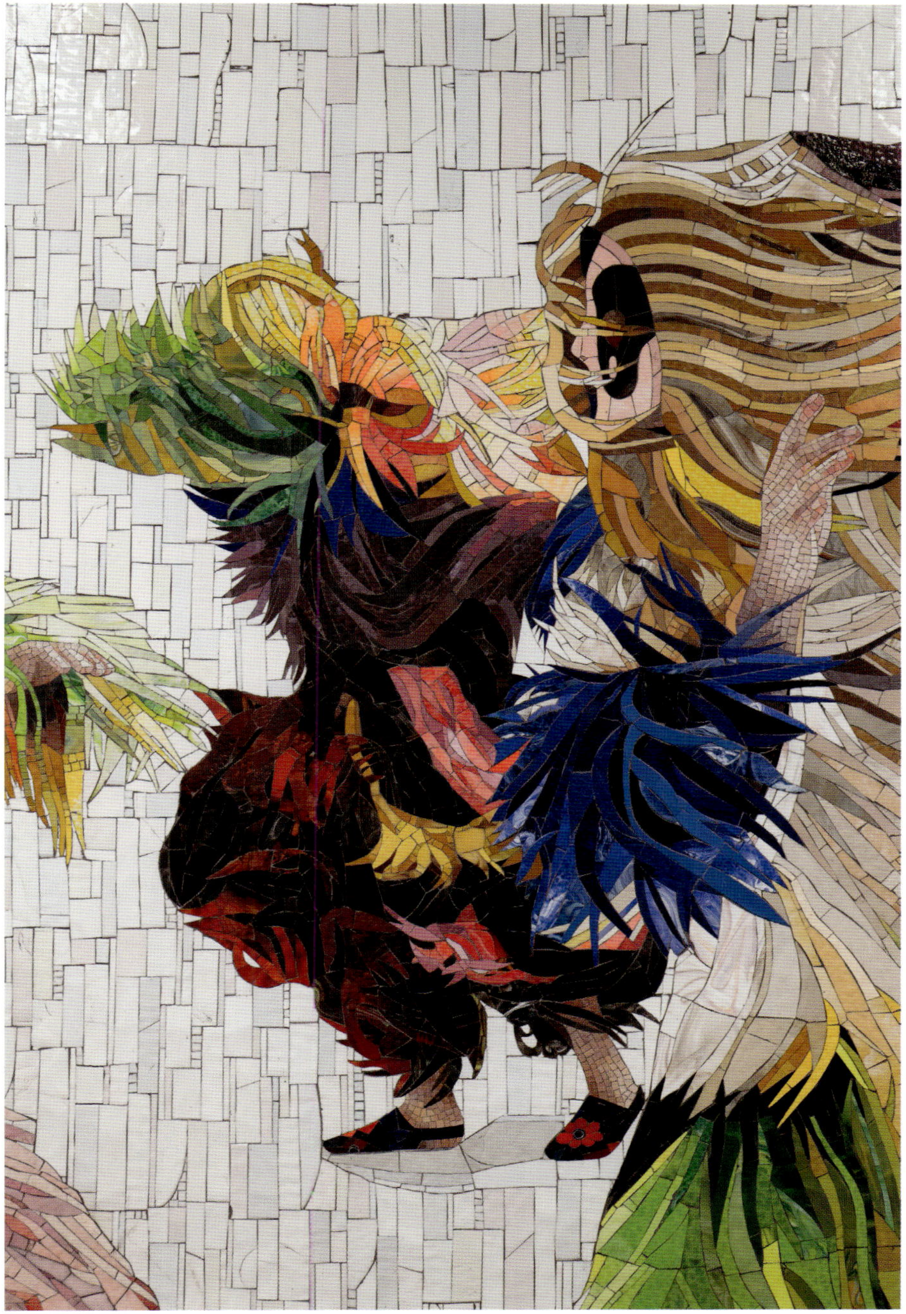

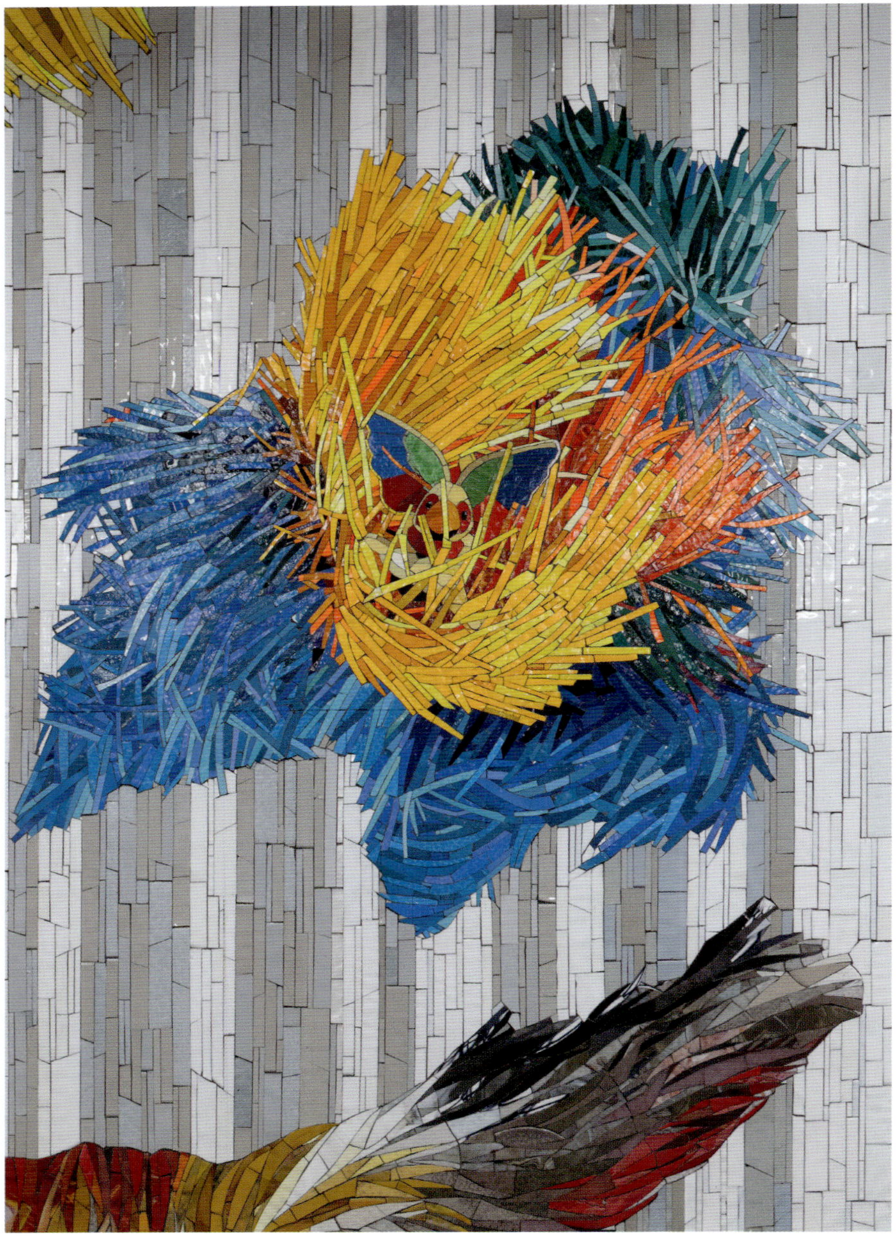

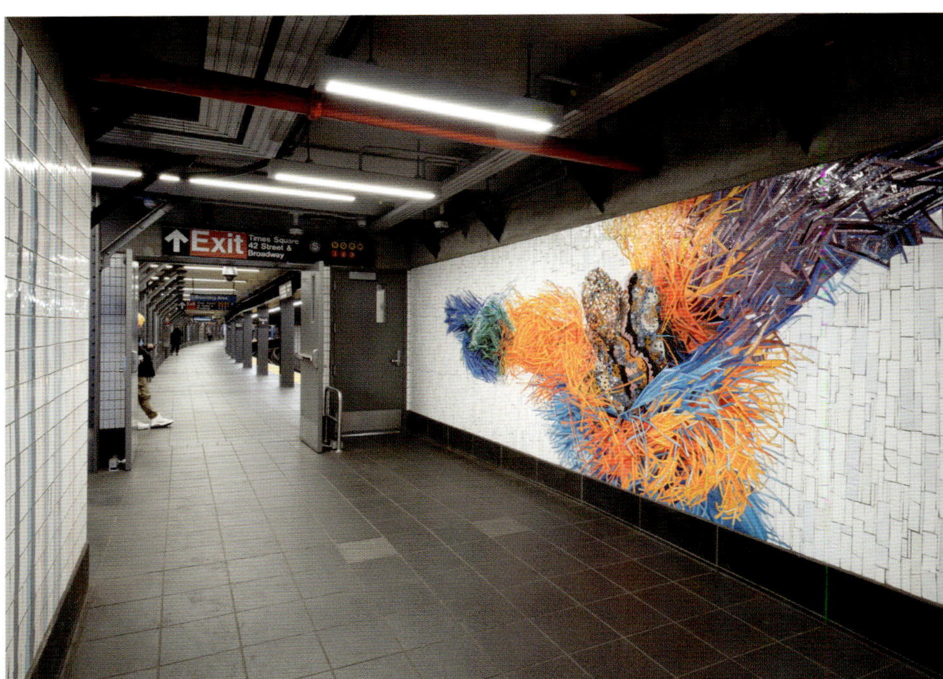
Exit
Times Square
42 Street &
Broadway

Nick Cave has been described as the most joyful artist, a man whose every performance aims to revive and unite performers and spectators alike in jubilant displays. Indeed, his works are often a riot of color, textures, and materials, but they are grounded in the harsh realities of racial injustice, gender oppression, and violence. His Soundsuits were almost an instinctual reaction to the Rodney King beating and the subsequent acquittal of the police responsible. His vibrant costumes shielded the wearer from the constant barrage of violence and hatred inflicted on the Black body, and serves both as an armor enabling anonymity and a loud declaration of oneself with the suit's bold extravagance. In hiding the body and any markers of identification, one can freely celebrate the self abashedly and without prejudice, drawing from the traditions of drag performance as well as the ceremonial practices of cultures around the world that often use costuming in their rituals. Cave has always been a collaborative artist, working with choreographers, designers, and even the public itself to enhance his work and deepen his message of healing, rejuvenation, and contemplation. At the Park Avenue Armory in 2018, he put on a show that was essentially a prolonged dance party, where various forms of expressions (hula dancers, yoga practitioners, DJs) mixed with his own Up Right performers and members of the general public.

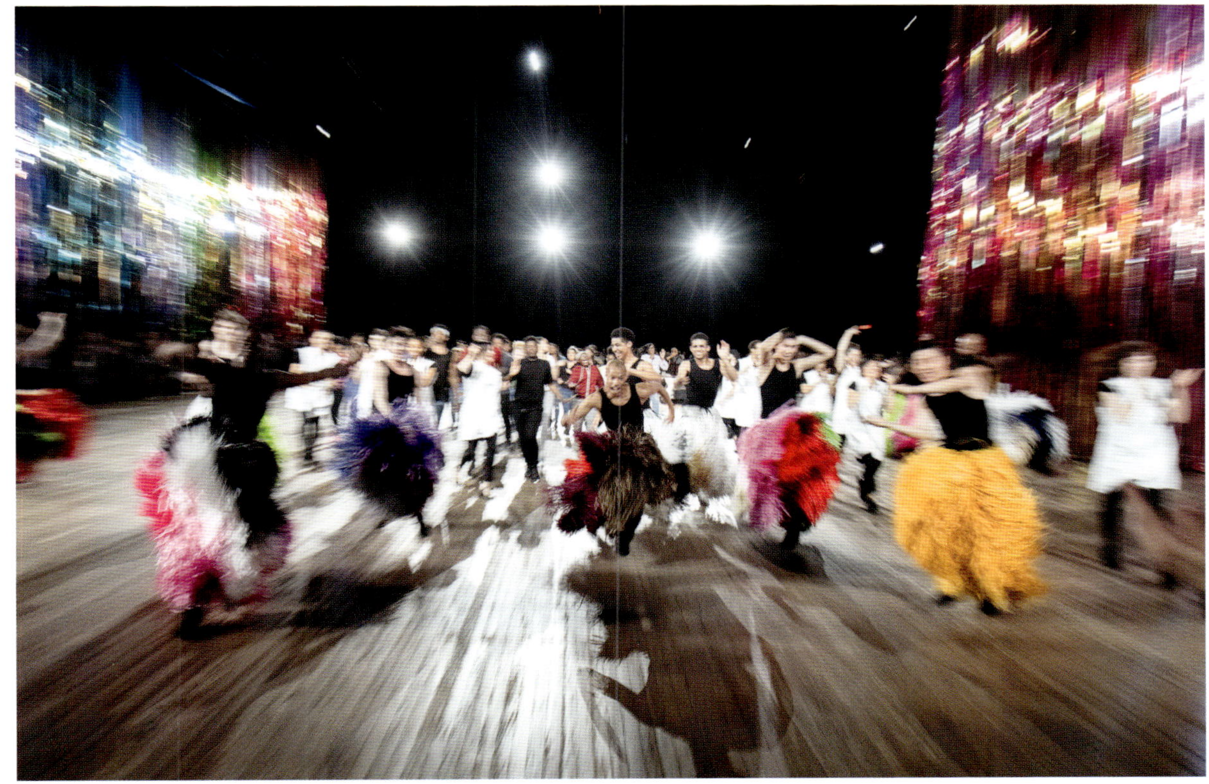

***The Let Go*, 2018**
Collaborative performance at
the Park Avenue Armory, New York City
Courtesy of the artist and Jack Shainman Gallery

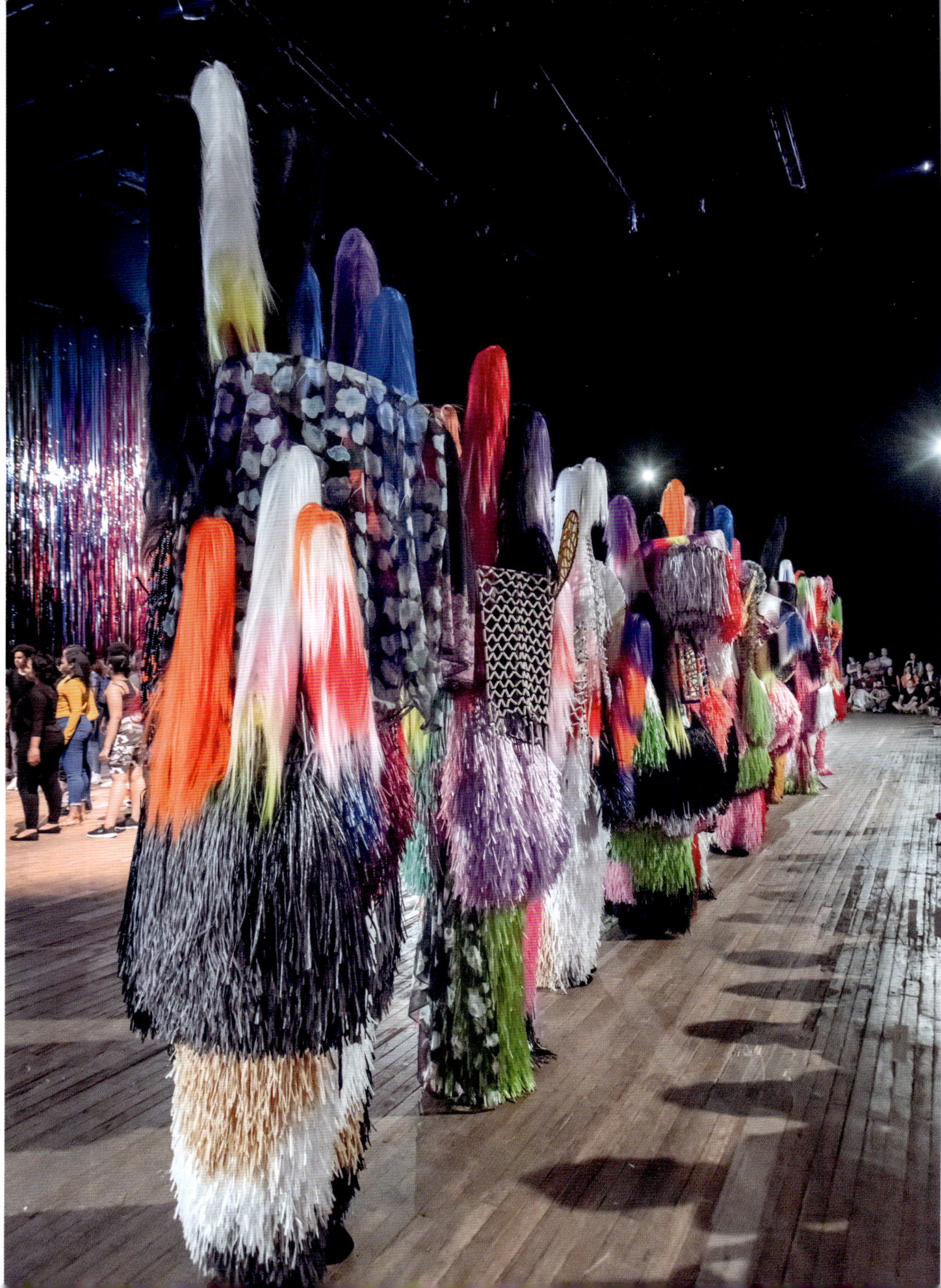

***Soundsuit*, 2006**

Cotton, twigs, mannequin, and armature

Courtesy of the artist and Jack Shainman Gallery

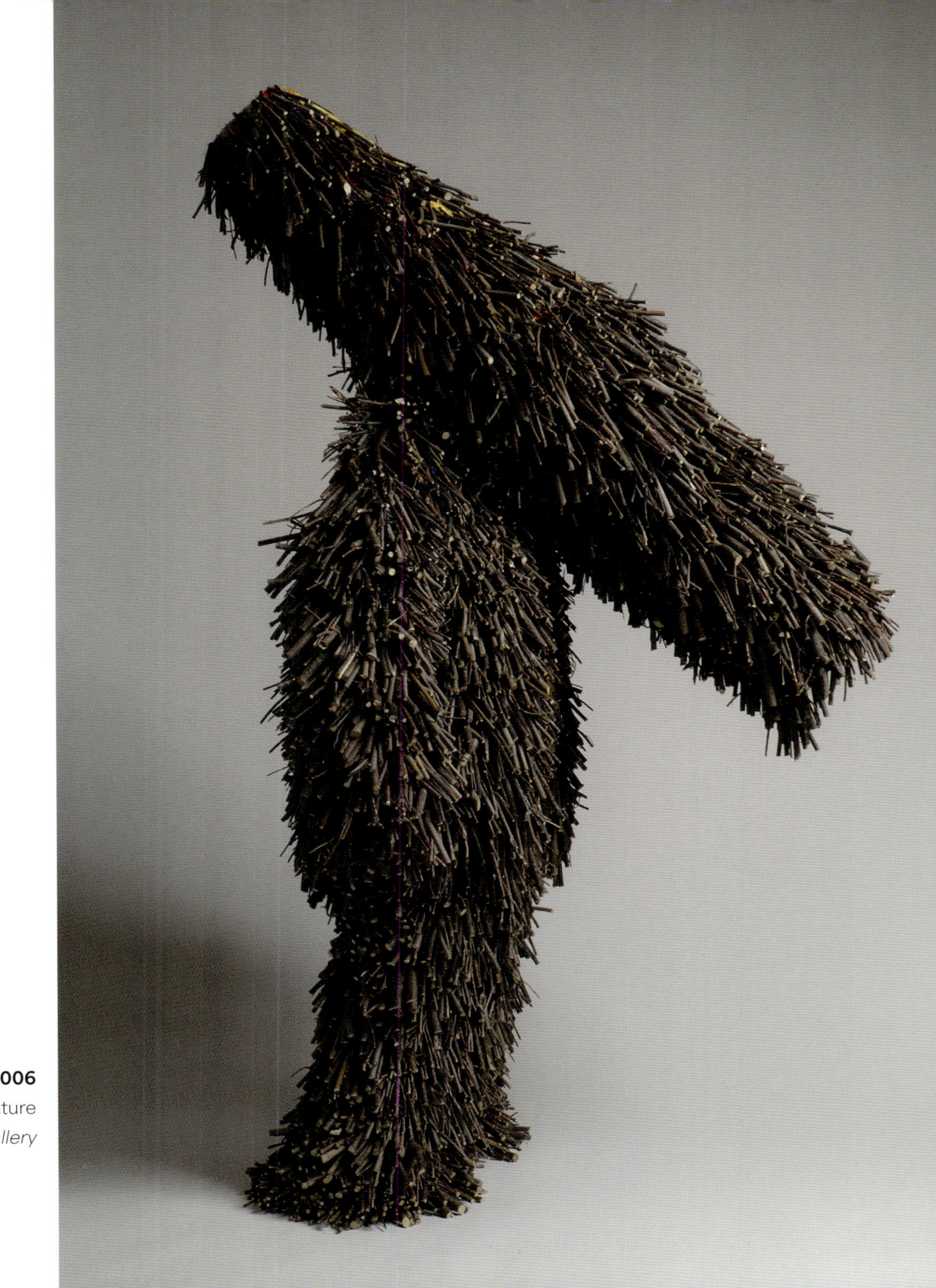

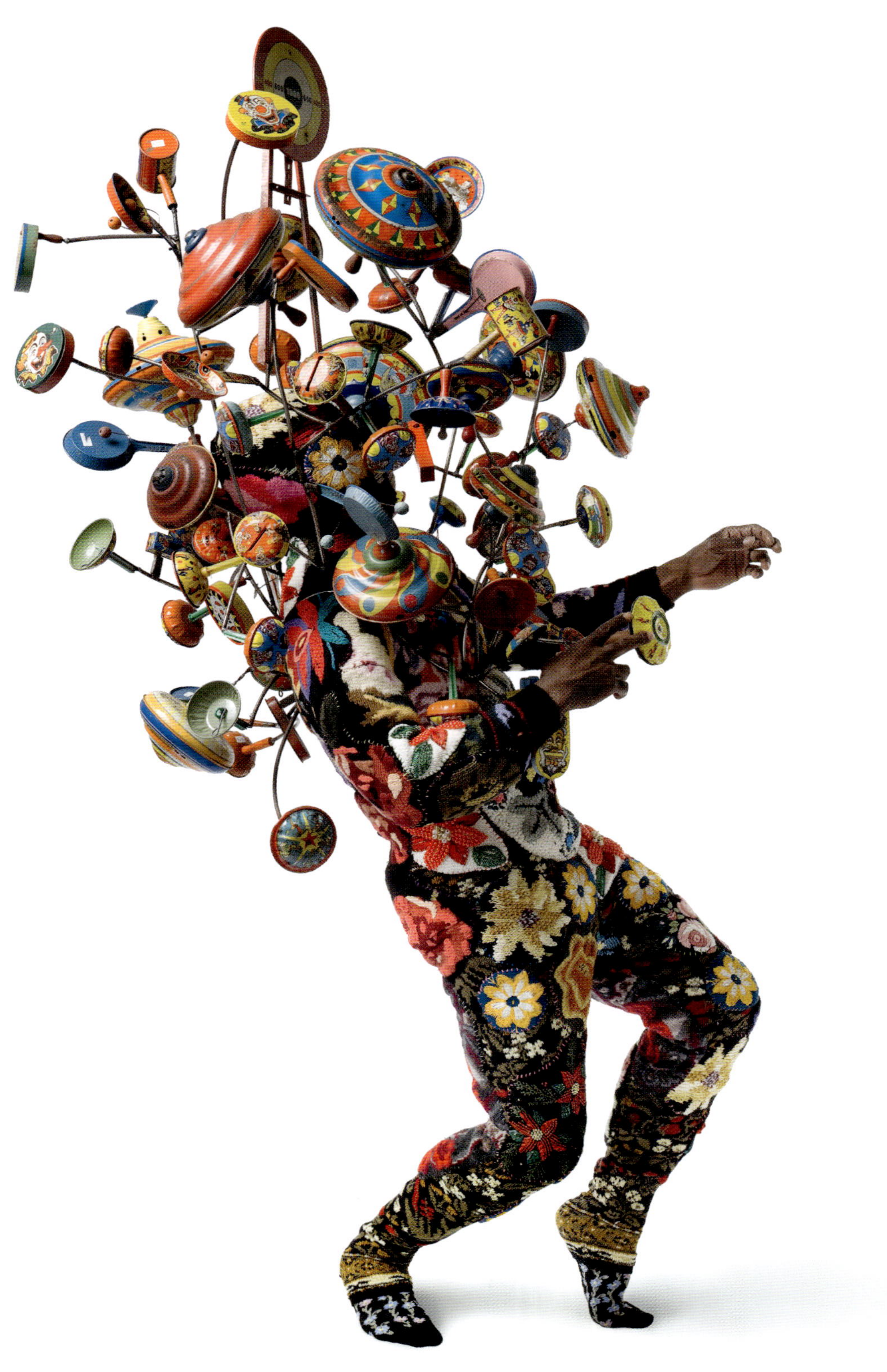

***Soundsuit*, 2008**
Embroidery, fabric, vintage toys, and mannequin
Courtesy of the artist and Jack Shainman Gallery

One particular public intervention directly informed his Times Square commission. In 2013, Creative Time and the MTA copresented *HEARD•NY*, a twice-daily performance at Grand Central Station's Vanderbilt Hall. With accompanying live music and dancers from the Alvin Ailey School, thirty elaborately costumed "horses" galloped and danced across the hall. *HEARD* was in the moment; you had to "catch" it on your commute. It raised the question of how do you take something like that in as you are on the go? Cave explains that he wanted to capture commuters' attention but also leave them with this experience where the usual drudgery of the routine became infused with splendor and joy. The performance took over the attention of commuters, in the same way that the walls of the Times Square subway, consumed by this abundance of colorful tile, dominate a rider's field of vision.

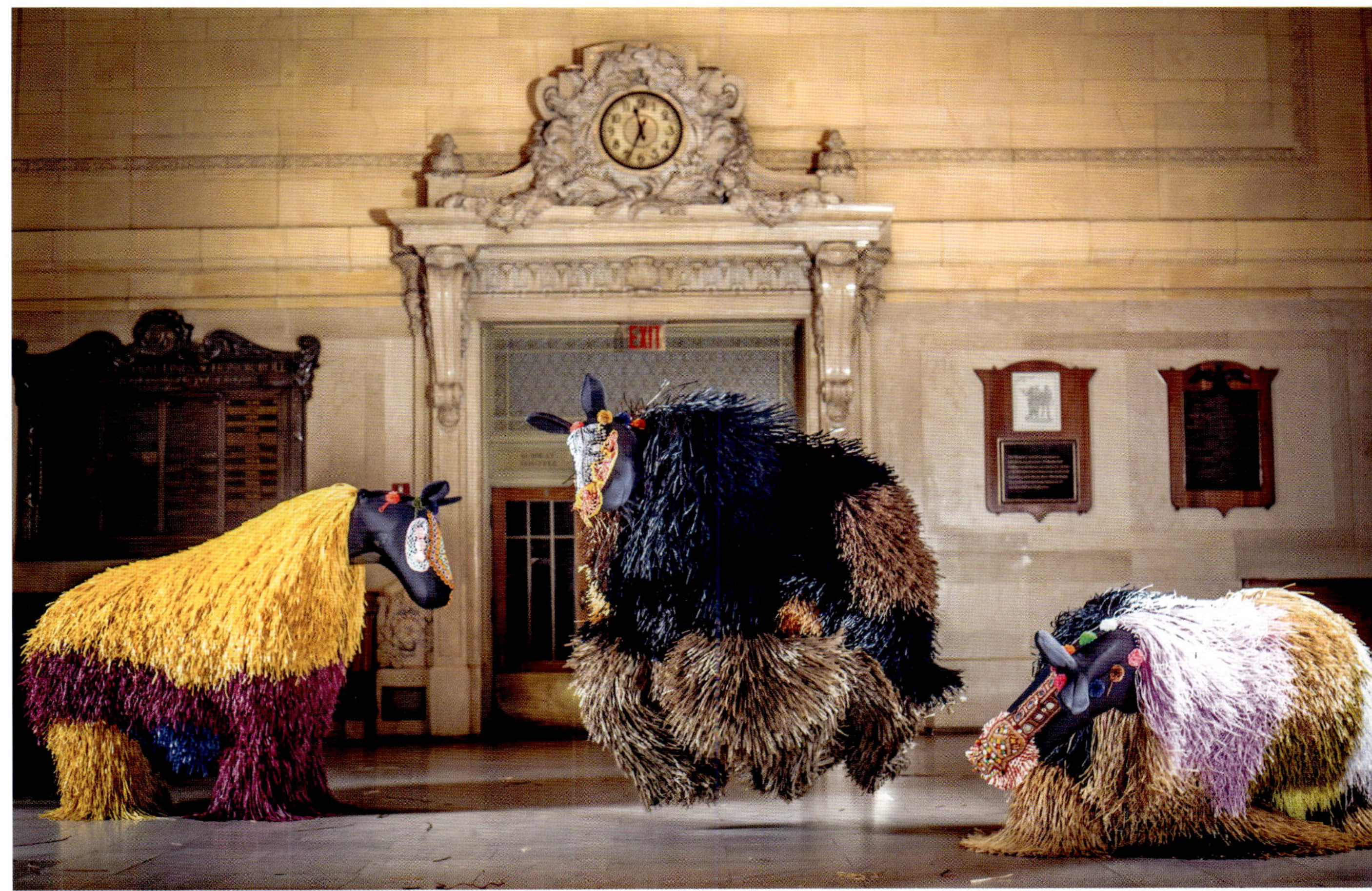

***HEARD•NY*, 2013**
Collaborative public performance with the Alvin Ailey School, choreographer William Gill, and musicians Shelley Burgon, Mary Lattimore, Robert Levin, and Junior Wedderburn. Copresented by Creative Time and MTA Arts for Transit in Grand Central Station, Vanderbilt Hall.

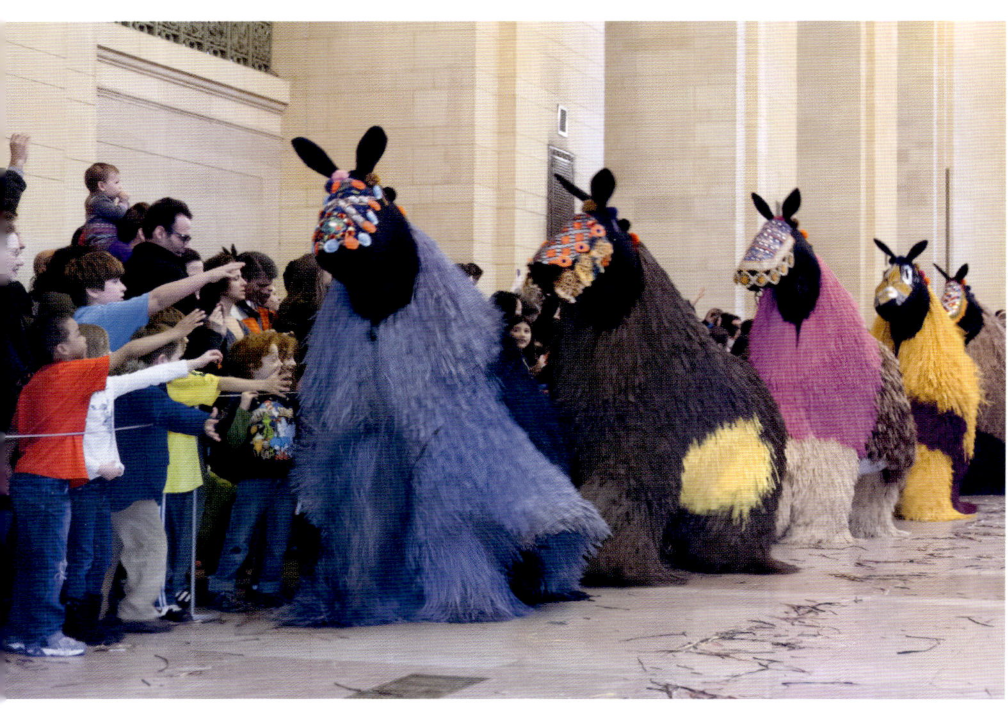

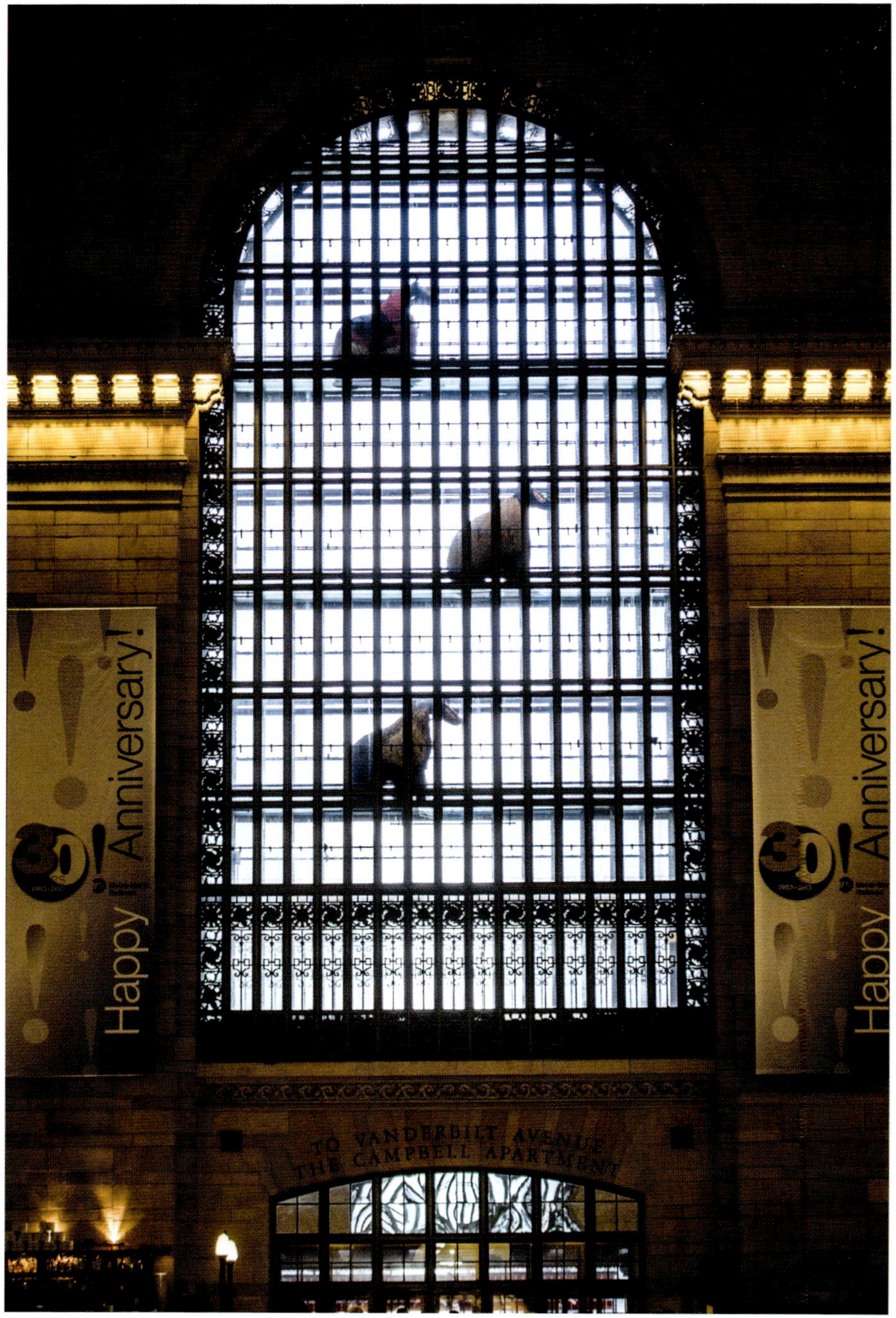

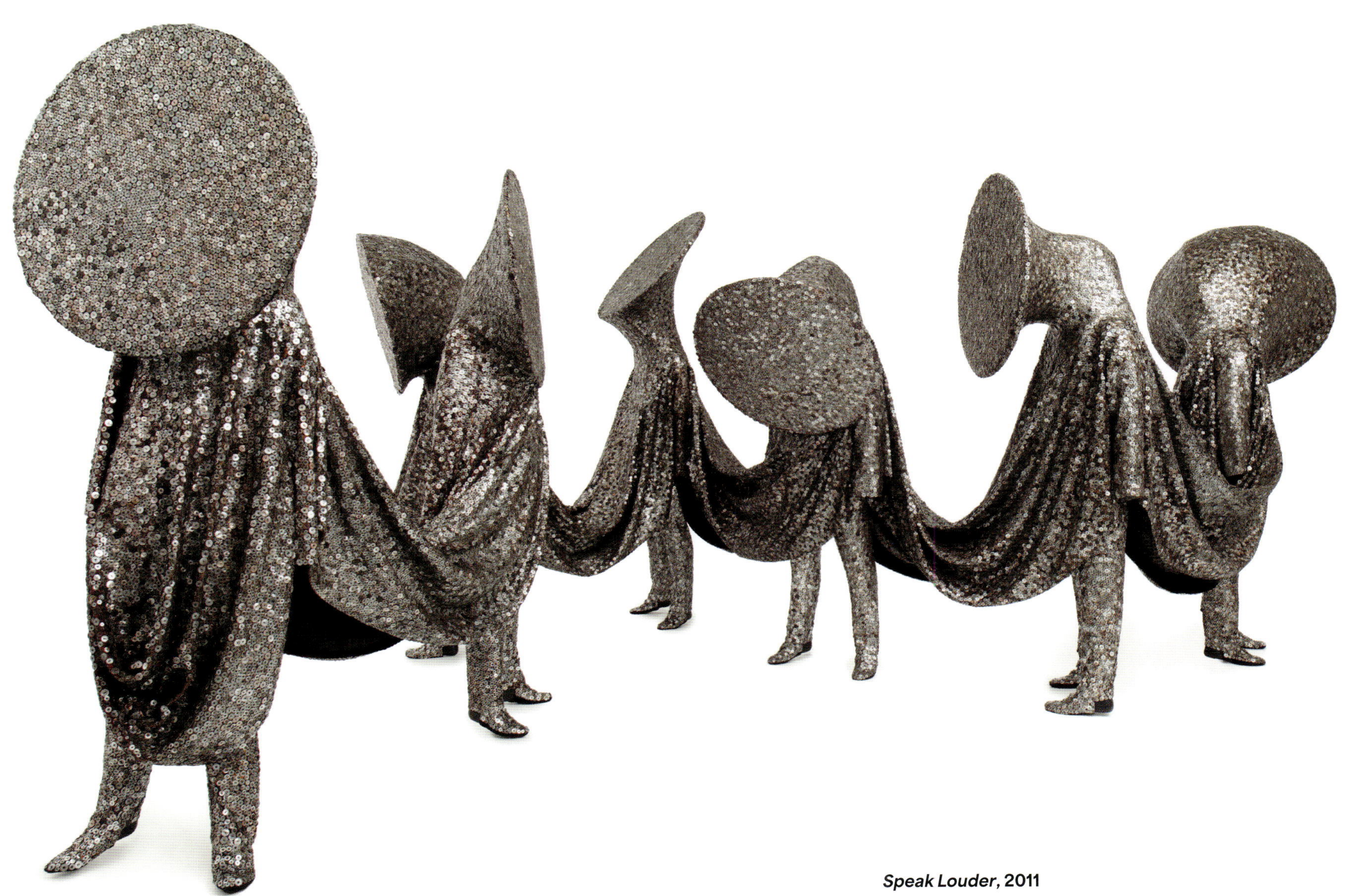

***Speak Louder*, 2011**
Black mother-of-pearl buttons, embroidery floss, upholstery, metal armature, and mannequins
Courtesy of Jack Shainman Gallery

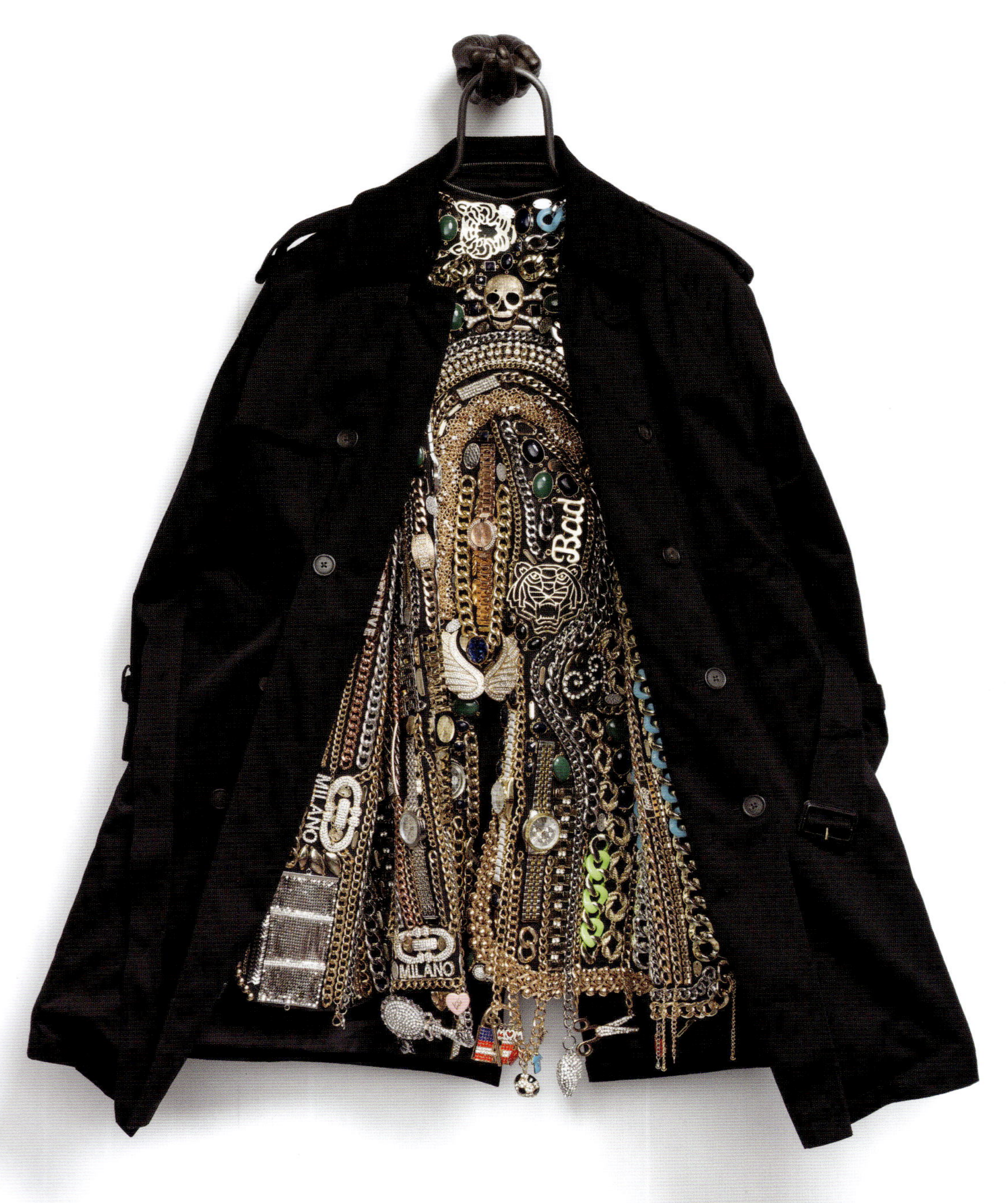

***Hustle Coat*, 2017**

Trench coat, cast-bronze hand, metal, costume jewelry, watches, and chains

Courtesy of Jack Shainman Gallery

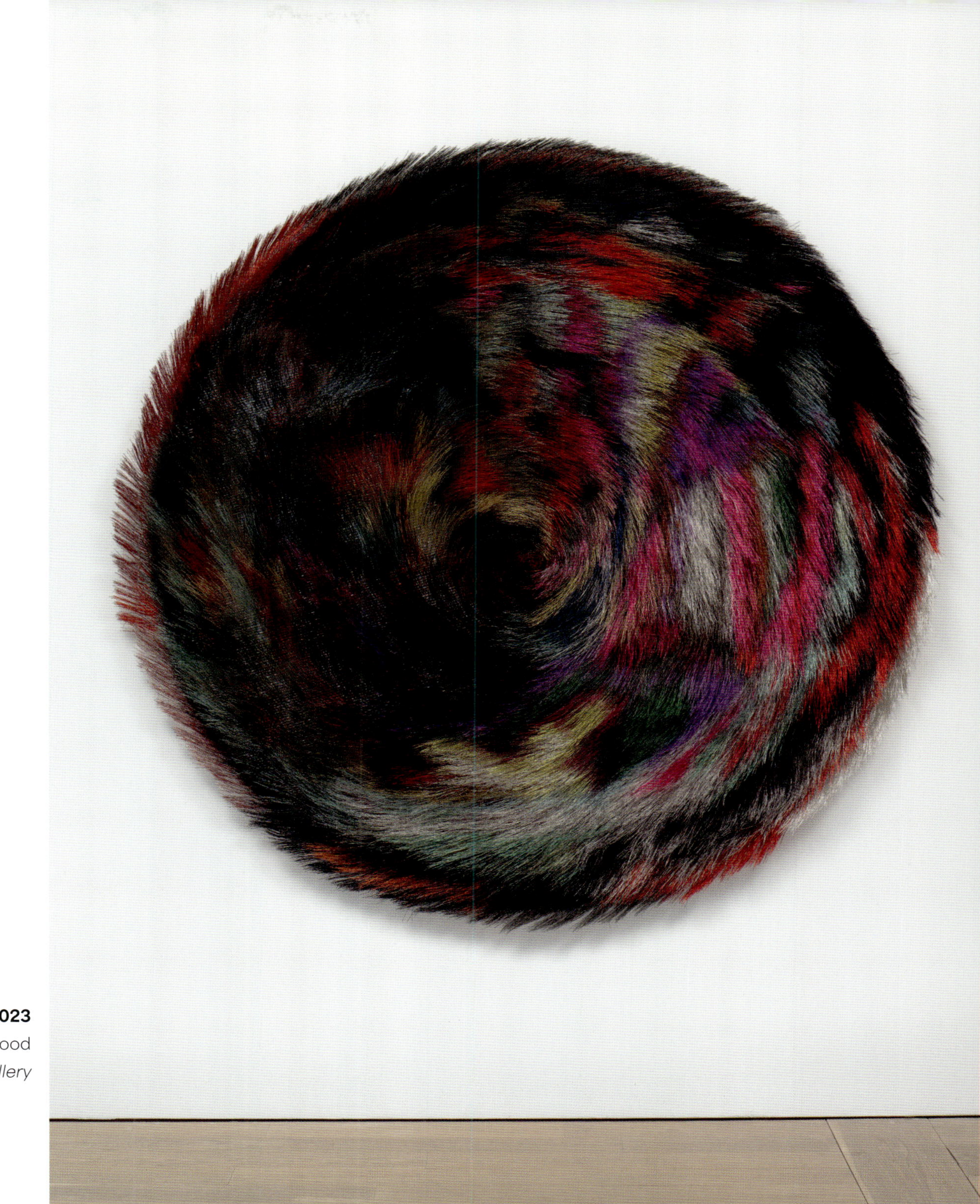

***Tondo*, 2023**
Wire, bugle beads, sequined fabric, and wood
Courtesy of Jack Shainman Gallery

Jane Dickson (b. 1952)

TIMES SQUARE STATION

***Revelers*, 2008**

Perhaps no other place exemplifies the mythology of New York City than Times Square. It looms large in the imagination of visitors as representative of the city at large: a gritty, colorful, flashy crossroads of humanity that is home to vice, entertainment, and commerce in equal measures. And no other artist captures the complexities of this area as well as Jane Dickson, who was a long-time resident of Times Square and as such is deeply attuned to the rhythms of the neighborhood. Her commission for the MTA, titled *Revelers*, is scattered throughout the mezzanine level connecting the 1/2/3 platform with the 7 train and partway to Port Authority. It celebrates the area as a place of joyful, raucous gatherings every New Year's Eve; revelers dance, blow horns, laugh, and drunkenly kiss; mosaic confetti are sprinkled among the work, connecting the many different figures that enliven the walls and tunnels. Observing people on New Year's Eve when she lived there, Dickson was fascinated by how people were acting out interpersonal relations so openly: People were kissing, or pulling on each other, dancing, and laughing. To prepare for the commission, she went to Times Square one New Year's Eve to photograph suitable subjects that she would then use in her mosaics. Dickson was unsatisfied with the resulting photographs, most of which depicted people only from the waist up. She pivoted to inviting models to her studio, mostly friends, family, and students, allowing them to create their own characters and reenact how they would celebrate New Year's Eve. In the process of pantomiming having fun, the models ended up genuinely having fun, imparting a realism to the subway figures.

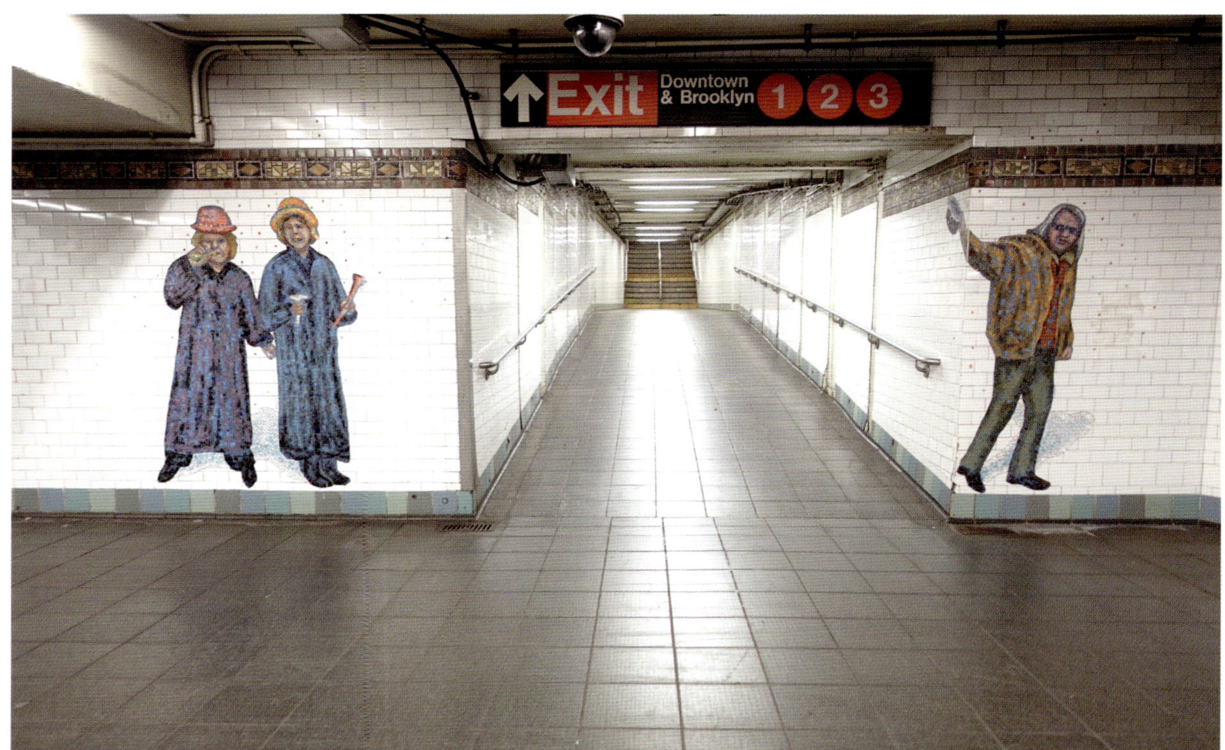

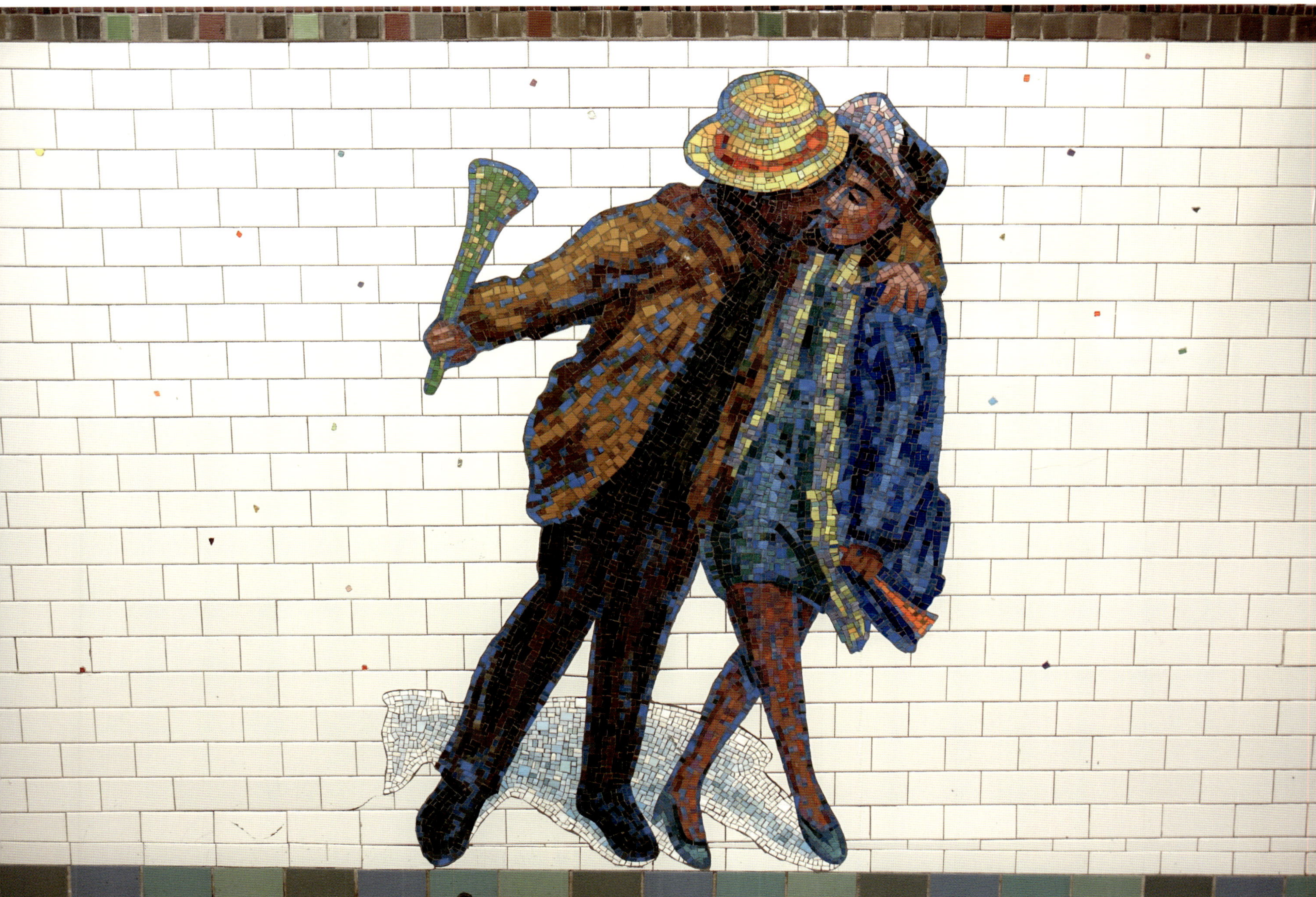

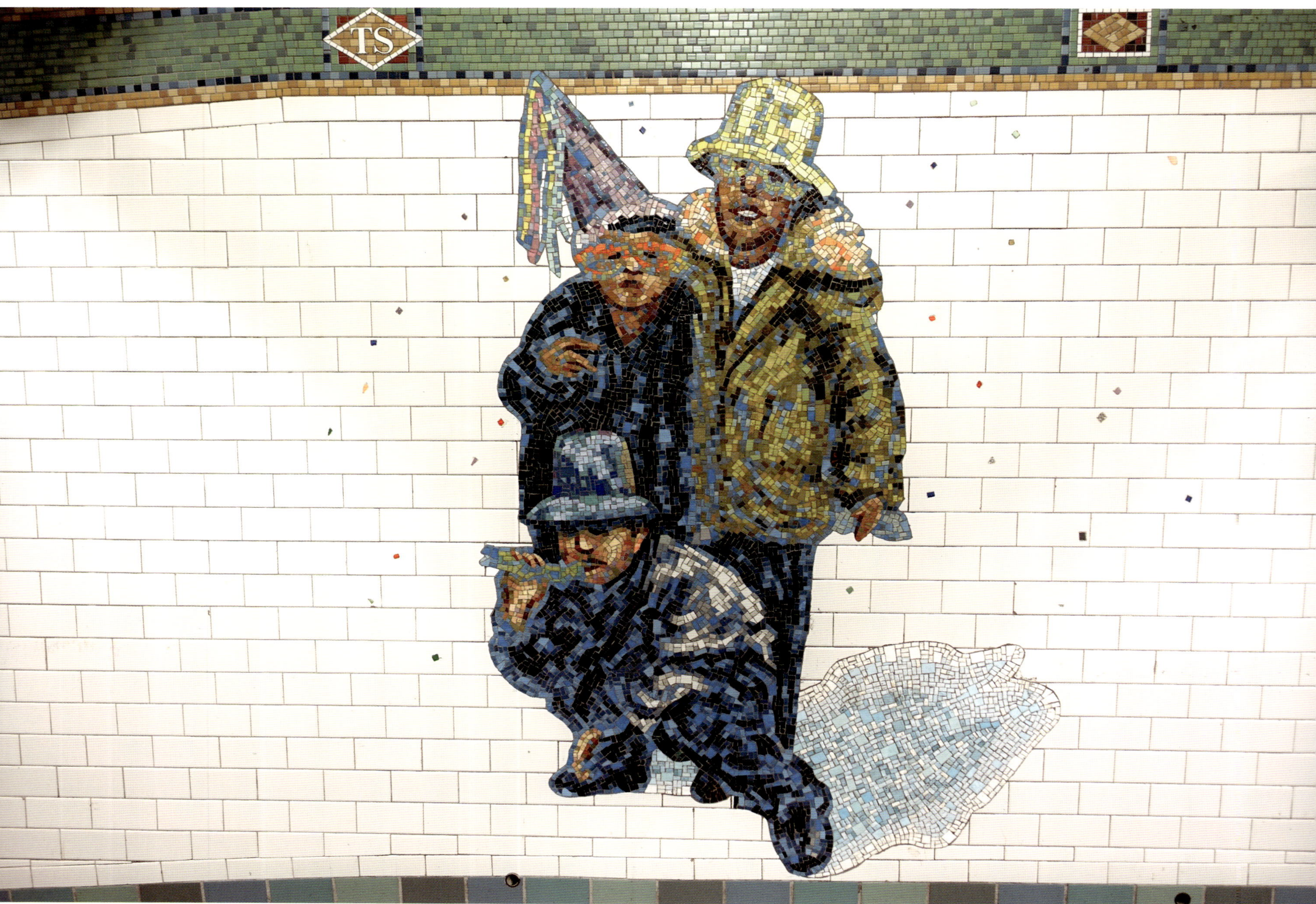
TS

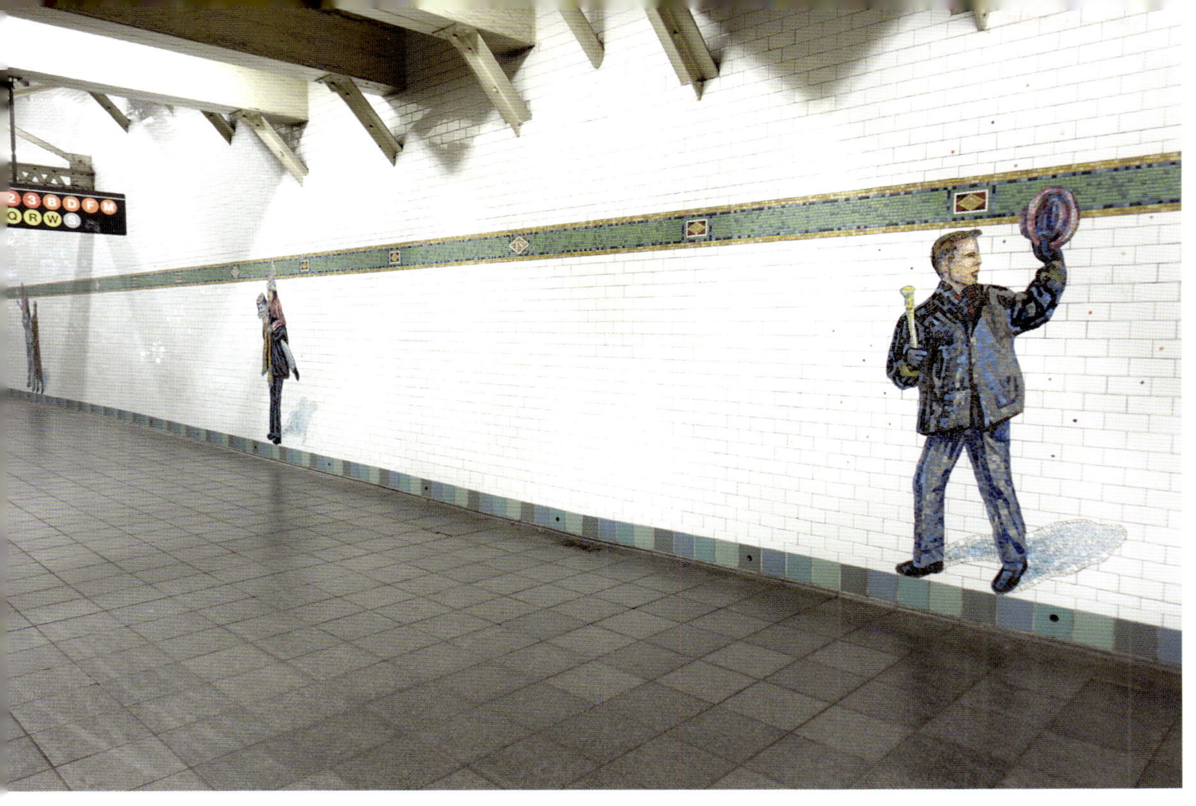

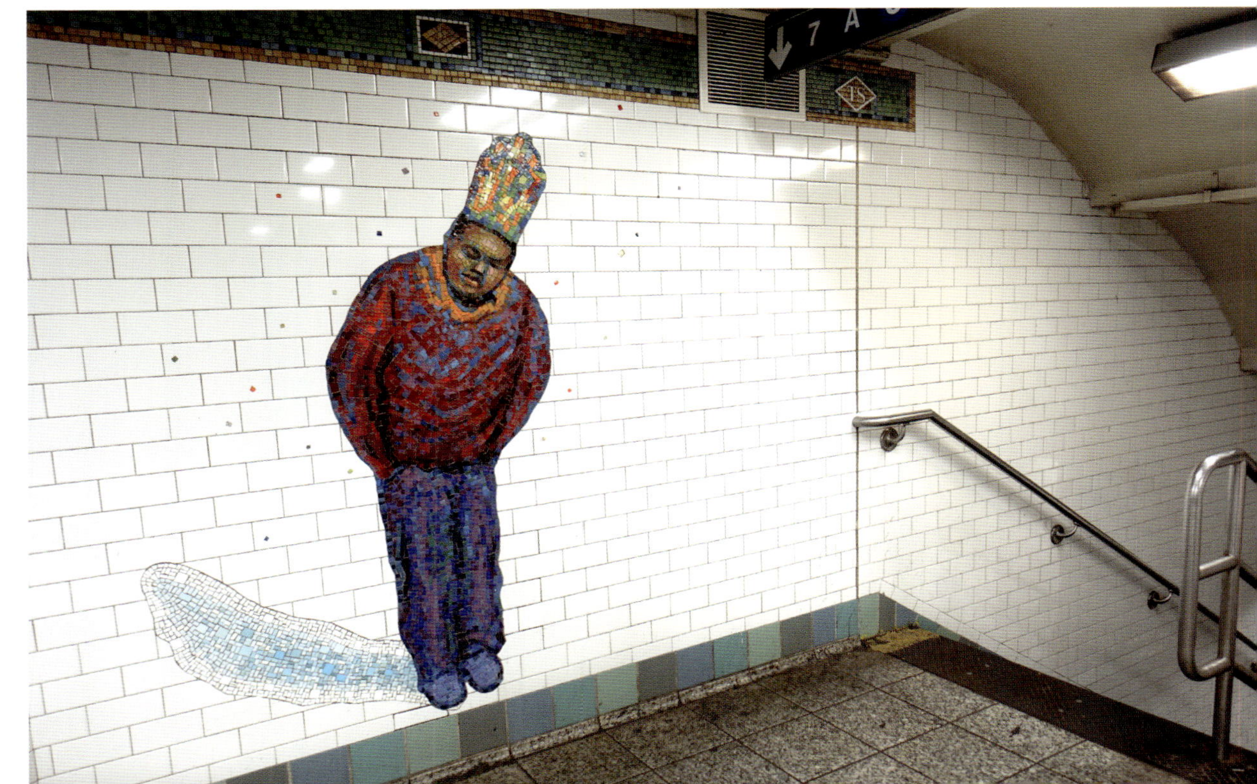
7 A

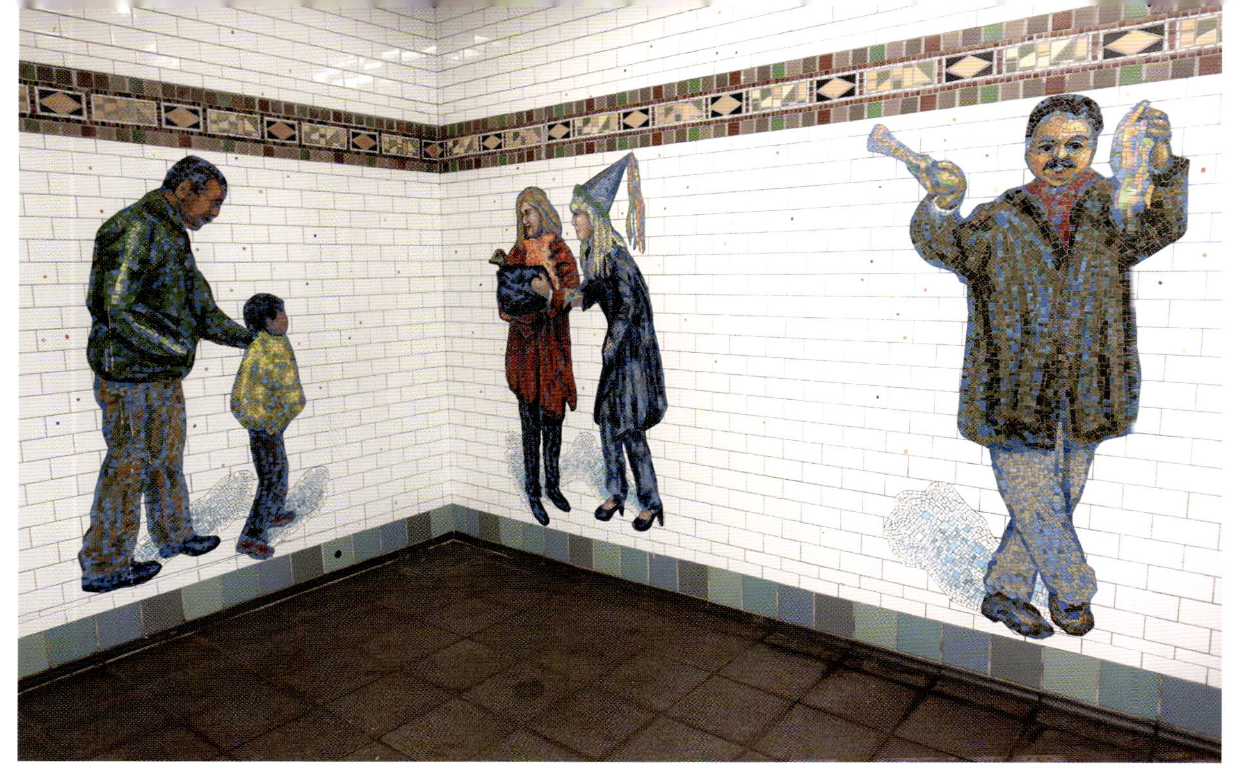

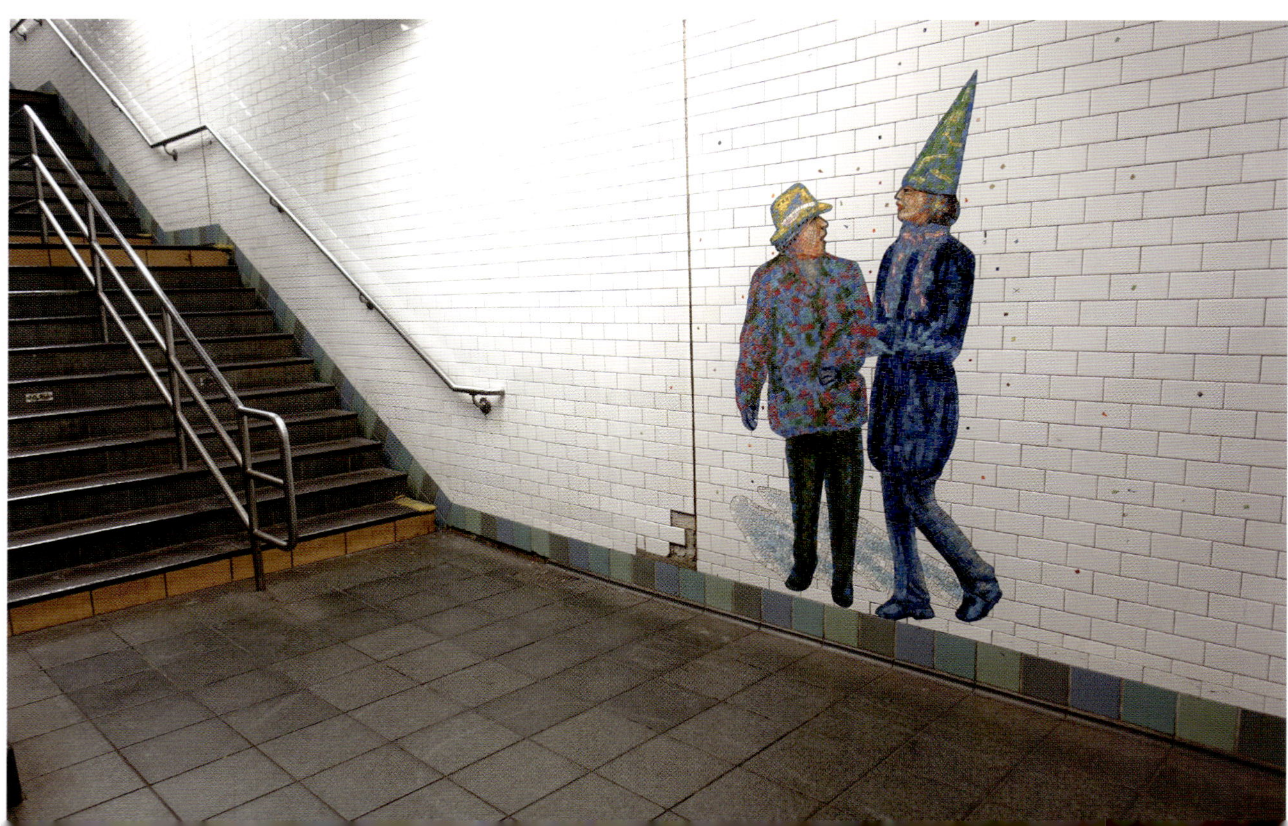

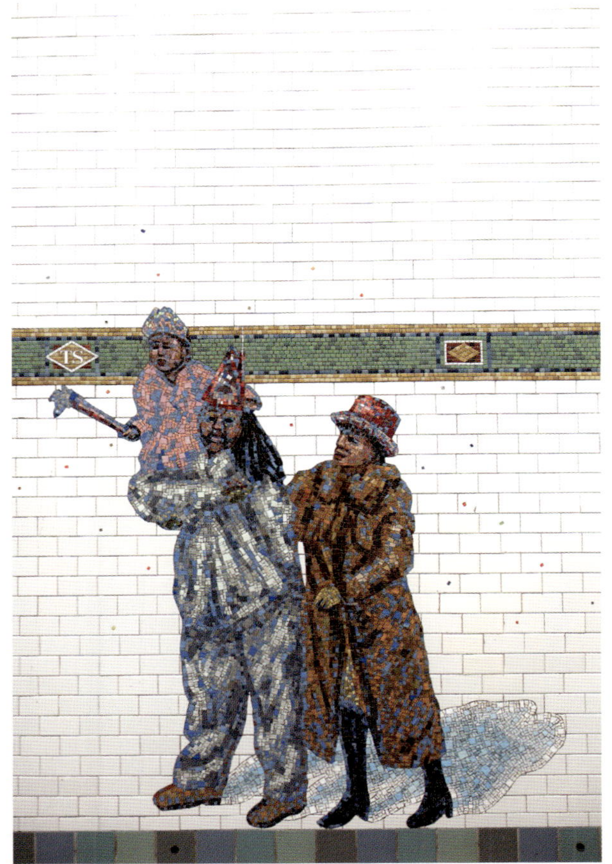
TS

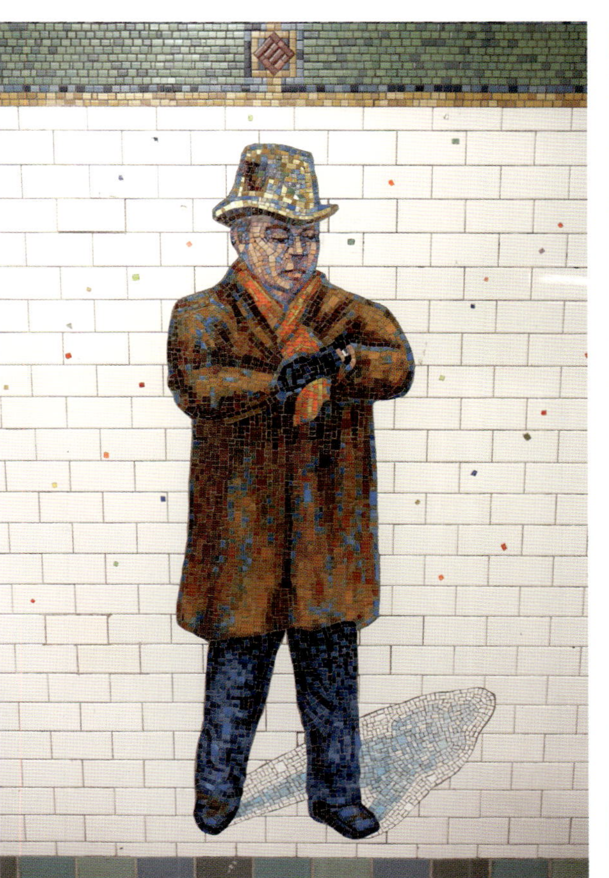

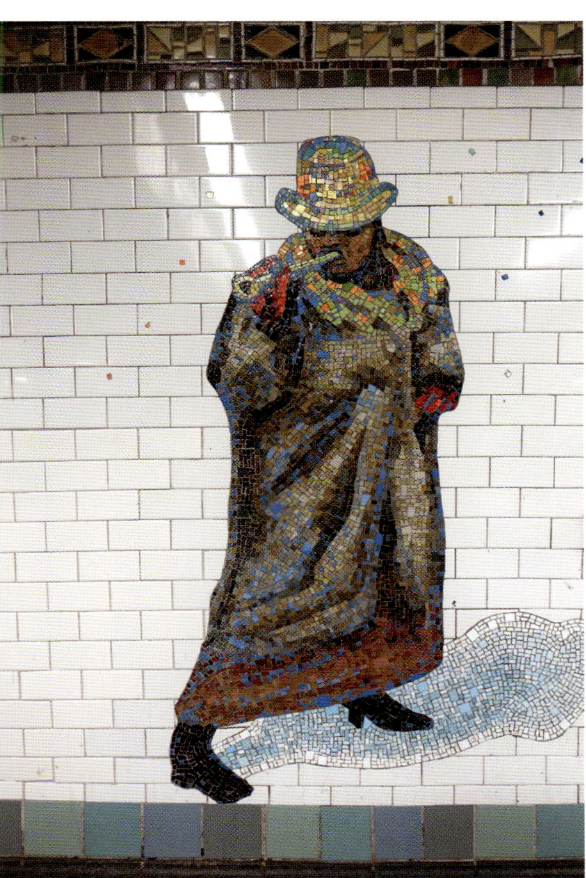

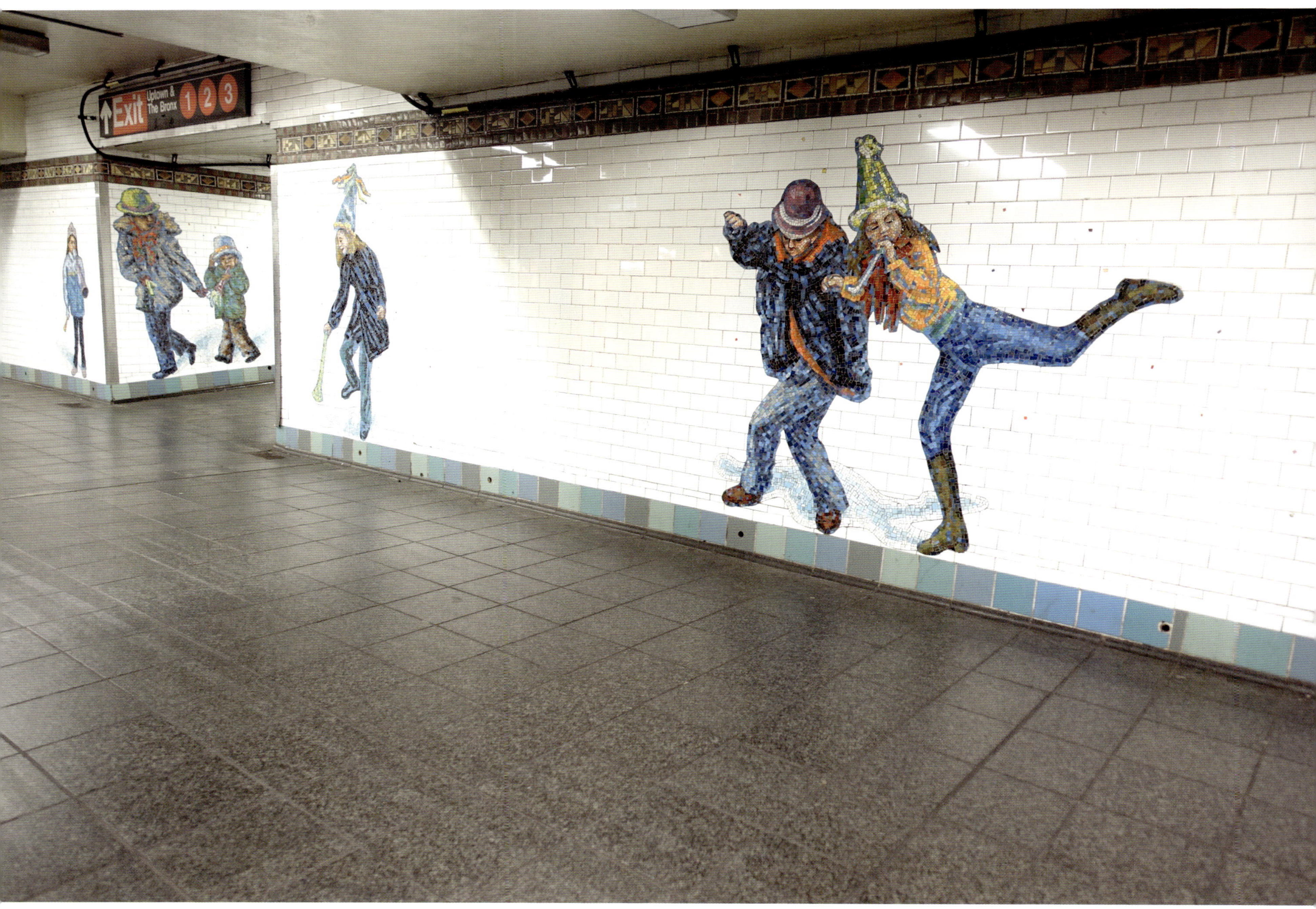
Exit
Uptown &
The Bronx
1 2 3

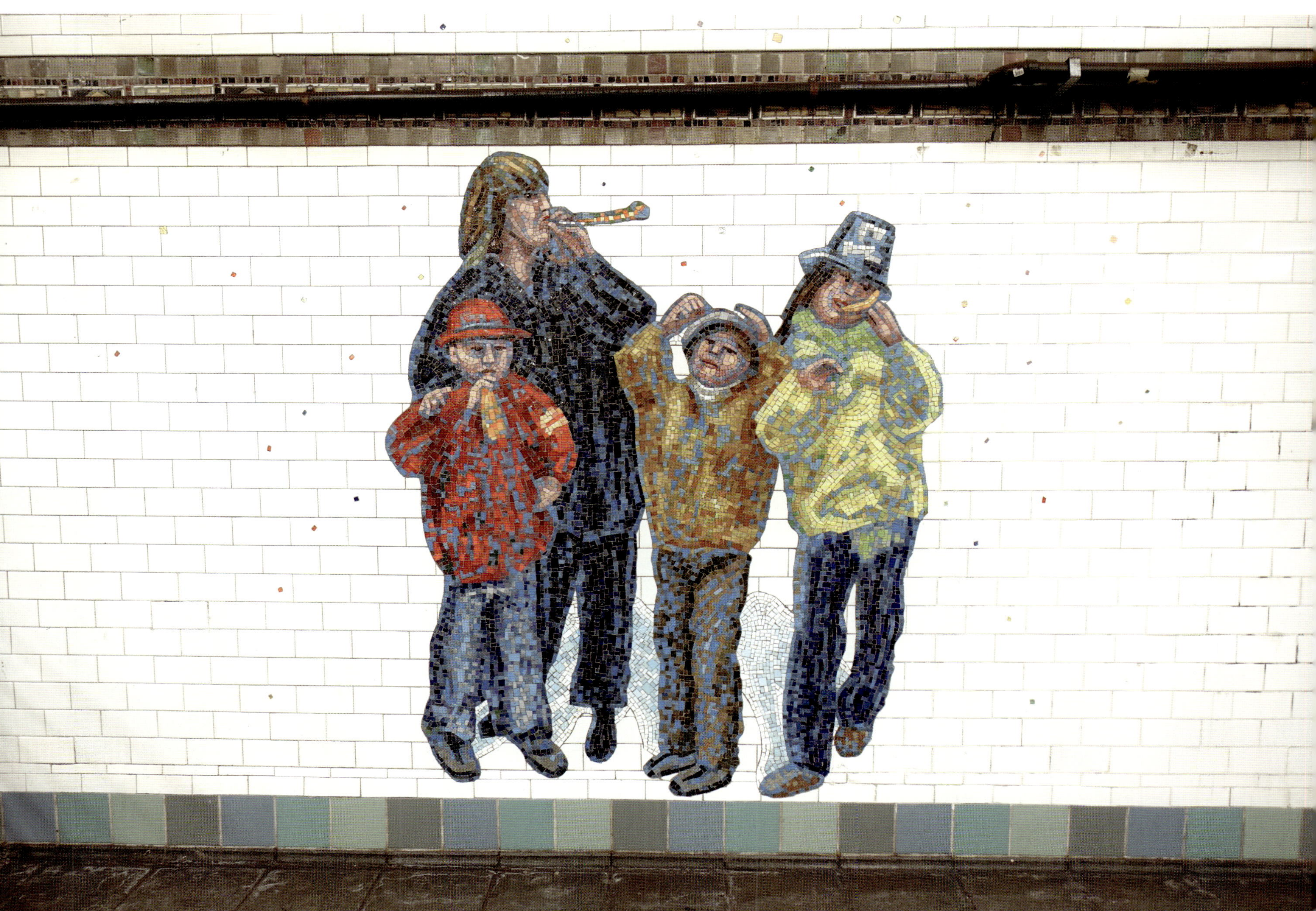

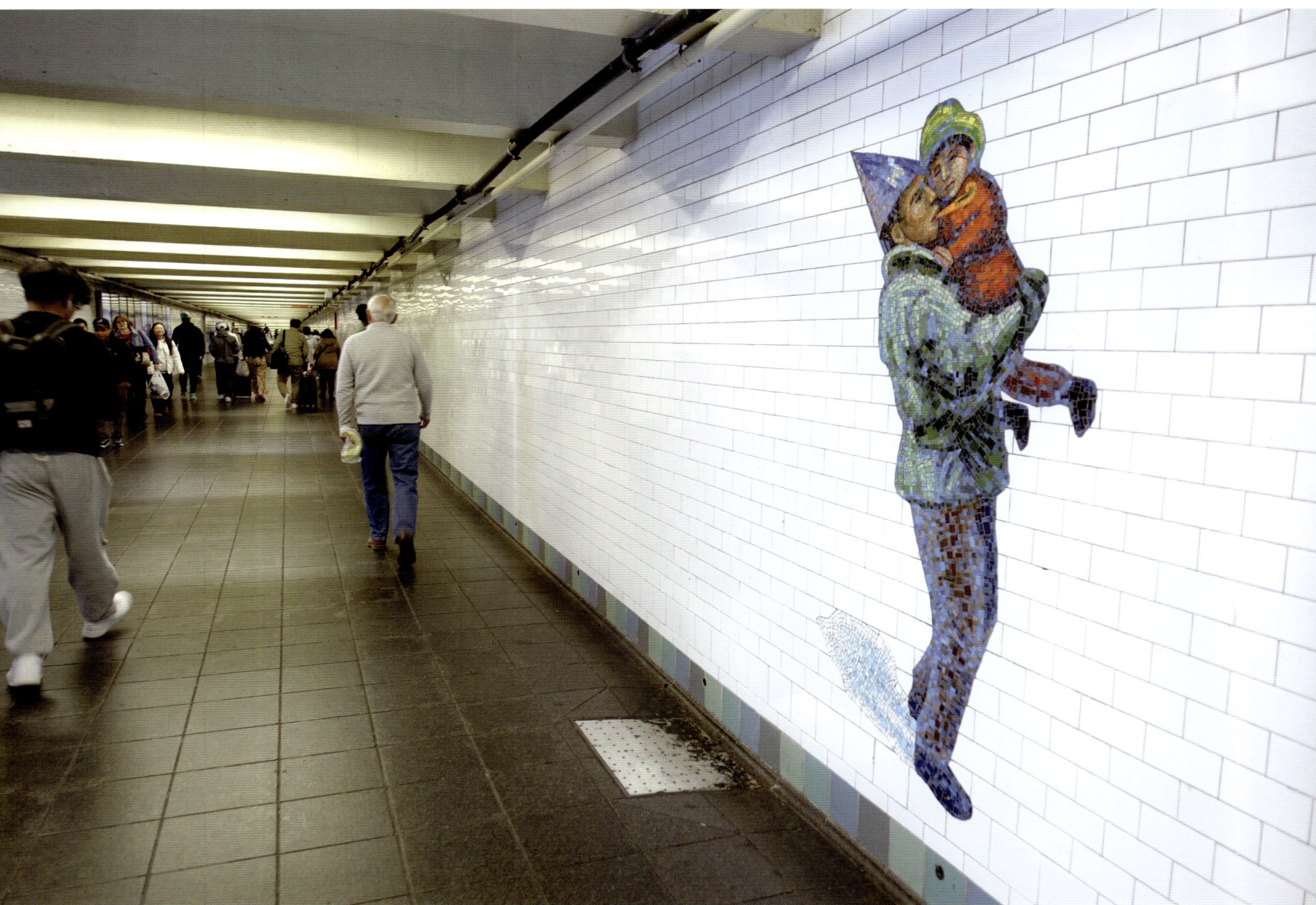

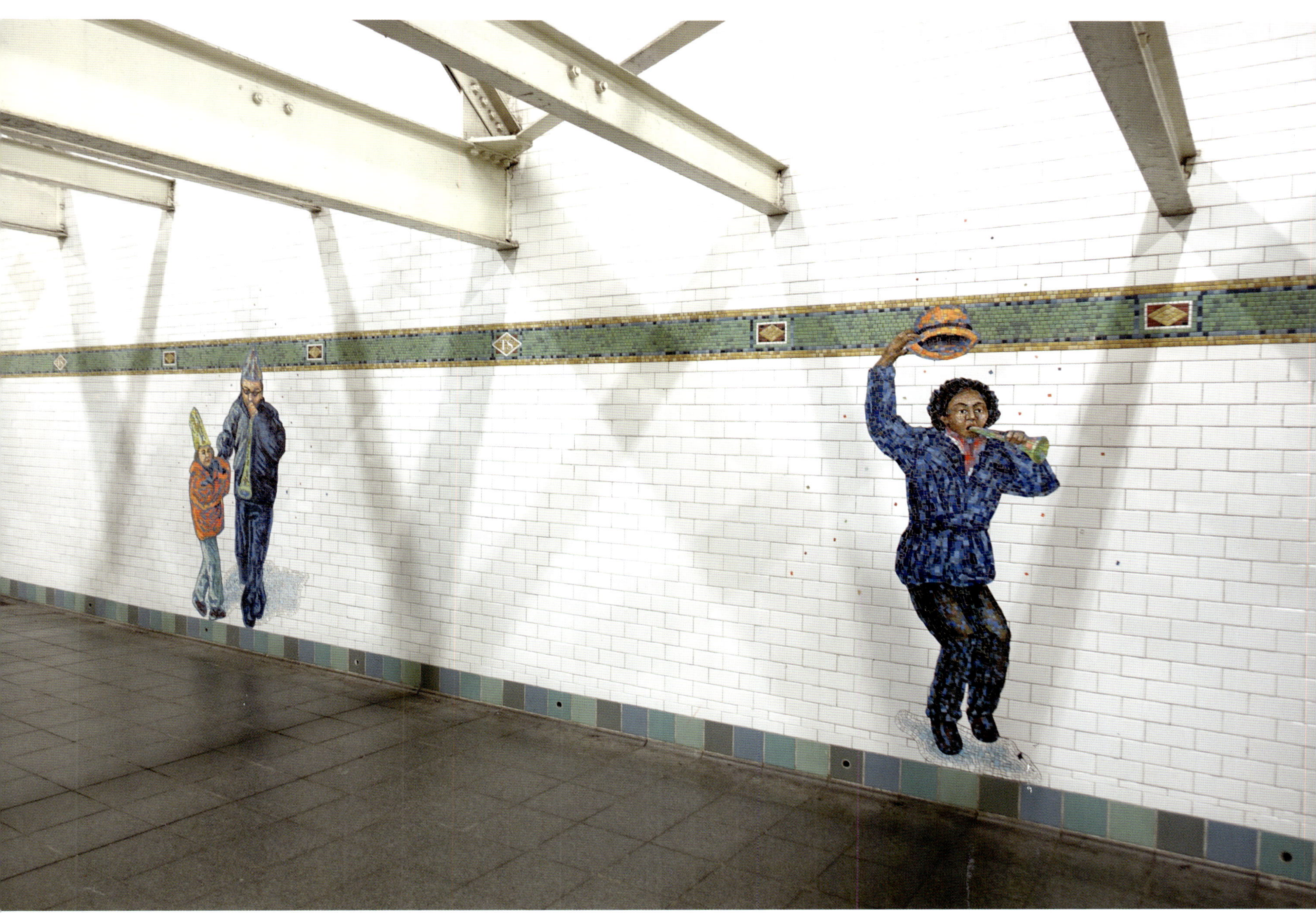

Jane Dickson was born in Chicago and moved to New York City in the late 1970s, choosing the Times Square area because "all the issues and problems of society are out on display. They may exist [elsewhere] but in Times Square they're right in front of you." She began her career as a figurative painter but found that life outside her studio was a lot more interesting than the still-lifes she had set up. Dickson worked for a time as a designer and animator at Spectracolor, the first digital billboard that loomed over Times Square. She came up in the wildly creative and productive downtown art scene in the 1970s and 1980s, organizing some of the most profound public exhibitions, including *Messages to the Public*, which broadcasted various digital artworks from different artists on the Spectracolor light board at One Times Square. Organized in conjunction with the Public Art Fund, the project ran from 1982 to 1990 and blurred the line between art, propaganda, and advertisement.

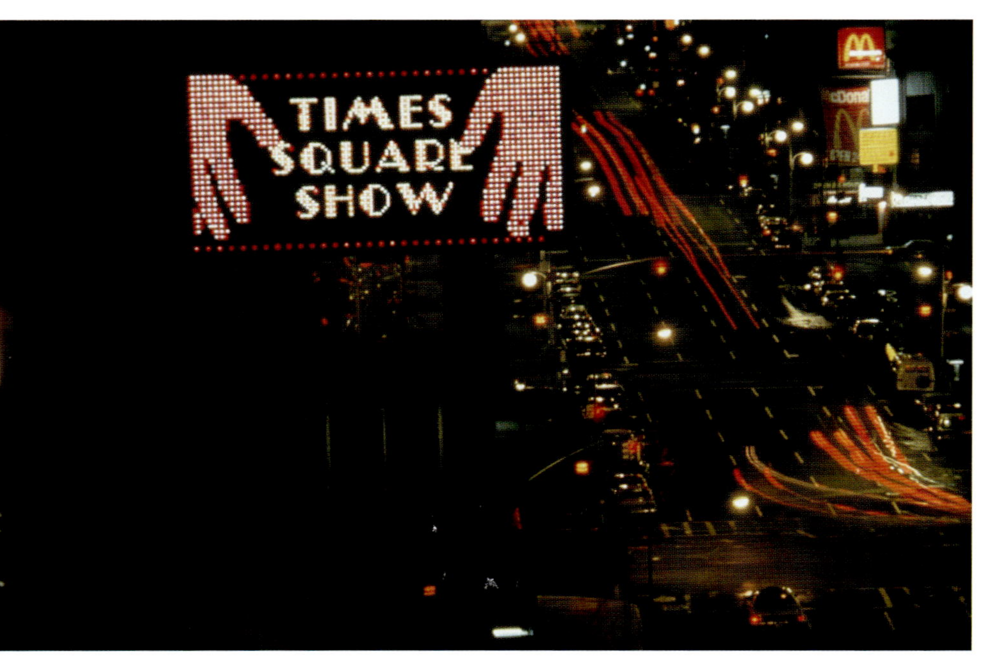

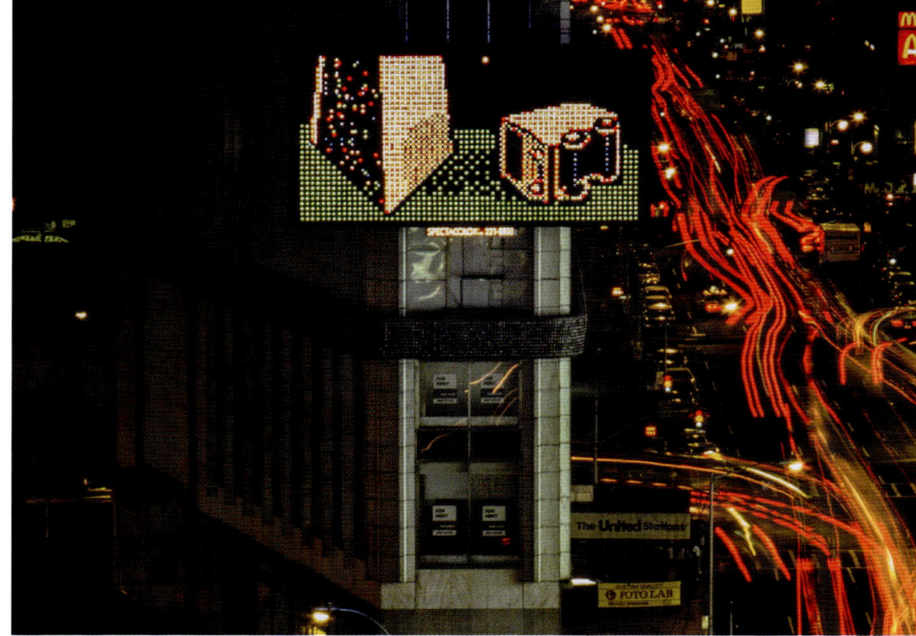

***Messages to the Public*, 1982**
Digital animation on Spectracolor billboard
Courtesy of the artist and Karma Gallery

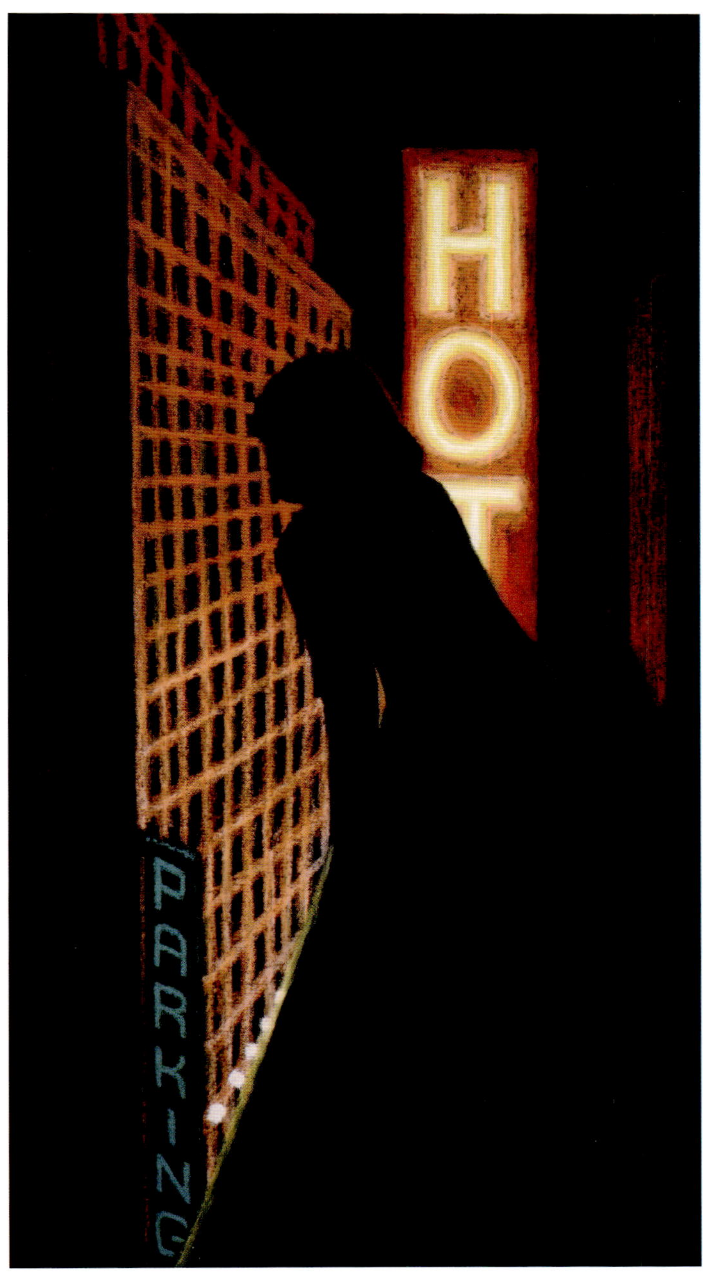

***Hotel Girl*, 1983**
Oil stick on canvas
Courtesy of the artist and Karma Gallery

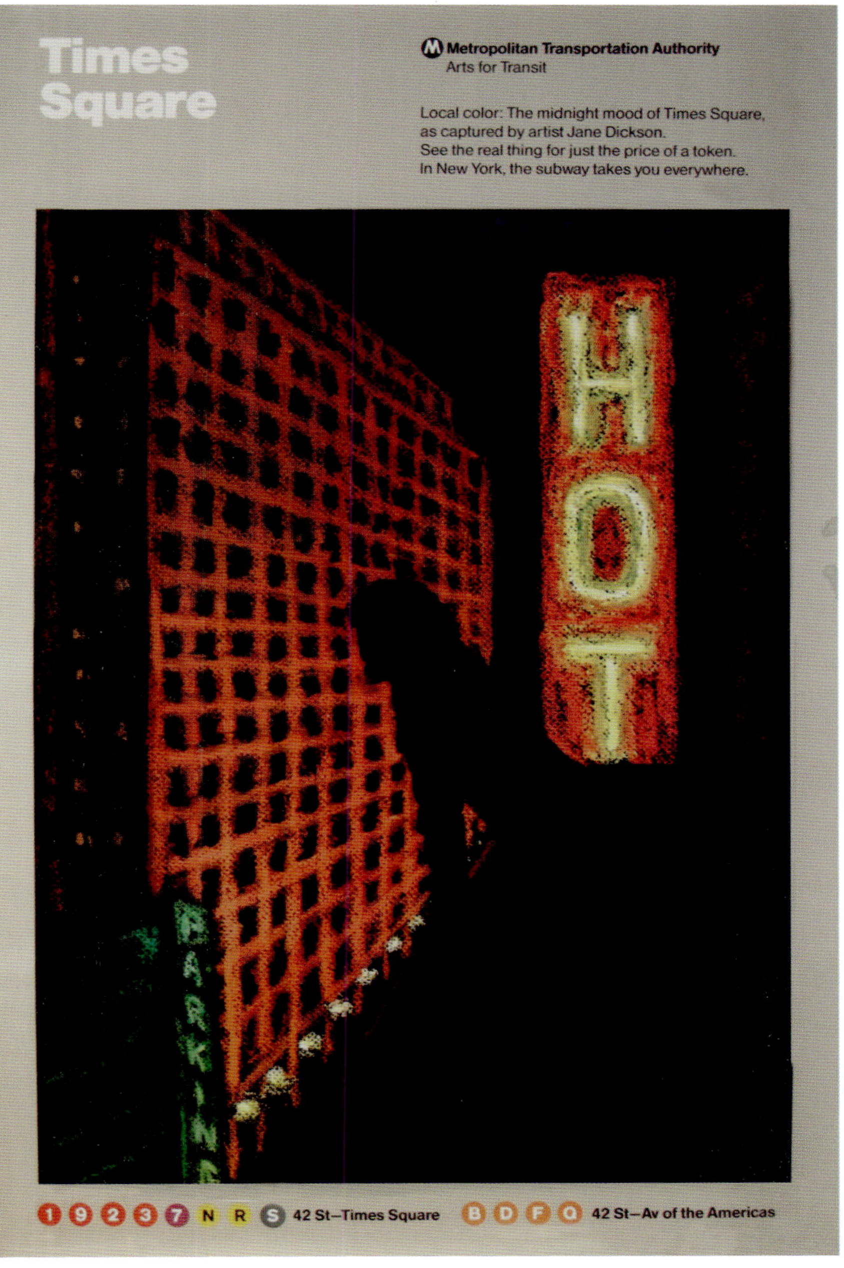

***Times Square Station Poster for MTA Arts for Transit*, 1991**
Courtesy of the artist and Karma Gallery

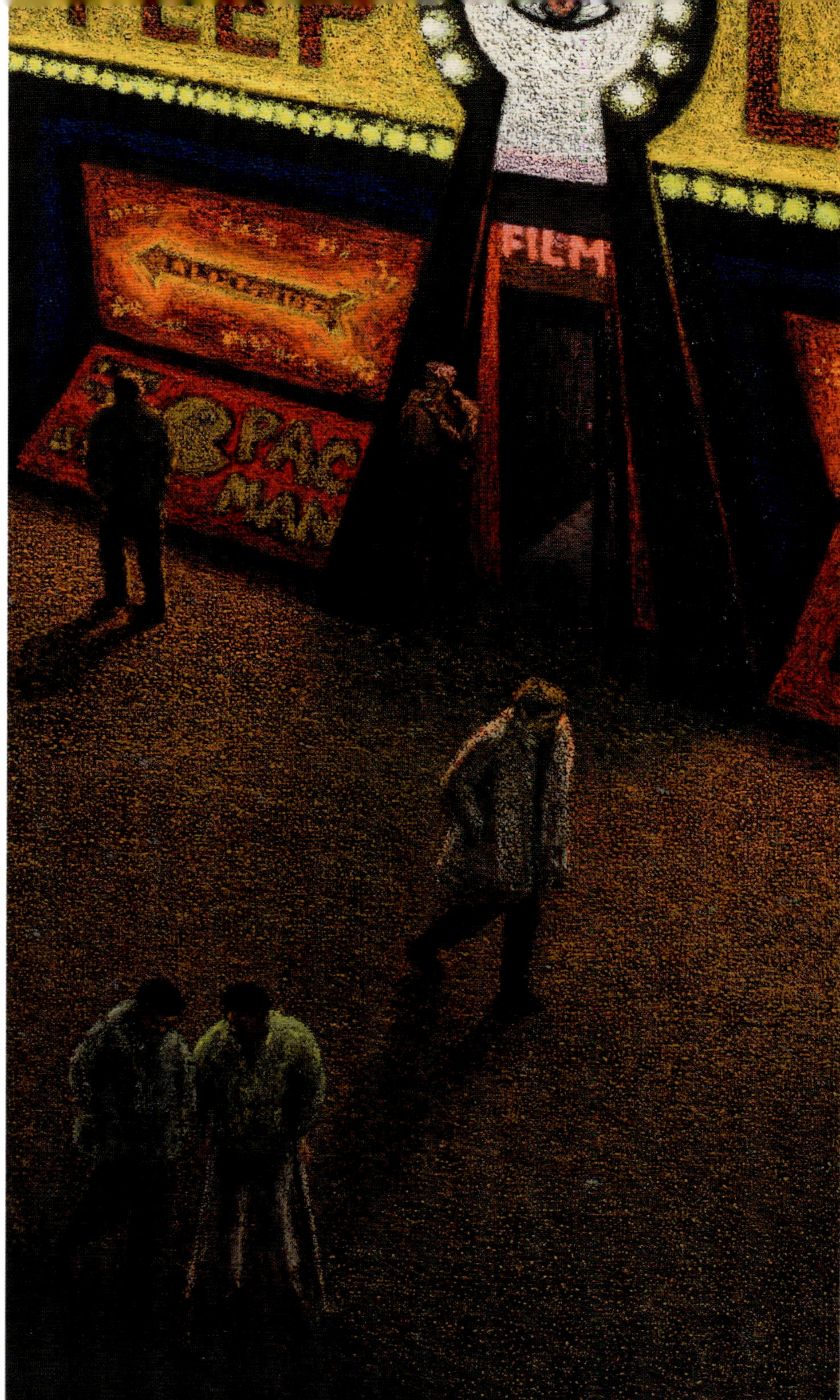

When Dickson lived in Times Square, she worked primarily at night so her view of the city was one cloaked in artificial light, glaring neon signs, and anonymous figures rushing down dark streets. It was also there that she began taking snapshots of the streets below, which became a seemingly endless source of material for her paintings and drawings. She used oil stick and acrylic on unconventional materials with distinct tactile qualities–astroturf, vinyl, sandpaper, any material that she could find and afford–that brought alive the implied drama of the scenes she captured, and imparted a grainy quality, as if seen through the screen of an analog television. *Peepland Conversation* (1988) epitomizes Dickson's distinct ability to capture the seediness of Times Square through this beautifully grainy lens, the rough materiality emphasizing the grim realities of life on the streets. Two men are deep in conversation outside a peep show, their bodies lit up by the neon glare of the establishment; elsewhere, a man contemplates the wares advertised, while another figure walks away, hunched and seemingly craving anonymity. Though all their faces are obscured or otherwise blurred, one can imagine their expressions implied from their body language and the atmospheric haze of an urban night.

***Peepland Conversation*, 1988**
Oil on linen
Courtesy of the artist and Karma Gallery

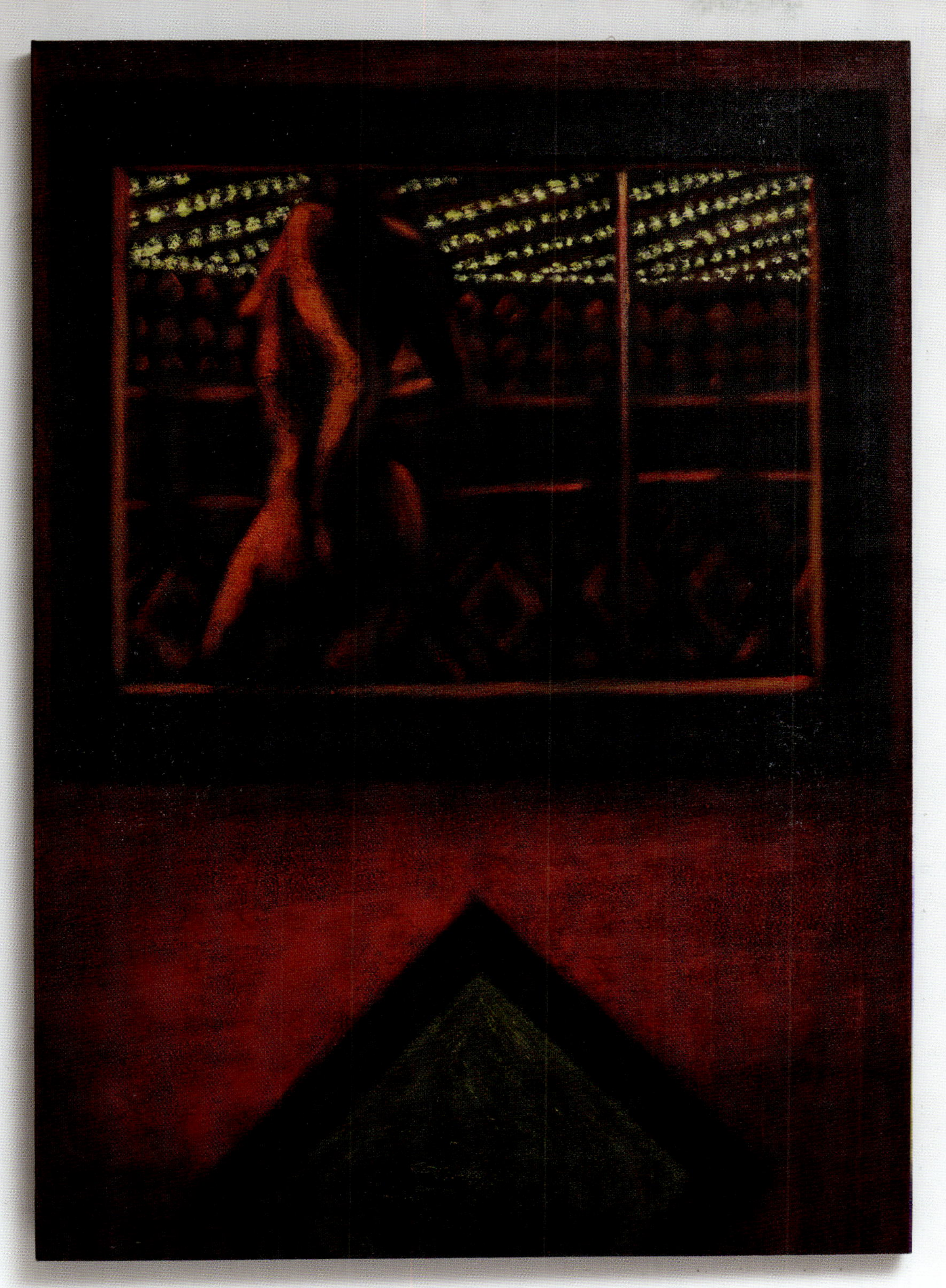

***Peep 3*, 1993**
Oil and pumice on canvas
Courtesy of the artist and Karma Gallery

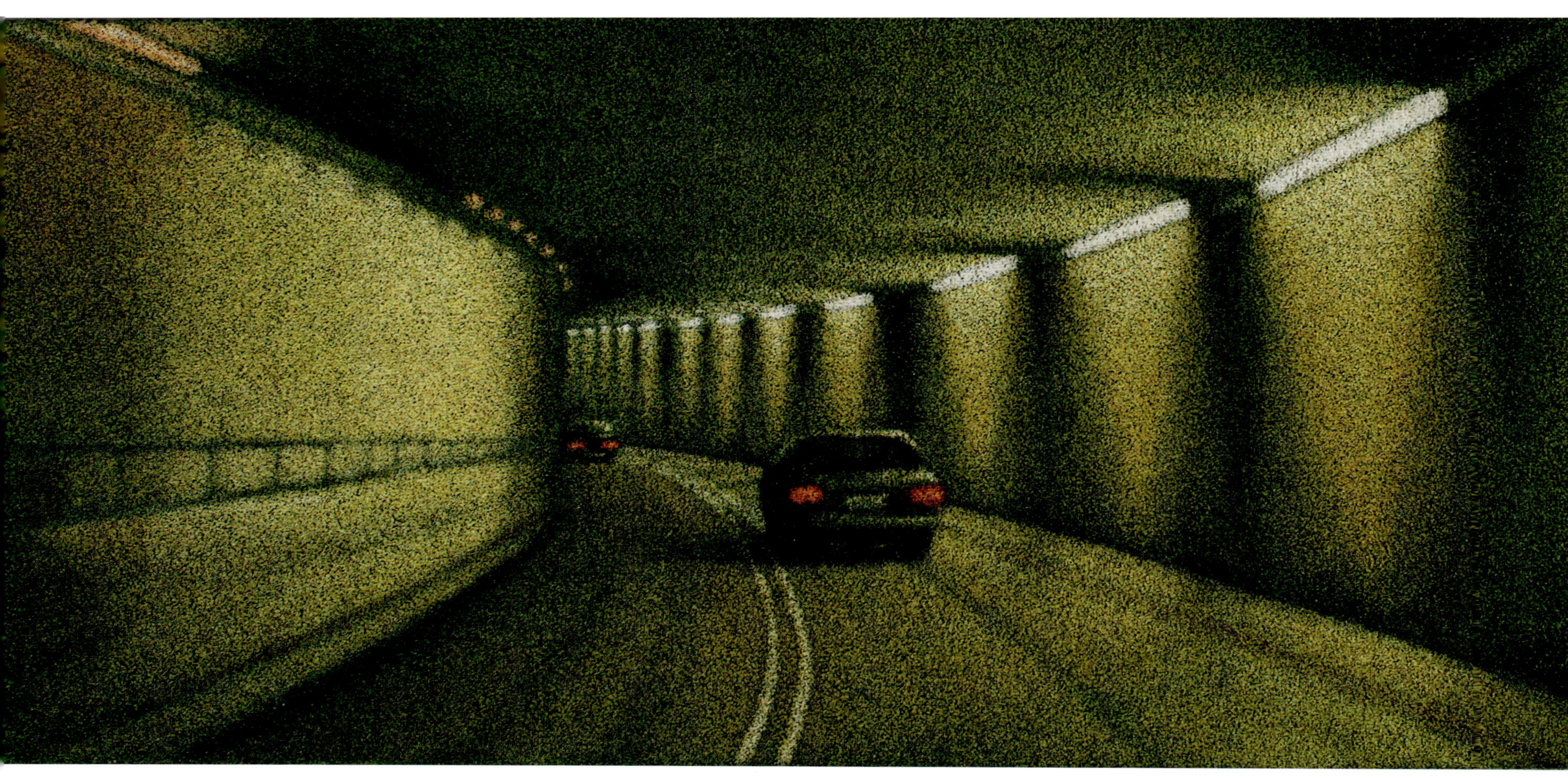

***Heading in–Lincoln Tunnel*, 2003**
Oil on Astroturf
Courtesy of the artist and Karma Gallery

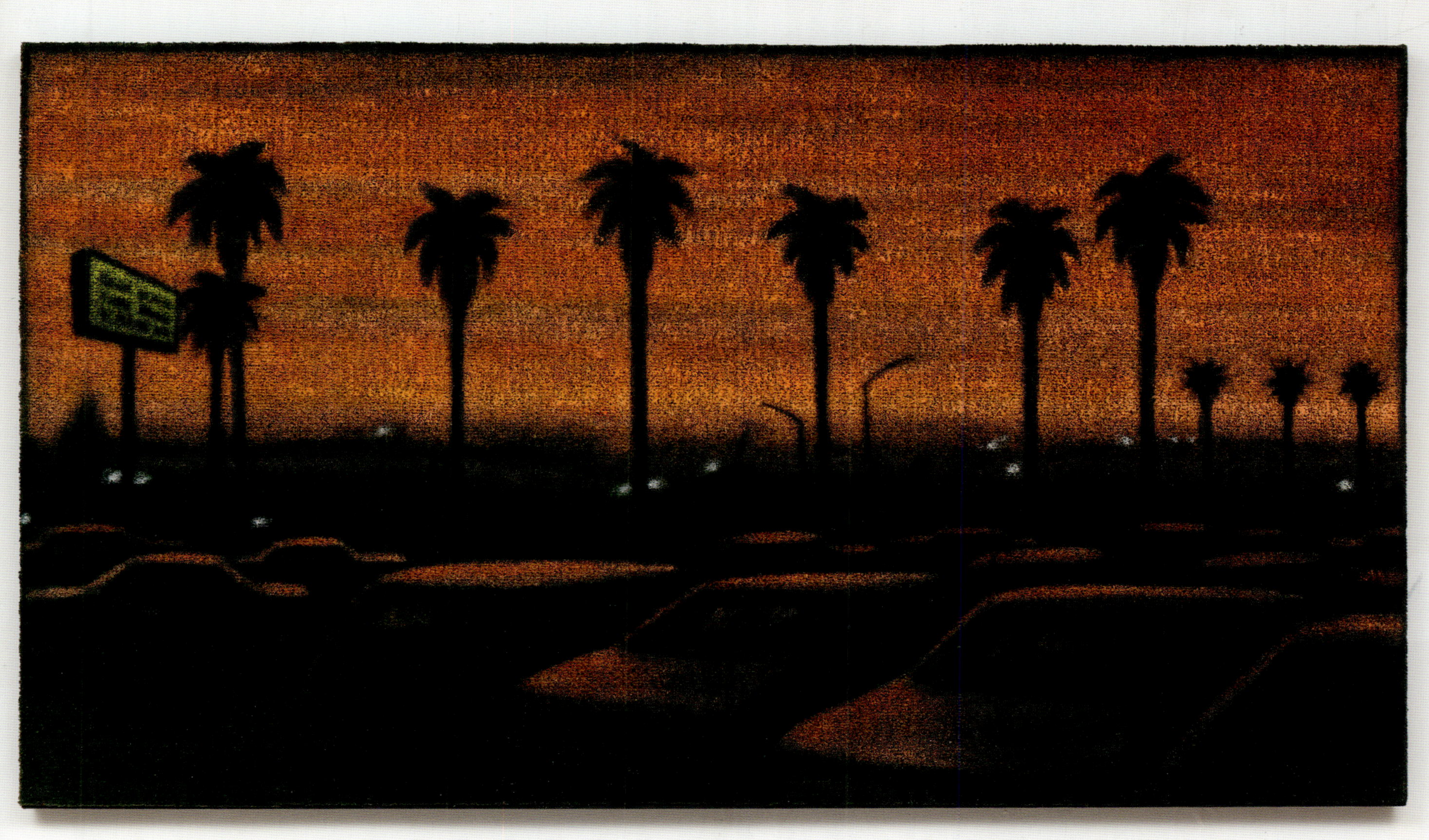

***Long Beach Lot Sunset*, 1999**
Oil on Astroturf
Courtesy of the artist and Karma Gallery

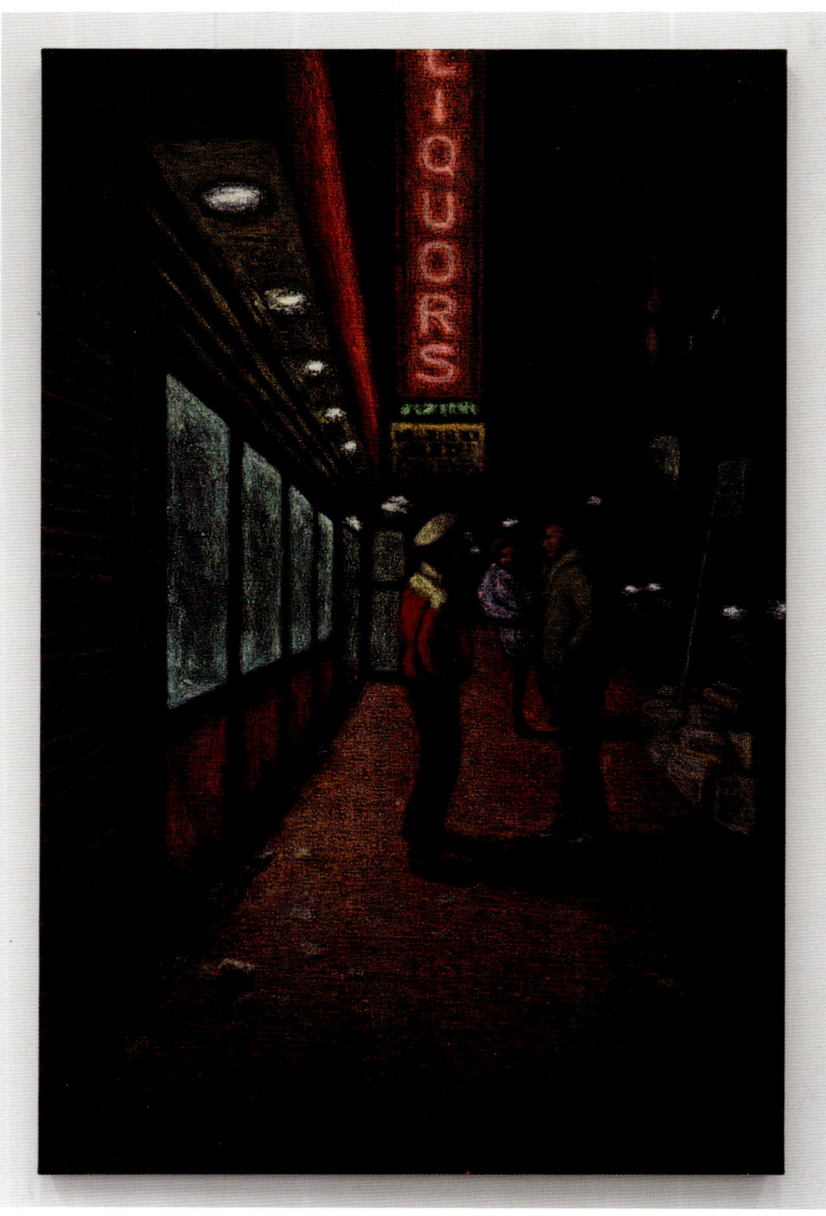

***Liquor Conversation*, 2020**
Oil stick on linen
Courtesy of the artist and Karma Gallery

***Dreams*, 2023**
Oil stick on linen
Courtesy of the artist and Karma Gallery

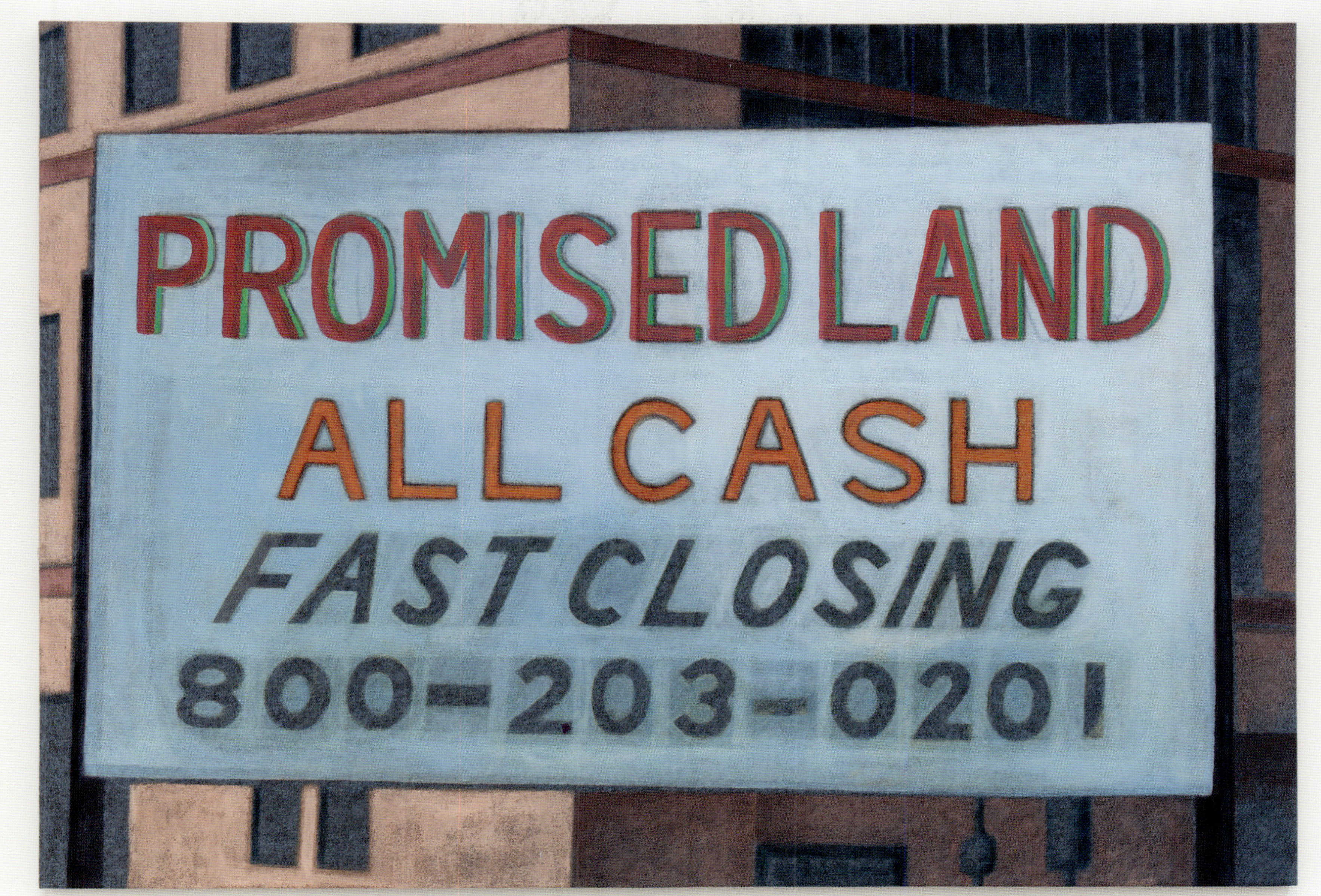

***Promised Land 1*, 2023**
Acrylic on felt mounted on canvas
Courtesy of the artist and Karma Gallery

Marcel Dzama (b. 1974)

BEDFORD AVENUE (L TRAIN)

***No Less Than Everything Comes Together*, 2021**

At the Bedford Avenue stop in Brooklyn, Marcel Dzama created theatrical tableaus filled with masked dancers, some performing under a vibrant sun, some beneath the moon, representing the passage of time in a commuter's day. The dancers wear costumes with polka-dot and spiral designs, which are a direct link to costumes that Dzama designed for the New York City Ballet in 2016. Accompanying the dancers are figures that reference famous Brooklynites, such as the mobster Bugsy Siegel (played by his young son in mafioso costume) and Peter Criss, drummer and founding member of the band Kiss, and a whimsical assortment of animal figures (including his own cat). The work, *No Less than Everything Comes Together*, is inspired by the Walt Whitman poem "Crossing Brooklyn Ferry," in which the protagonist describes not just what he sees but also feels when riding the ferry from Brooklyn to Manhattan, relating this small but significant journey to the progress of mankind itself. This poem was especially significant for Dzama, since it encapsulated his own sense of excitement riding the subway for the first time, especially coming from rural Winnipeg, Canada. The murals play out like a musical, with the artist casting the commuters into characters in his own theatrical creation, coming together in a dreamy homage to the vibrant culture and people of Brooklyn.

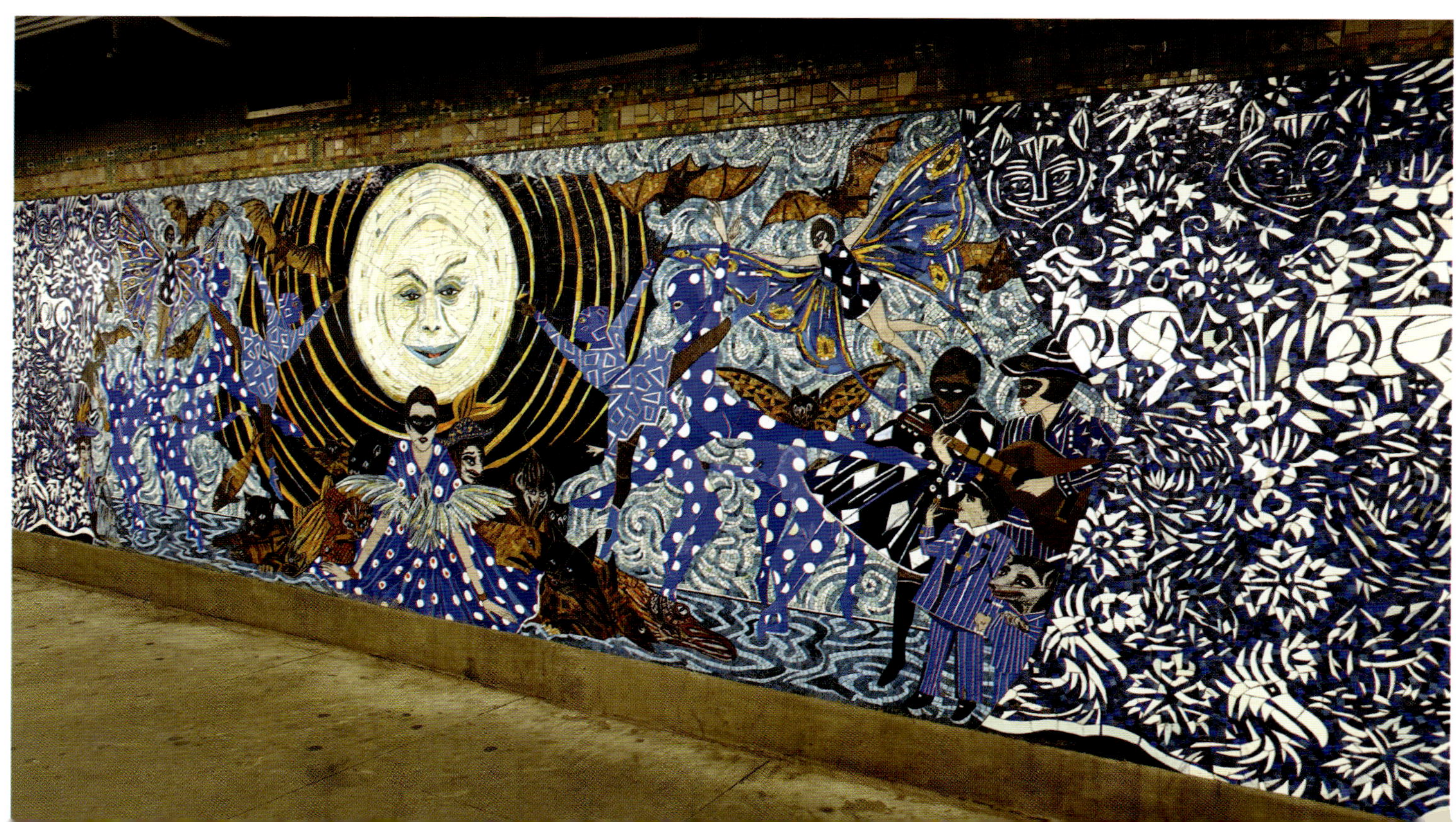

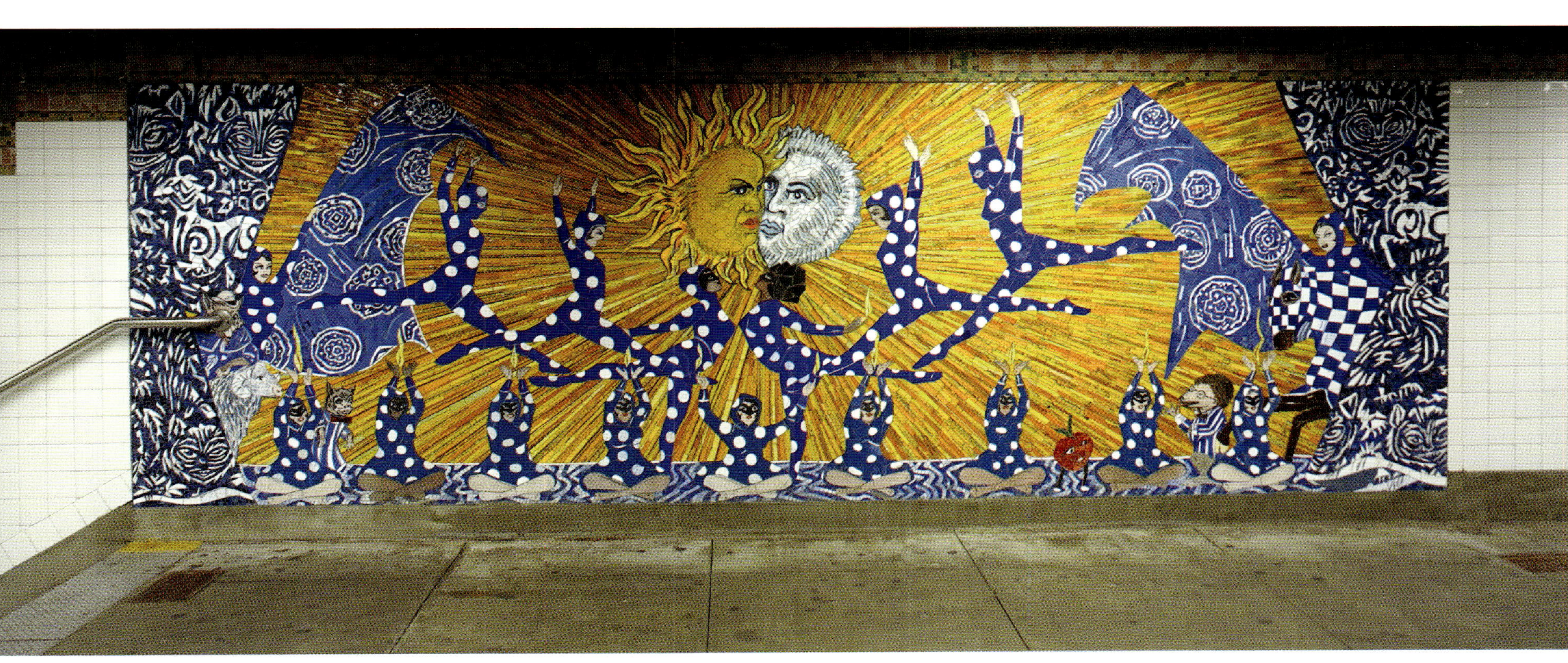

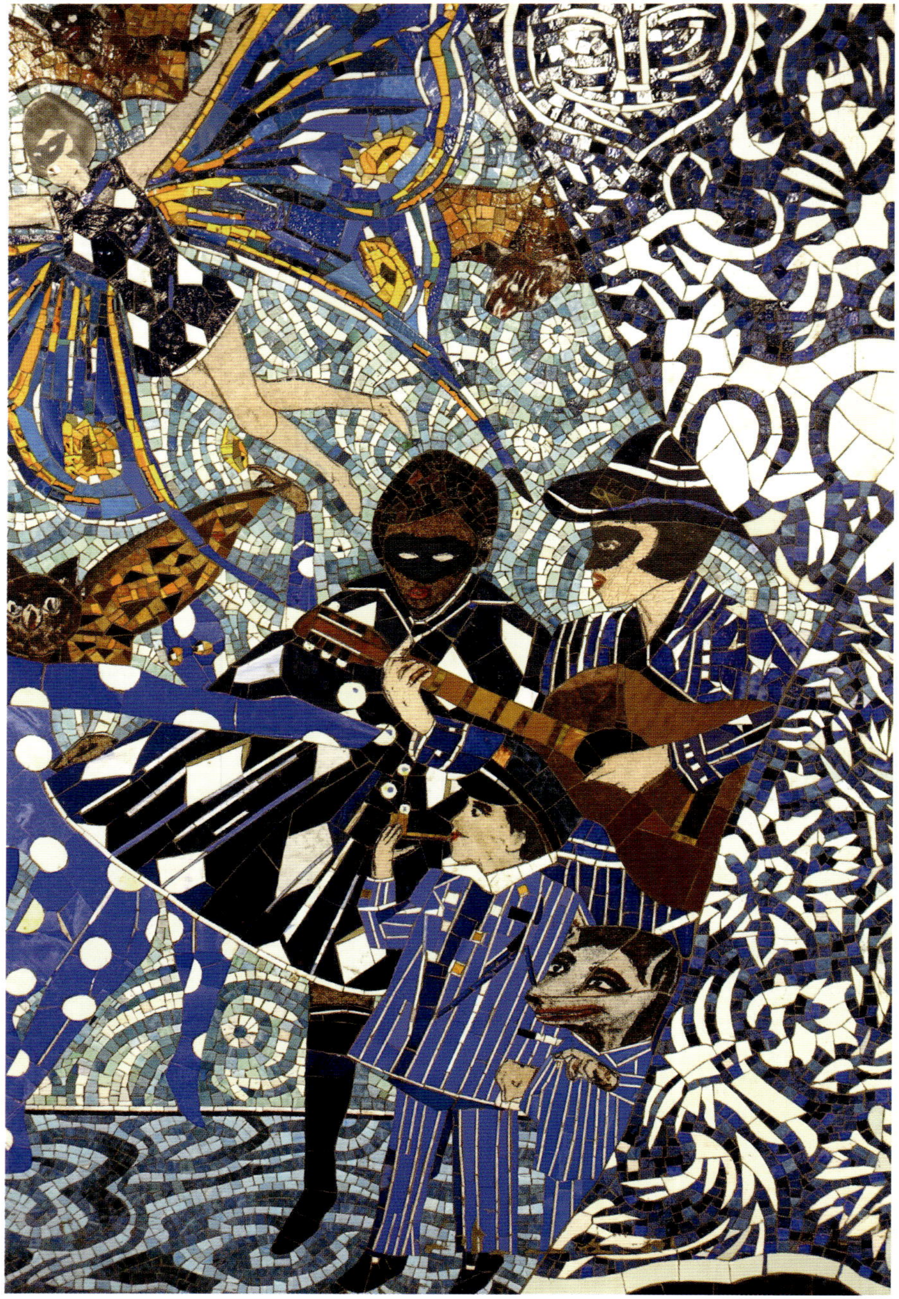

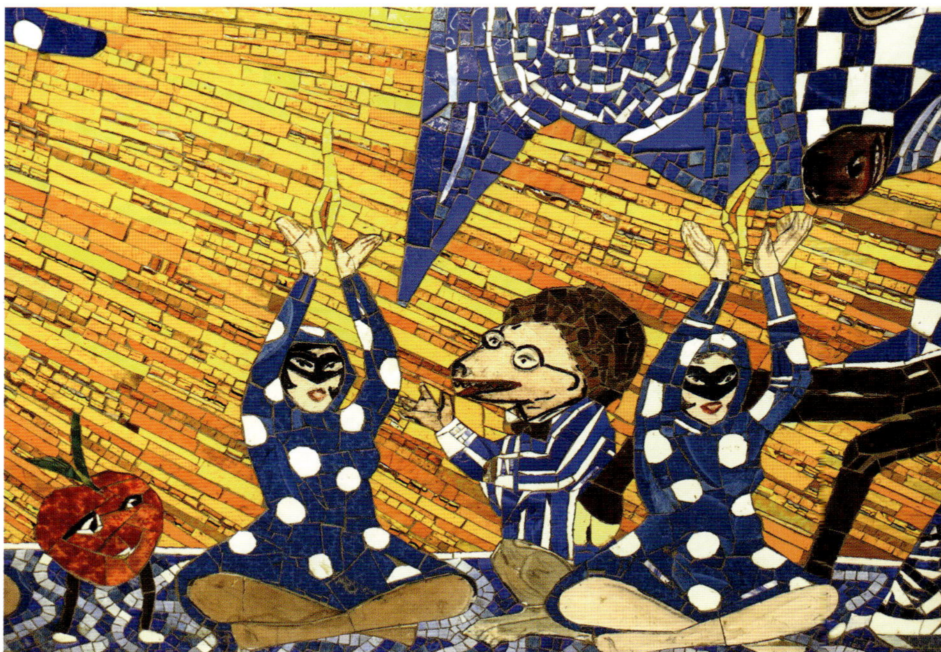

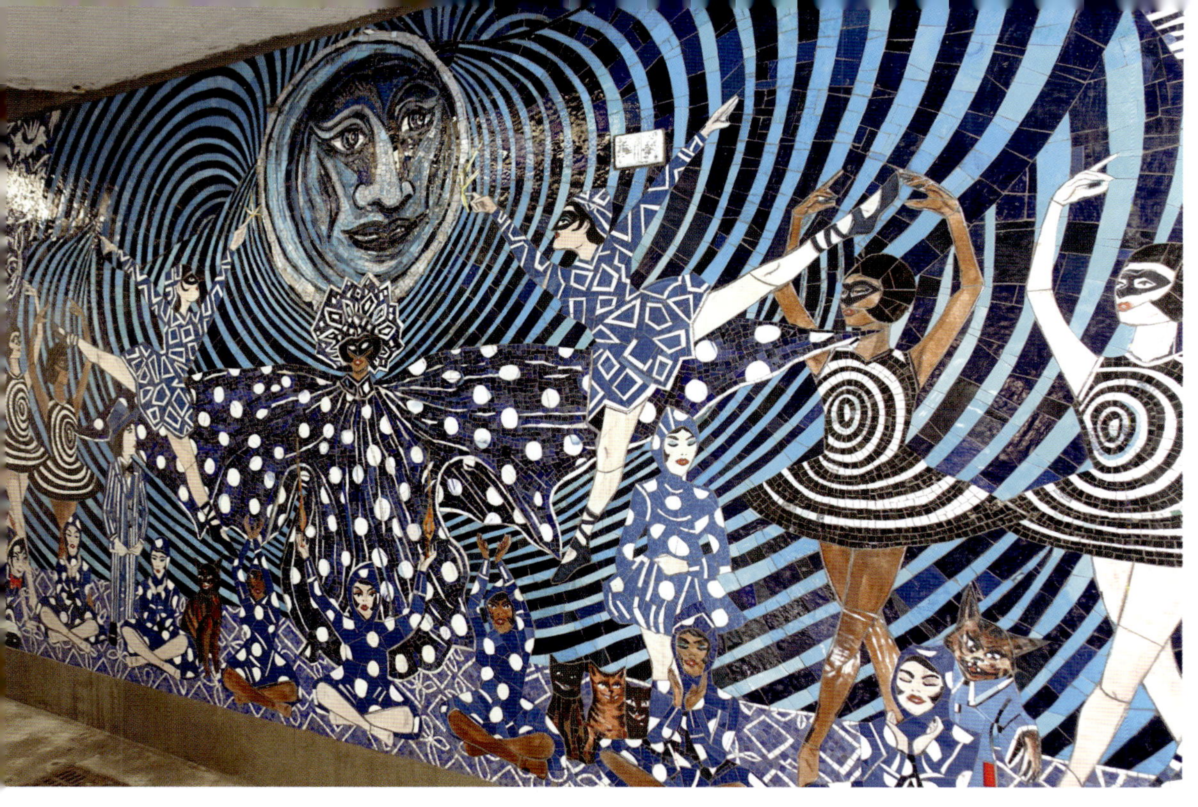

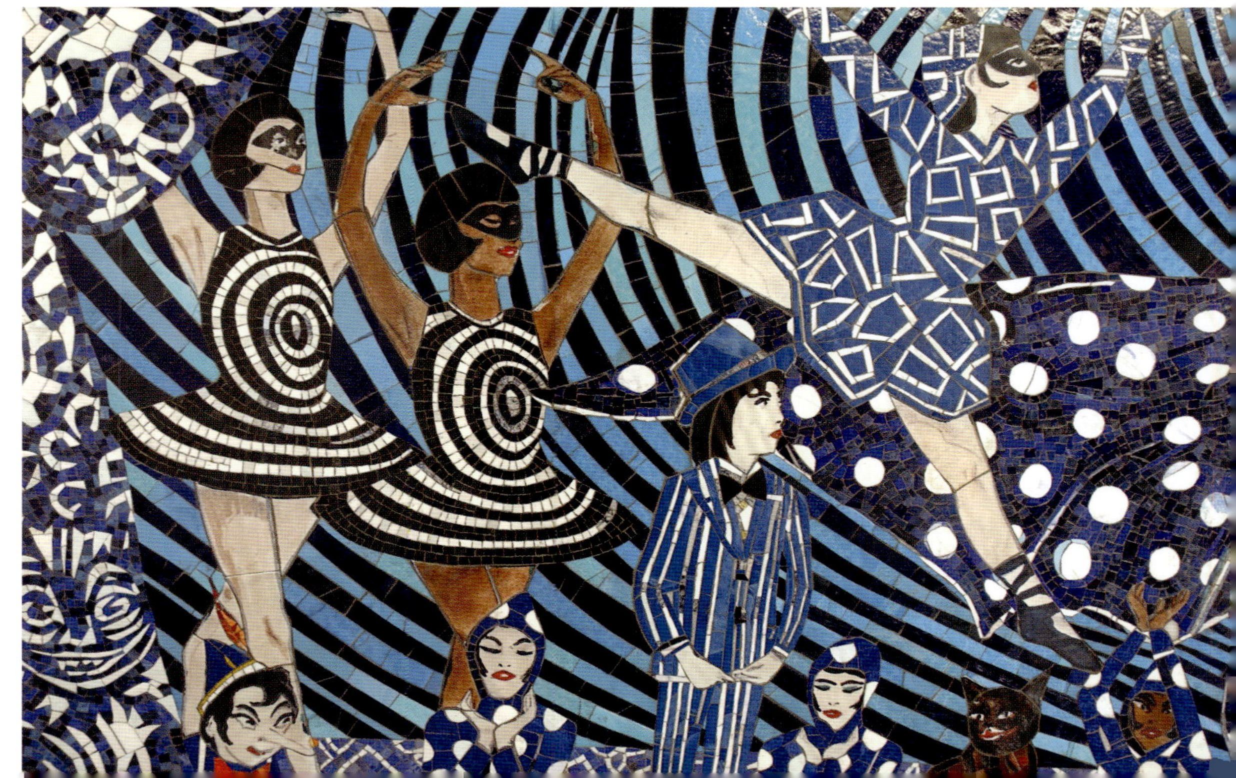

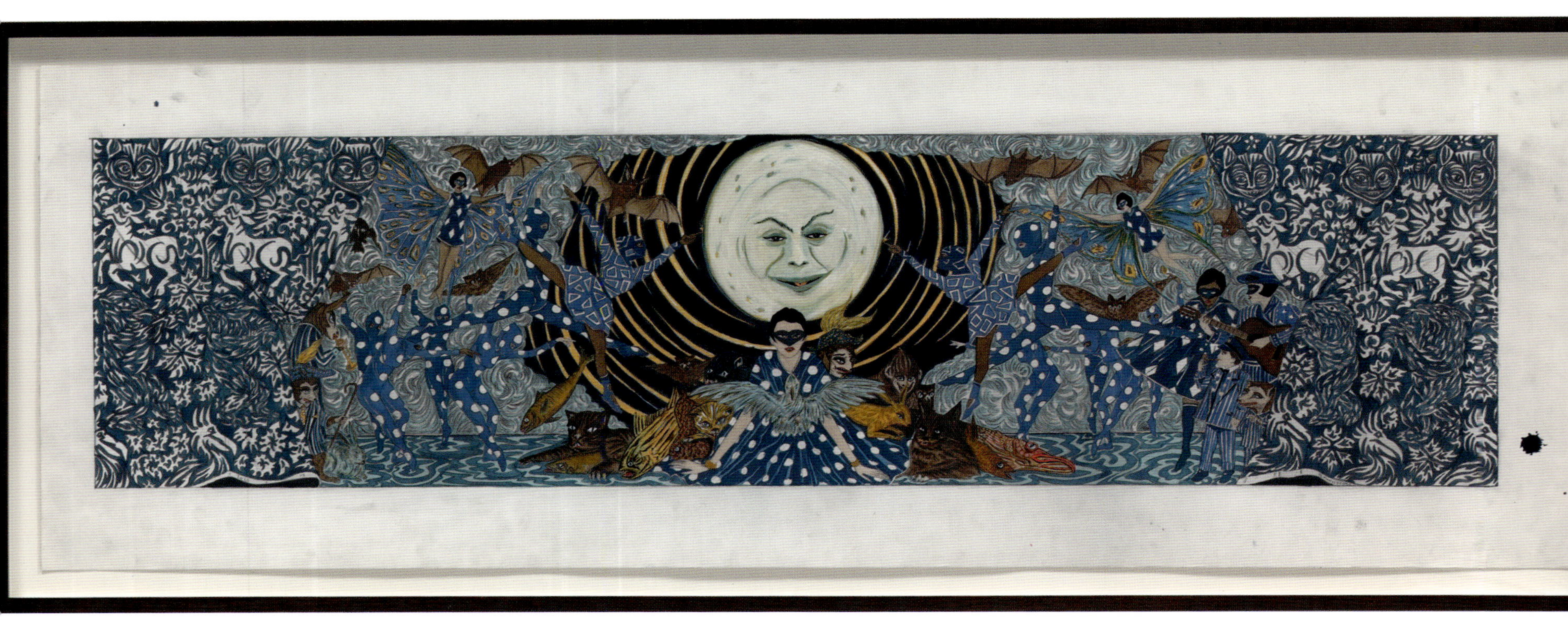

***Blue Moon*, 2020**

Ink, gouache, and graphite on paper

Courtesy of the artist and David Zwirner Gallery

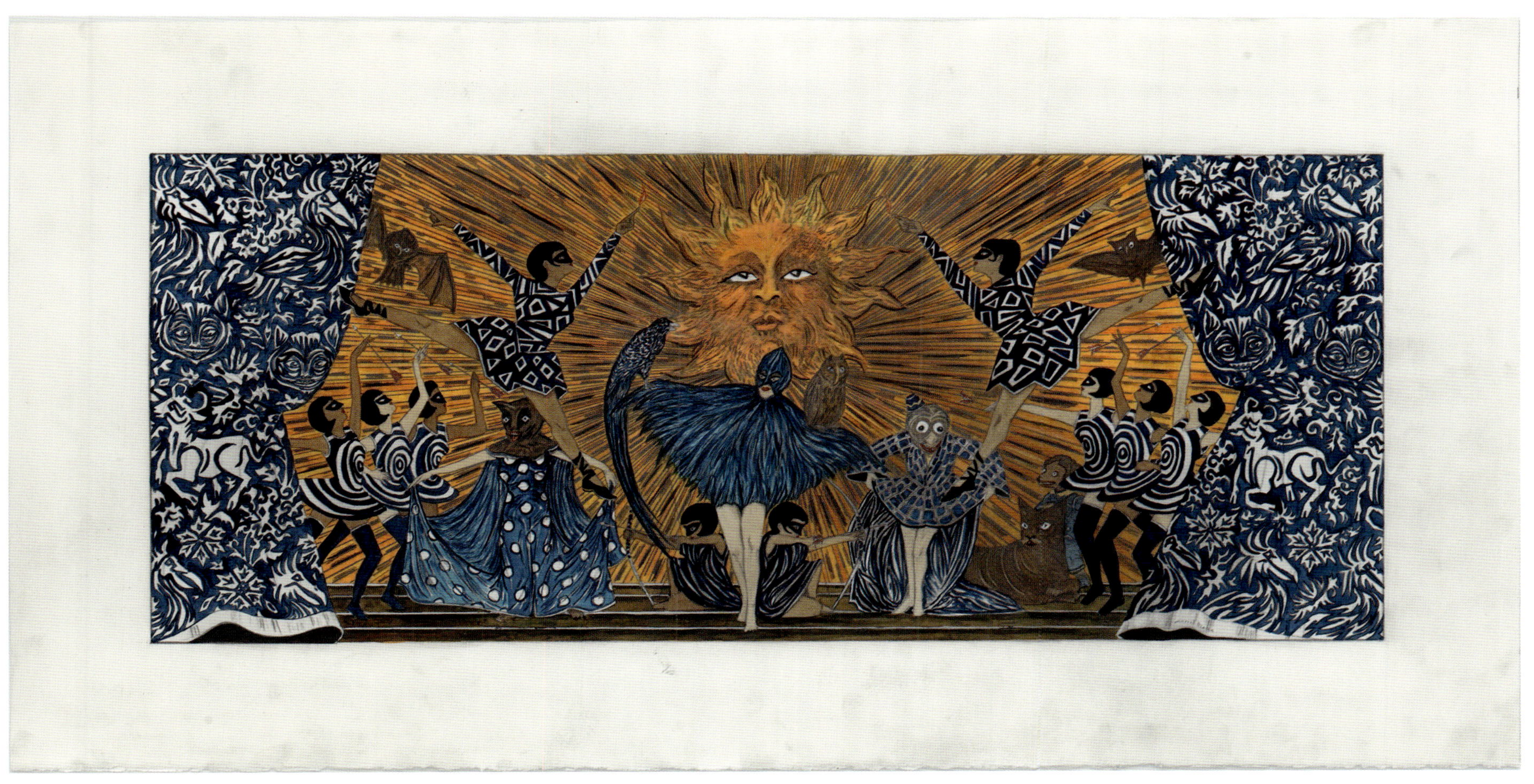

***Who Loves the Sun*, 2020–2021**
Ink, gouache, and graphite on paper
Courtesy of the artist and David Zwirner Gallery

Looking at this richly detailed mural, it is clear that Dzama is an artist who draws inspiration from a vast creative well. Art history, poetry, and music comingle with political movements, personal experiences, and mythology. He is equally influenced by Dada artists such as Francis Picabia and contemporary peers such as Raymond Pettibone (whom he collaborates with often). He is known for his vivid, layered paintings and illustrations, poetically titled and brimming with whimsical figures in surreal situations. In earlier works that are more outright political and dark, Dzama clad figures in polka-dotted costumes that dance across the paper to cleverly draw the viewer into a foreboding world. He worked in somber, moody tones of maroon and brown. After trips to Morocco in 2018 and Mexico in 2020, his palette brightened and took on a vibrancy that emphasized his play with contrasts more pointedly. In *Our father was a beast, mother a beauty, and grandpa was a vampire* (2021), two masked children ride astride a hairy creature under the blue glow of a grinning moon. The beach on which they reside is a golden yellow, the sea a vibrant blue that matches the figures' clothing. Framed by lush green foliage like stage curtains, the scene is at once peculiar and inviting; there is a hint of violence, with the beast standing on top of a bloody bat, that belies the benign cheerfulness of the smiling figures.

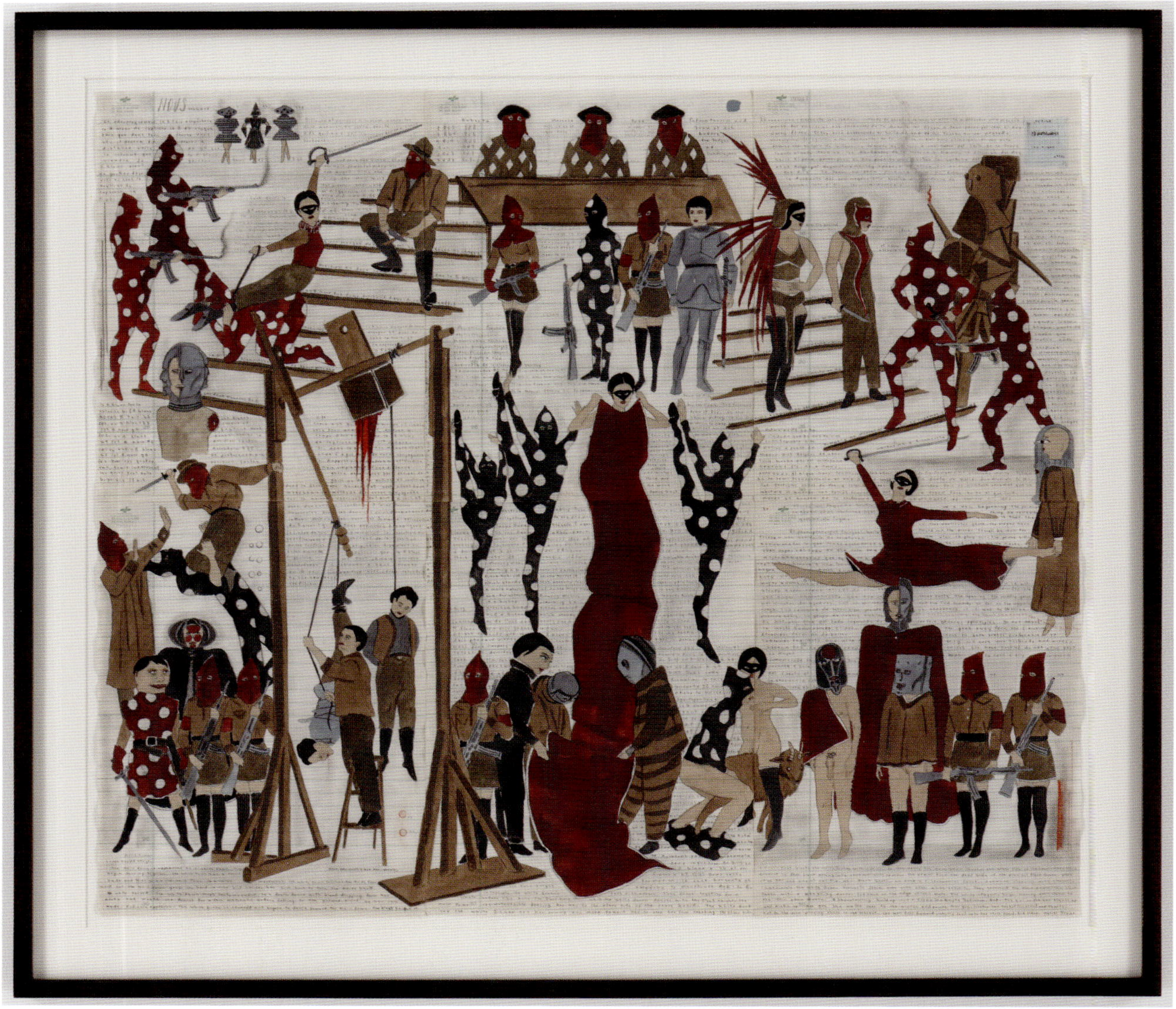

***Potnia Theron and Joan of Arc before the judges of Guadalupe*, 2010**
Graphite, watercolor, and ink on paper
Courtesy of the artist and David Zwirner Gallery

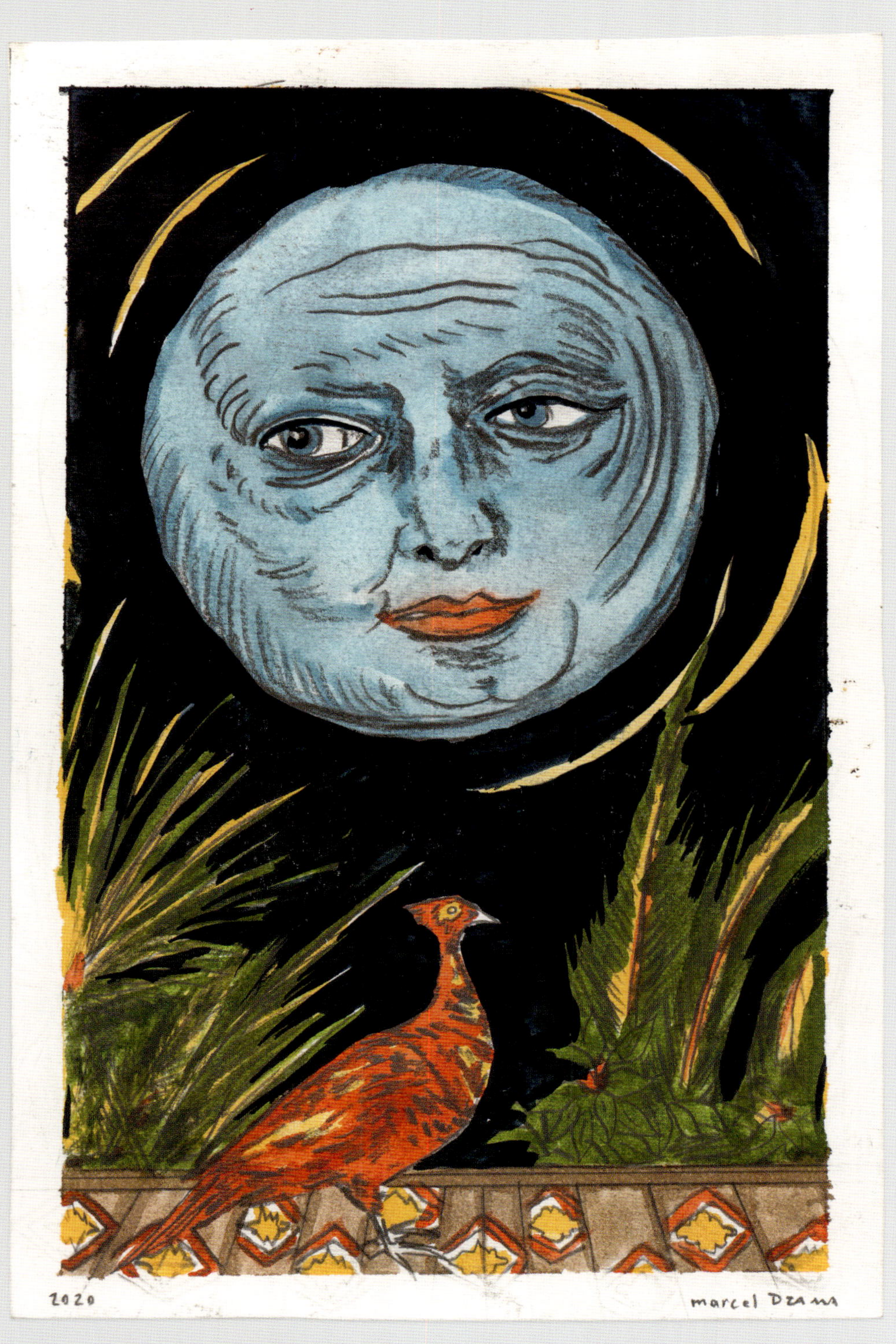

***Blue Moon of Morocco*, 2020**

Watercolor, ink, and graphite on paper

Courtesy of the artist and David Zwirner Gallery

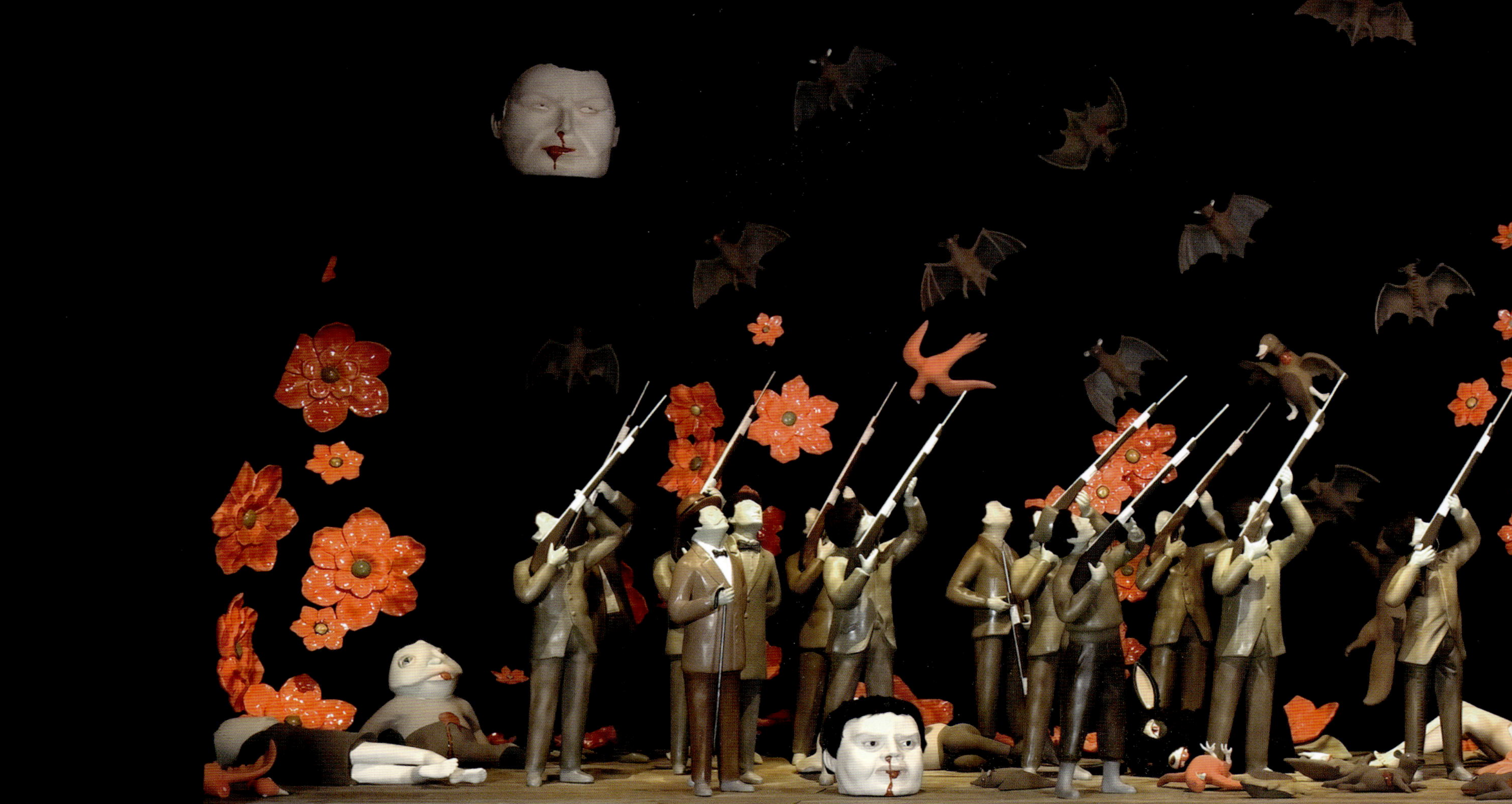

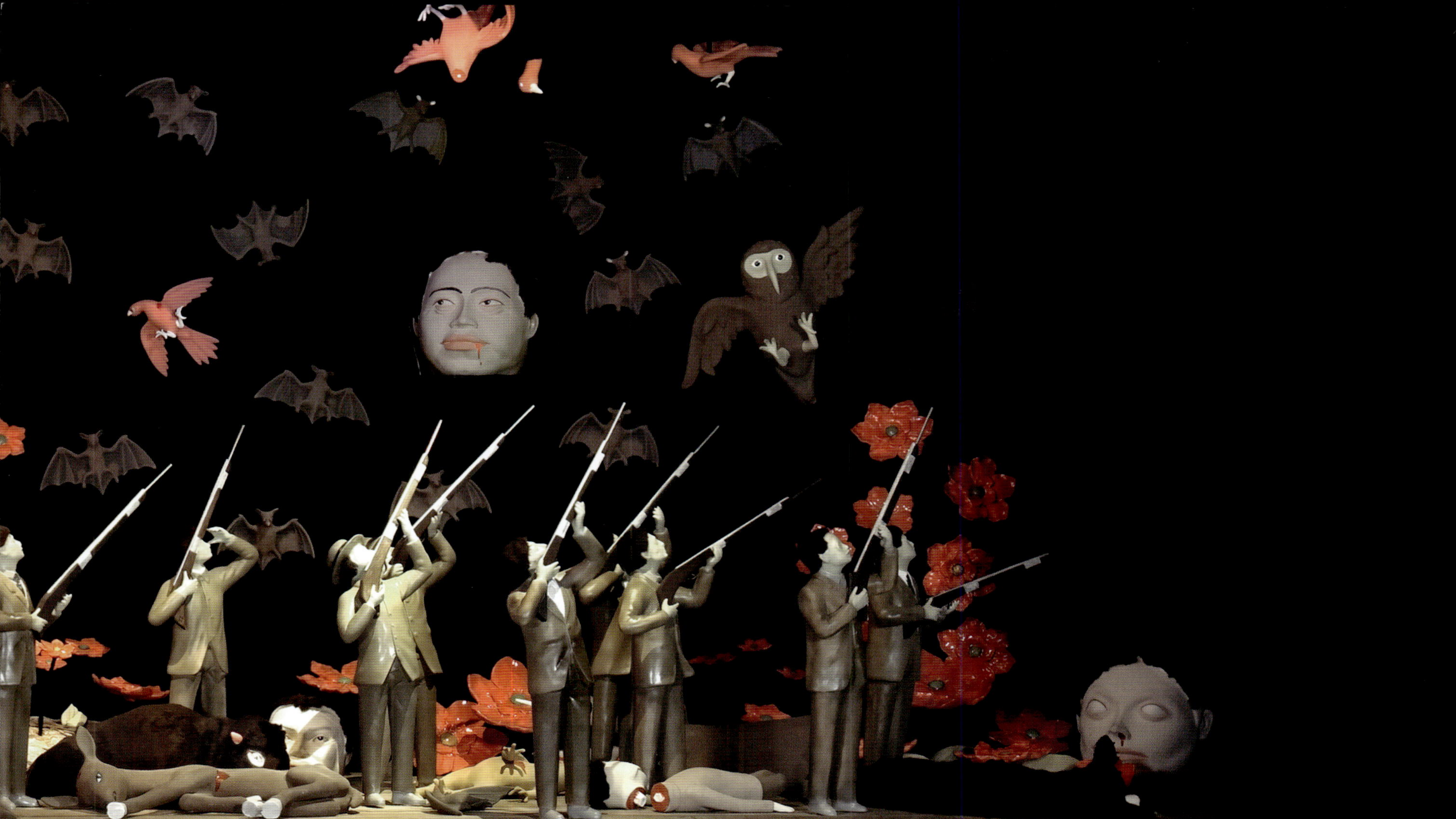

***On the banks of the Red River*, 2008**
Diorama: wood, glazed ceramic sculptures, metal, fabric
Courtesy of the artist and David Zwirner Gallery

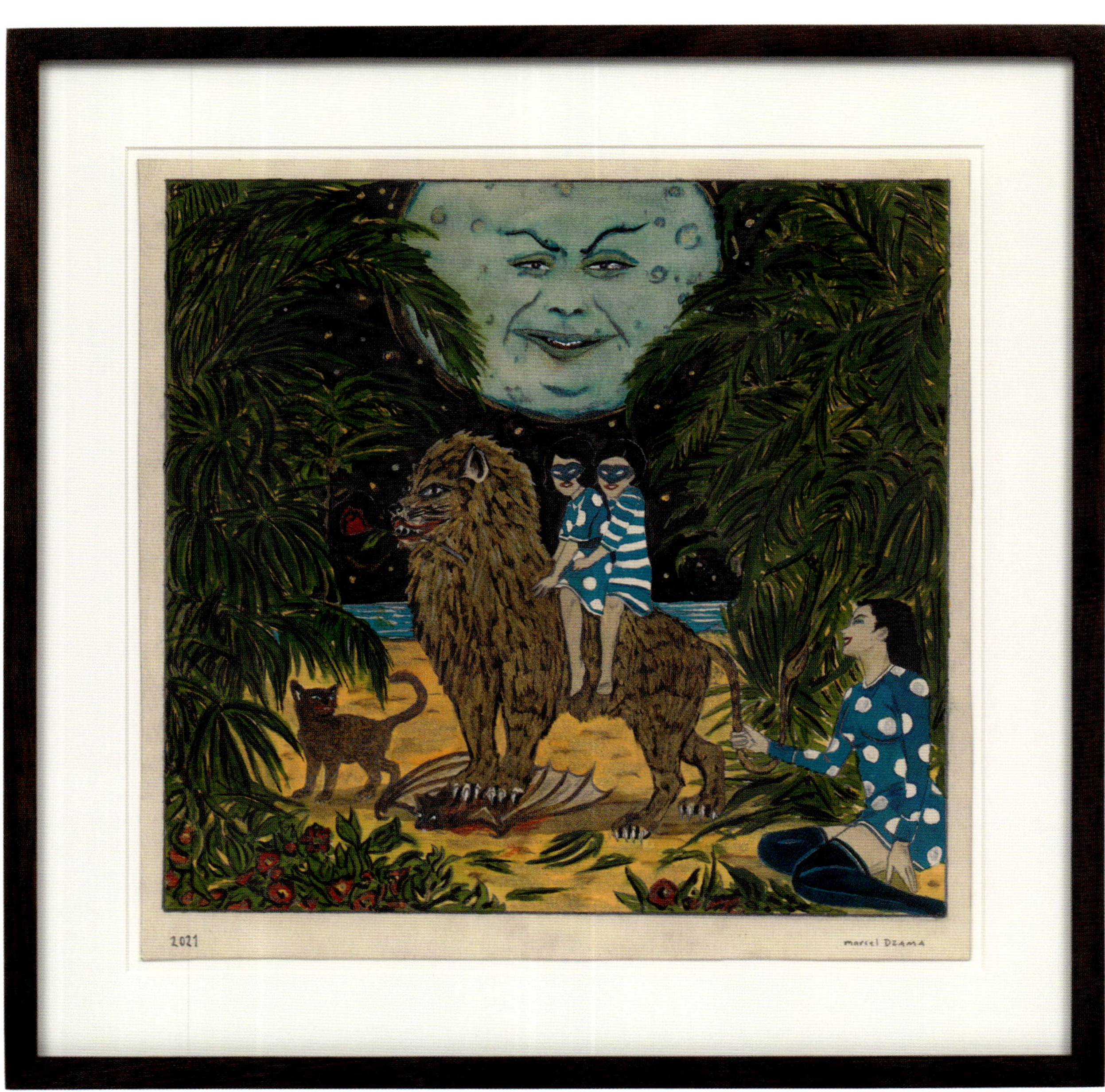

***Our father was a beast, mother a beauty, and grandpa was a vampire*, 2021**
Ink, gouache, and graphite on paper
Courtesy of the artist and David Zwirner Gallery

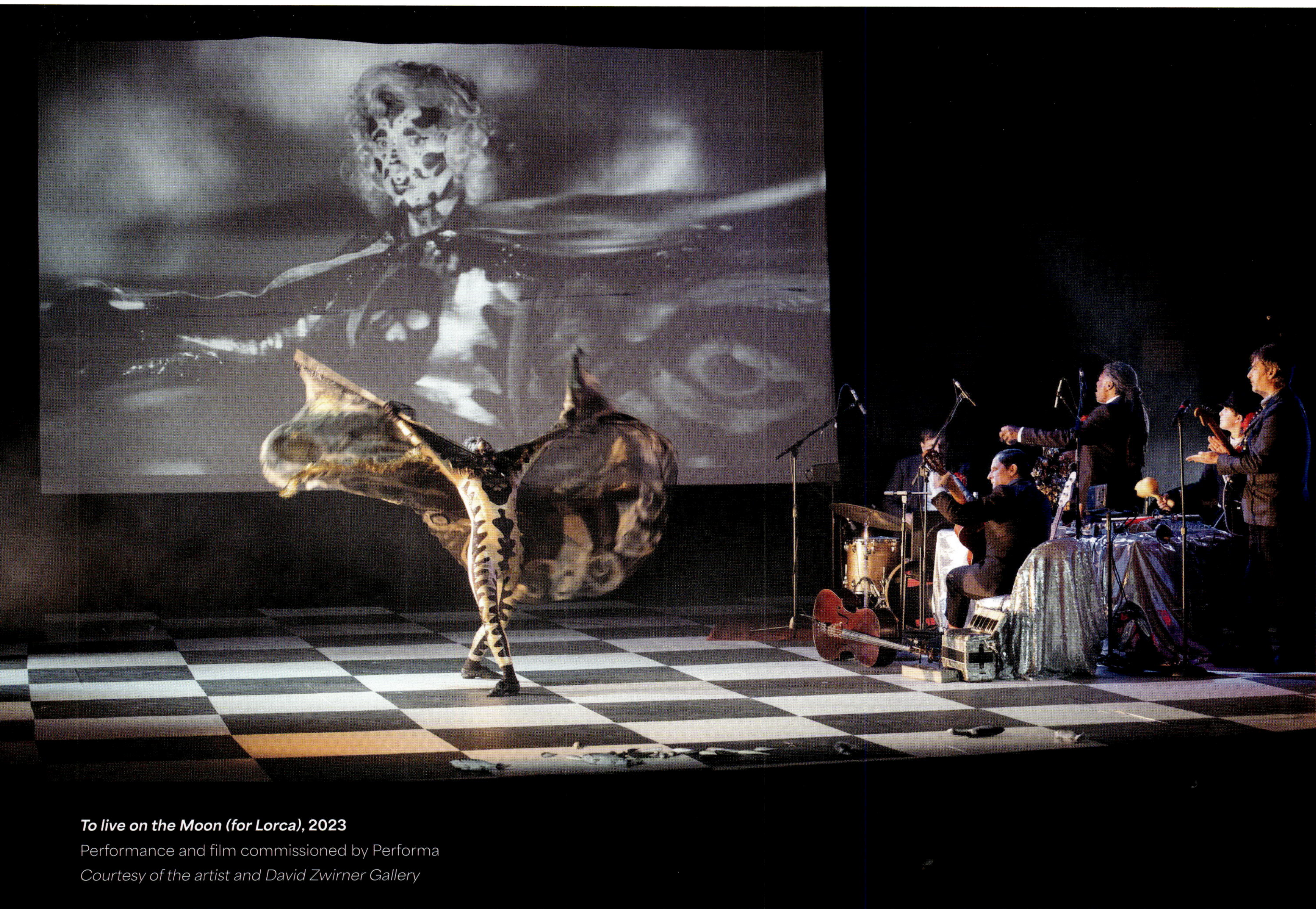

***To live on the Moon (for Lorca)*, 2023**
Performance and film commissioned by Performa
Courtesy of the artist and David Zwirner Gallery

Jeffrey Gibson (b. 1972)

ASTORIA BOULEVARD

***I AM A RAINBOW TOO*, 2020**

At Astoria Blvd., Jeffrey Gibson loudly declares I AM A RAINBOW TOO in a series of multicolored glass panels, installed throughout the station. At the time of the commission, Gibson had lived in New York City for twelve years and wanted to represent the diversity of his adopted hometown into abstract designs that reference many things without being too specific. He deliberately pushed the number of different color combinations to encompass as many cultural heritages as possible, echoing the vast multicultural communities of Queens. The sunlight that passes through a tunnel of windows leaves gorgeous reflections on the ground, the intense vibrancy imparting a brilliant glow to the drab walkway. His color wheels recall traditional motifs of Indigenous weaving, with its geometric patterning and color gradients. The effect is nothing short of joy and elation. These panels were fabricated by another MTA artist, glass maven Tom Patti (74th St. and Broadway), whose experiments in new techniques in glasswork melded well with Gibson's approaches to paint and color.

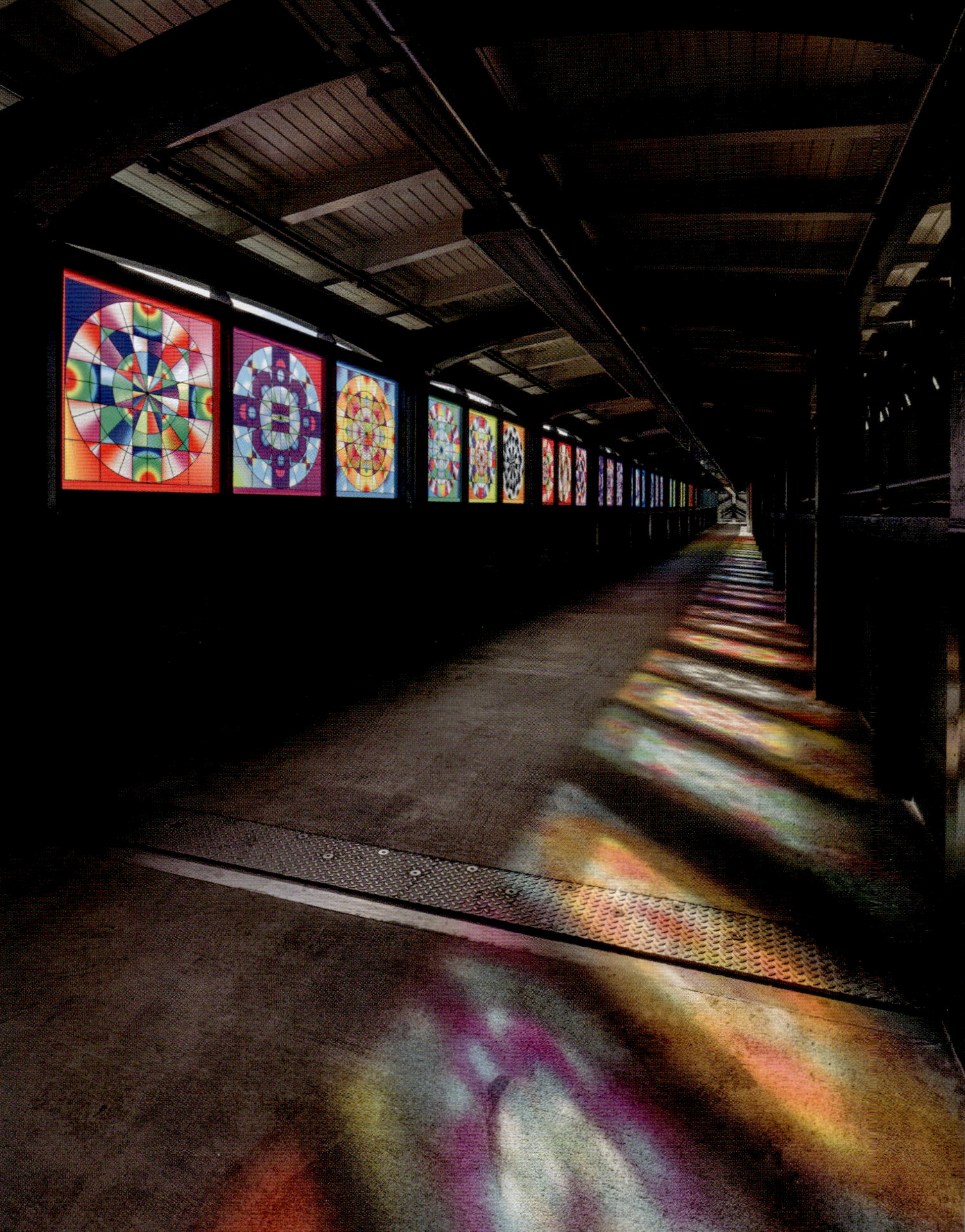

Photos by Etienne Frossard
Courtesy of the artist

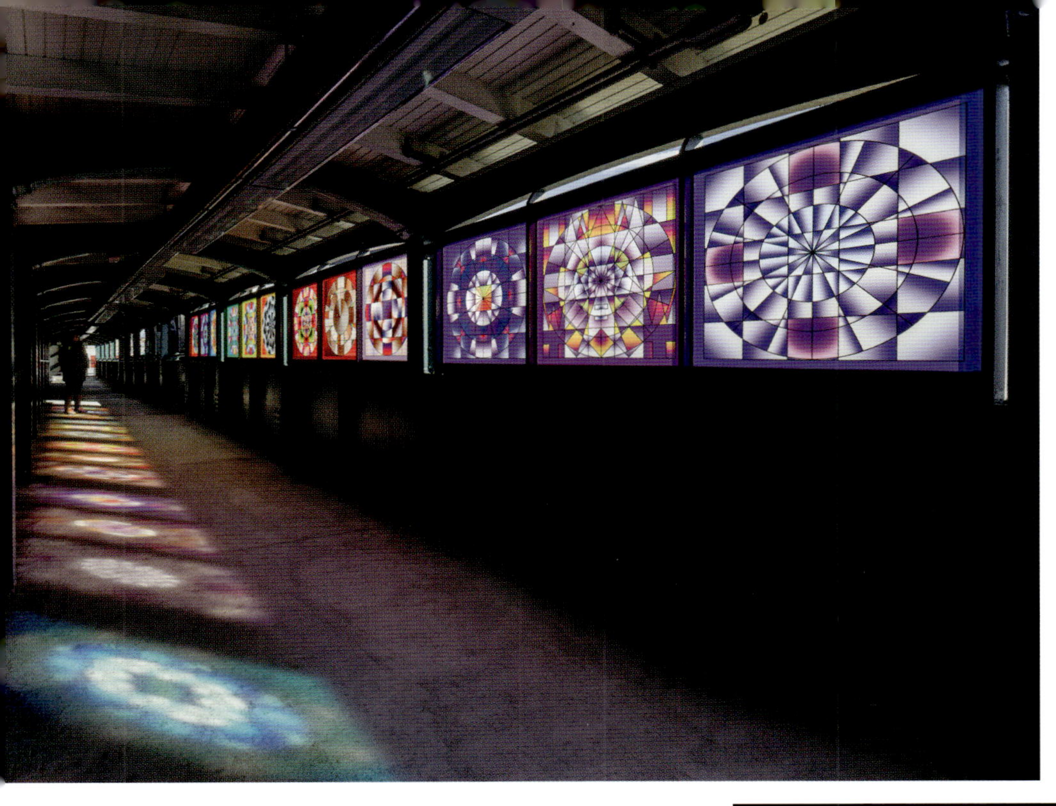

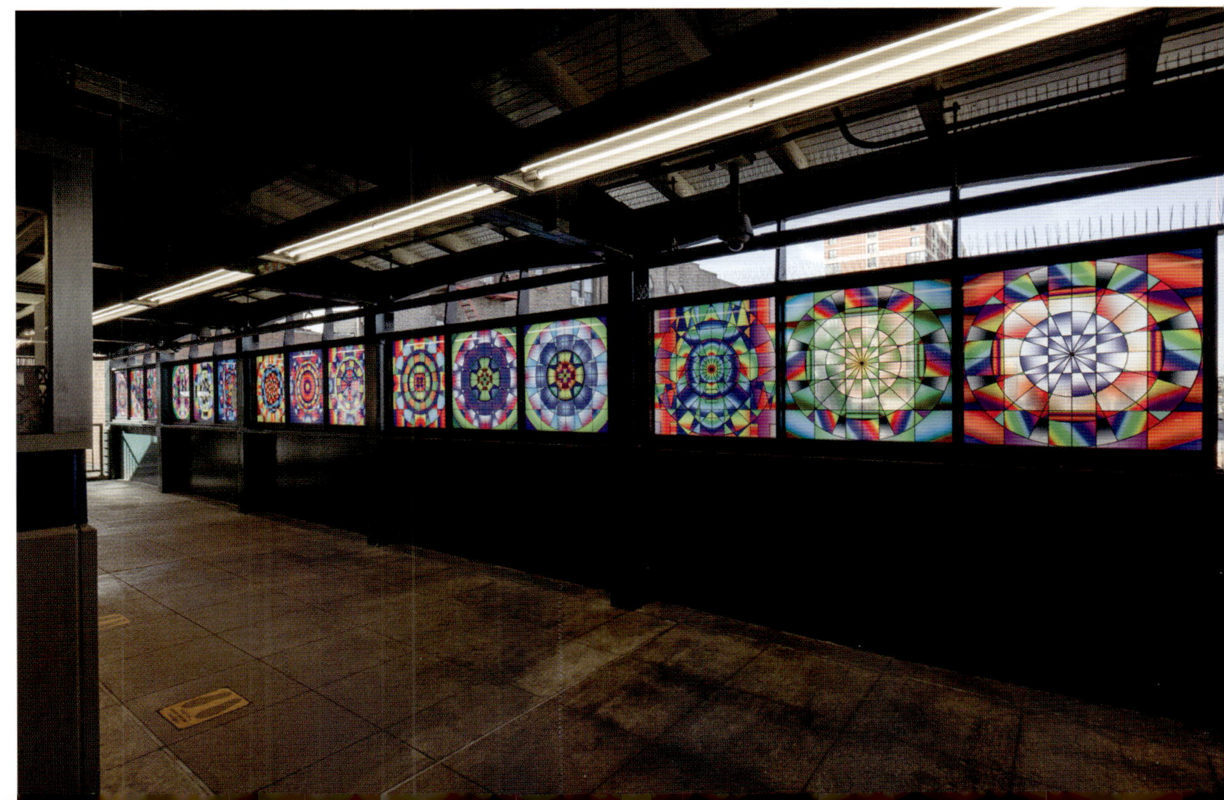

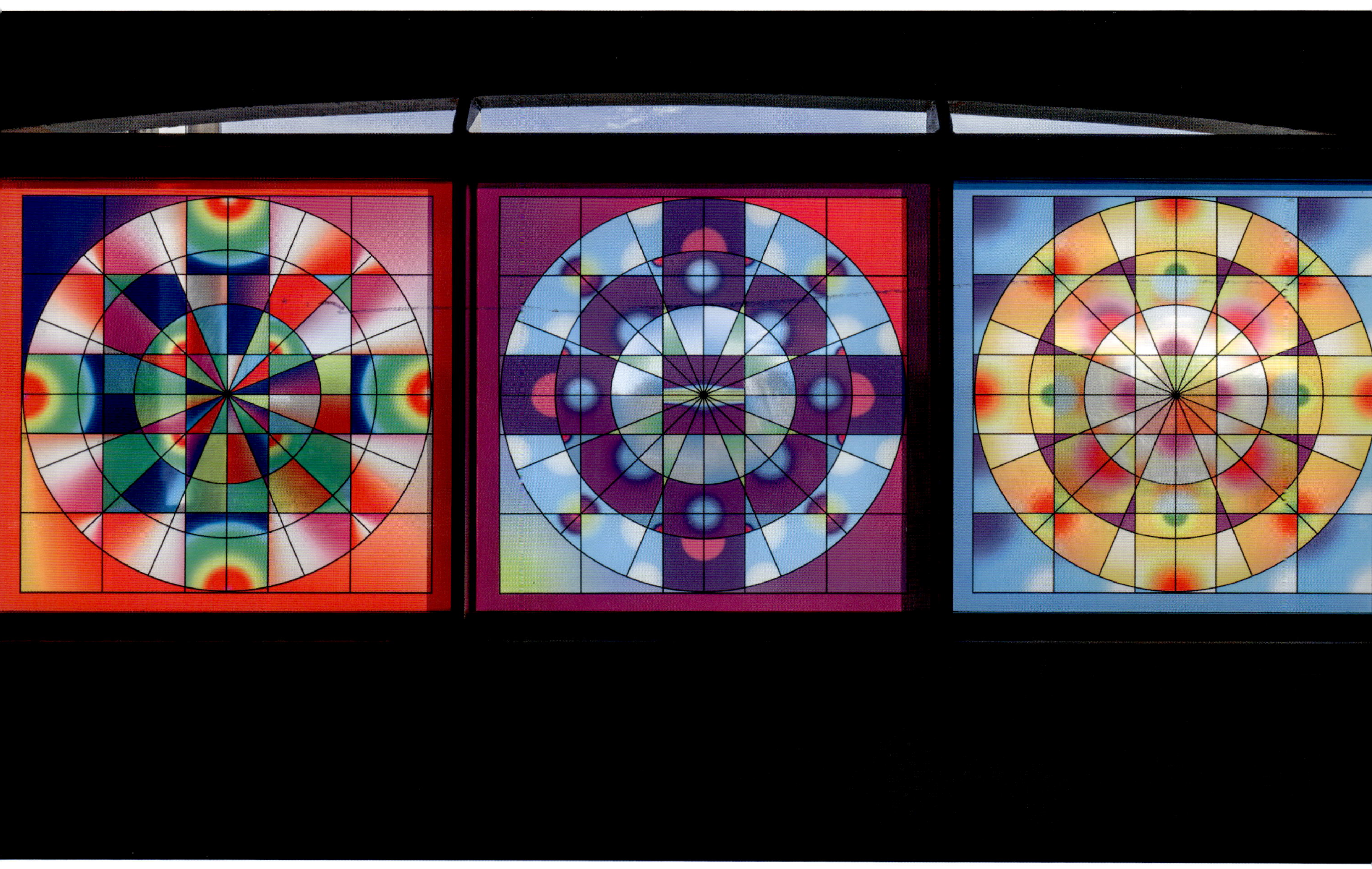

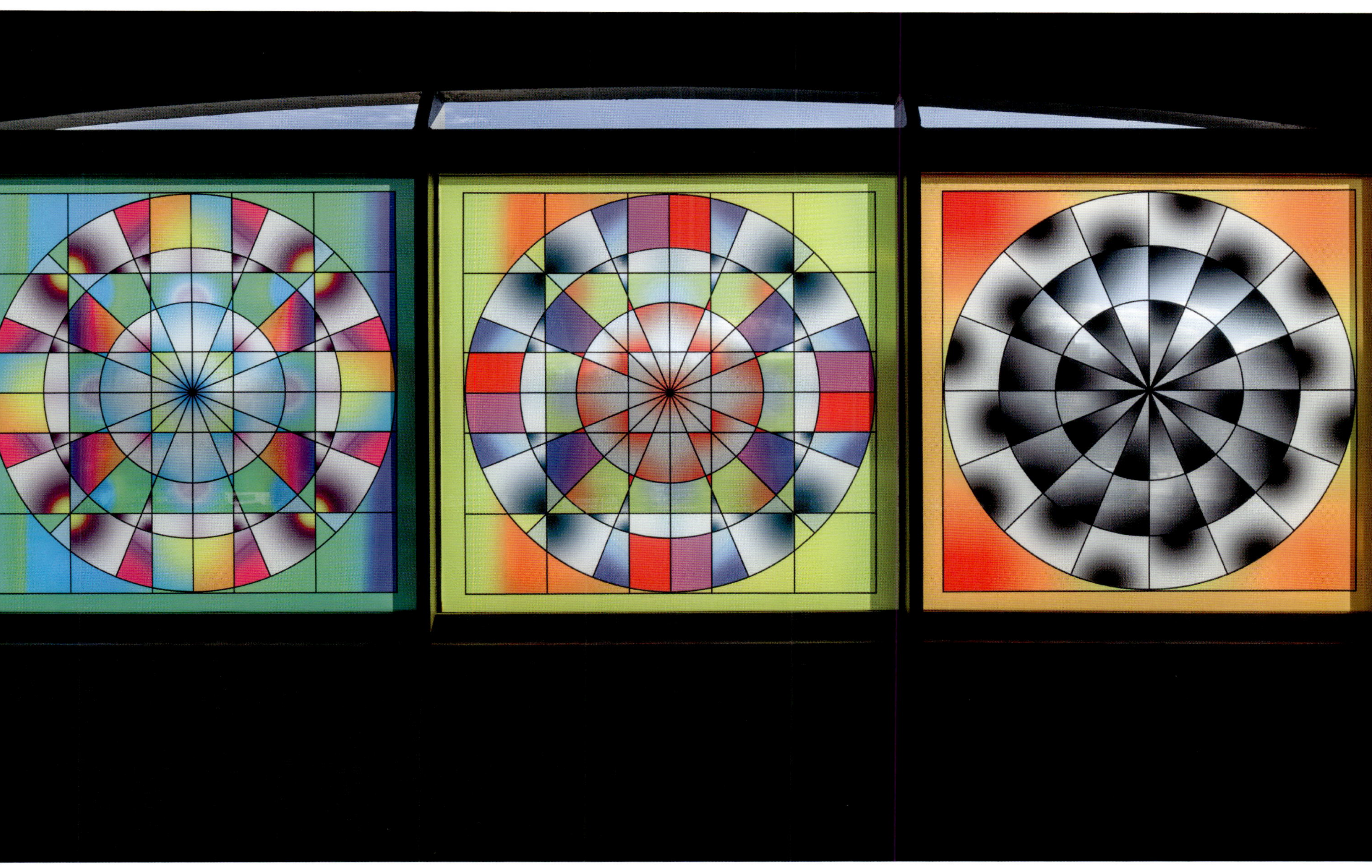

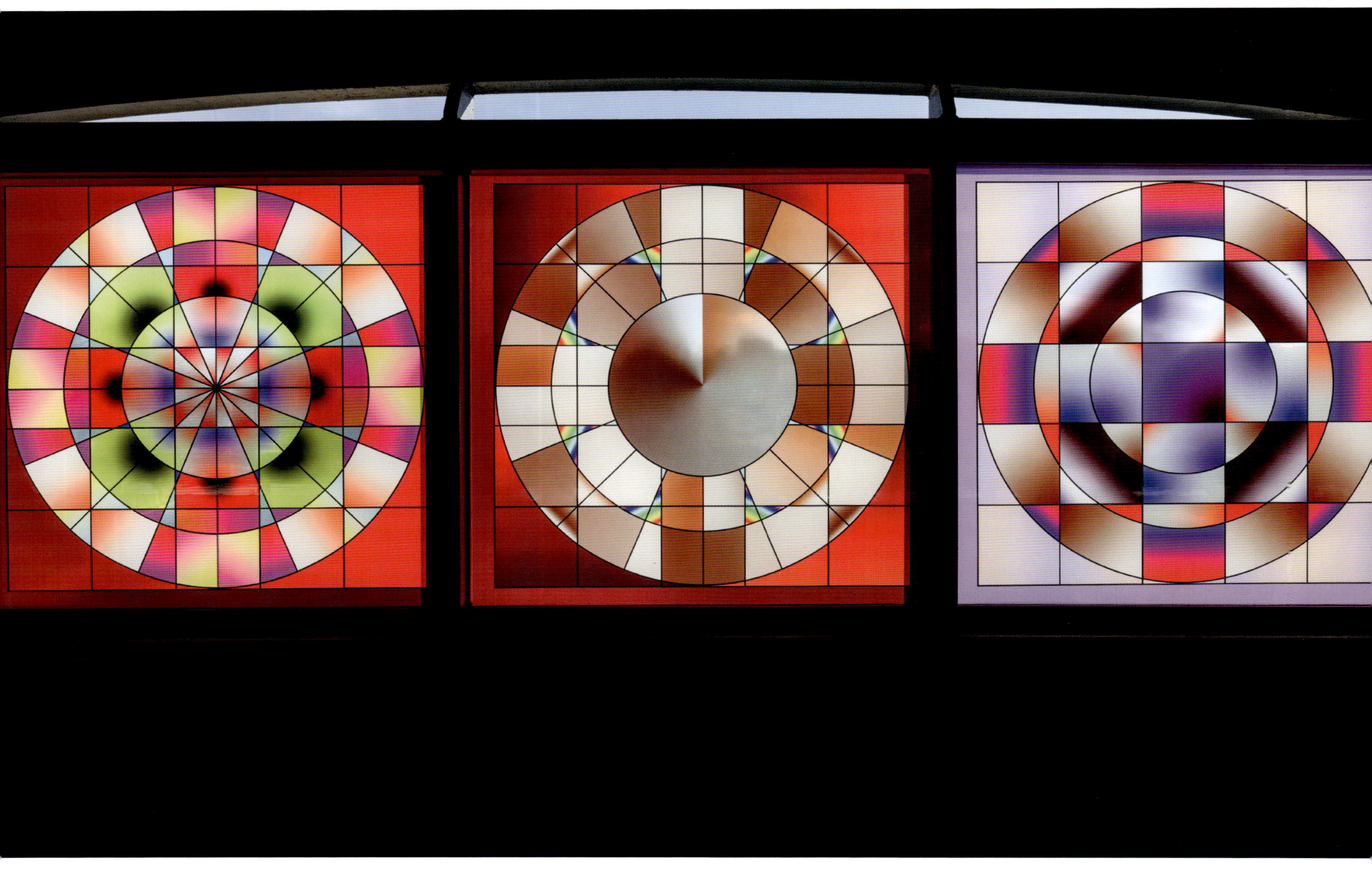

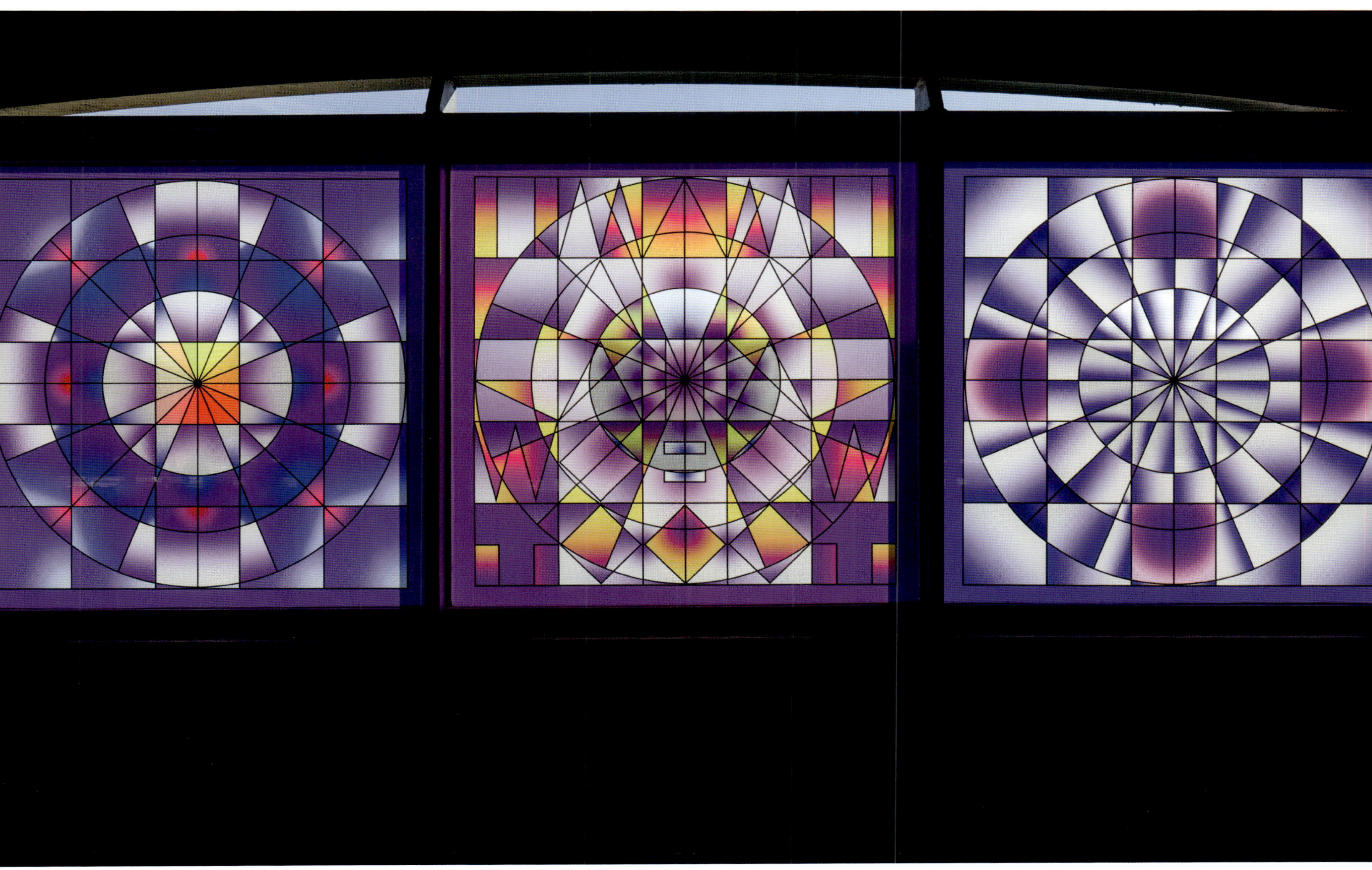

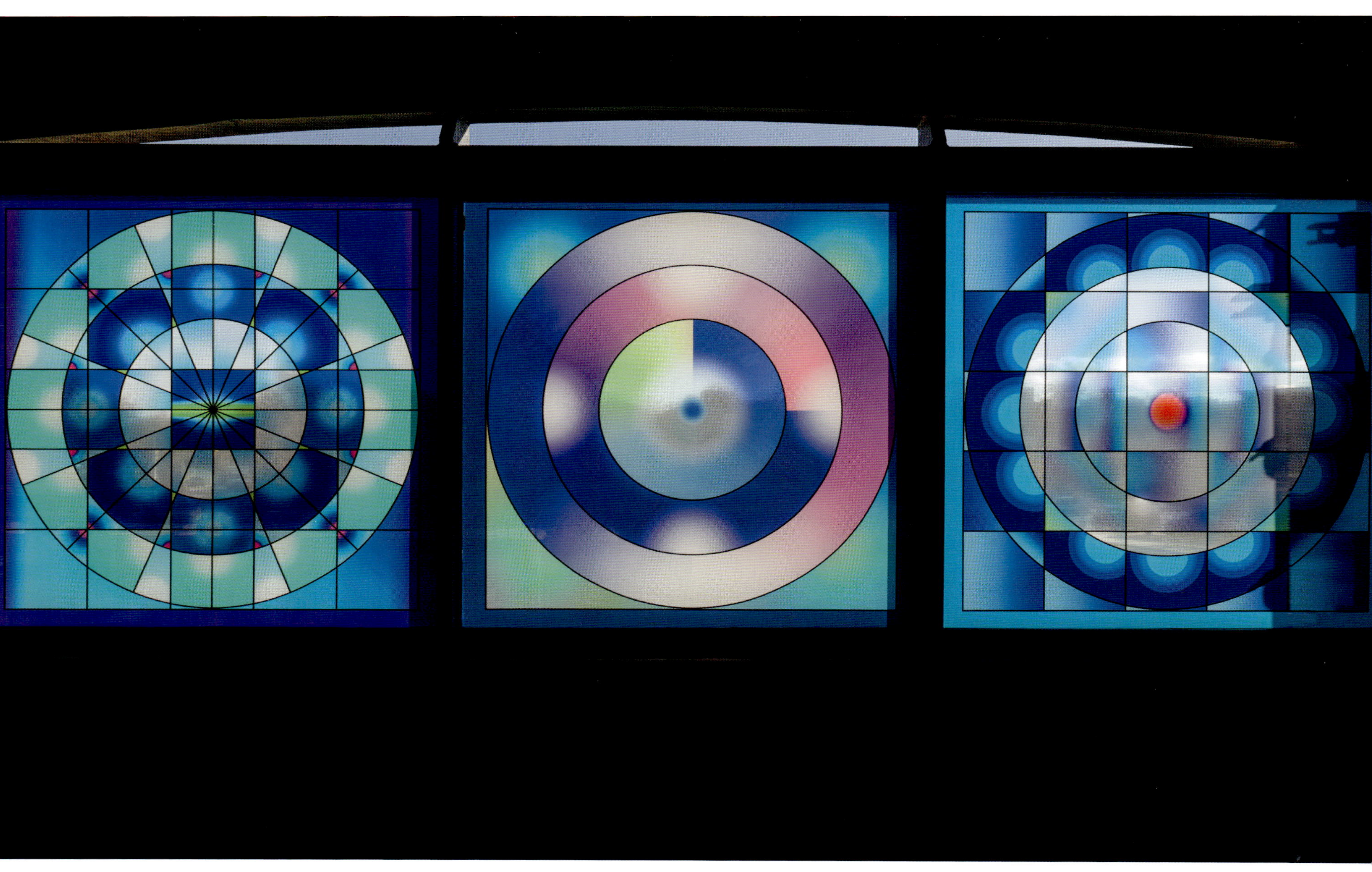

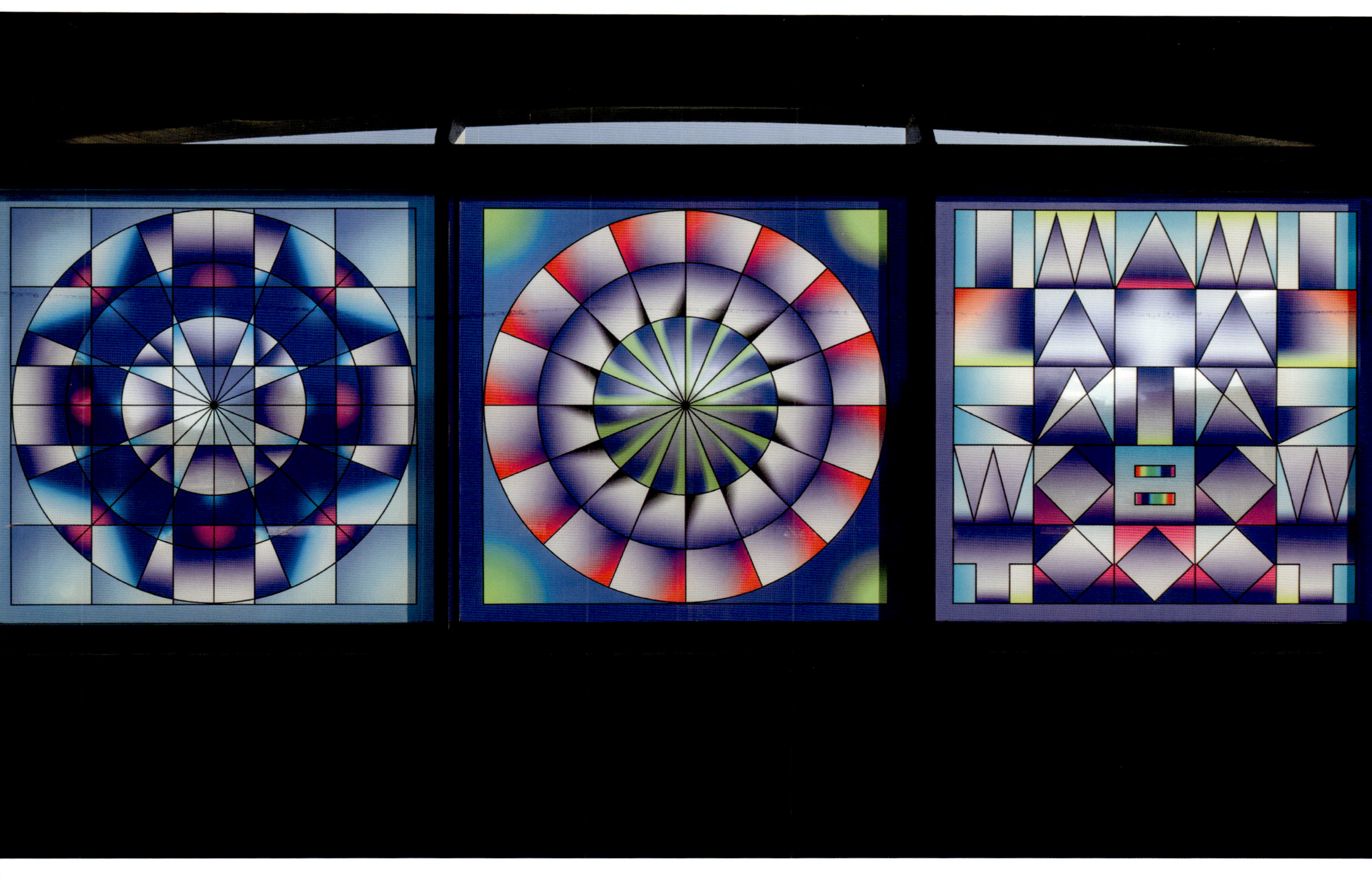

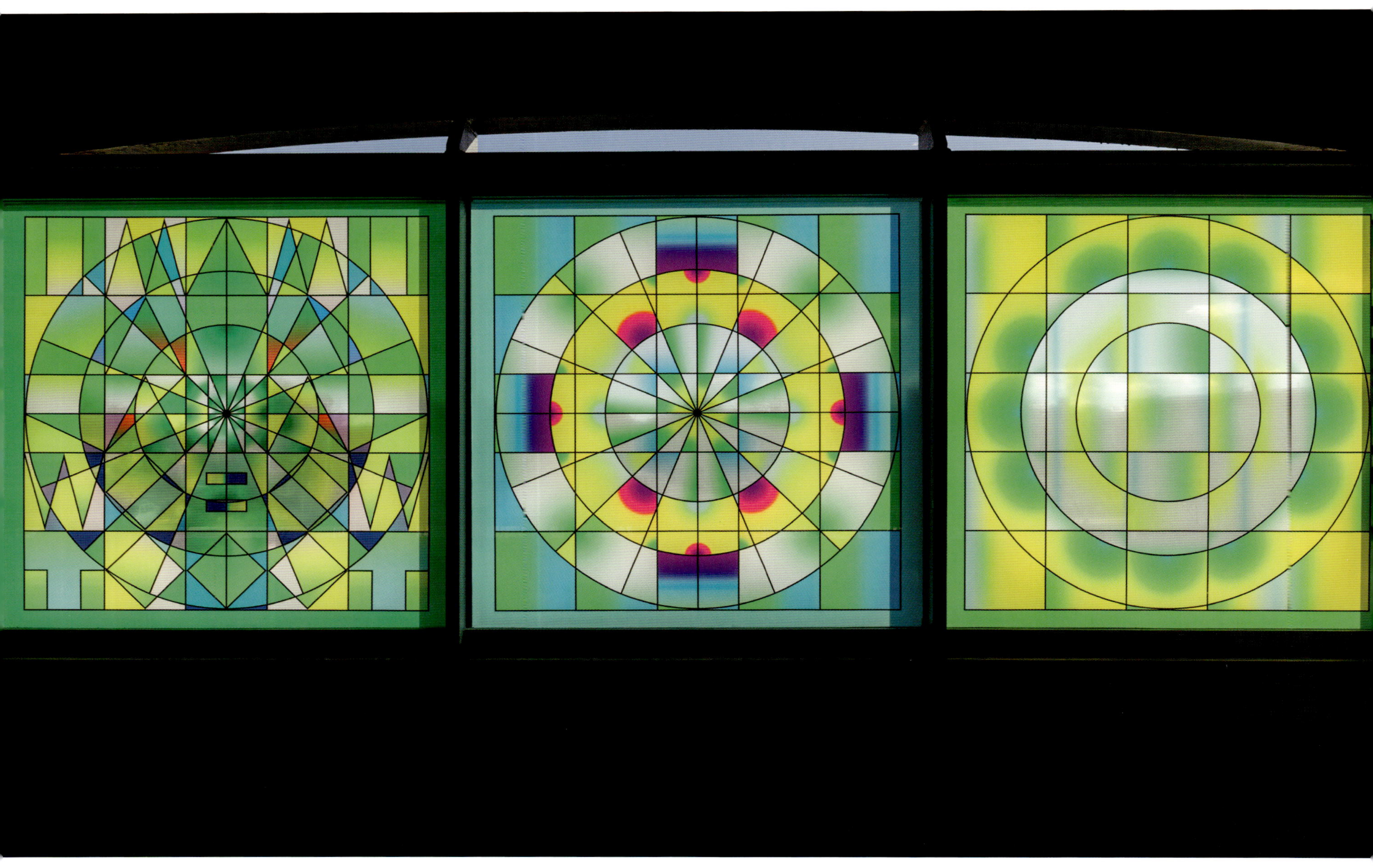

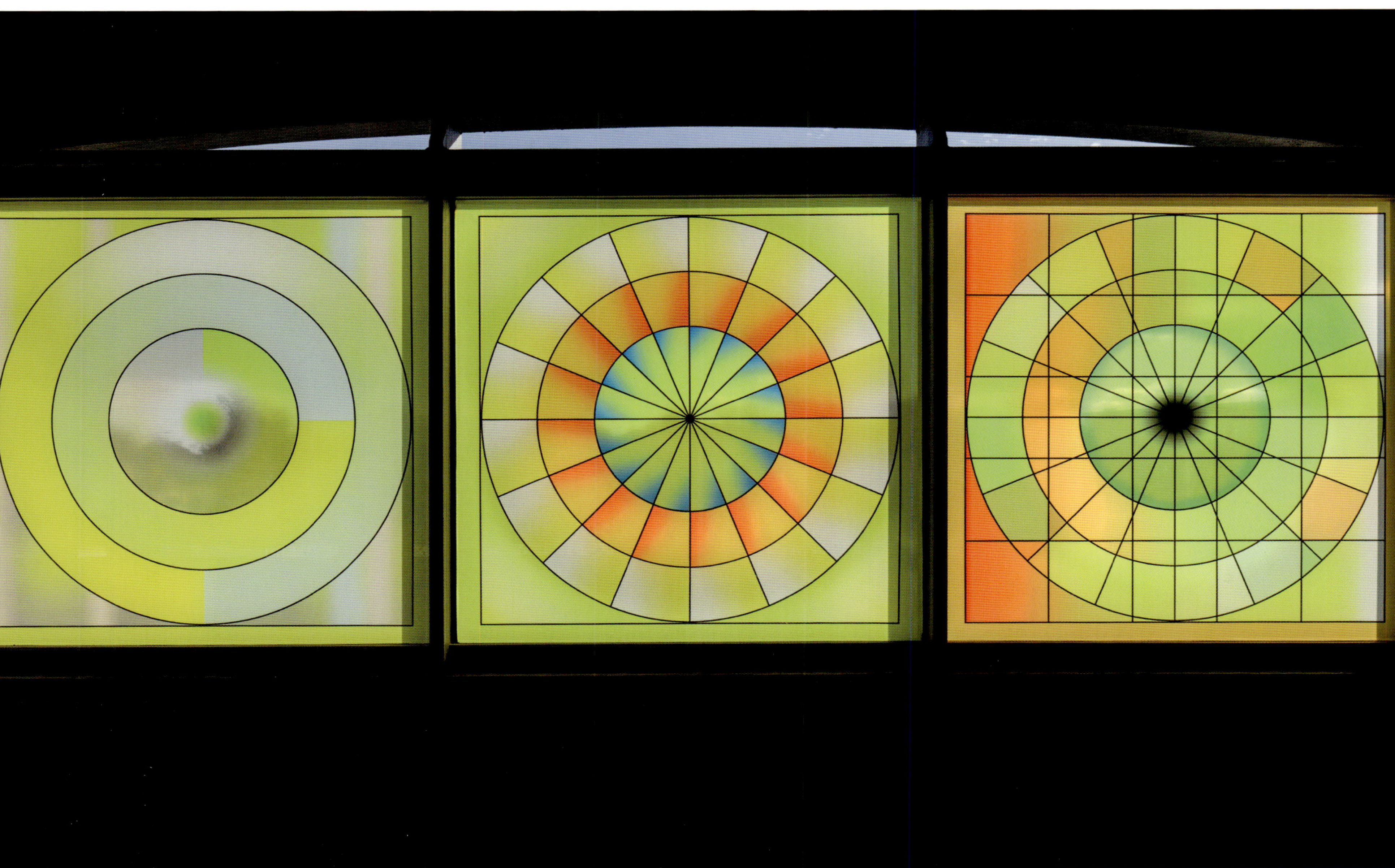

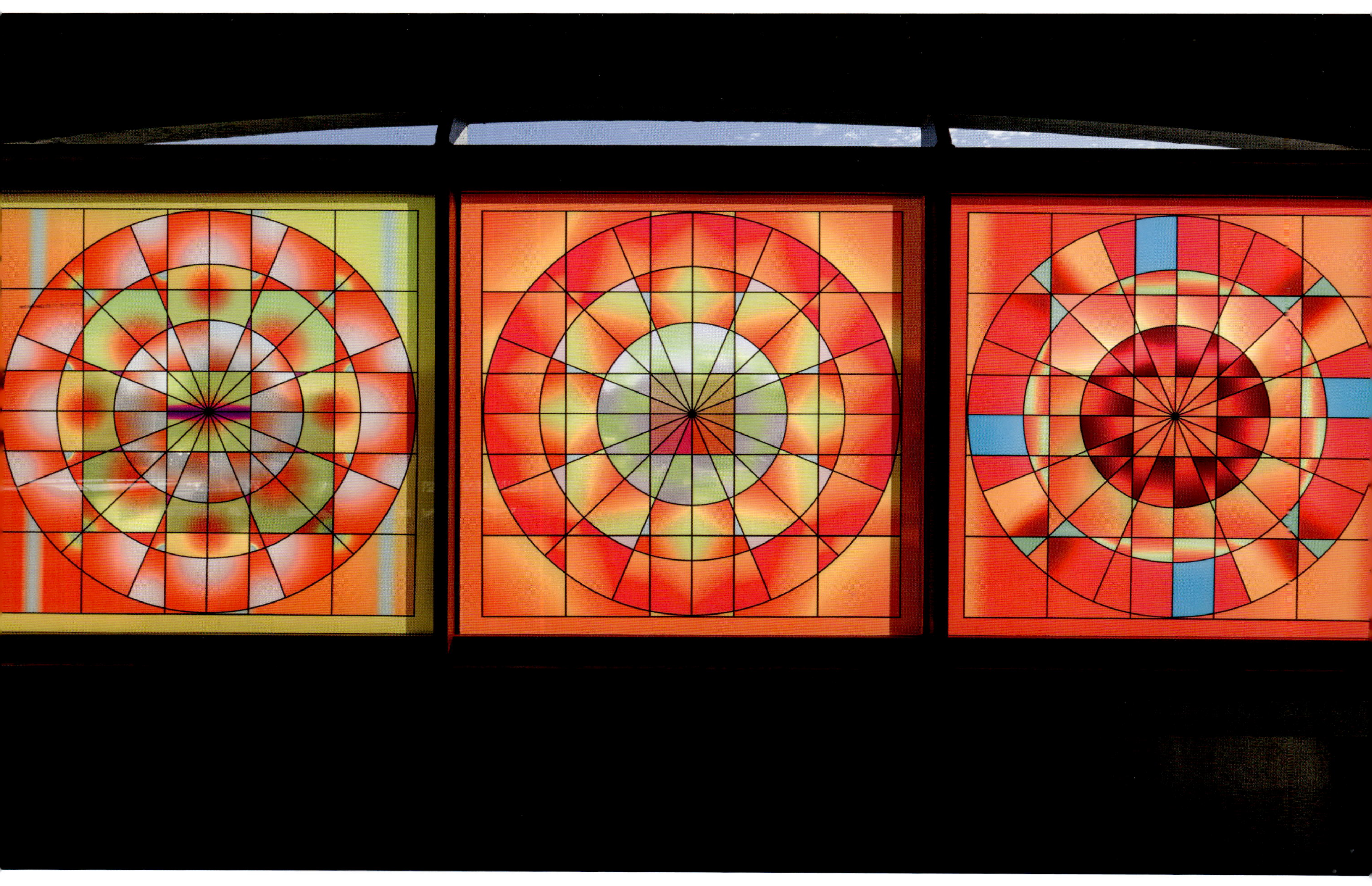

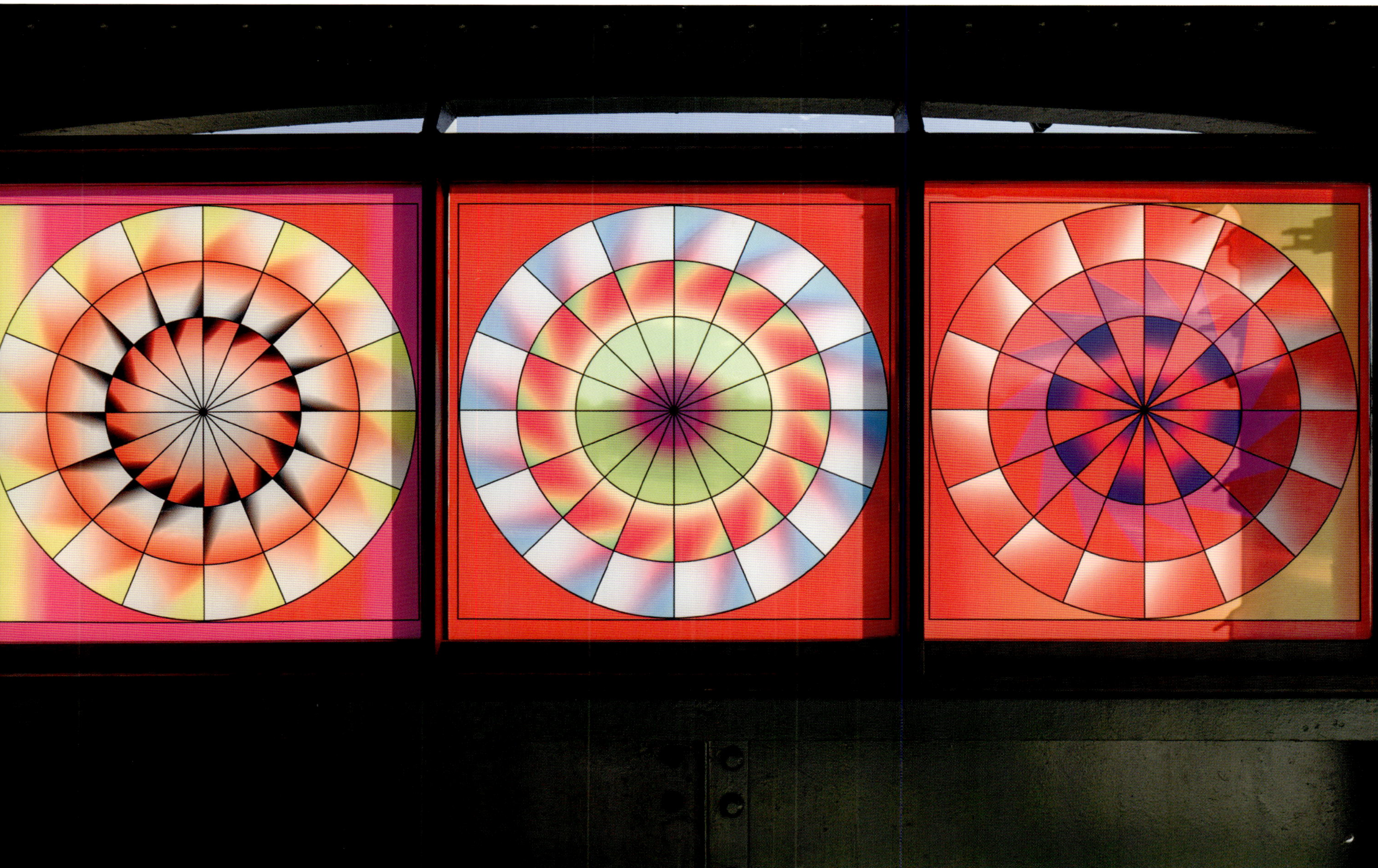

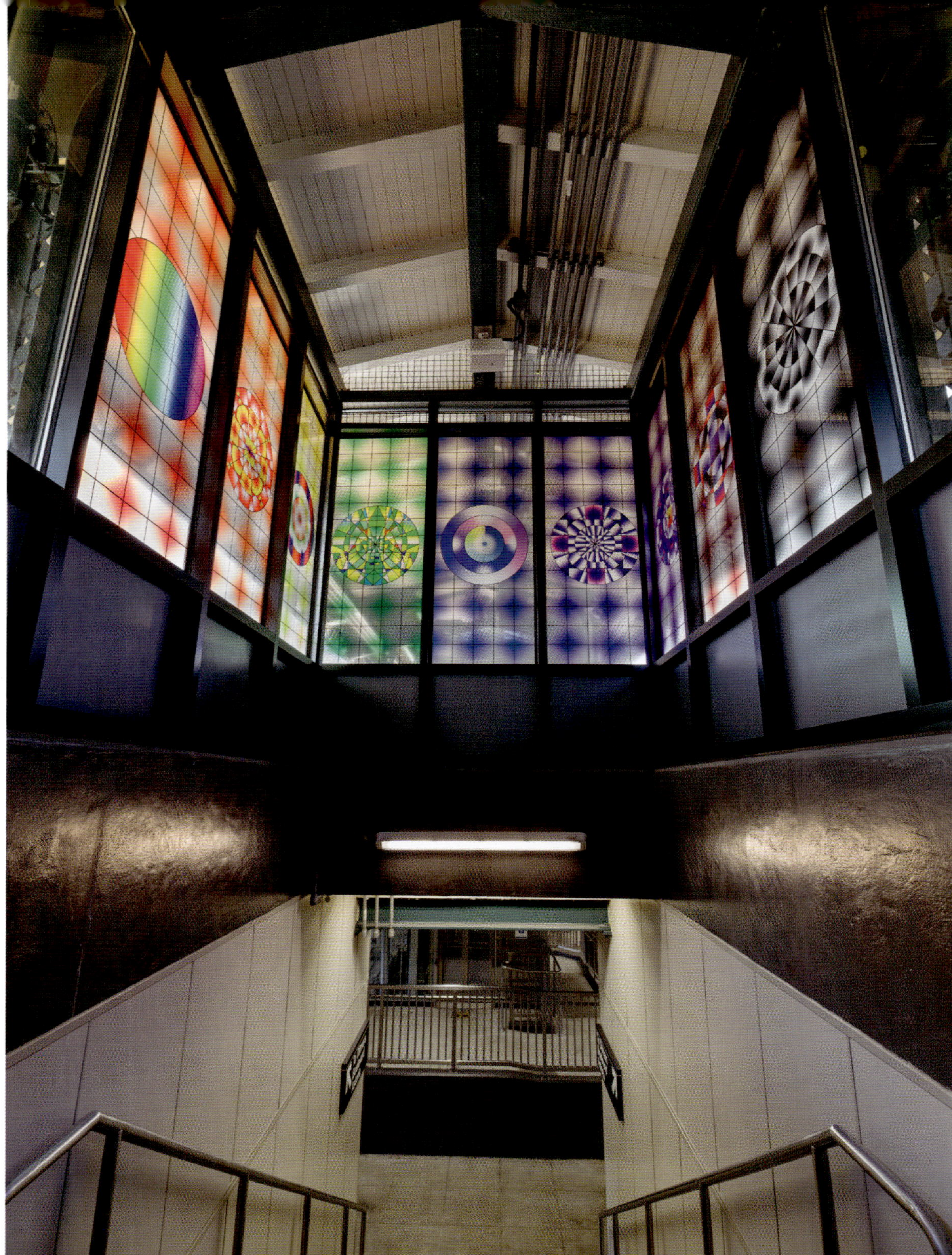

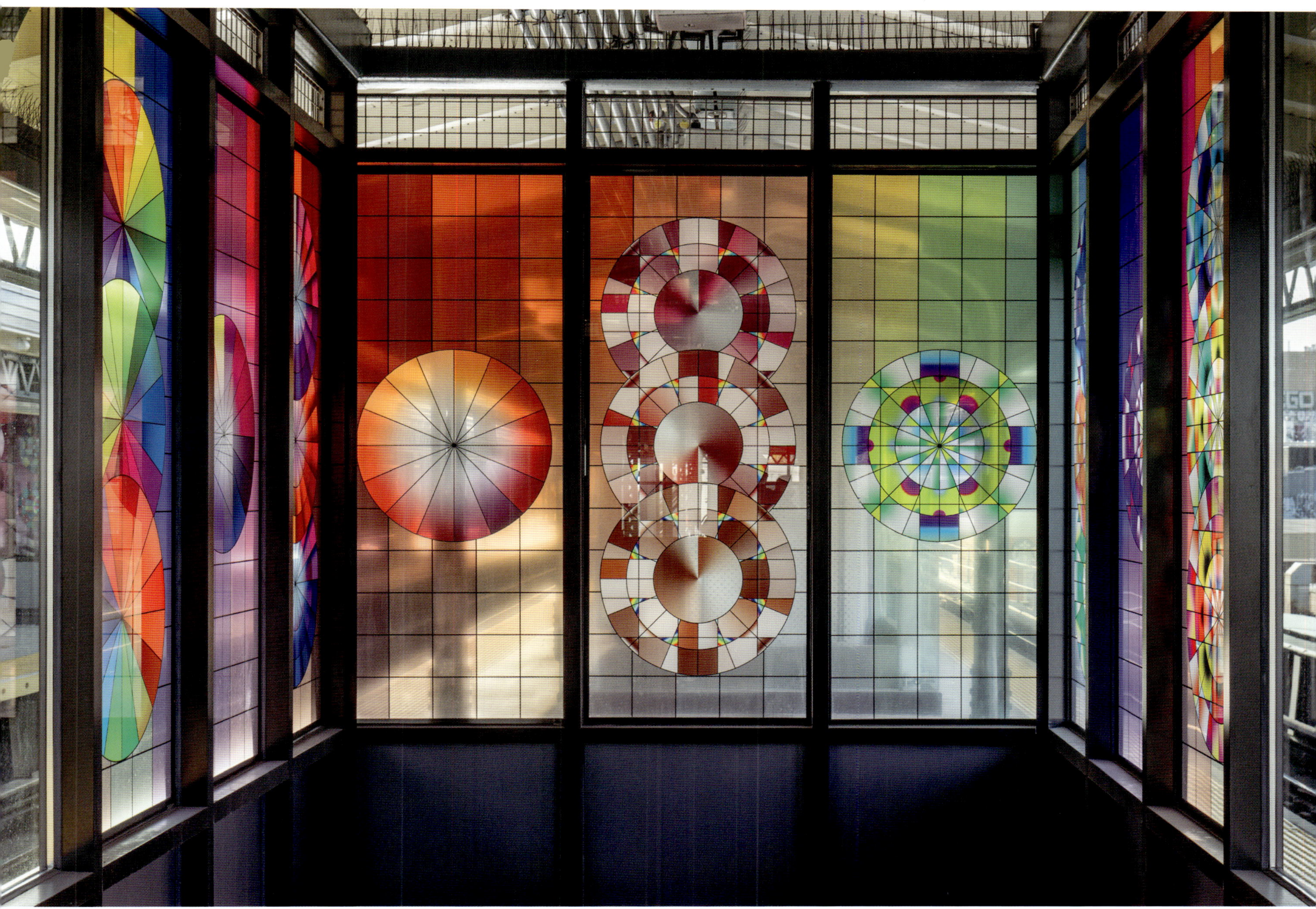

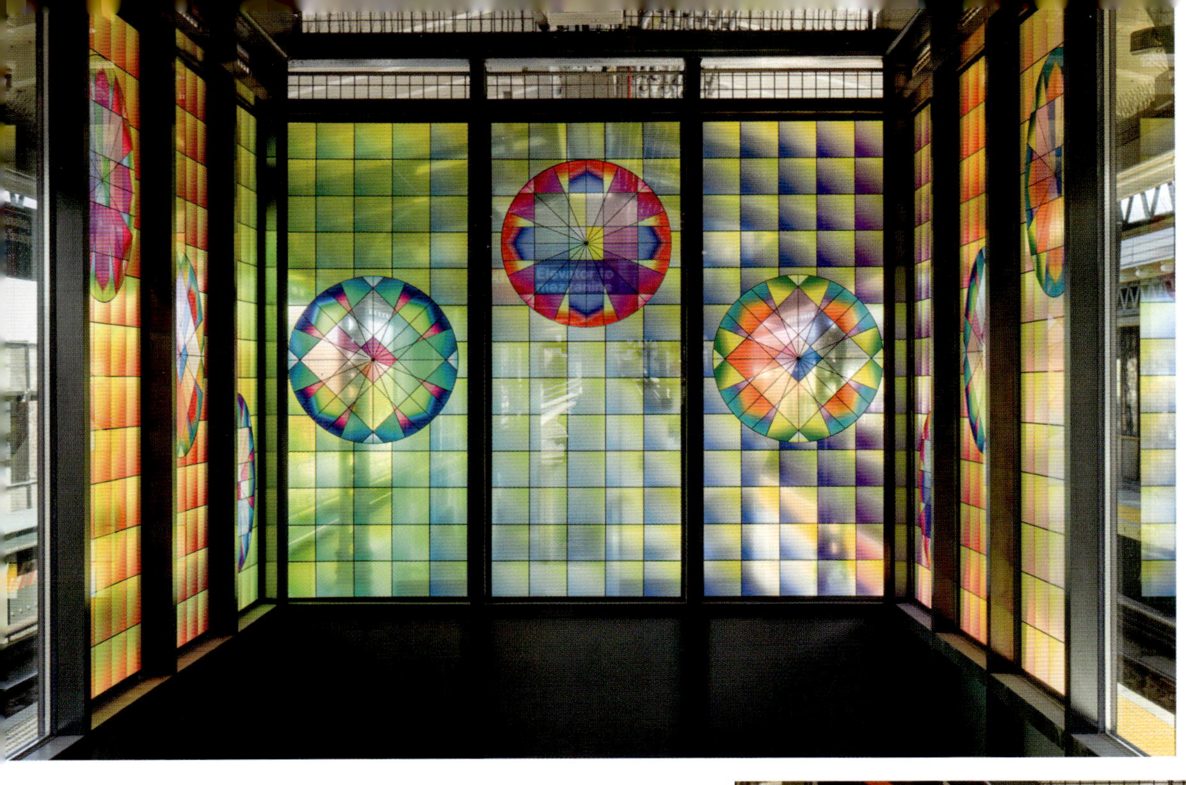

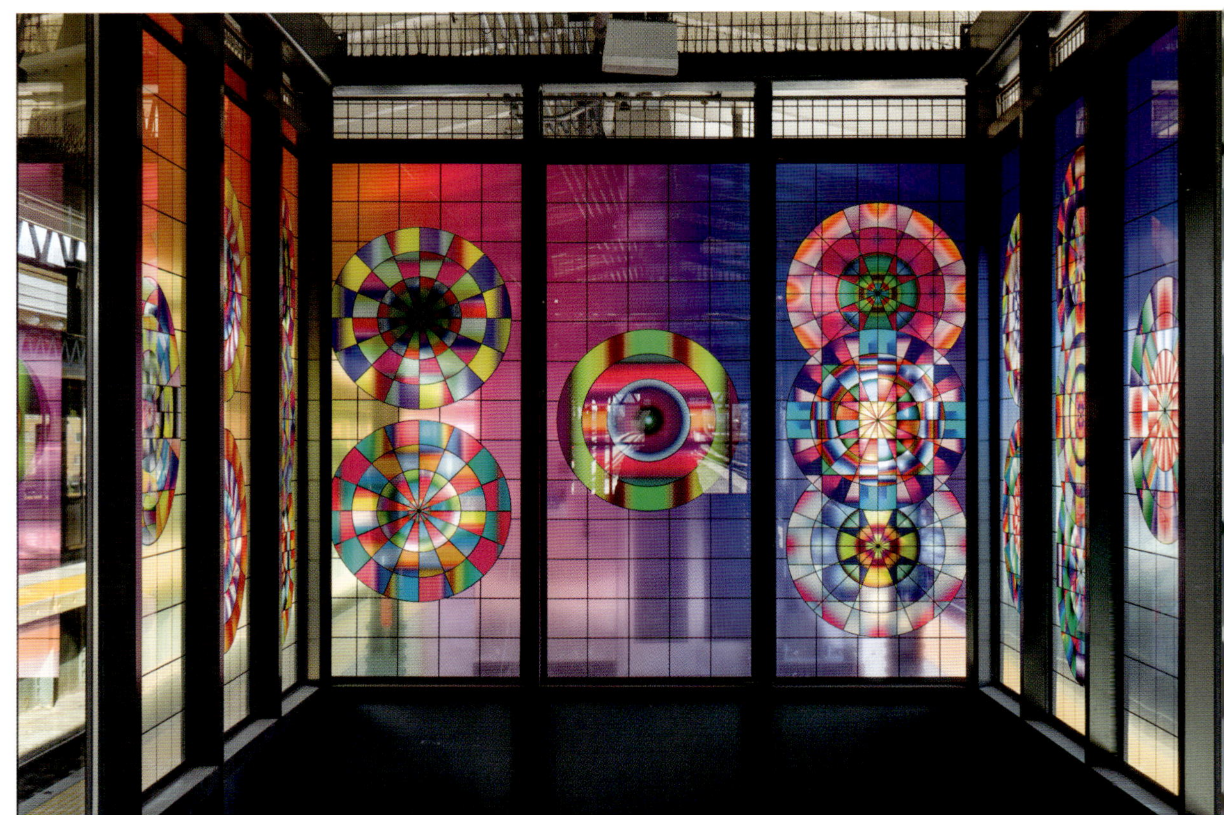

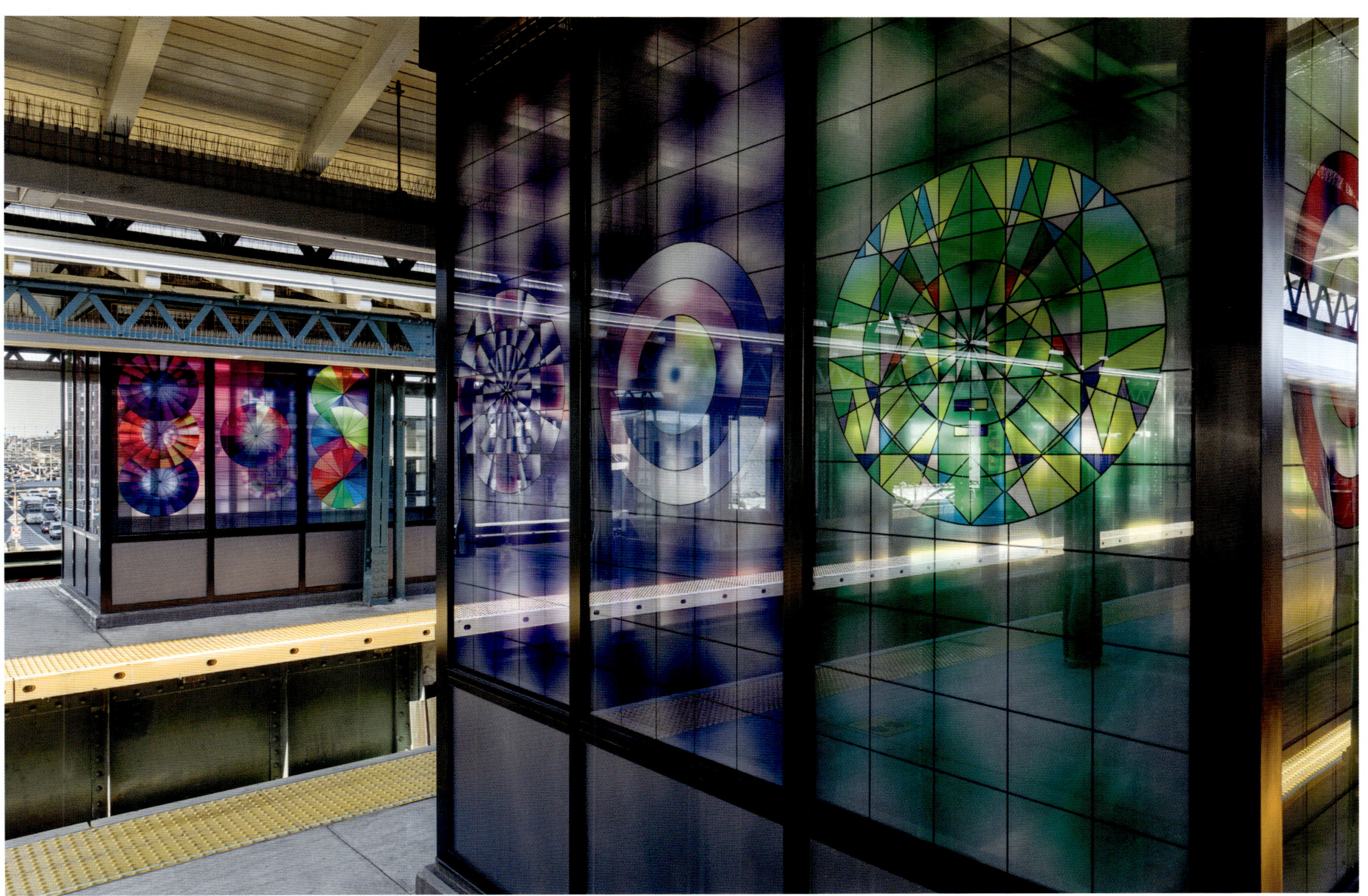

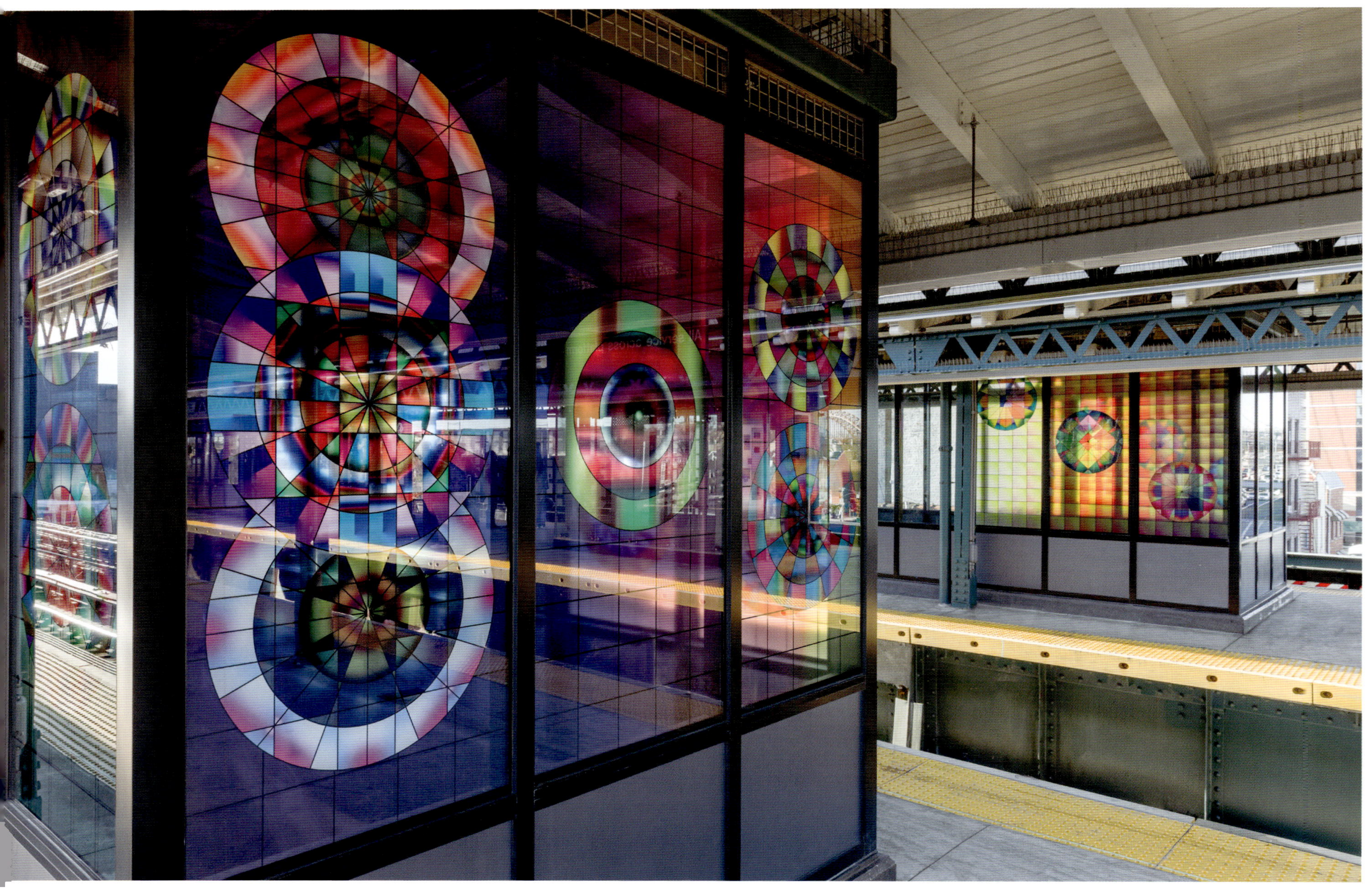

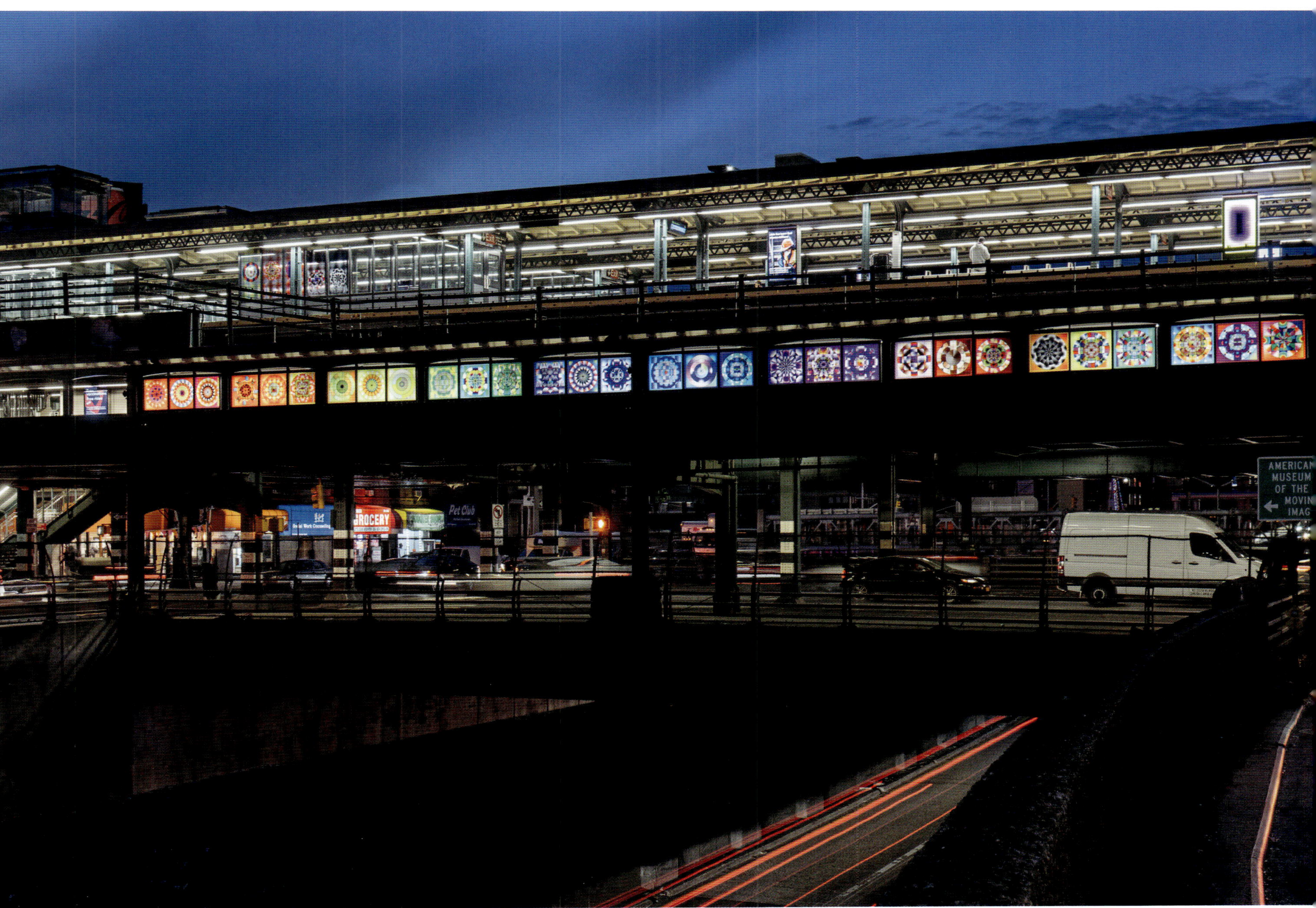
AMERICAN
MUSEUM
OF THE
GROCERY
Pet Club

I AM A RAINBOW TOO is also the name of a seven-part work from 2018, geometric acrylic paintings incorporating text and bordered by colorful glass beads. Gibson is known for striking works that are brilliantly colored and extravagantly adorned with beads and fabric, be they works on canvas or traditional costumes or sculpture. His works are both a defiant declaration of identity and a jubilant celebration of it. Gibson is an American queer artist of Choctaw and Cherokee descent who grew up abroad (Germany, Korea); his embrace of these exuberant forms of expression comes from his investigation into how Indigenous cultures made beautiful, elaborate objects even in, or especially during, times of great duress. Realizing that this impulse was a sign of survival, defiance, and cultural continuity, he adopted this approach of beautifying what is ugly, adorning what is dark–it has become a defining quality of his work. At the same time, his ideas of identity and community extend beyond his Native roots. The unabashed embrace of the vibrant colors speaks to Gibson's boosting of the queer community, especially in an era where the devastation of the AIDS epidemic can still be felt and the rights of LGBTQ people are once again put into question.

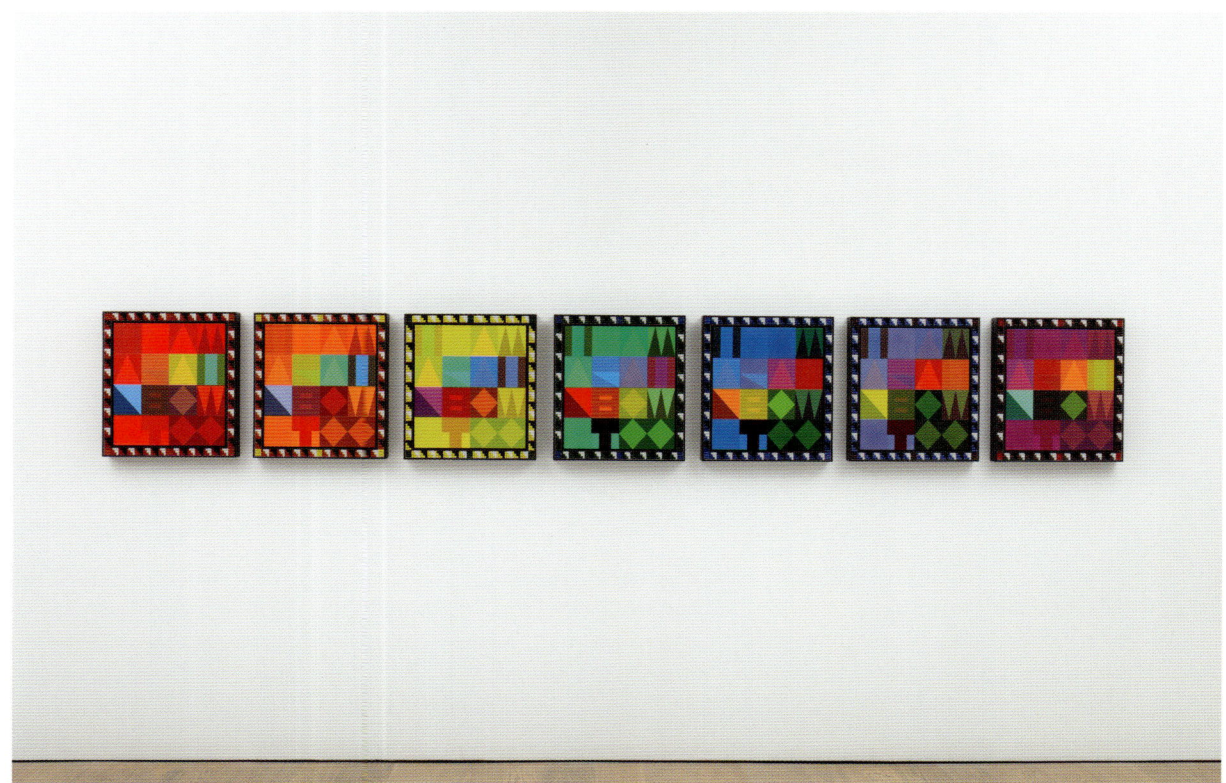

***I AM A RAINBOW TOO*, 2018**
Acrylic on canvas, glass beads, and artificial sinew inset into wood frame
Courtesy of the artist and Sikkema Jenkins Gallery

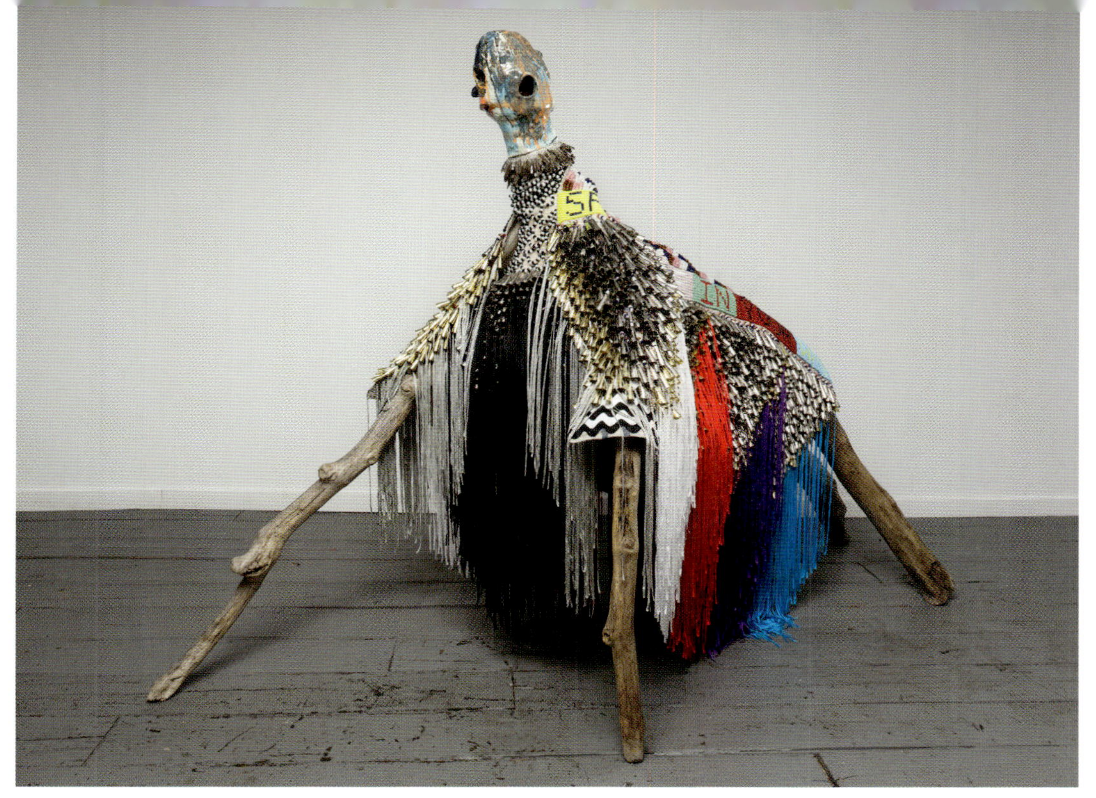

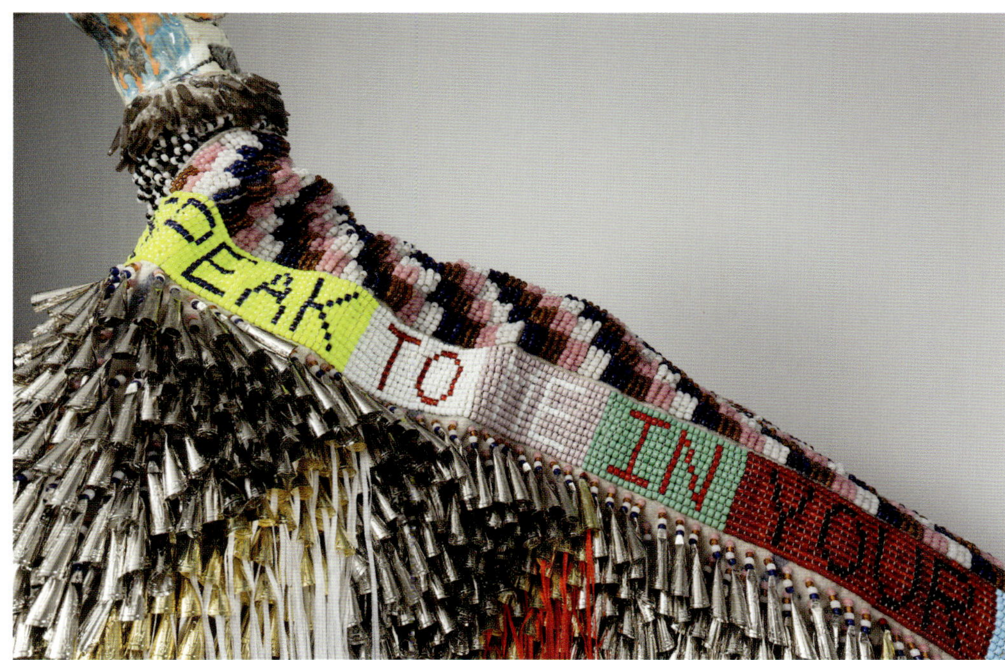

***SPEAK TO ME IN YOUR WAY SO I CAN HEAR YOU*, 2015**

Driftwood, glazed ceramics, beads, bells, ribbon

Courtesy of the artist and Hauser & Wirth Gallery

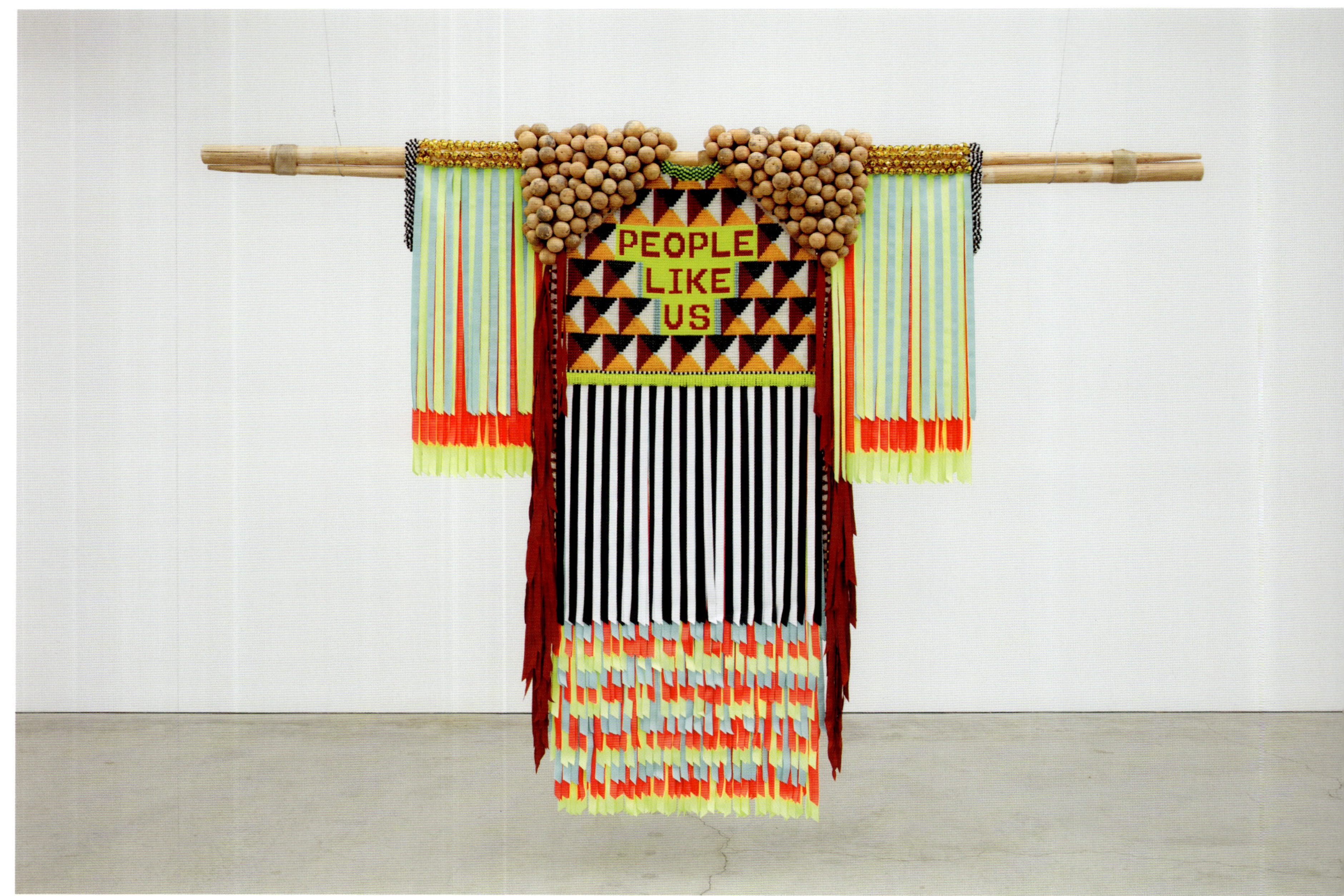

***PEOPLE LIKE US*, 2019**

Canvas, glass and plastic beads, artificial sinew, dried pear gourds, bells, ribbon, and tipi pole

Courtesy of the artist and Sikkema Jenkins Gallery

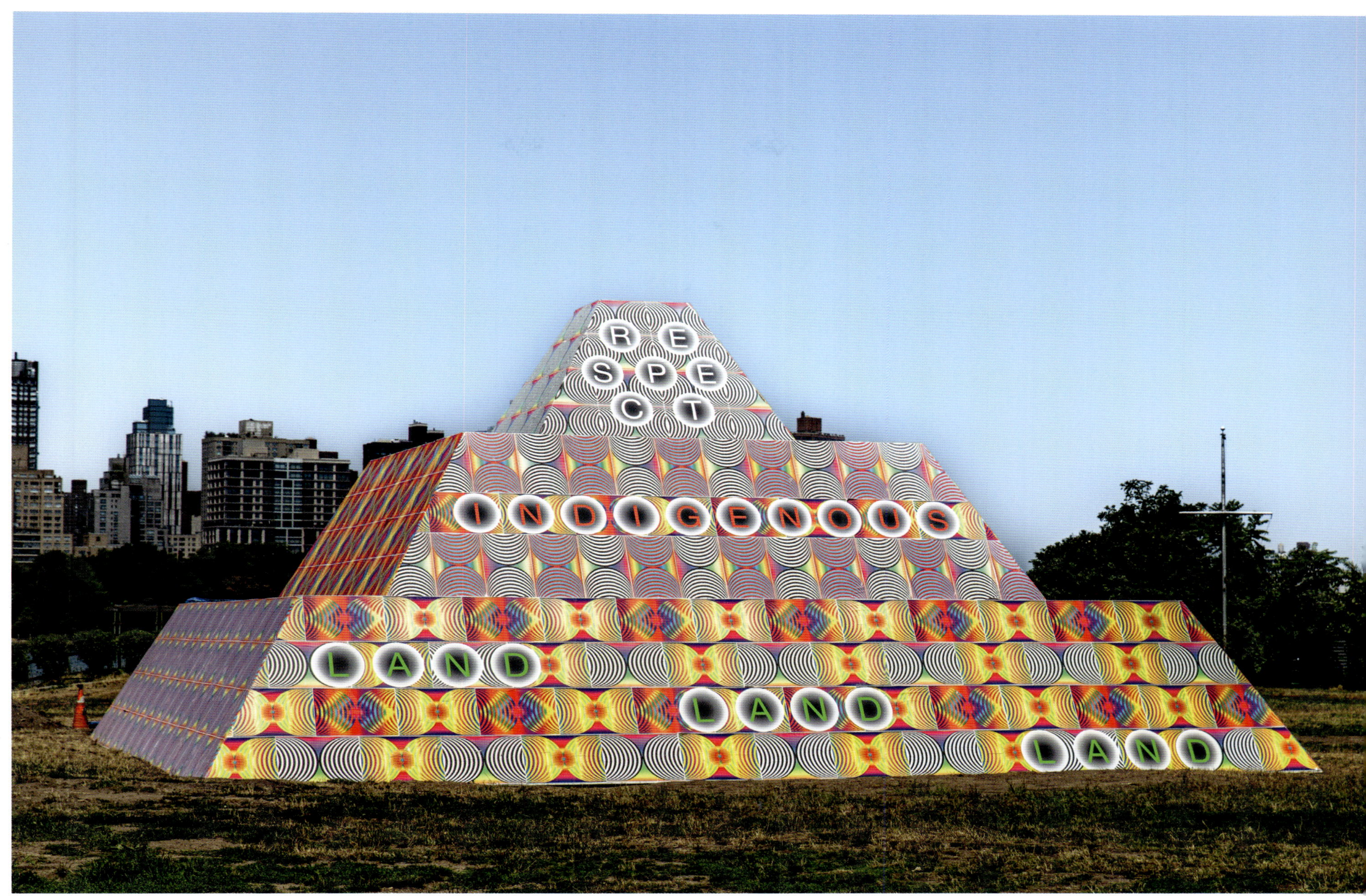

***BECAUSE ONCE YOU ENTER MY HOUSE IT BECOMES OUR HOUSE*, 2020**
Plywood, posters, steel, and LEDs
Installation at Socrates Sculpture Park with performances, Queens, New York
Courtesy of the artist and Hauser & Wirth Gallery

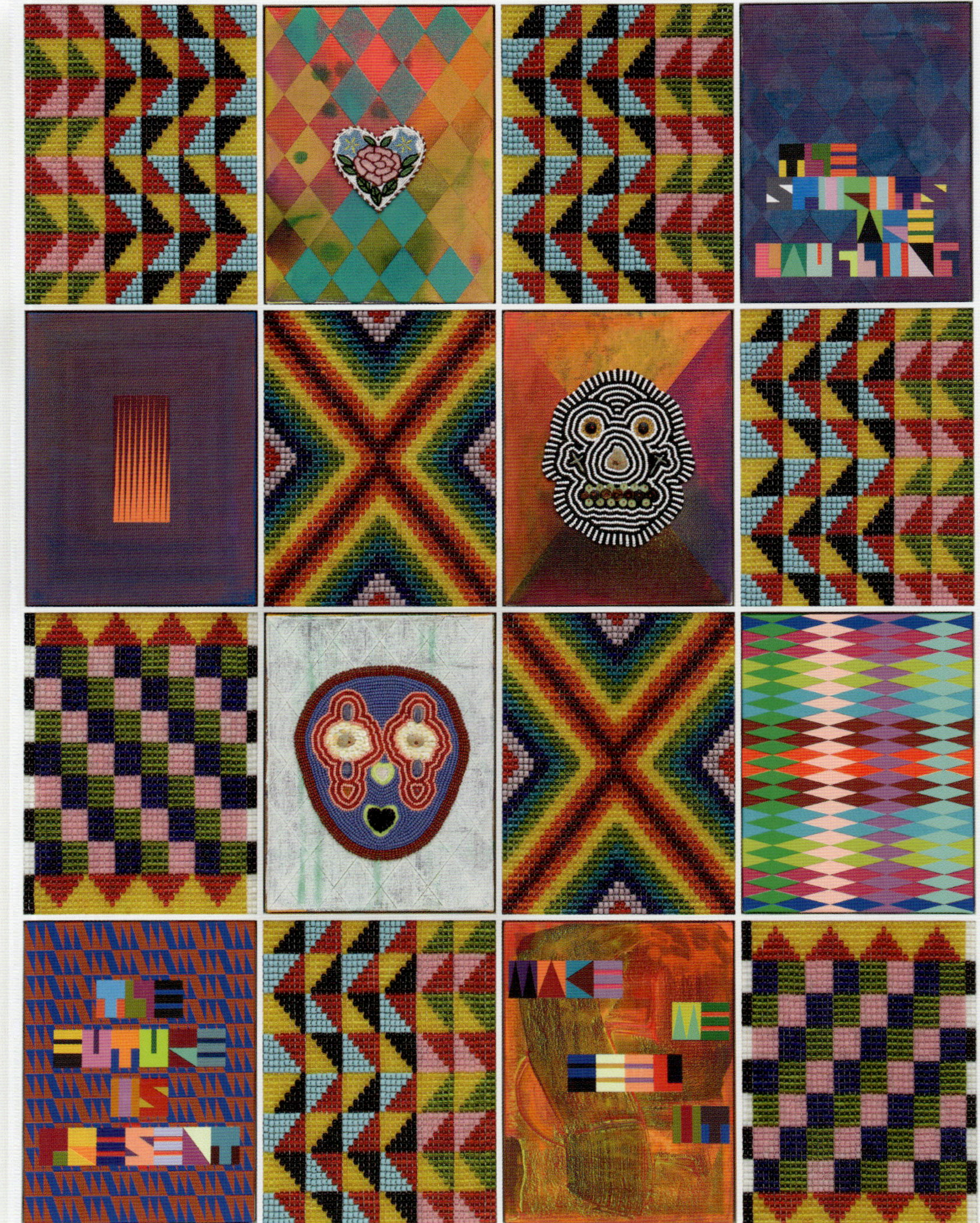

***MAKE ME FEEL IT*, 2021**

Acrylic on canvas, artificial sinew, glass beads

Courtesy of the artist and Hauser & Wirth Gallery

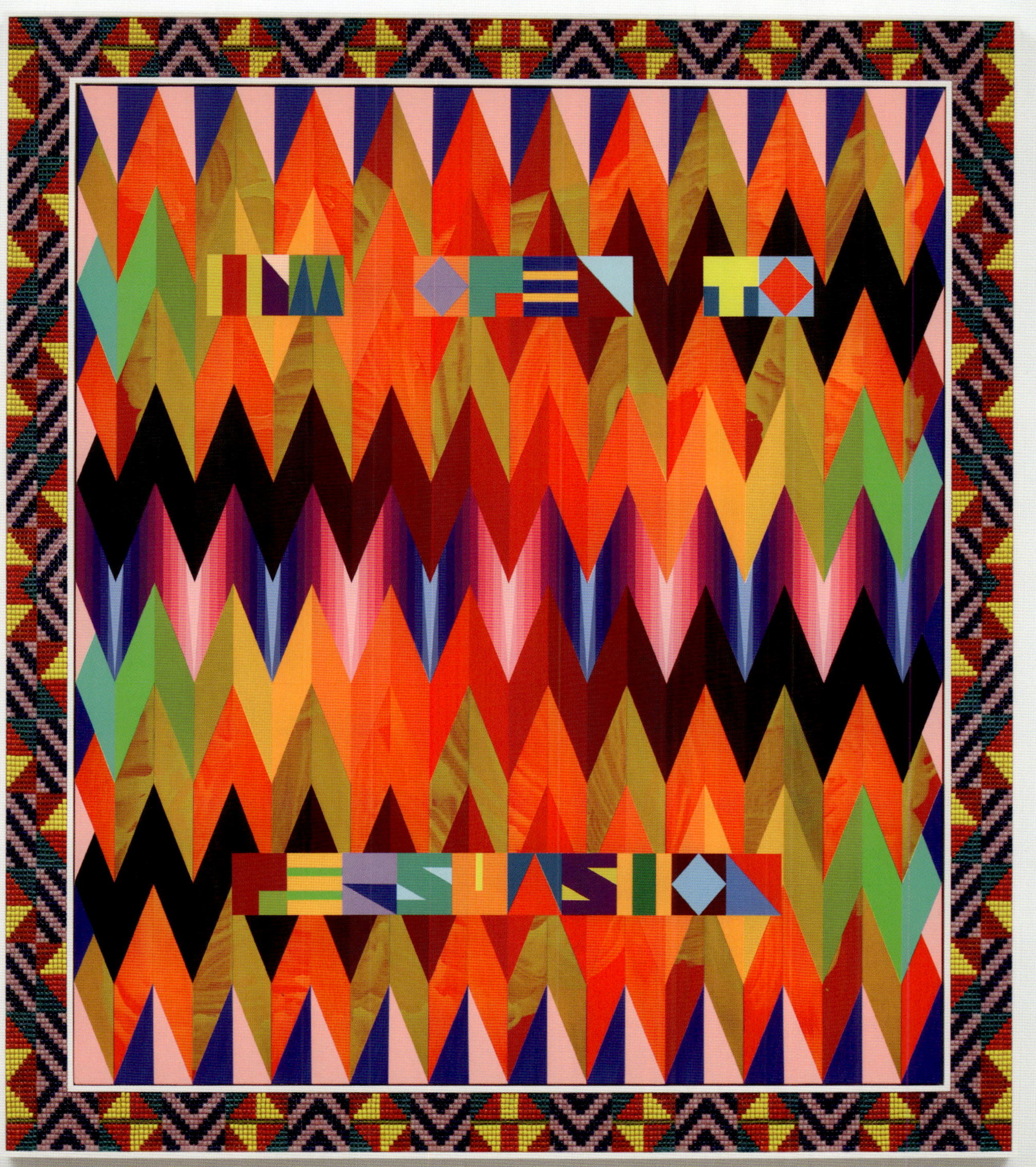

***I'M OPEN TO PERSUASION*, 2023**
Acrylic on canvas, artificial sinew, glass beads
Courtesy of the artist and Hauser & Wirth Gallery

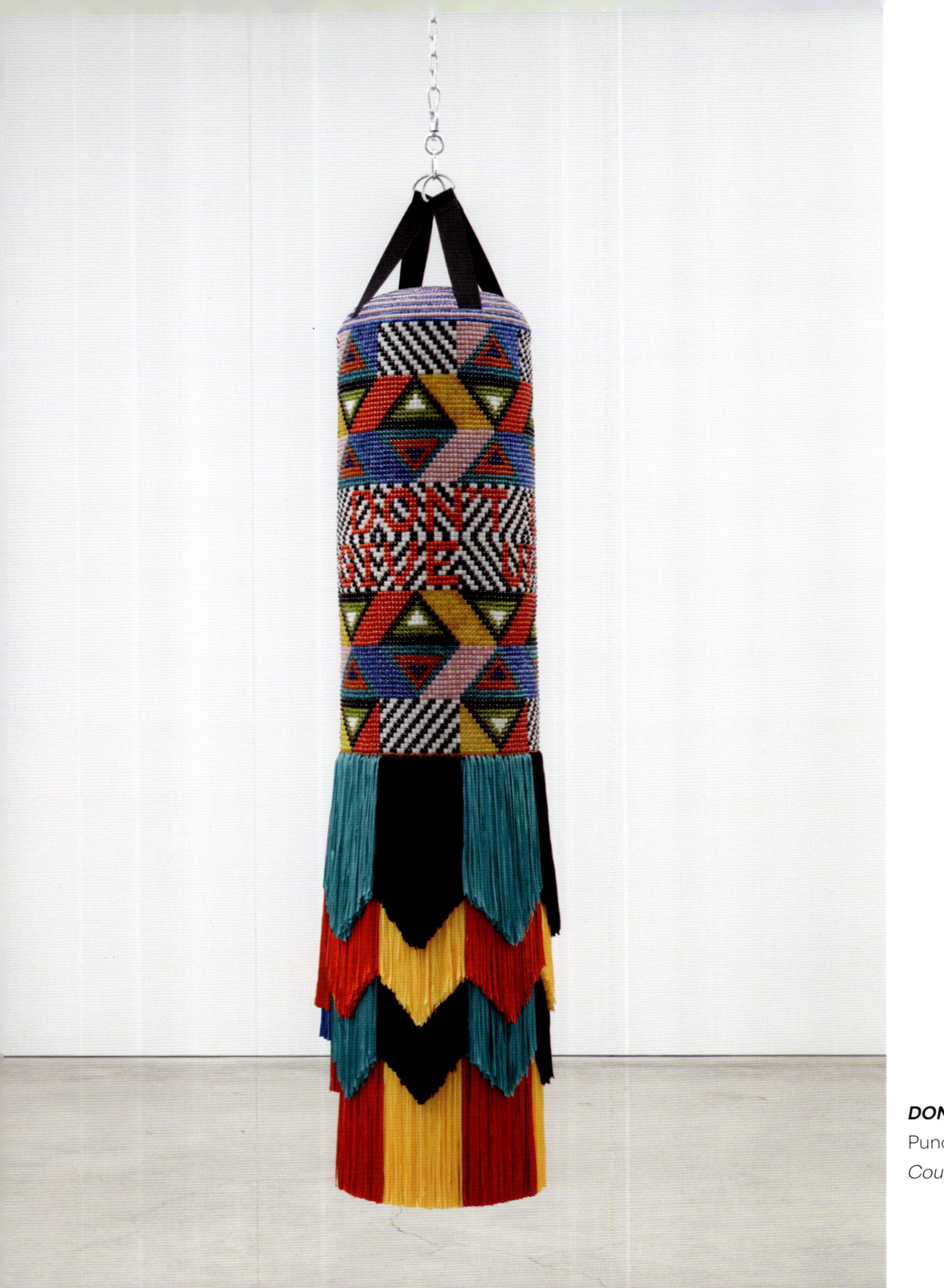

***DON'T GIVE UP*, 2023**

Punching bag, glass beads, fabric tassles

Courtesy of the artist and Hauser & Wirth Gallery

In 2024, Gibson became the first Indigenous artist to represent the United States at the 60th Venice Biennale. For this commission, he transformed the interior and exterior of the neoclassical pavilion into a Technicolored celebration of Native American culture and history. Bright paintings and beaded sculptures were shown against vividly painted walls, reassessing the traditional narrative of his roots by mixing modern references—Nina Simone lyrics sewn onto costumes, political pins affixed to sculptures—with traditional craftsmanship. The exterior in particular puts into question the lens in which we view the history of the US in relation to Indigenous groups. Modeled after Monticello, Thomas Jefferson's primary residence, the US pavilion's architecture favors a Western vision of culture. By updating the colonial architecture with colorful murals and flags, Gibson shifts the view away from a Eurocentric one to one that includes, and highlights, oppressed groups. A cluster of empty plinths in particular underscores the way in which monuments, so important in building national identity, excludes certain groups. Gibson defies this settled history and forces us to reevaluate who is American.

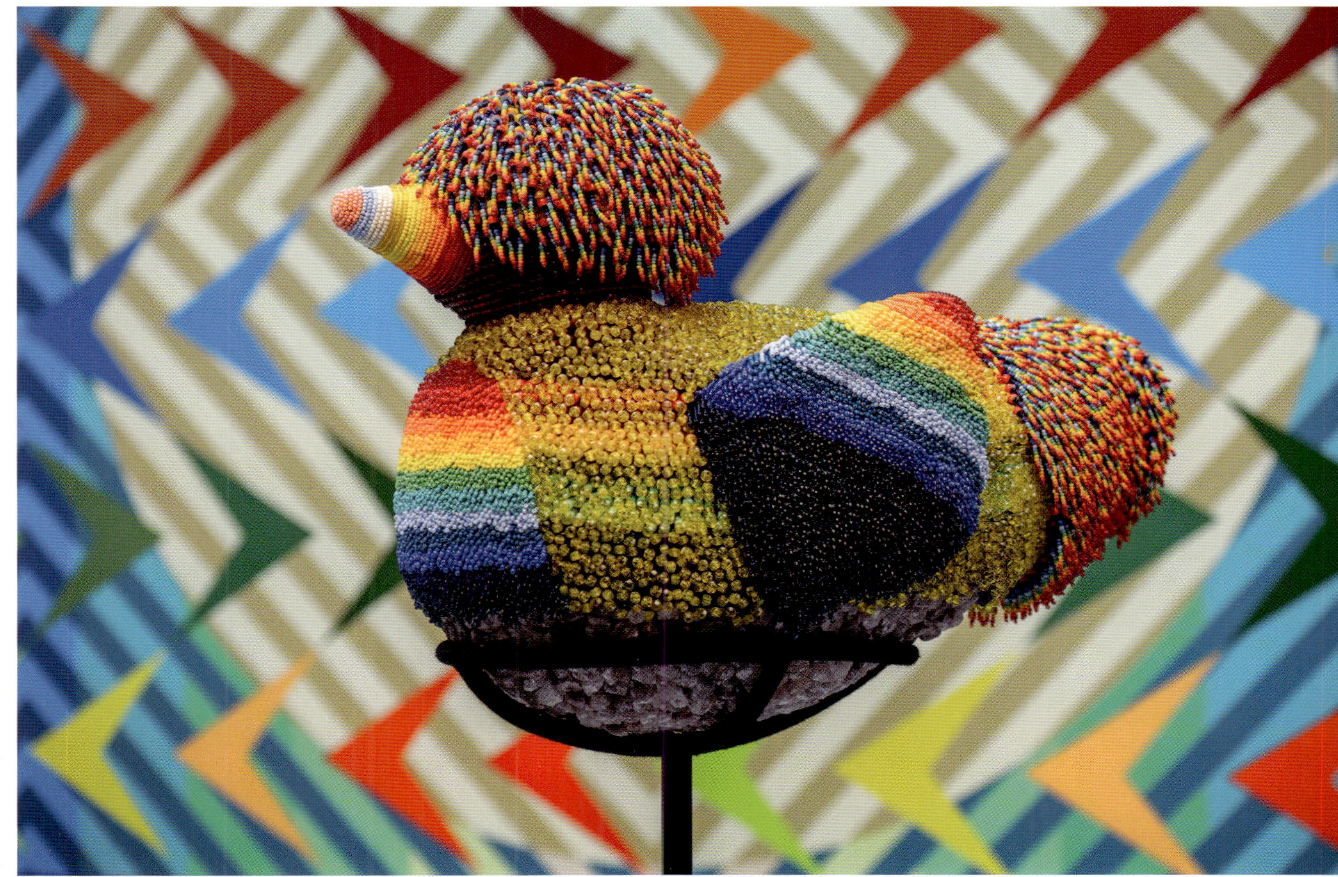

***the space in which to place me*, 2024**
Detail view
Commission for the United States Pavilion for the 60th International Art Exhibition of the La Biennale di Venezia, Venice, Italy
Courtesy of the artist and Hauser & Wirth Gallery

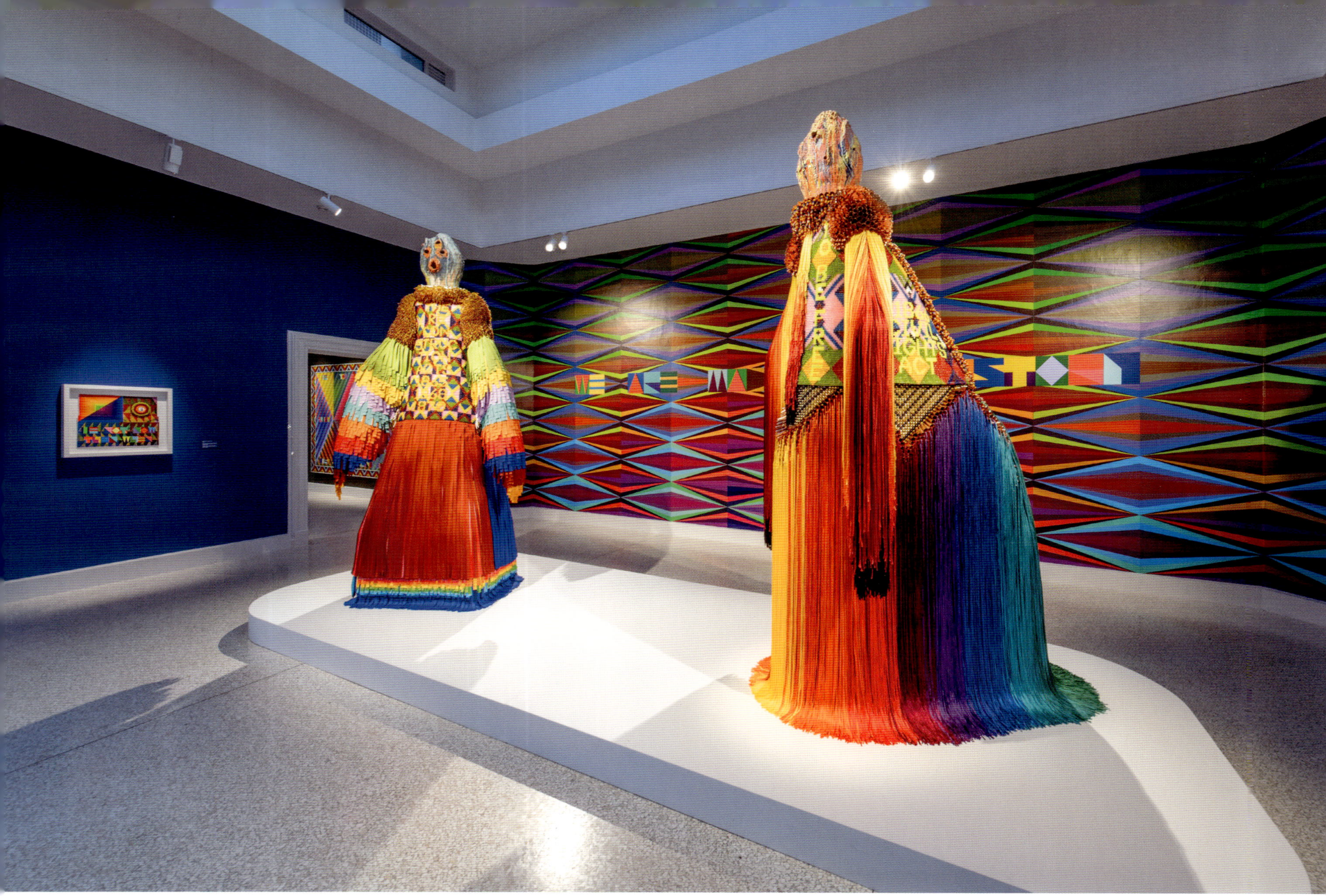

***the space in which to place me*, 2024**
Installation view
Courtesy of the artist and Hauser & Wirth Gallery

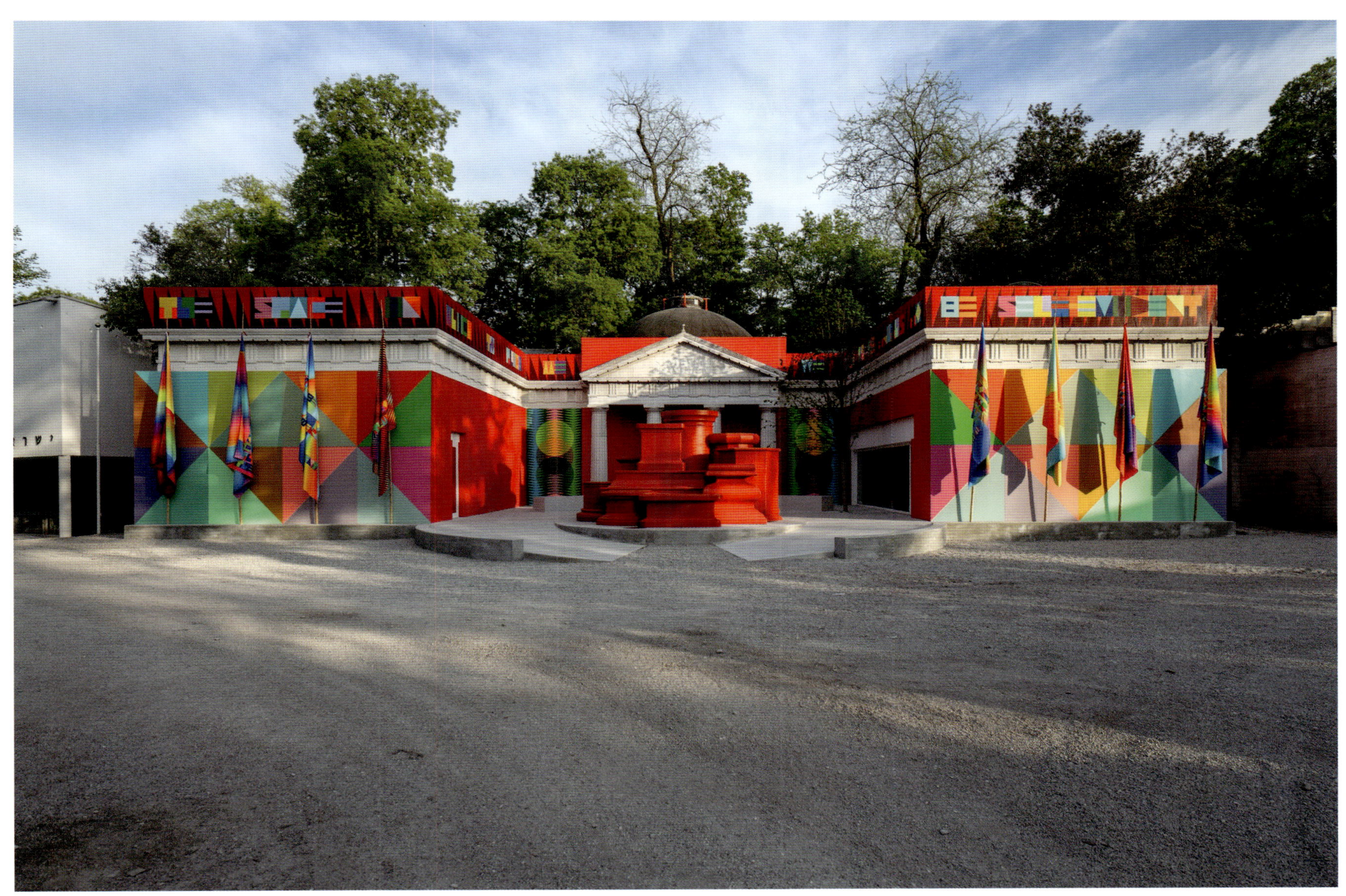

***the space in which to place me*, 2024**
Exterior view
Courtesy of the artist and Hauser & Wirth Gallery

Al Loving (1935-2005)

BROADWAY JUNCTION (L TRAIN)

***Brooklyn New Morning*, 2000**

Broadway Junction is a vast hub connecting many lines deep in Brooklyn. At every turn in the station, one can find the works of Al Loving, who created over seventy stained glass works and a mosaic mural that bear the marks of a long career exploring abstraction. His glass panels employ the use of circles and spirals that characterized his later works, which are a marriage of his early geometric forms and his later experiments with material traditions. They can be found on the stairwells, greeting riders as they enter and exit the platforms, as well as along the escalators, vibrant windows that impart a kaleidoscope of color onto commuters. The mosaic mural on the mezzanine is the center piece of this expansive project; spirals and swirls dance on top of a checkboard design like animated musical notes.

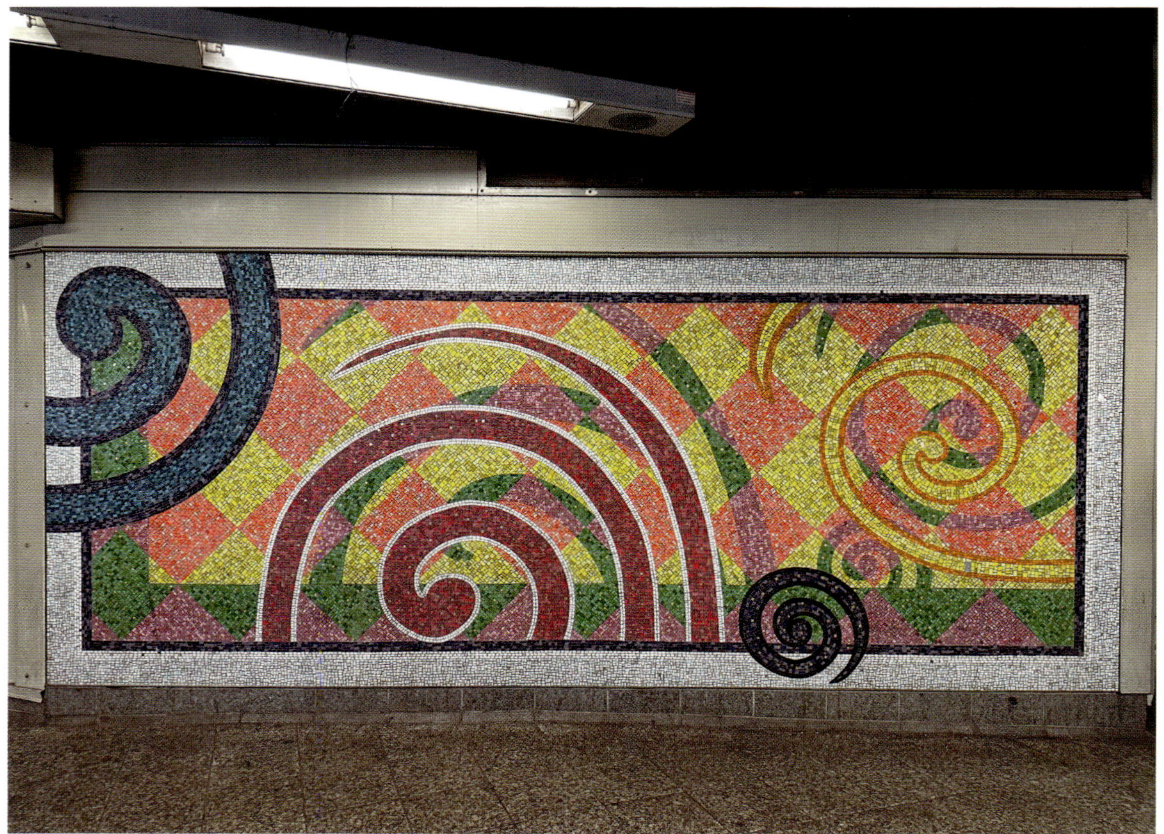

Photos: Adam Chitayat

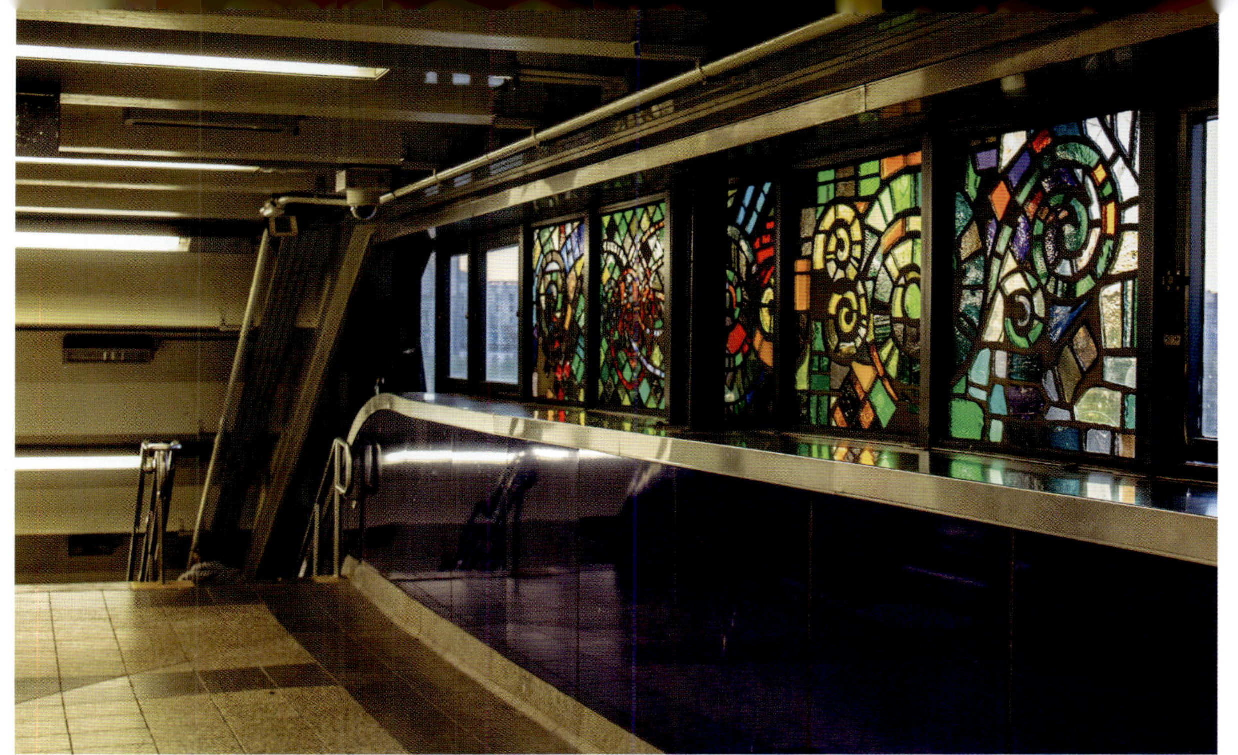

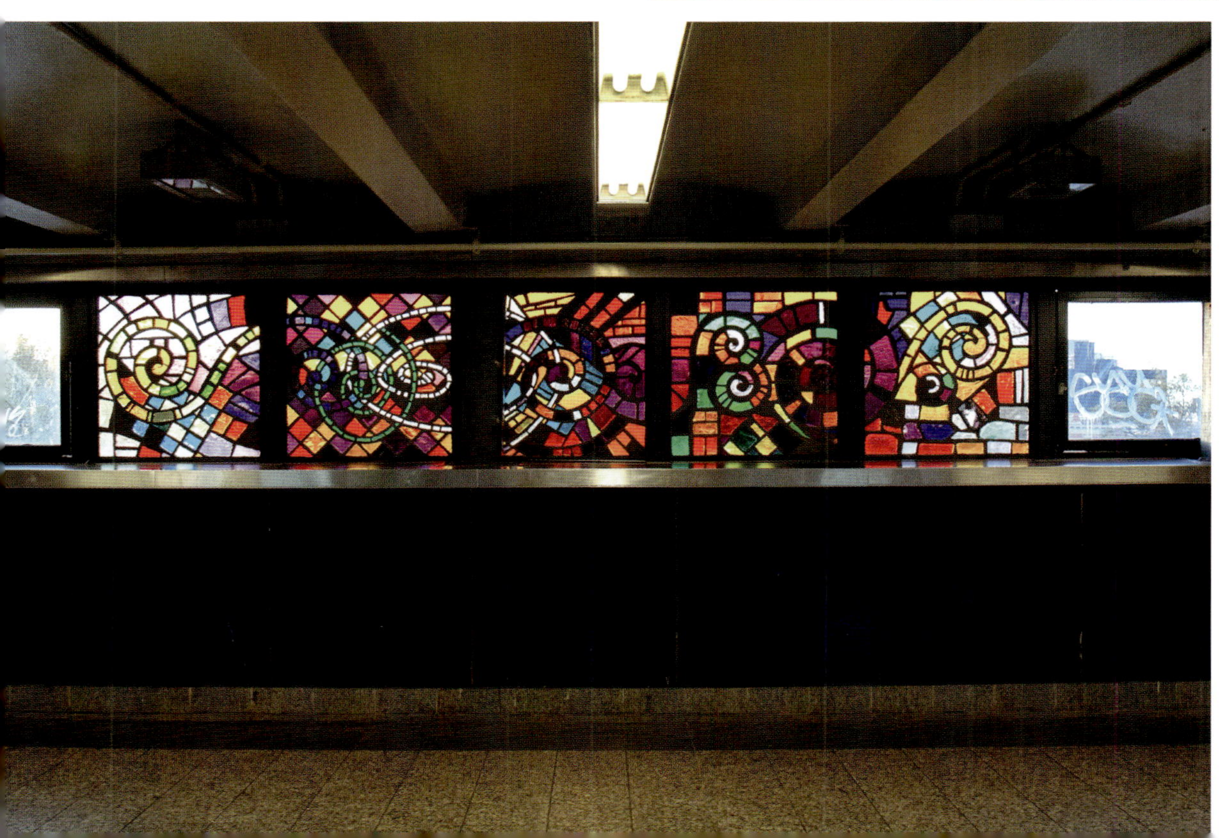

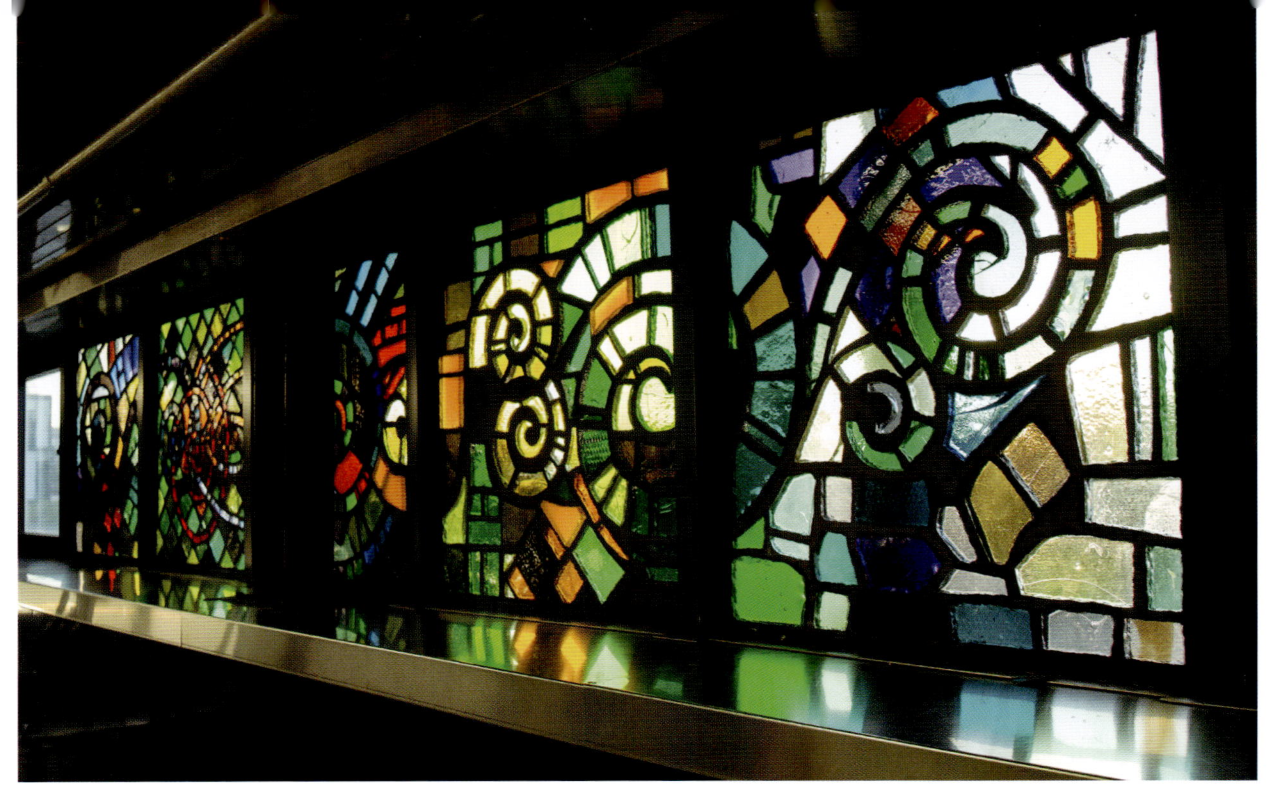

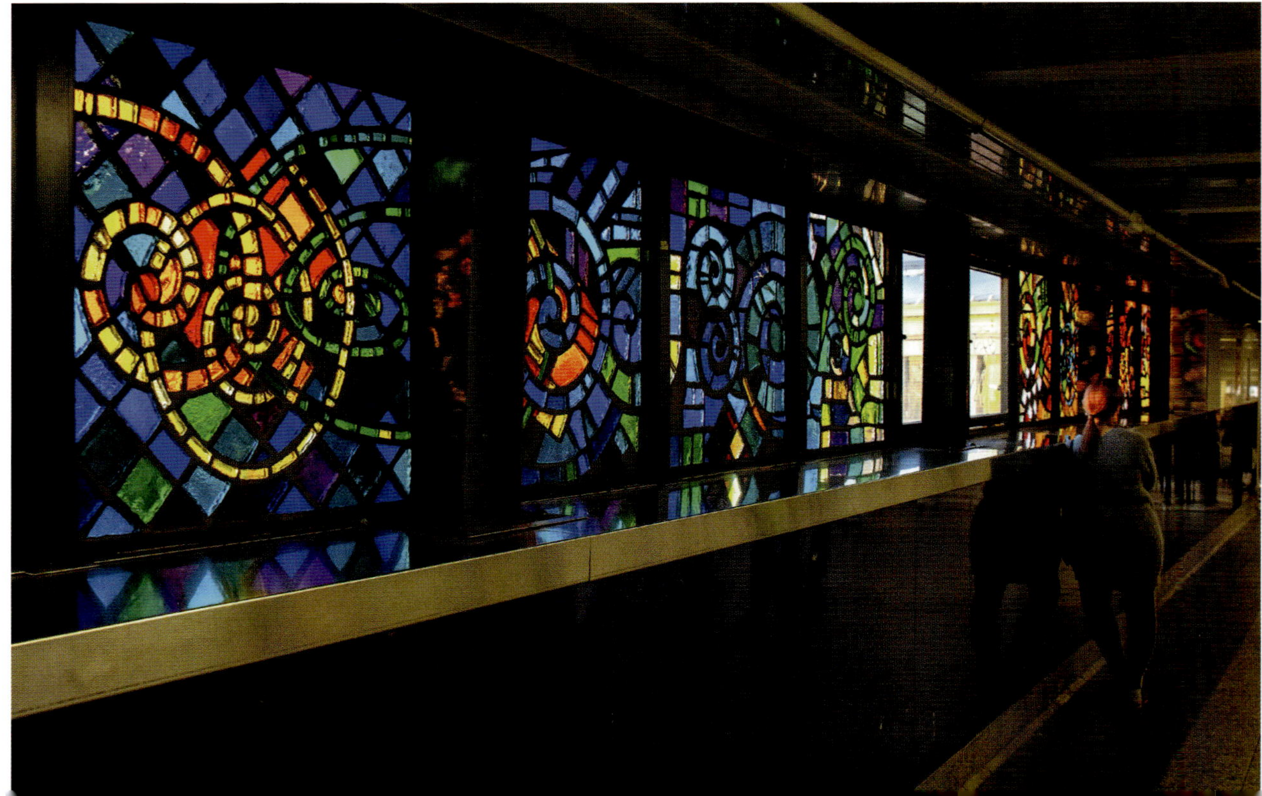

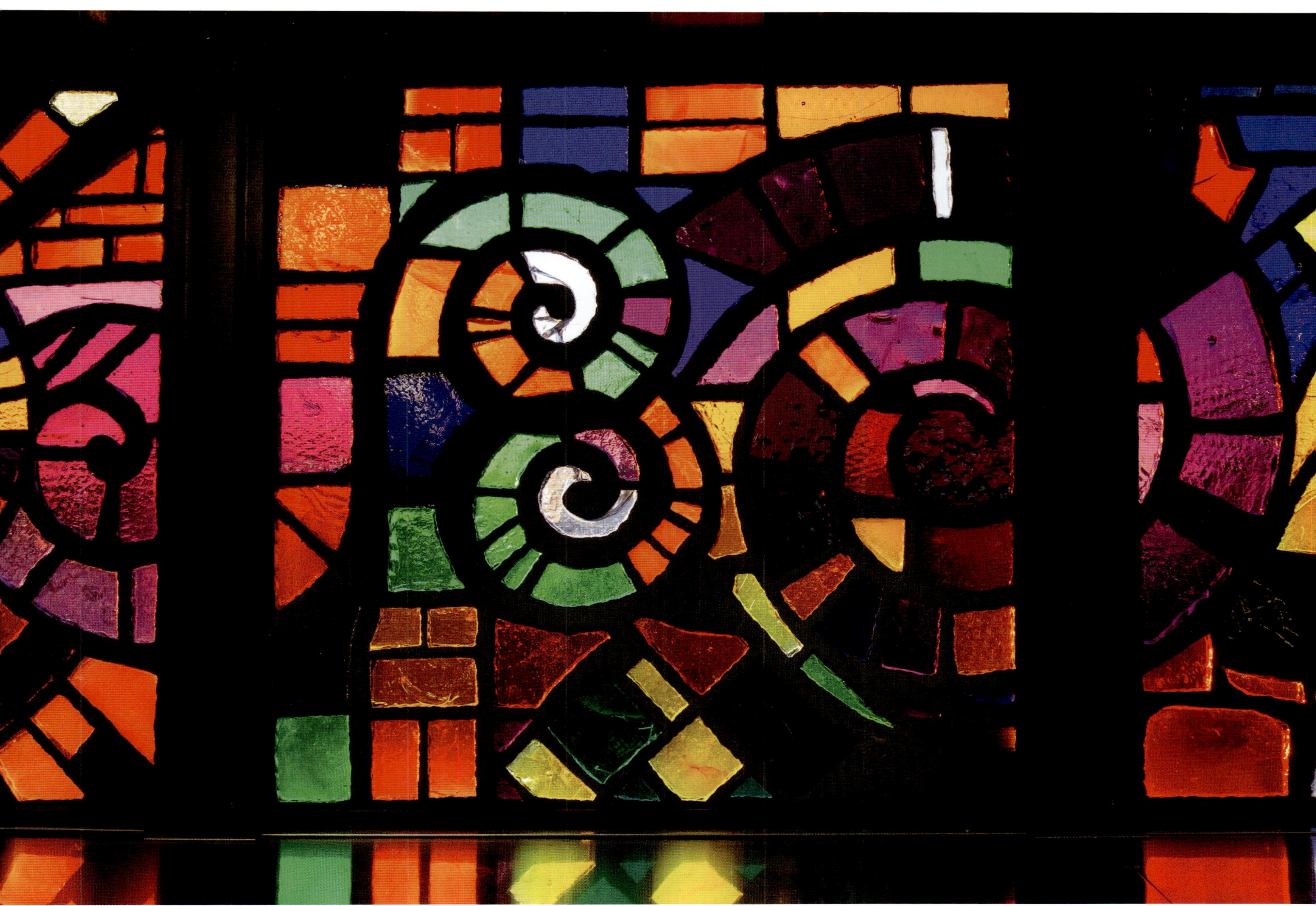

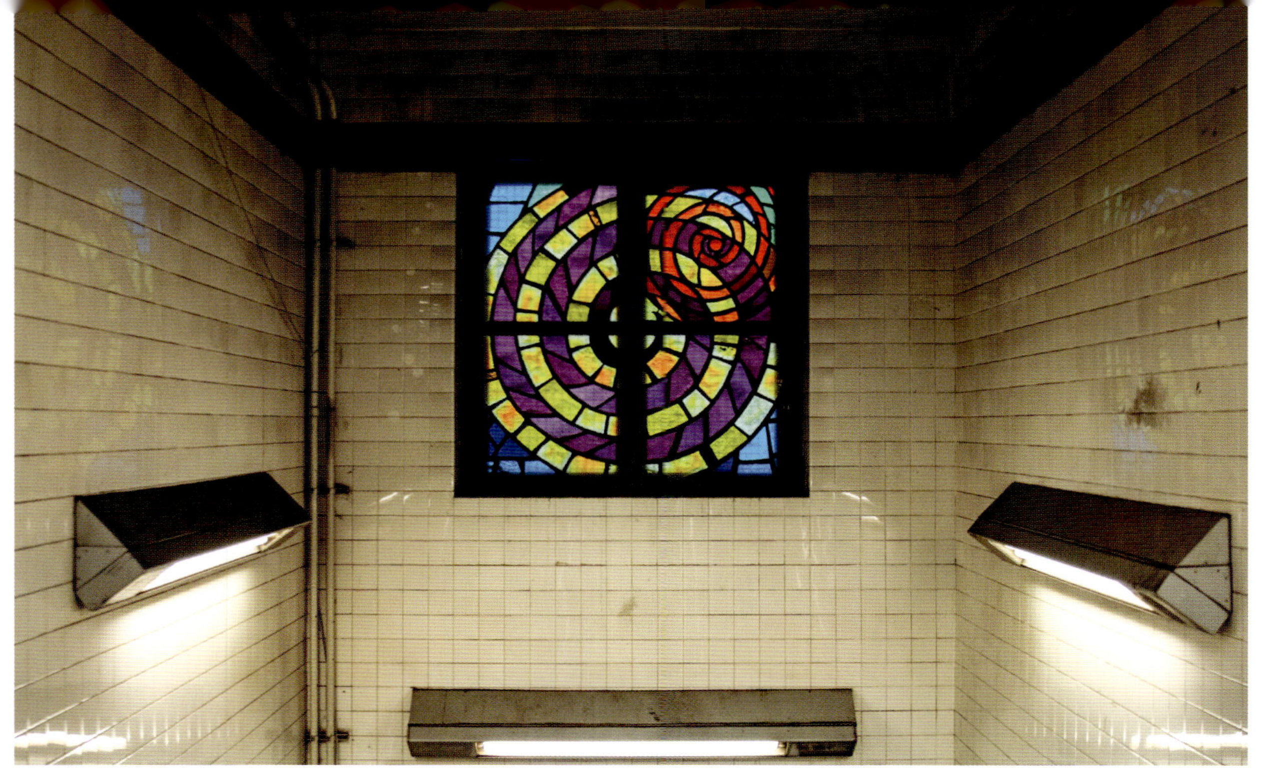

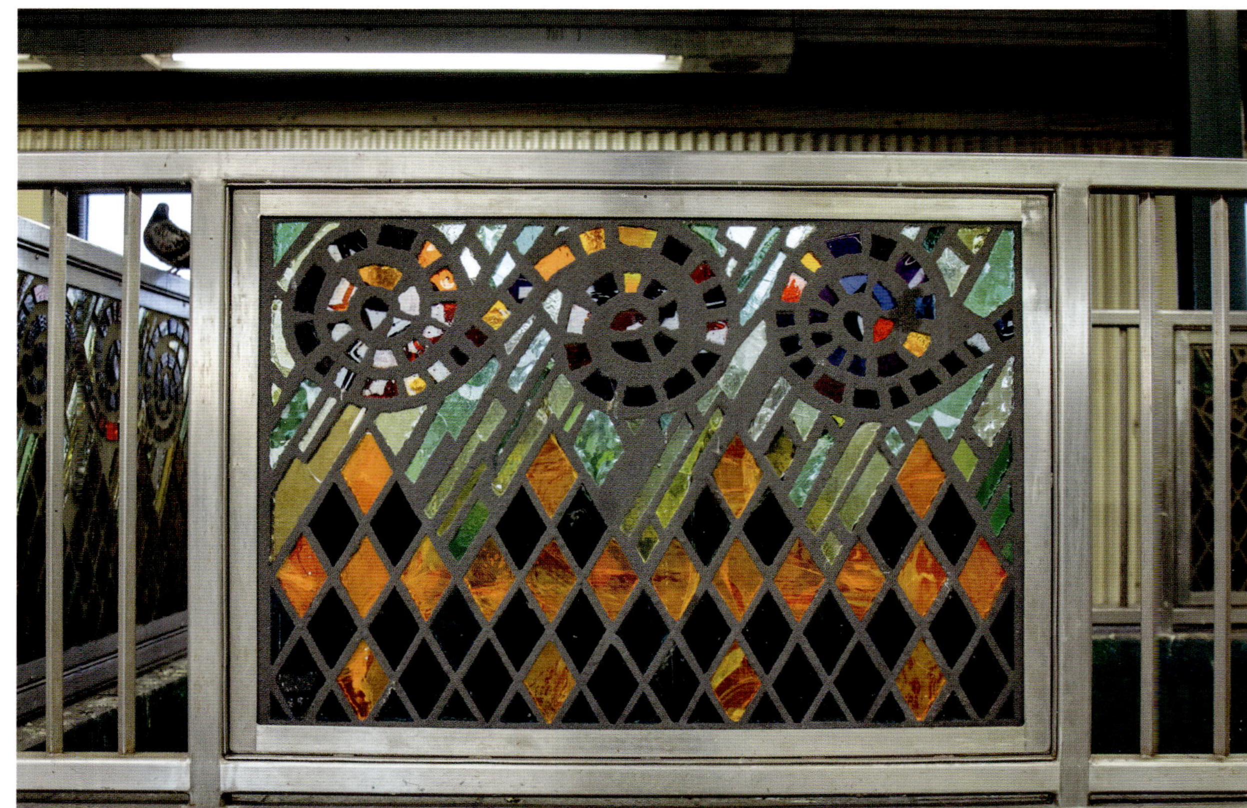

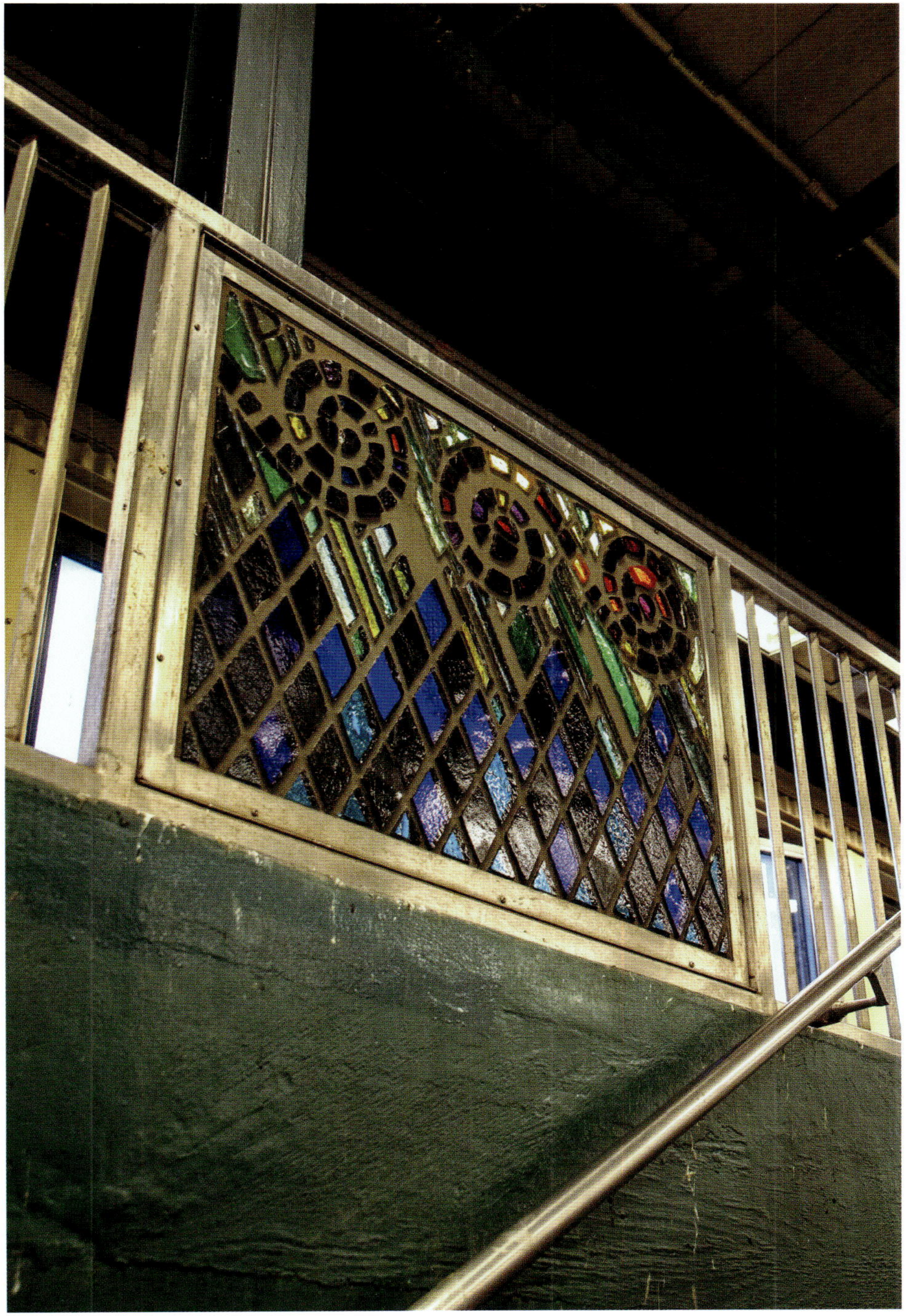

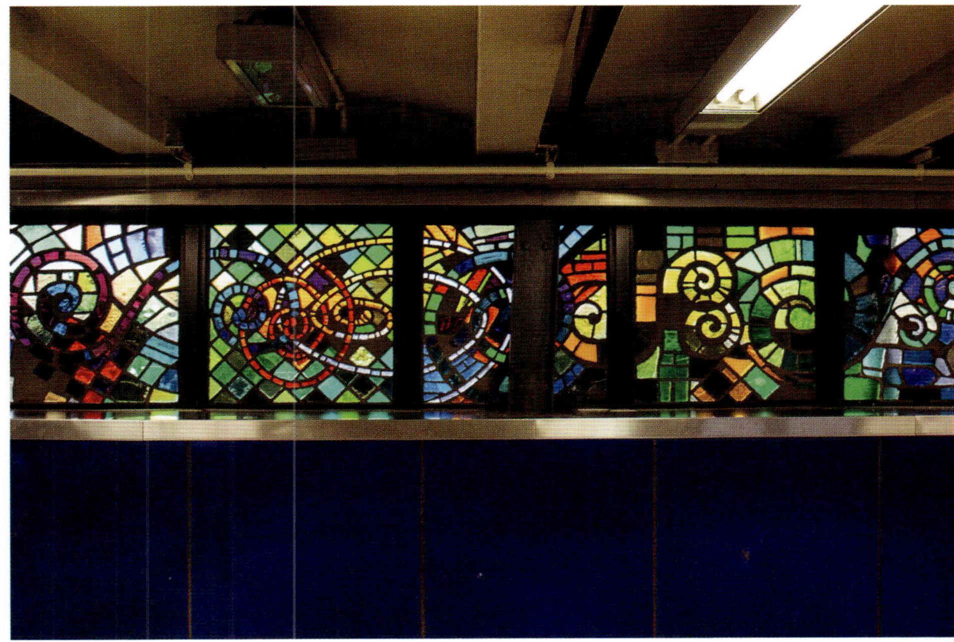

At a time when Black American artists were expected to consider the Black experience in their work, Loving defied conventions with his exploration into abstraction. His early works adhered to strict geometric forms—hard-edged paintings with crisp, vibrant colors, the irregularly shaped canvases often arranged into tight formations. These were rational works that showed an artist exploring the spatial possibilities of a two-dimensional space, creating illusions of three-dimensionality on the canvas. These were the works that were subject of his solo show at the Whitney Museum in 1969, the first Black artist to have their own show at the revered institution.

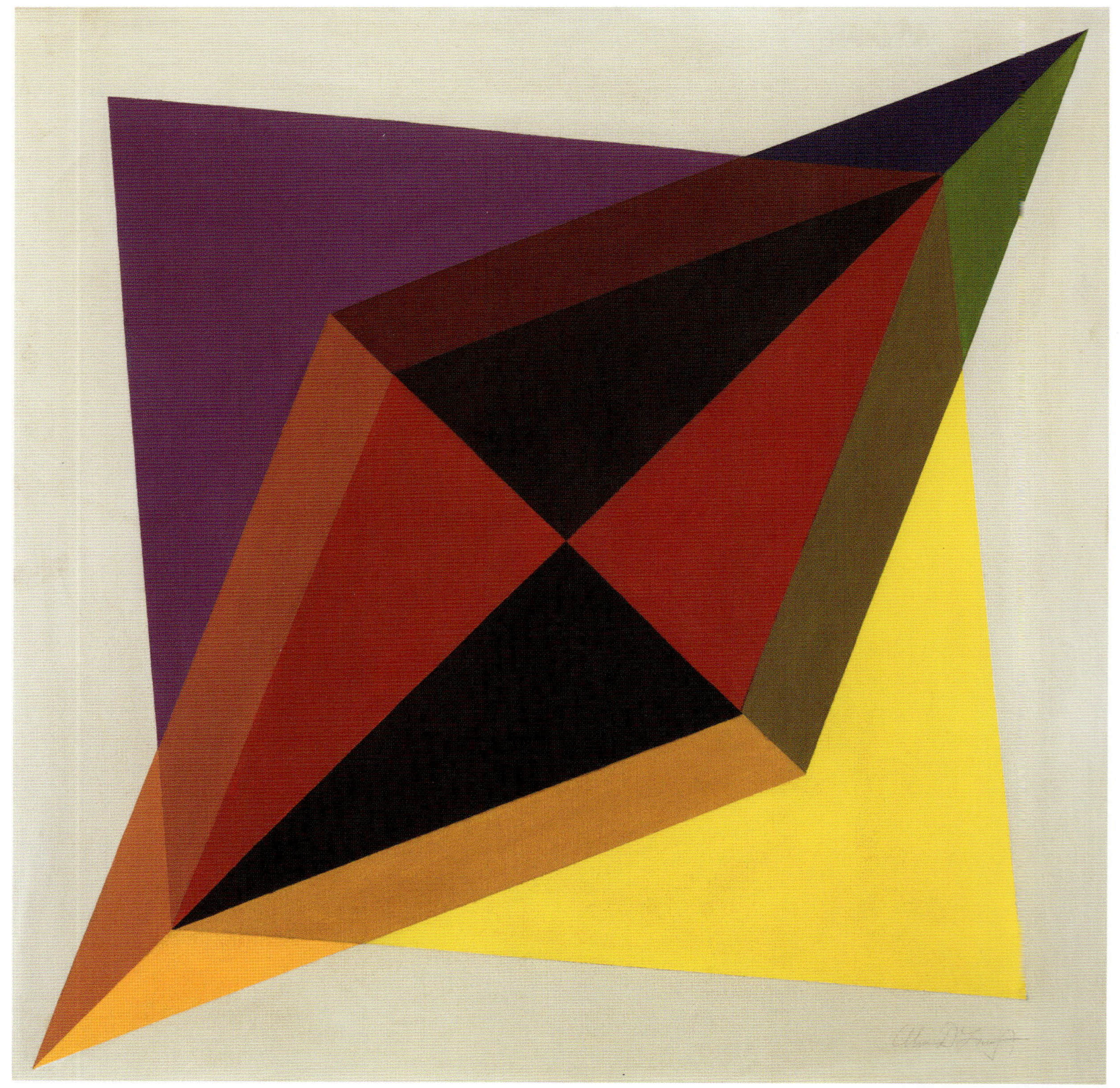

***Untitled*, 1967**
Acrylic on canvas
Courtesy of Garth Greenan Gallery

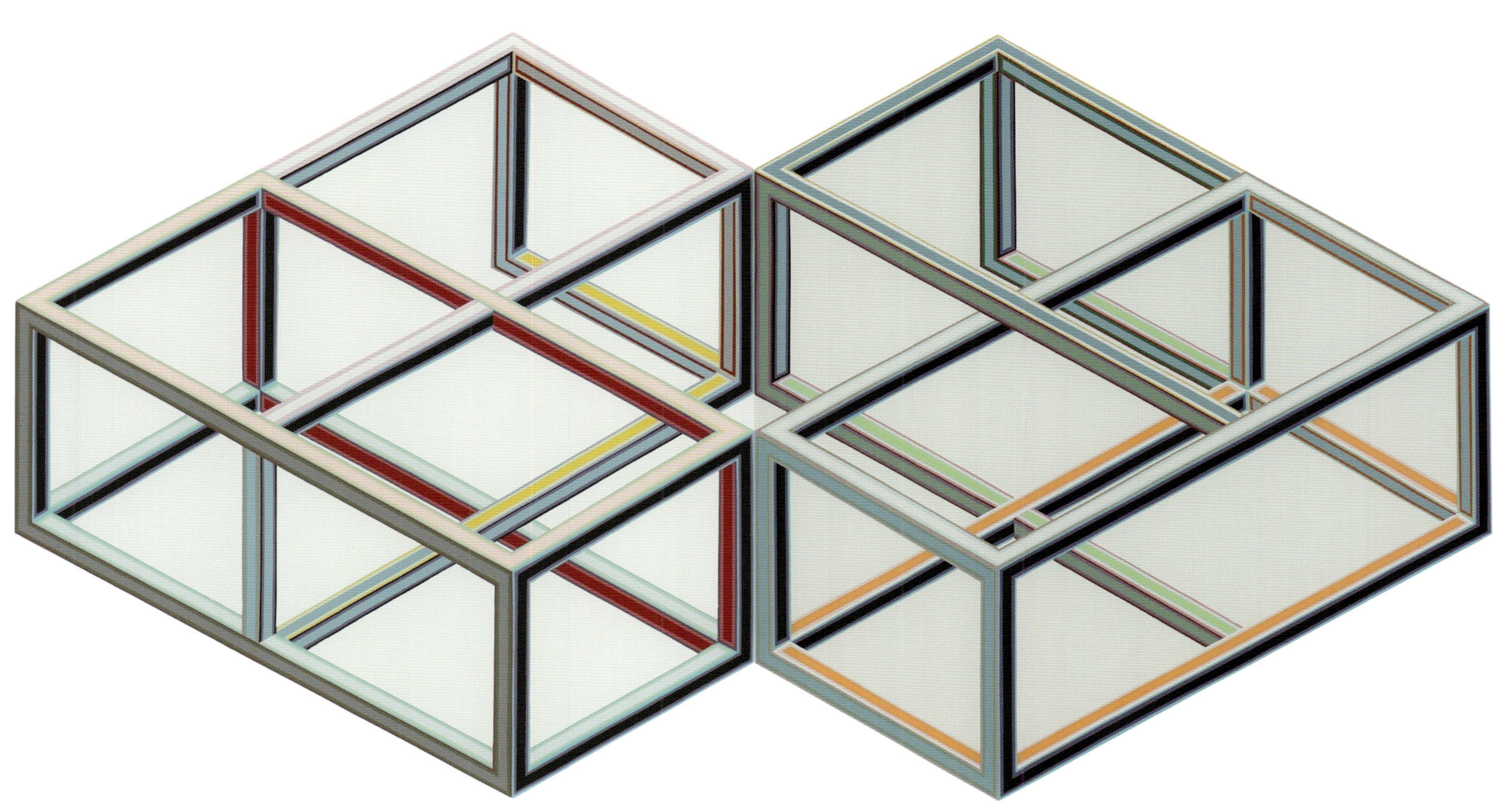

***White Rational Irrationalism*, 1969**
Acrylic on canvas
Courtesy of Garth Greenan Gallery

***Untitled*, 1969**
Acrylic on canvas
Courtesy of Garth Greenan Gallery

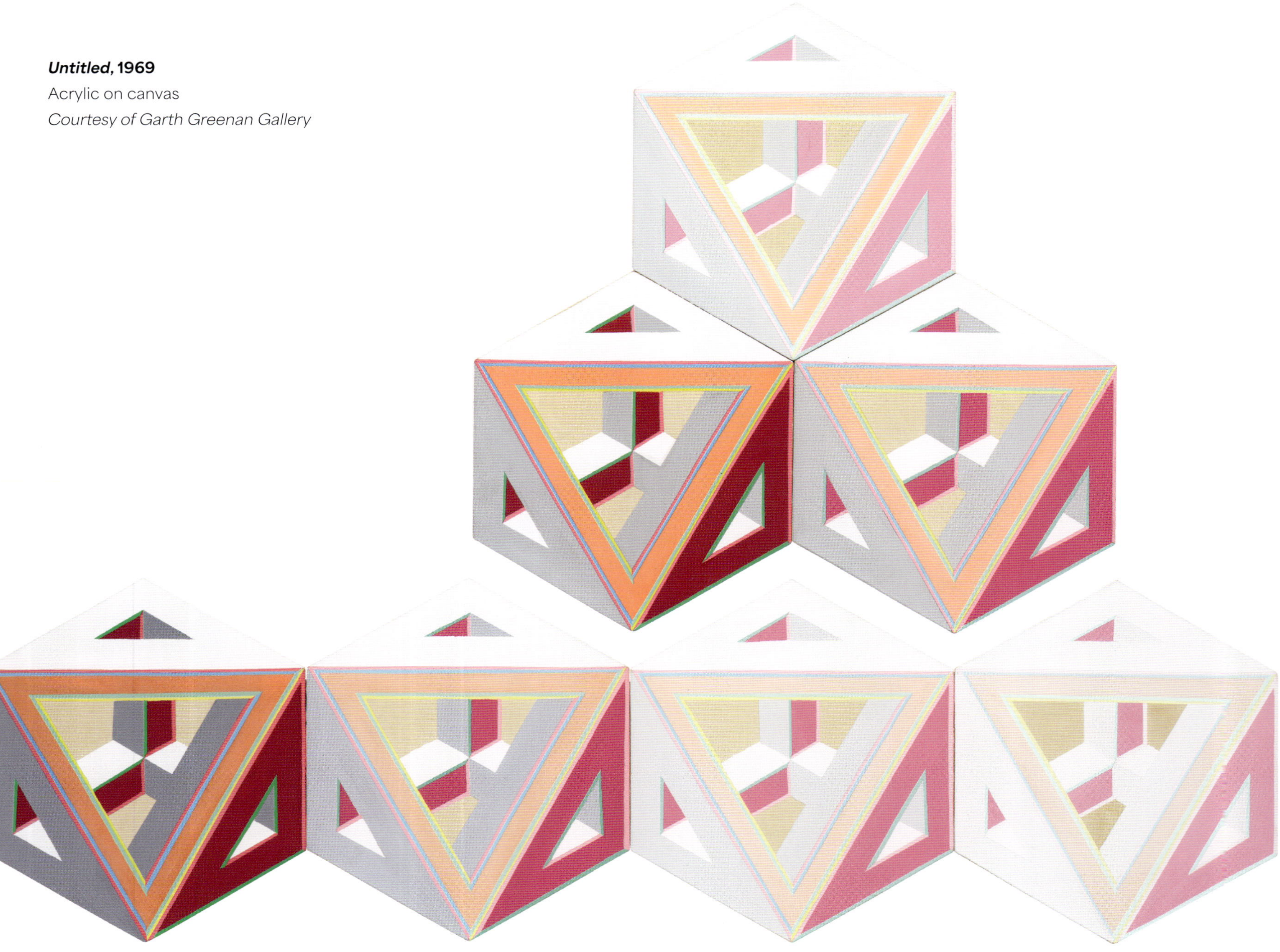

Not long after this exhibition, Loving made a radical change in his practice. He dispensed with hard-edged formalism, adapting a looser style that still had a basis in his early geometric works but without the rigid confines of those canvases. In a way rejecting the mid-century abstraction that he had immersed himself in, he found inspiration in the quilting traditions of Black American women such as his mother and grandmother, stitching strips of dyed canvas into informal compositions, his works taking on the energy of freehand sketches. There was an improvisational quality to them that nonetheless showed his thoughtful considerations of form and color. In one work from 1973 (*Untitled*), he arranged red- and peach-colored cloth into a rough shape of a face, flanked by dark-brown sheets that are tied and braided like hair. Loving also created collages on paper and cardboard, allowing him to play even more with shapes, adding spirals, squares, and grids. The spiral in particular is an important component to his later works, symbolizing to him affirmation and regeneration. As in his commission at Broadway Junction, these shapes are an important element to his experimentations with free-form compositions, like a jazz musician improvising.

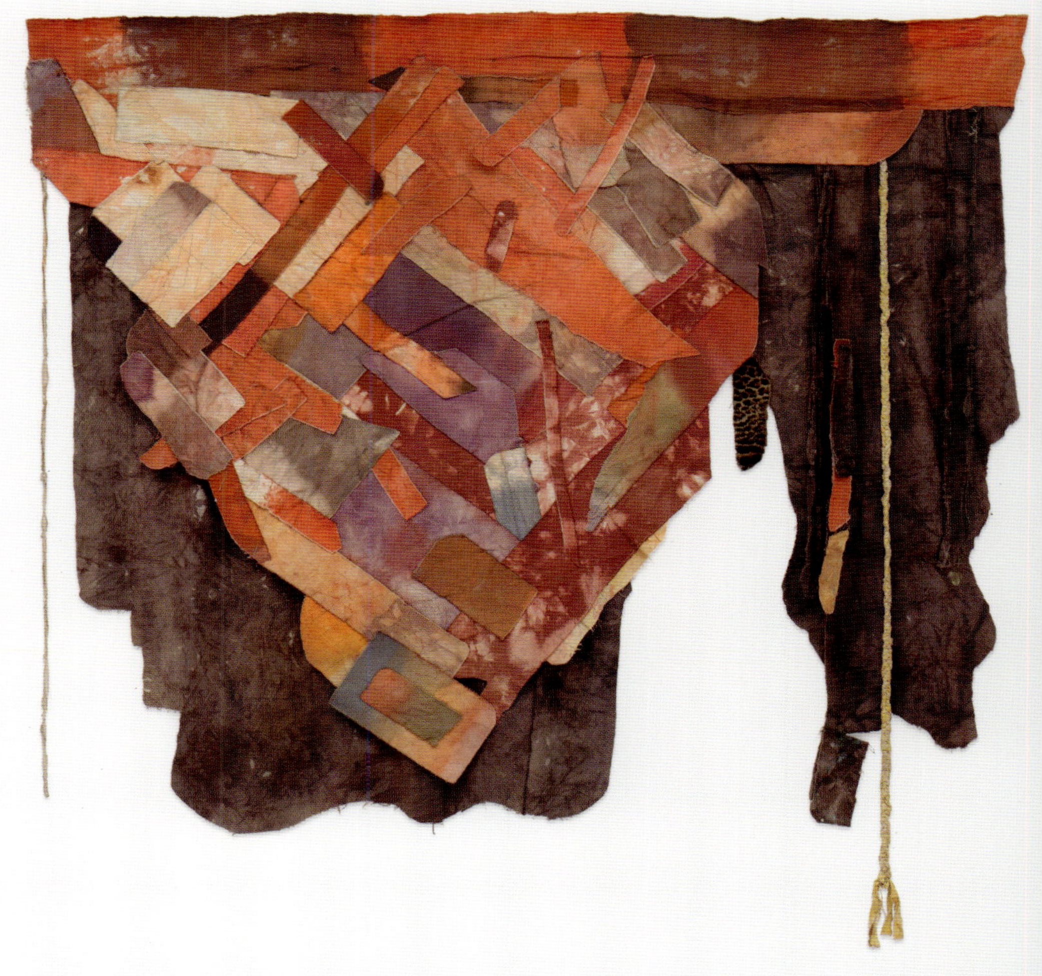

***Untitled*, 1973**
Mixed media on canvas
Courtesy of Garth Greenan Gallery

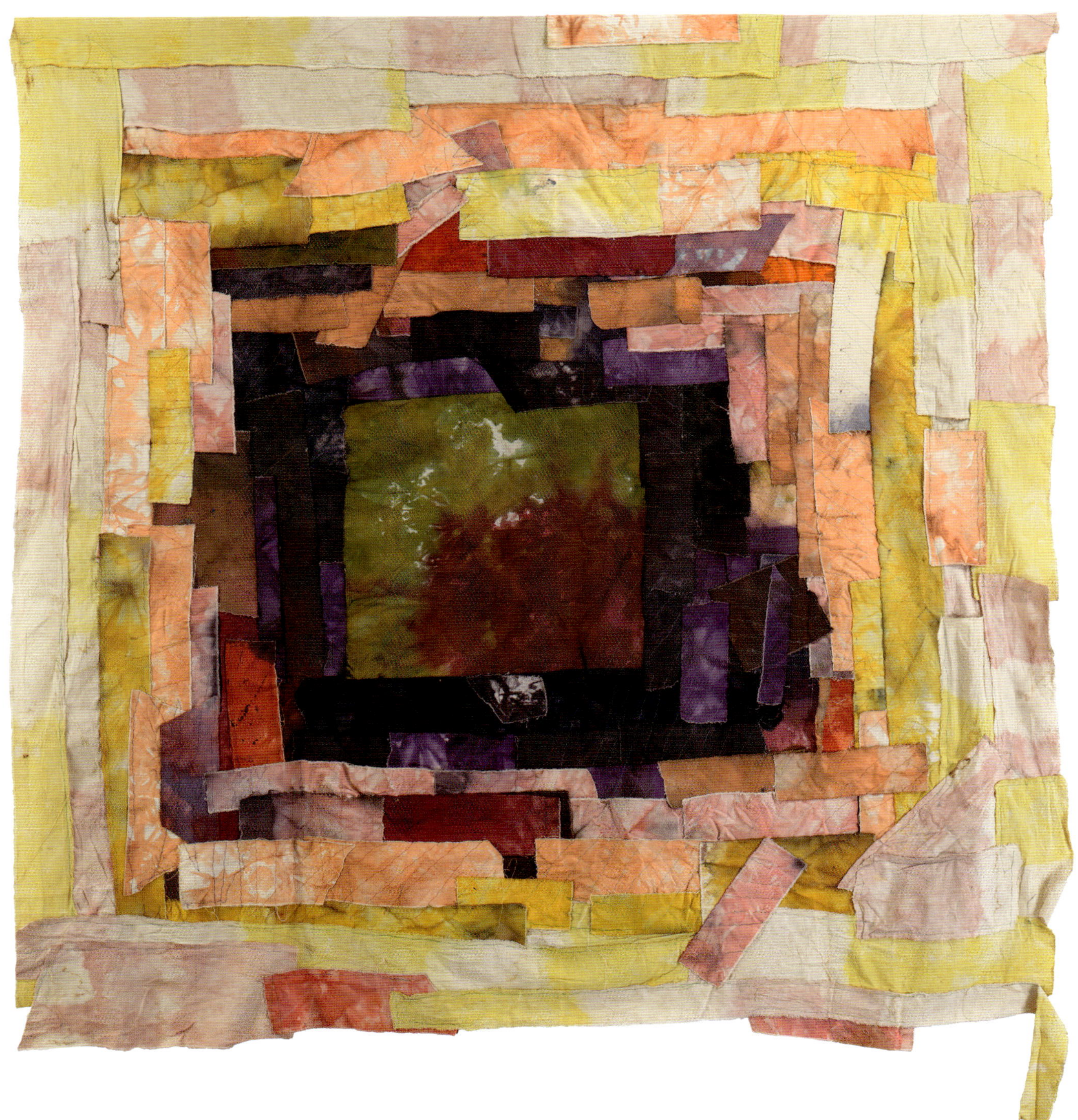

***Square*, 1973–1974**
Mixed media on canvas
Courtesy of Garth Greenan Gallery

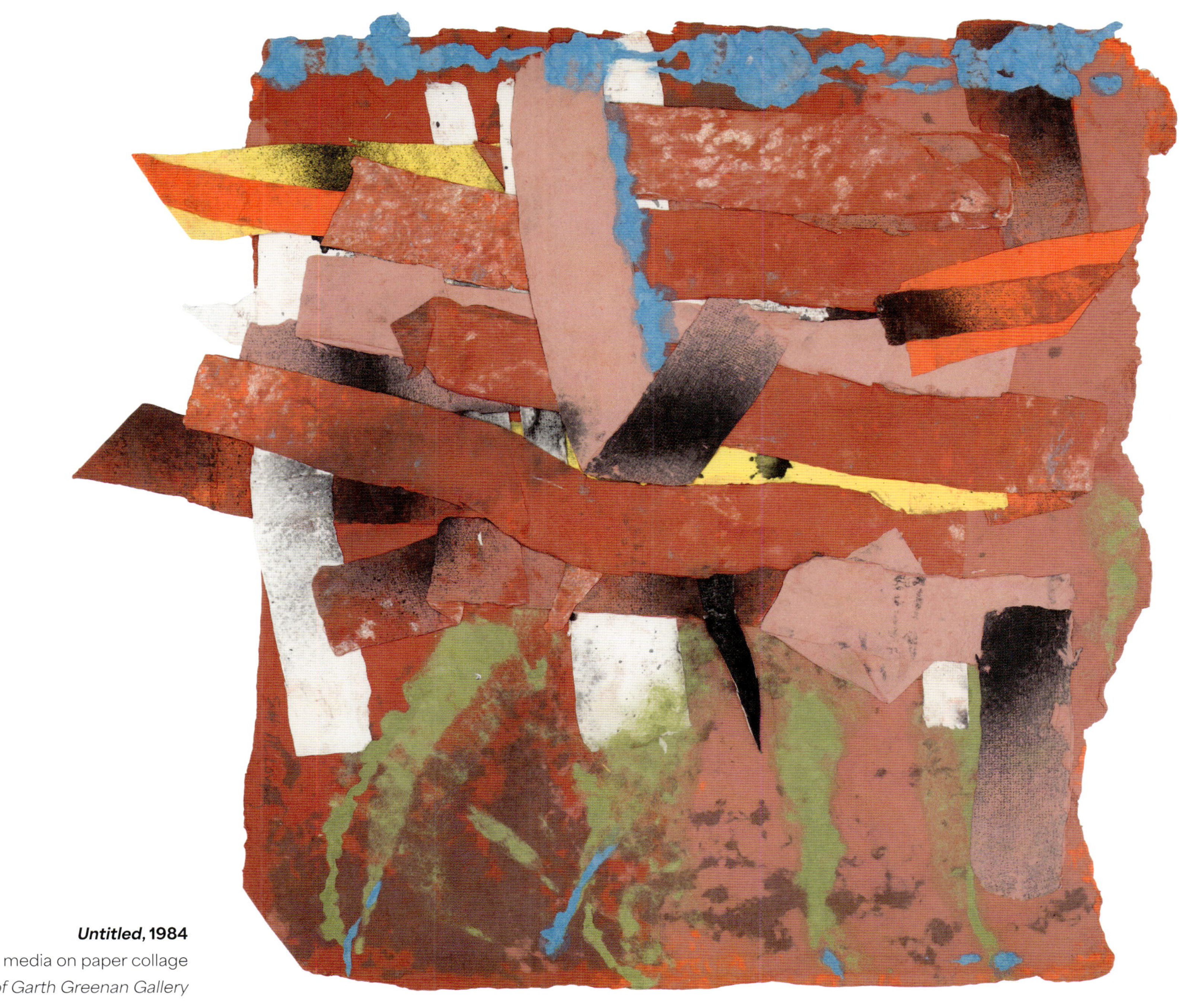

***Untitled*, 1984**
Mixed media on paper collage
Courtesy of Garth Greenan Gallery

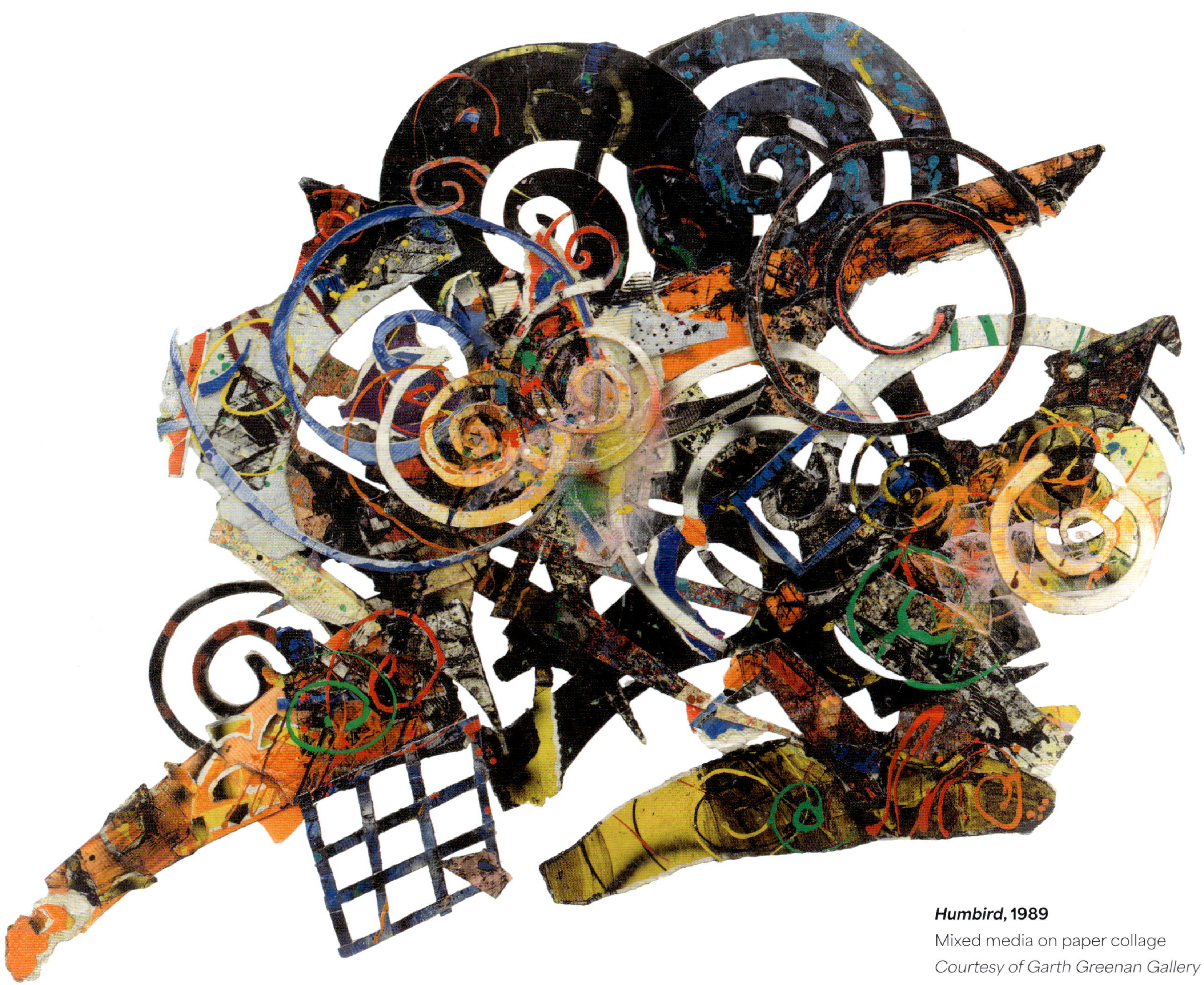

***Humbird*, 1989**
Mixed media on paper collage
Courtesy of Garth Greenan Gallery

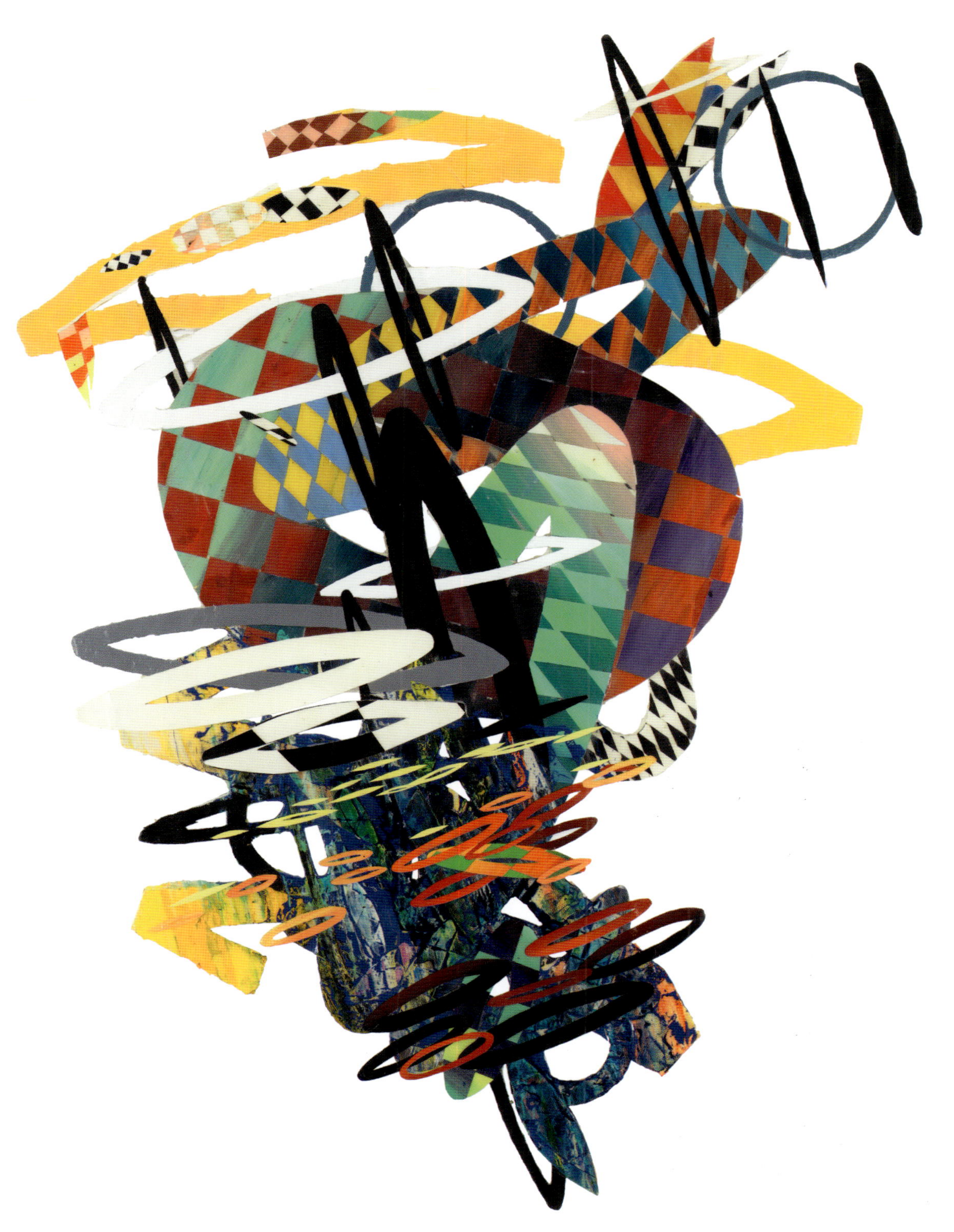

***Spatial Collage #3*, 2004**
Mixed media on paper collage
Courtesy of Garth Greenan Gallery

Portia Munson (b. 1961)

FORT HAMILTON PKWY. (D TRAIN)

***Gardens of Fort Hamilton Parkway Station*, 2012**

At the Fort Hamilton station, laminated glass windows feature lush blooms that can be found all over Brooklyn and are arranged throughout the station seasonally, from early spring to mid-autumn. Portia Munson first experimented with these mandala-like forms in the early aughts; they are a spiritual contrast to her installations that are heavy with plastic and man-made materials, though both her floral mandalas and installations are saturated with form and color. Not merely framing the blooms in the traditional sense, her mandalas present the flowers in startling detail; specimens are often pulled apart and rearranged, each petal and leaf playing a role in the overall composition. Though mandalas have a spiritual legacy, these works are almost scientific in their presentation of the subjects, every vein of the leaves, every bit of pollen laid bare. *Gardens of Fort Hamilton Parkway Station* take on the structure of a formal garden, with its specimens bounded into sections and thus mimicking the structure of the city and its architecture.

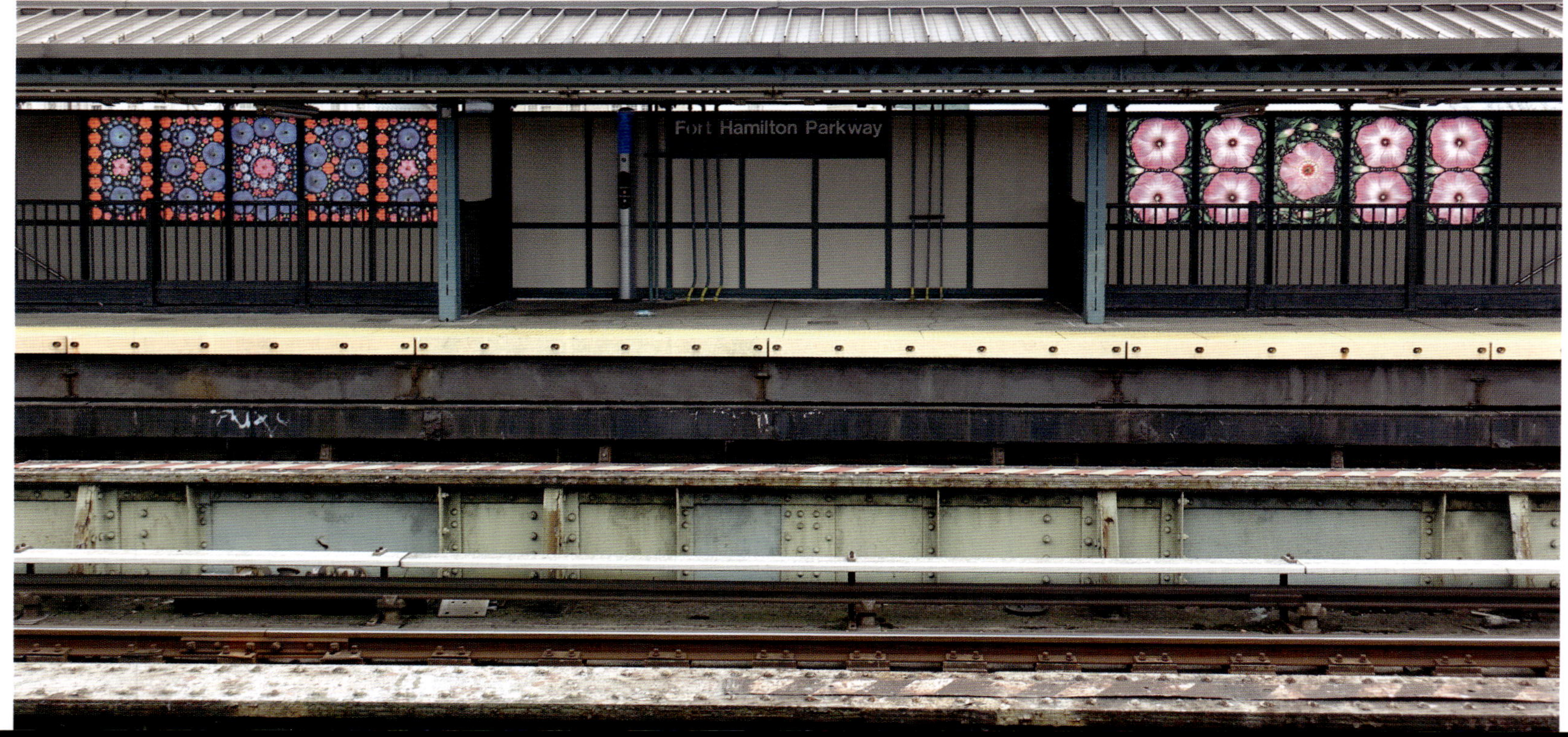

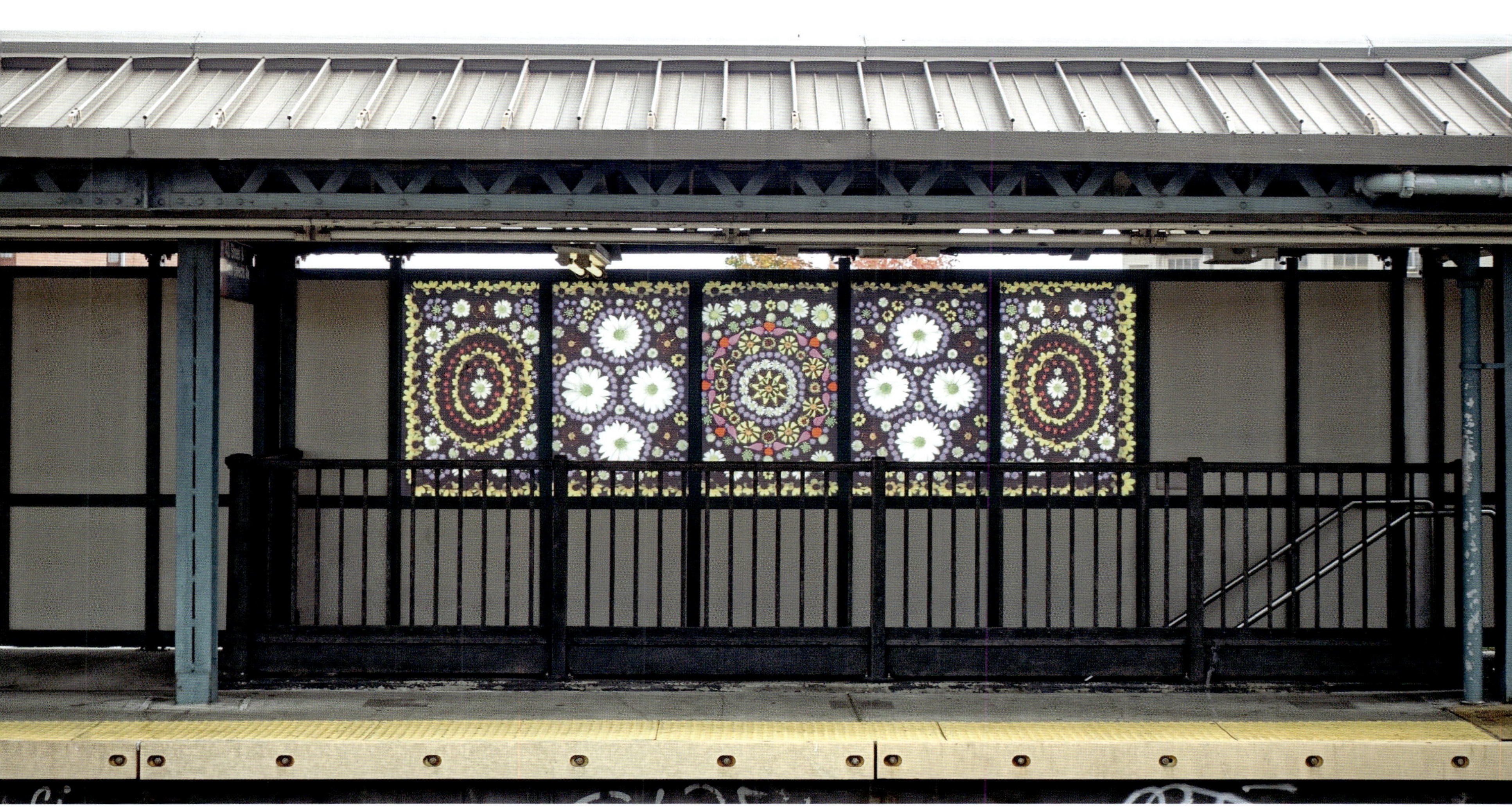

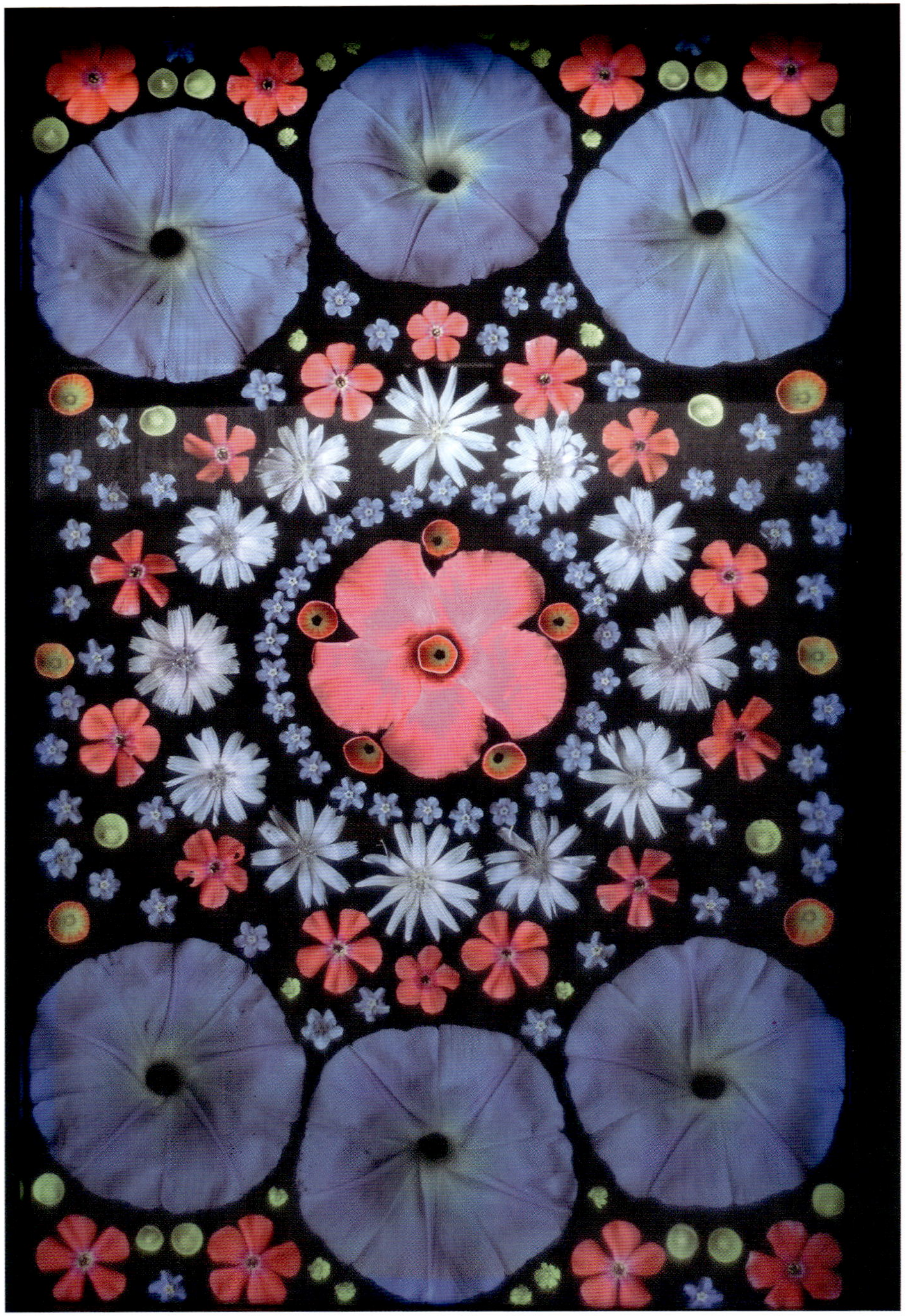

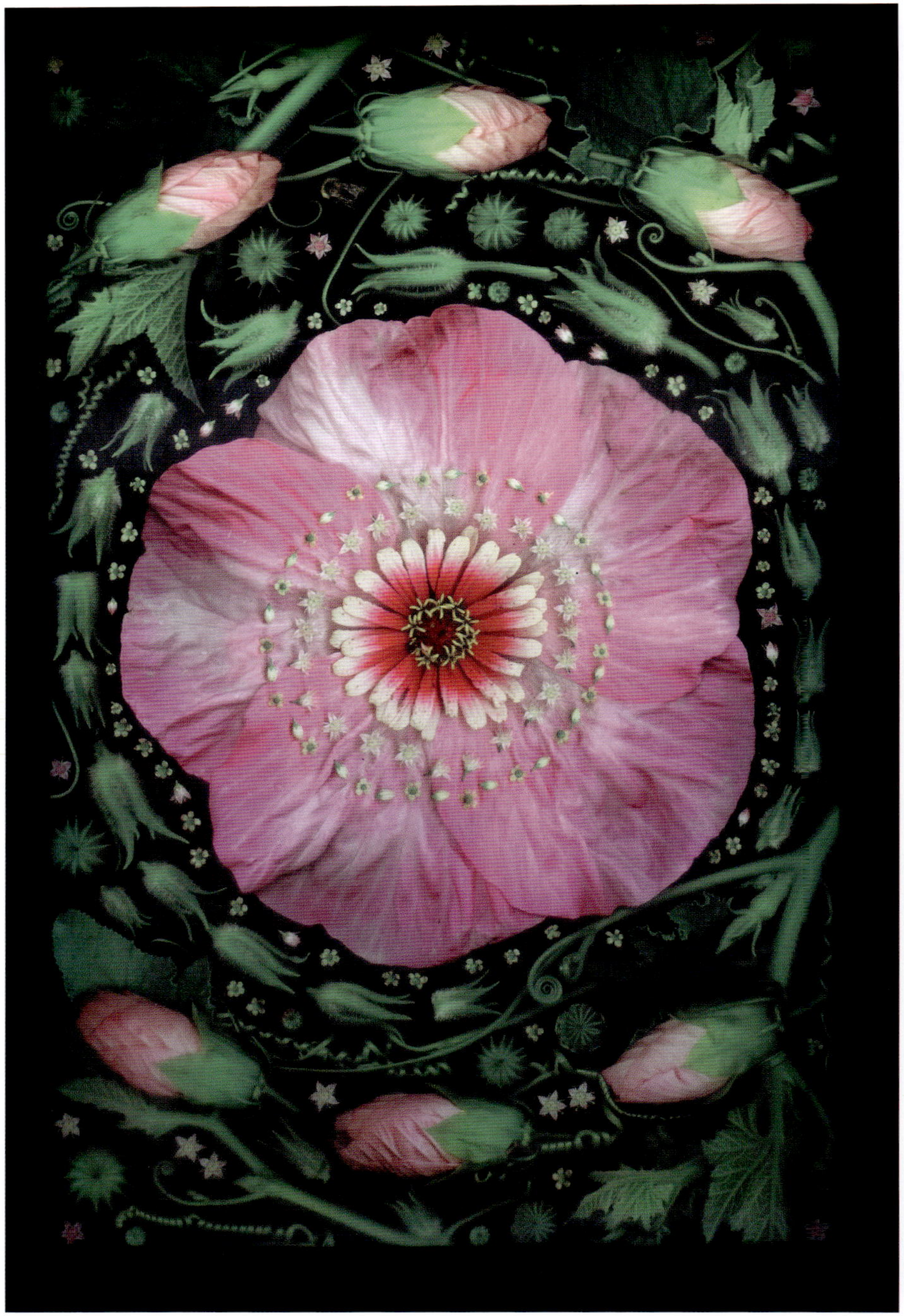

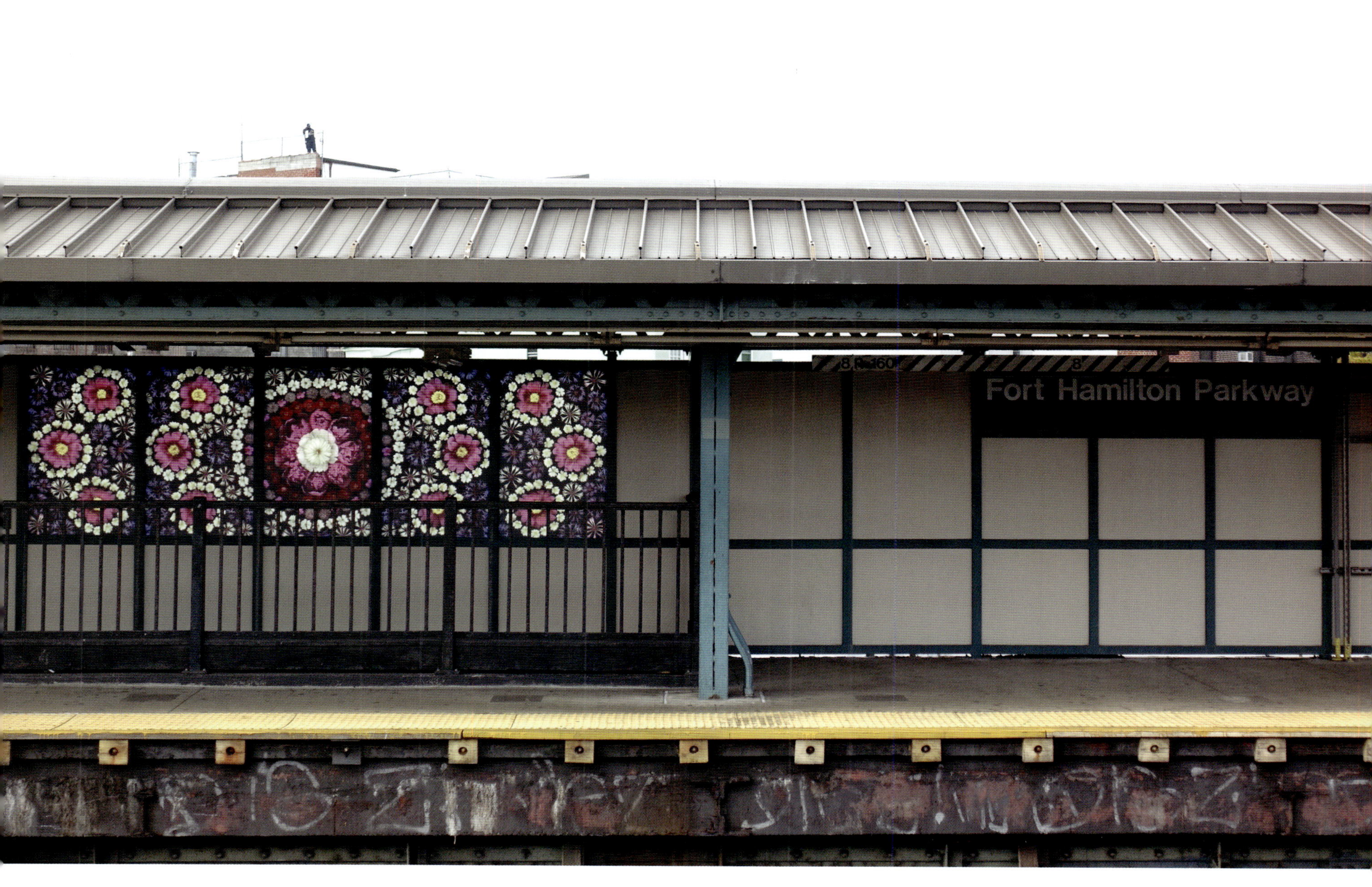
Fort Hamilton Parkway

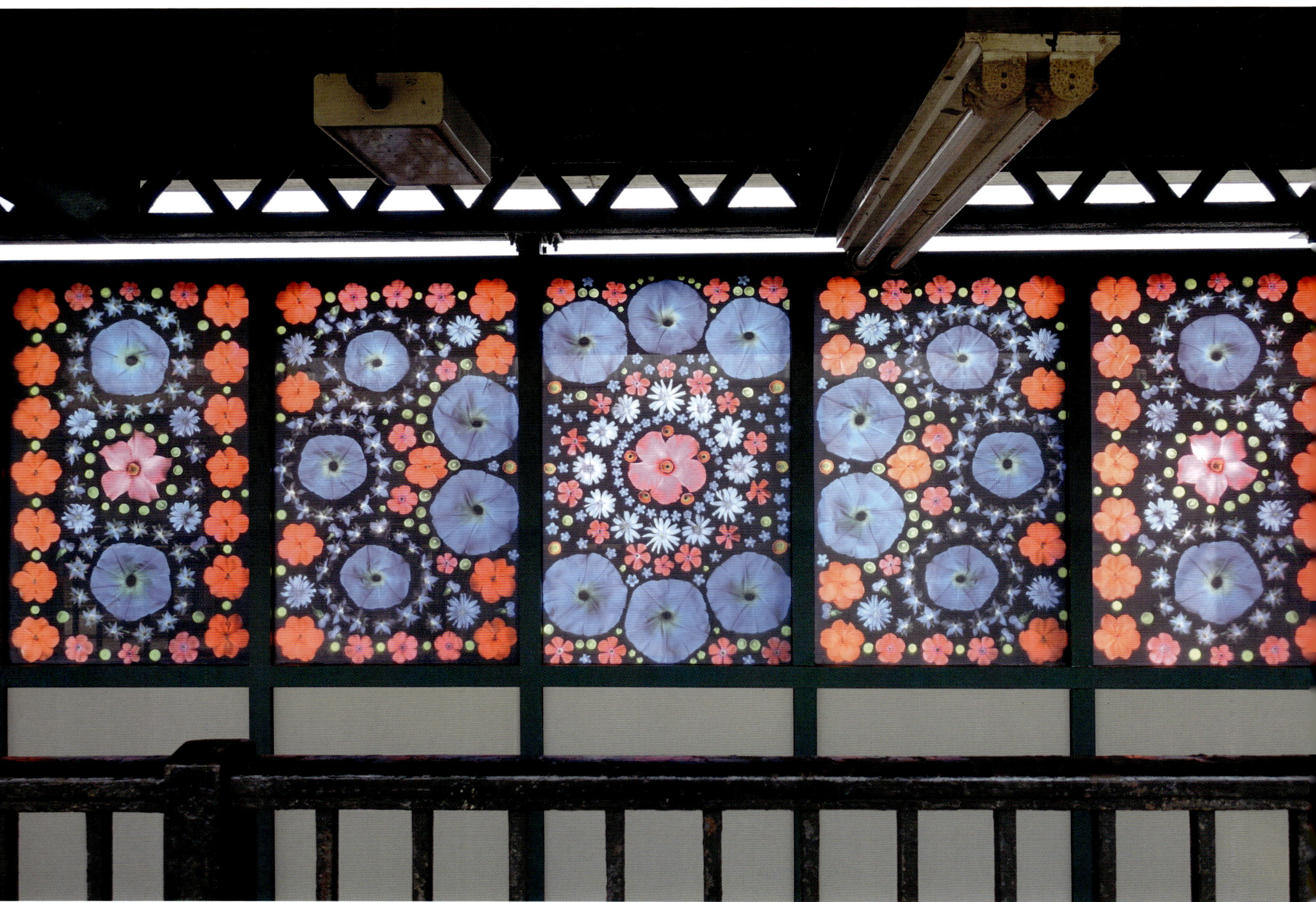

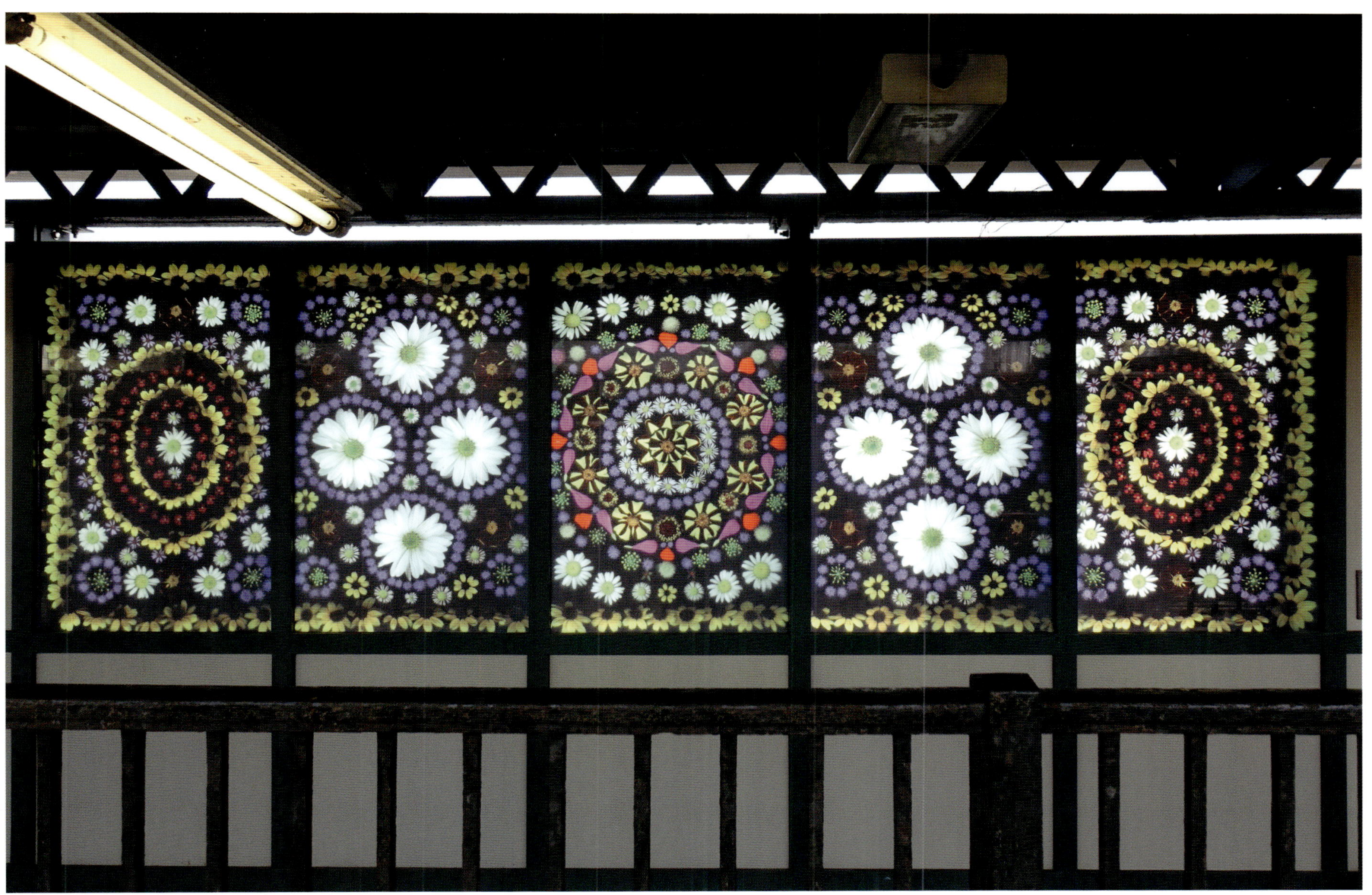

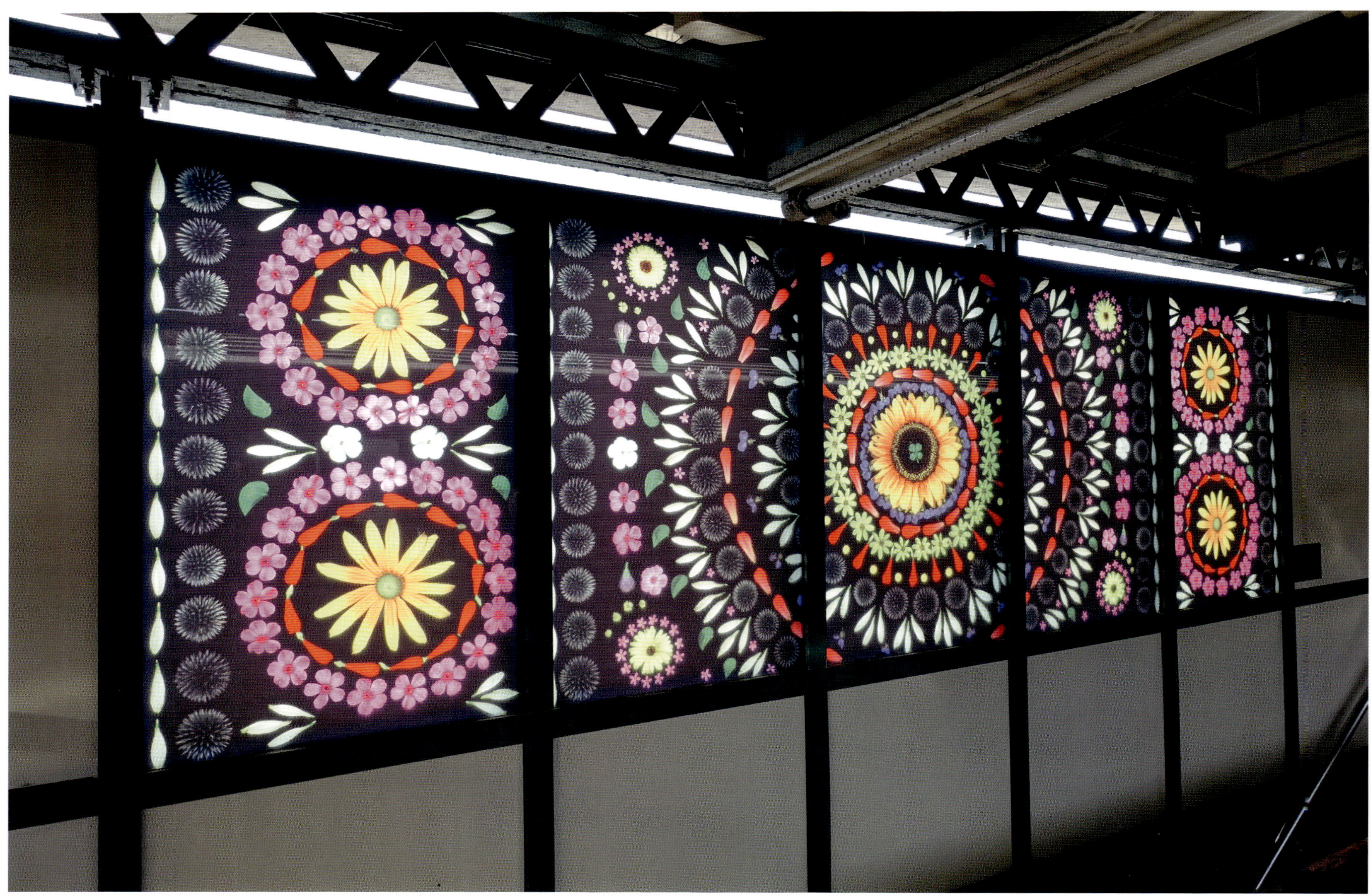

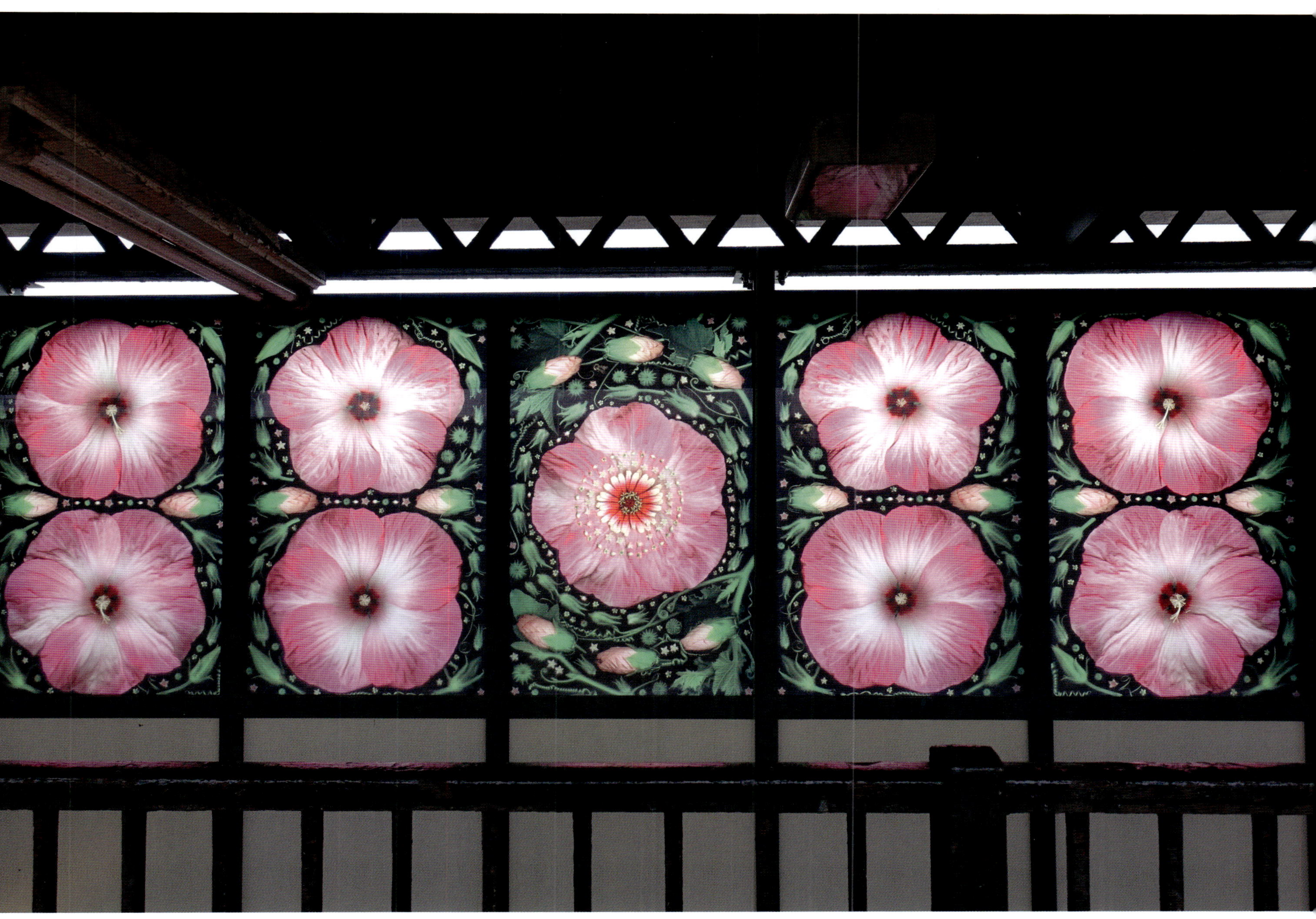

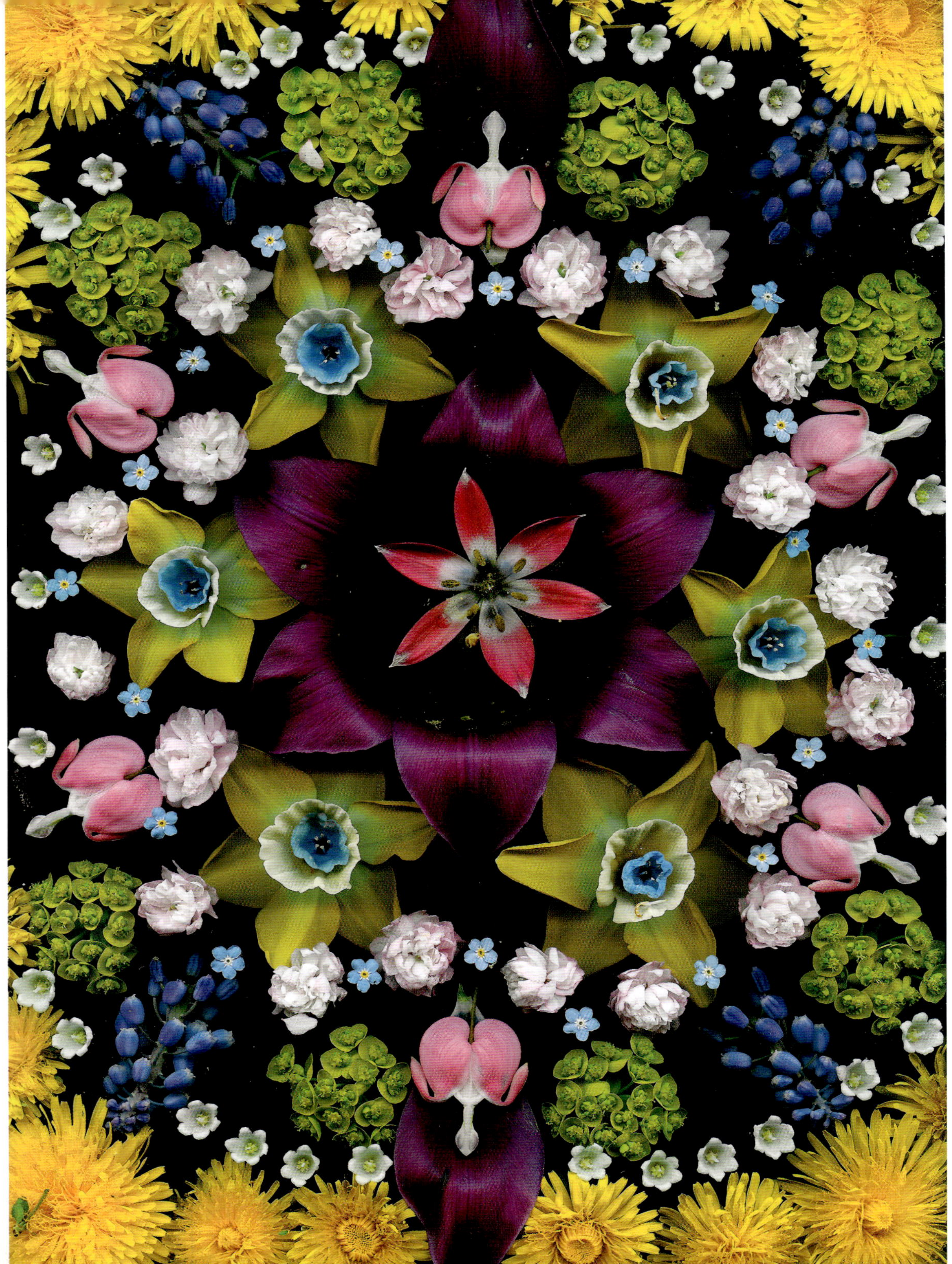

Portia Munson is an artist who defies categorization; she works in installation, photography, and painting, and her art lives in a vast area where consumer culture, feminism, and environmental anxieties intersect. Her installations are dizzying arrangements of objects that sometimes number in the thousands, categorized by color, and can fill a table or an entire room. In works such as *Pink Project* and *Bound Angel*, Munson explored the commoditization and dissemination of feminine ideals, often with profuse humor, even while scrutinizing the casual violence and misogyny of these objects. For her photographic works, she employs a similar strategy of gathering like objects in dense arrangements, usually inspired by the flora of her upstate New York home. This was the starting point for her work at the Fort Hamilton station.

***Wild Tulip*, 2004**
Pigmented ink on rag paper
Courtesy of the artist and P.P.O.W. Gallery

***Verdant Aftermath*, 2011**
Pigmented ink on rag paper
Courtesy of the artist and P.P.O.W. Gallery

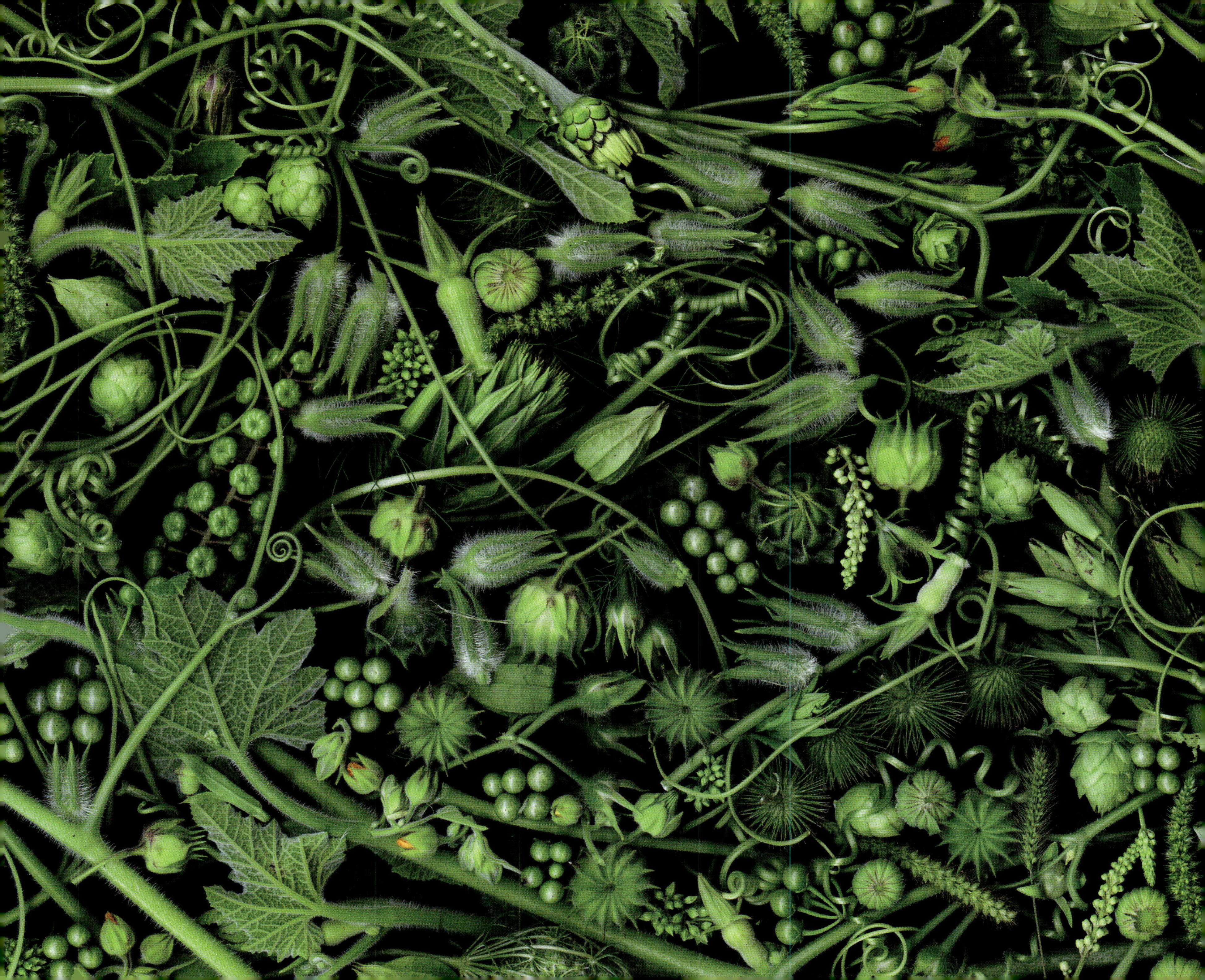

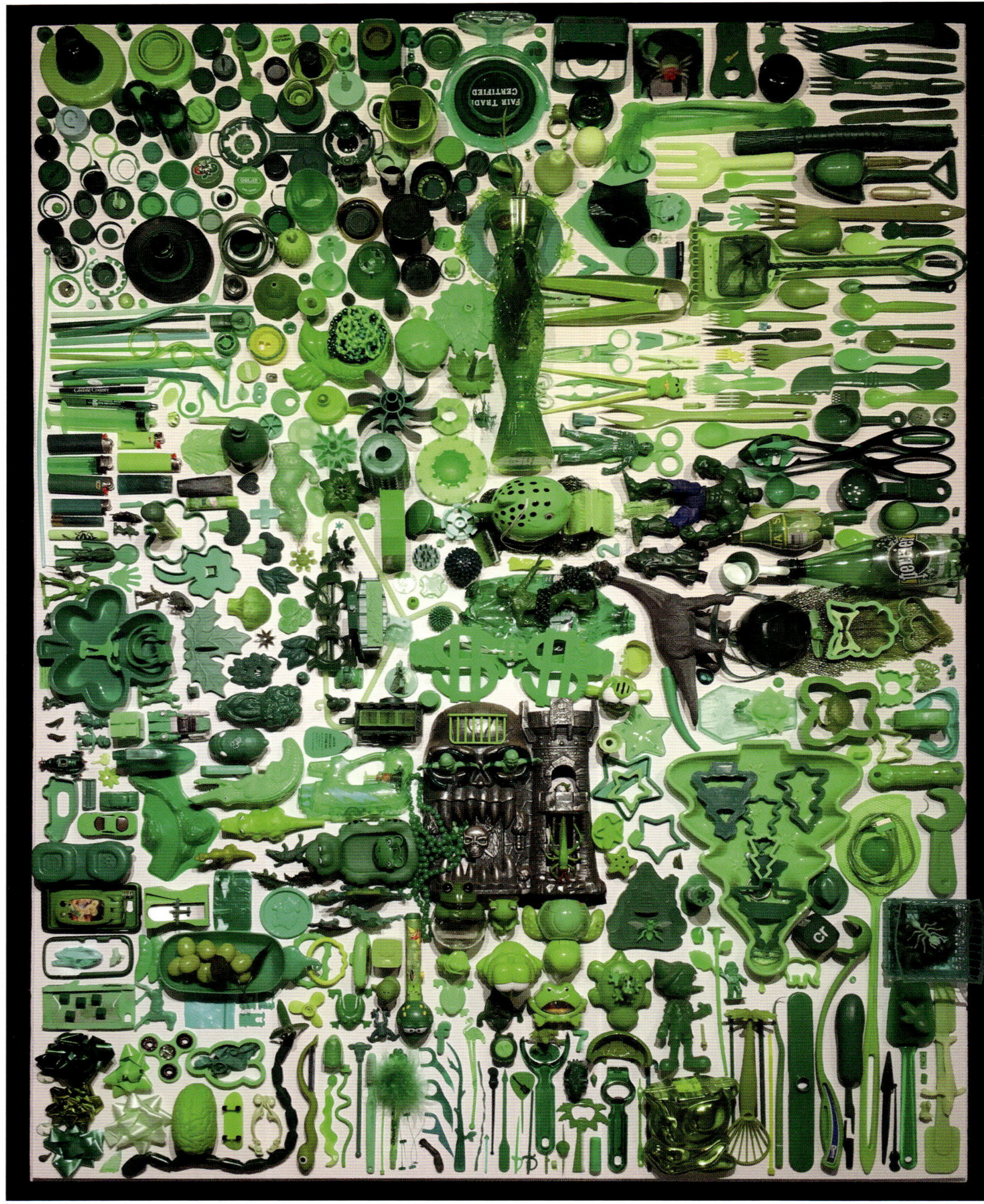

***Future Fossils*, 2018**

Found plastic

Courtesy of the artist and P.P.O.W. Gallery

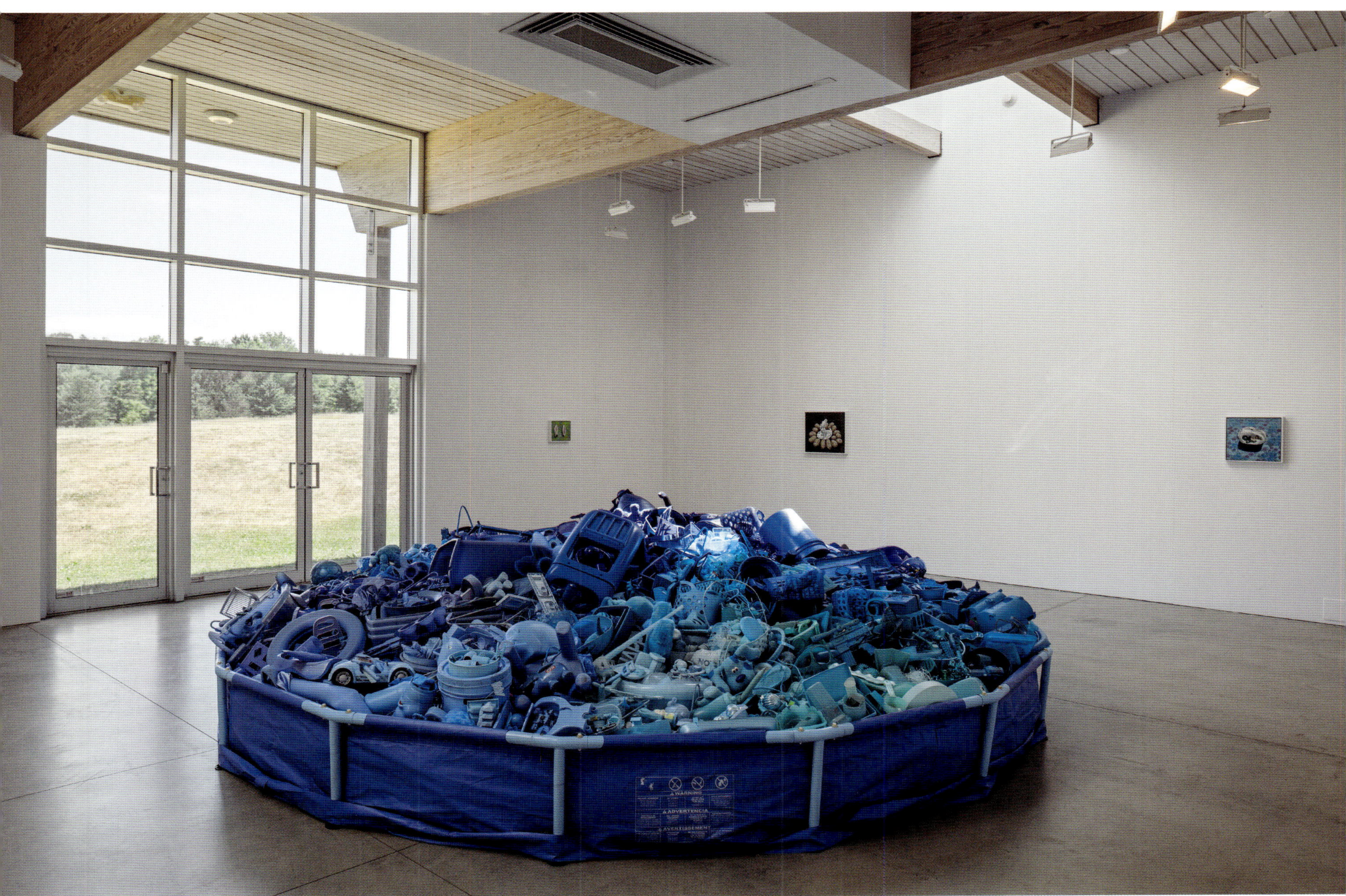

***Flood*, 2022**
Multimedia installation
Courtesy of the artist and P.P.O.W. Gallery

Munson herself has deep roots in Brooklyn, with several great-grandparents immigrating to the city in the late 1880s. There is a Munson family plot at Greenwood Cemetery, mere blocks from the station, with the family settling in the general neighborhood. A photograph from around 1900 of her grandfather and his brothers playing in what was then a forested Brooklyn had a strong influence on her exploration of change, especially the city's ability to consume nature. Just as profound is the move from our reliance on nature for pleasure and entertainment, as her grandfather did, to our consumption of artificially made objects and toys to keep our minds busy. Her ongoing Pink Room series and other monumental works such as *The Garden* are dense with plastic commodities, incisively exploring our consumer-driven society, which creates landscapes of artificiality. Particularly in *The Garden*, Munson presents a bedroom filled with plastic flowers, printed floral fabrics, stuffed animals, and other garish tchotchkes in a decidedly synthetic approximation of nature that has become our touchstone for natural and feminine ideals. While her mandalas celebrate and enshrine the beauty in nature, her densely packed installations capture our lost connection to the world outside our hermetic, urban existence.

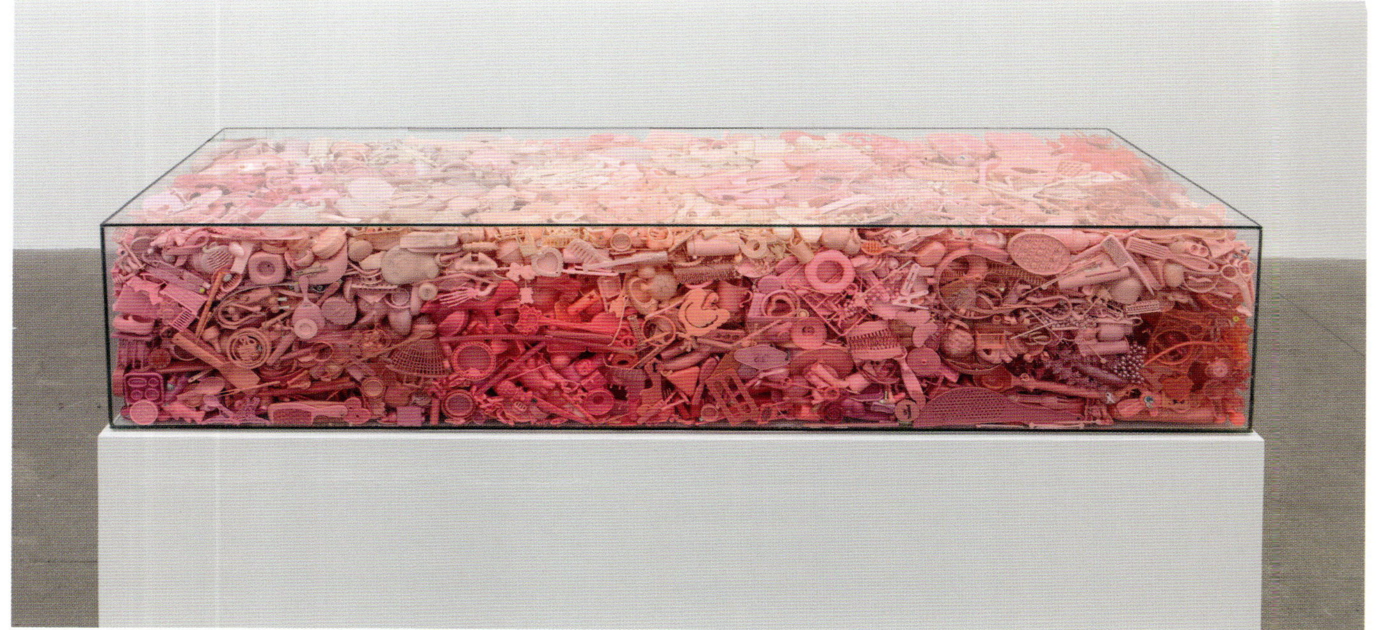

***Her Coffin*, 2016**
Multimedia installation
Courtesy of the artist and P.P.O.W. Gallery

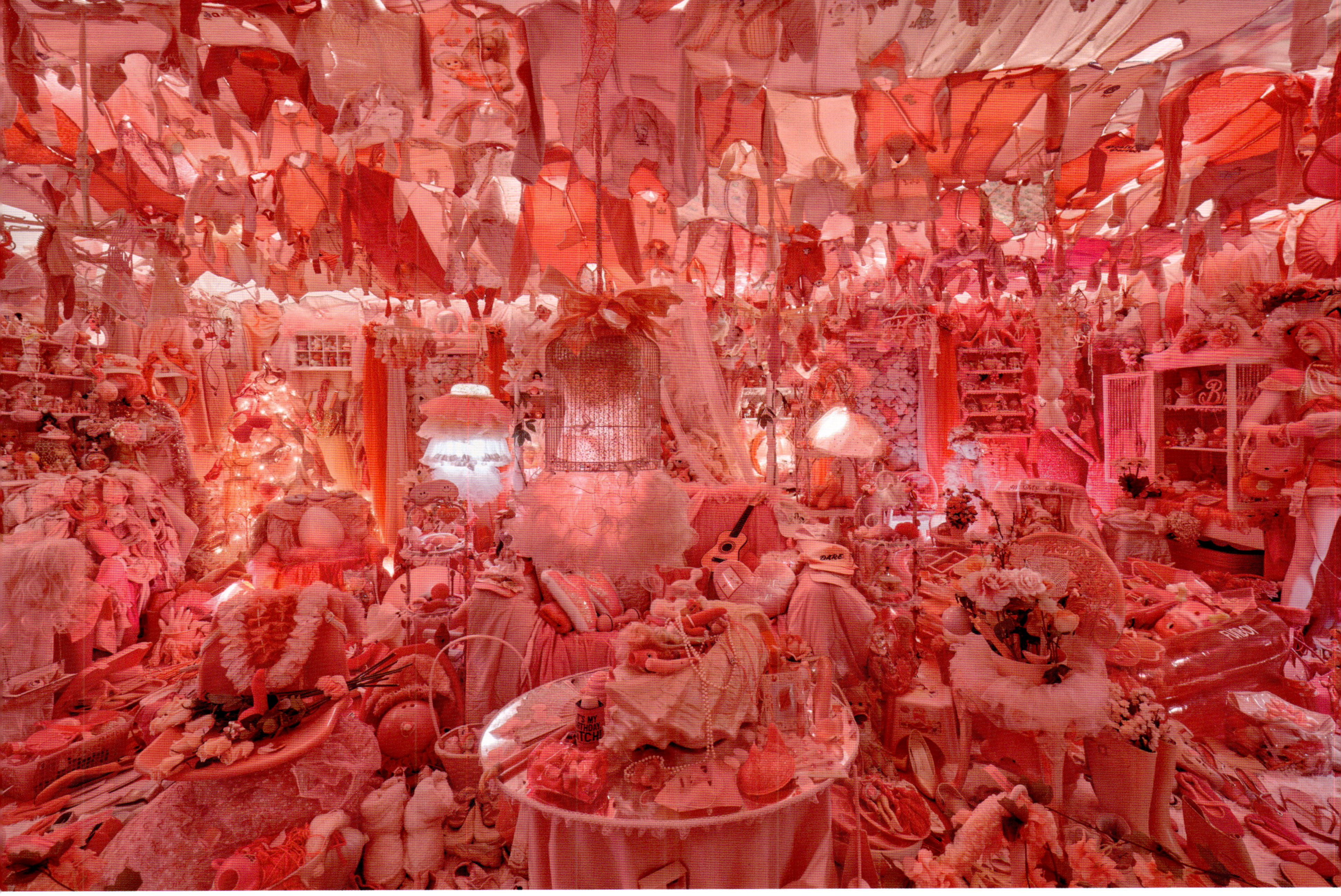

***Pink Room*, 2021 (ongoing)**
Multimedia installation
Courtesy of the artist and P.P.O.W. Gallery

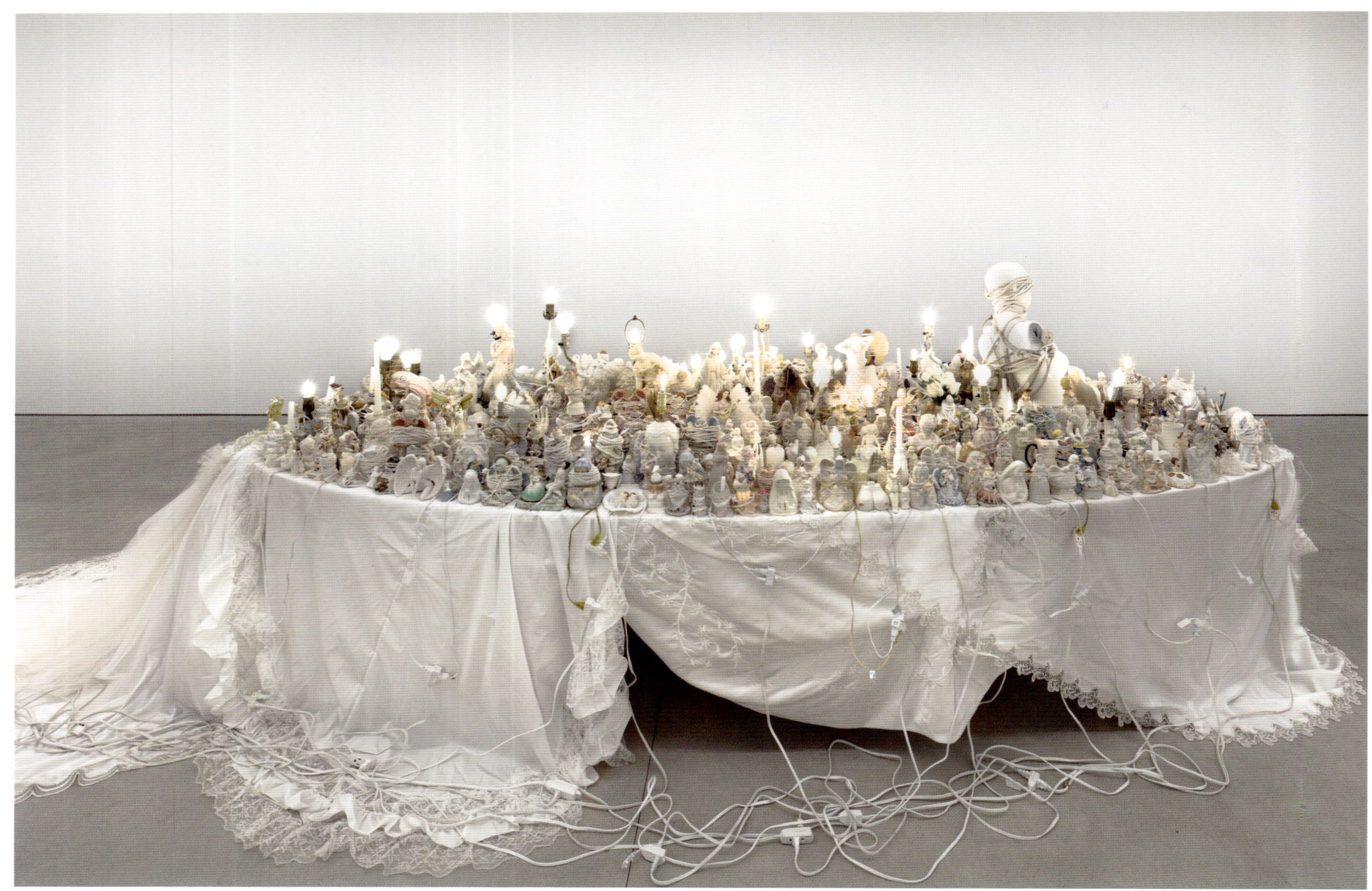

***Bound Angel*, 2021**
Multimedia installation
Courtesy of the artist and P.P.O.W. Gallery

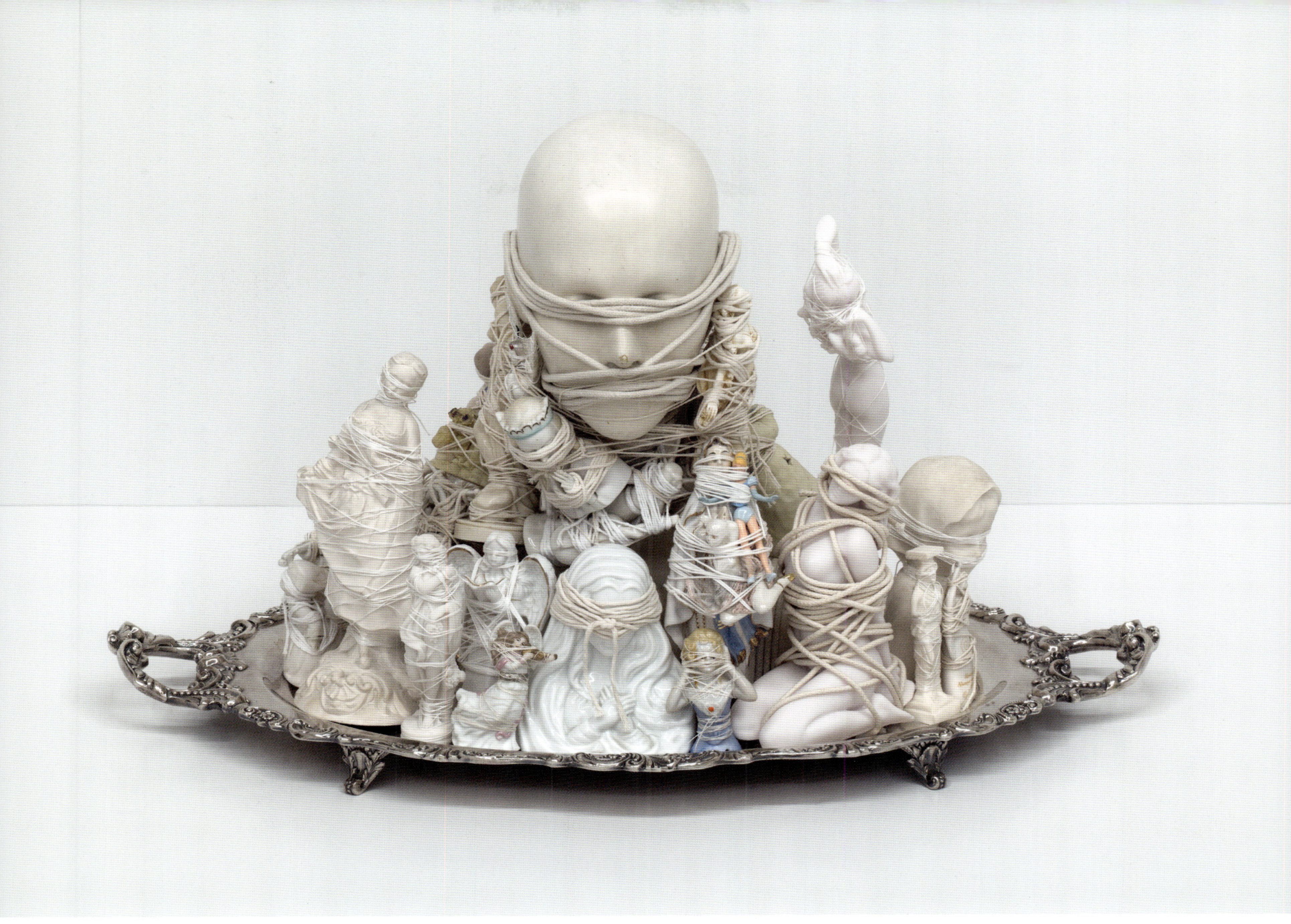

***Serving Tray #6*, 2022**
Found figurines, string, rope, serving tray
Courtesy of the artist and P.P.O.W. Gallery

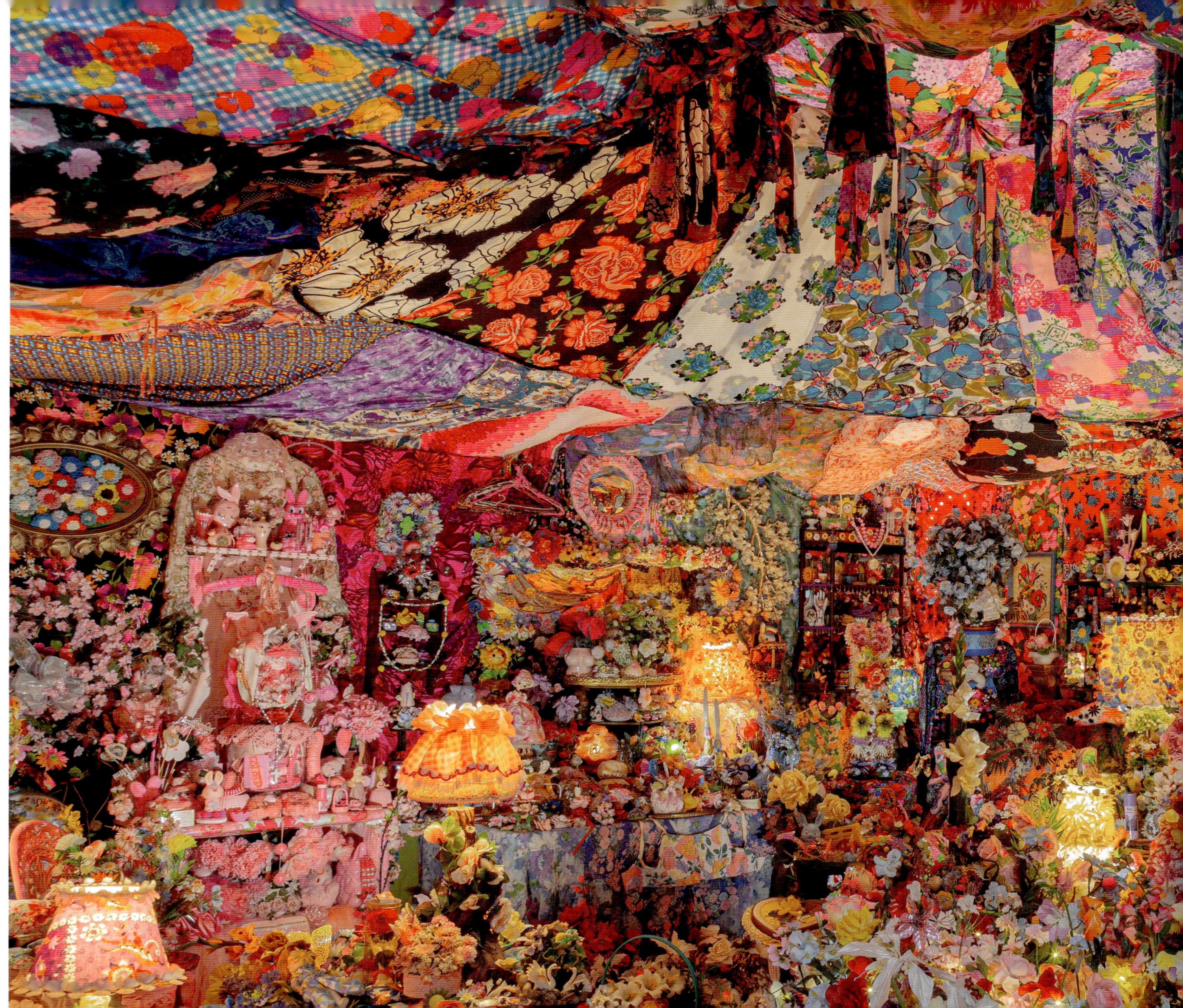

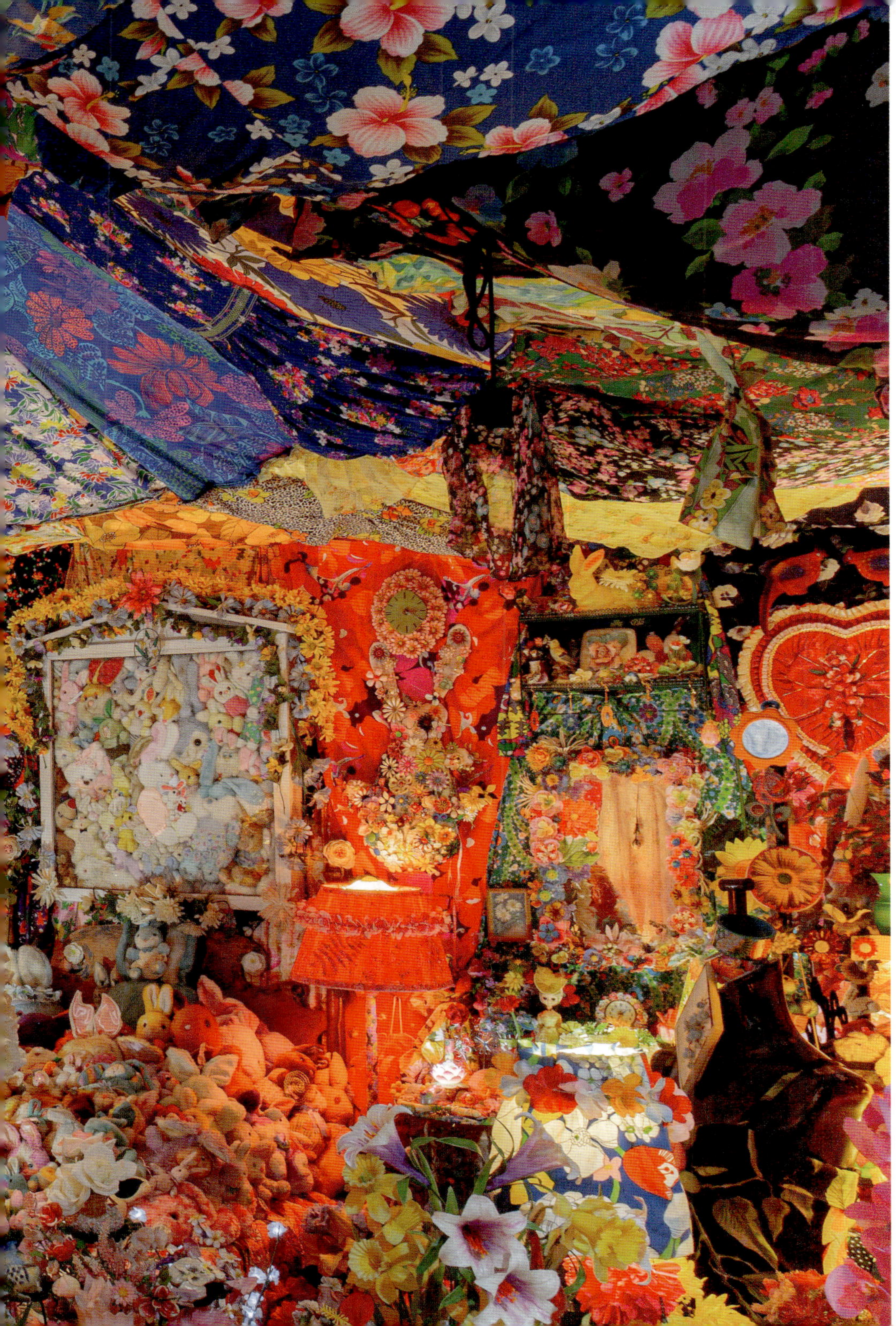

***The Garden*, 1996 (ongoing)**
Multimedia installation
Courtesy of the artist and P.P.O.W. Gallery

Eamon Ore-Giron (b. 1973)

BAY PARKWAY (N TRAIN)

***People's Instinctive Travels: Homage to the Tribe*, 2019**

At the Bay Pkwy. station, on the way to Coney Island, Eamon Ore-Giron created mosaic murals along the platform as an ode to a city that encompasses seemingly diametric identities. On the southbound platform, the murals have a fluidity to them that recalls movements in nature; lines arc like waves, or sea creatures swimming. The terminus of this particular line is the beach, and the southbound platform reflects that, with the abstracted whale forms leaping out of the water and the waves rolling along the walls. Going back into the city, the northbound platform is more rectilinear and geometric like the skyscrapers that loom in the distance. There is a mechanical quality to these murals, mimicking the industrial forms of the subway trains and the urban environment. The colorful forms move across panels, breaking up into spectrums like light refracted through a prism; it is as if they are animating the movement of passing trains with their dynamic lines and circles.

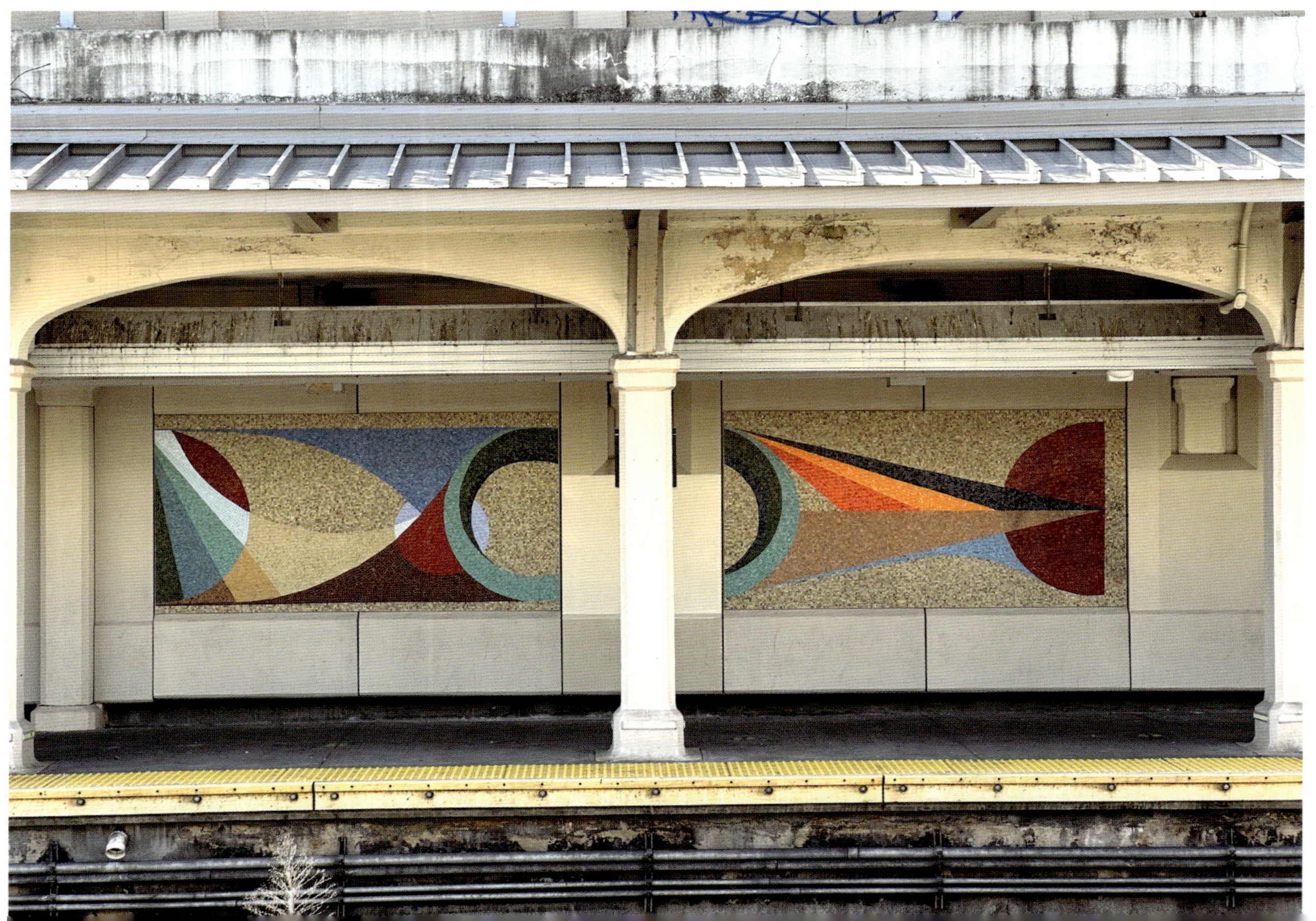

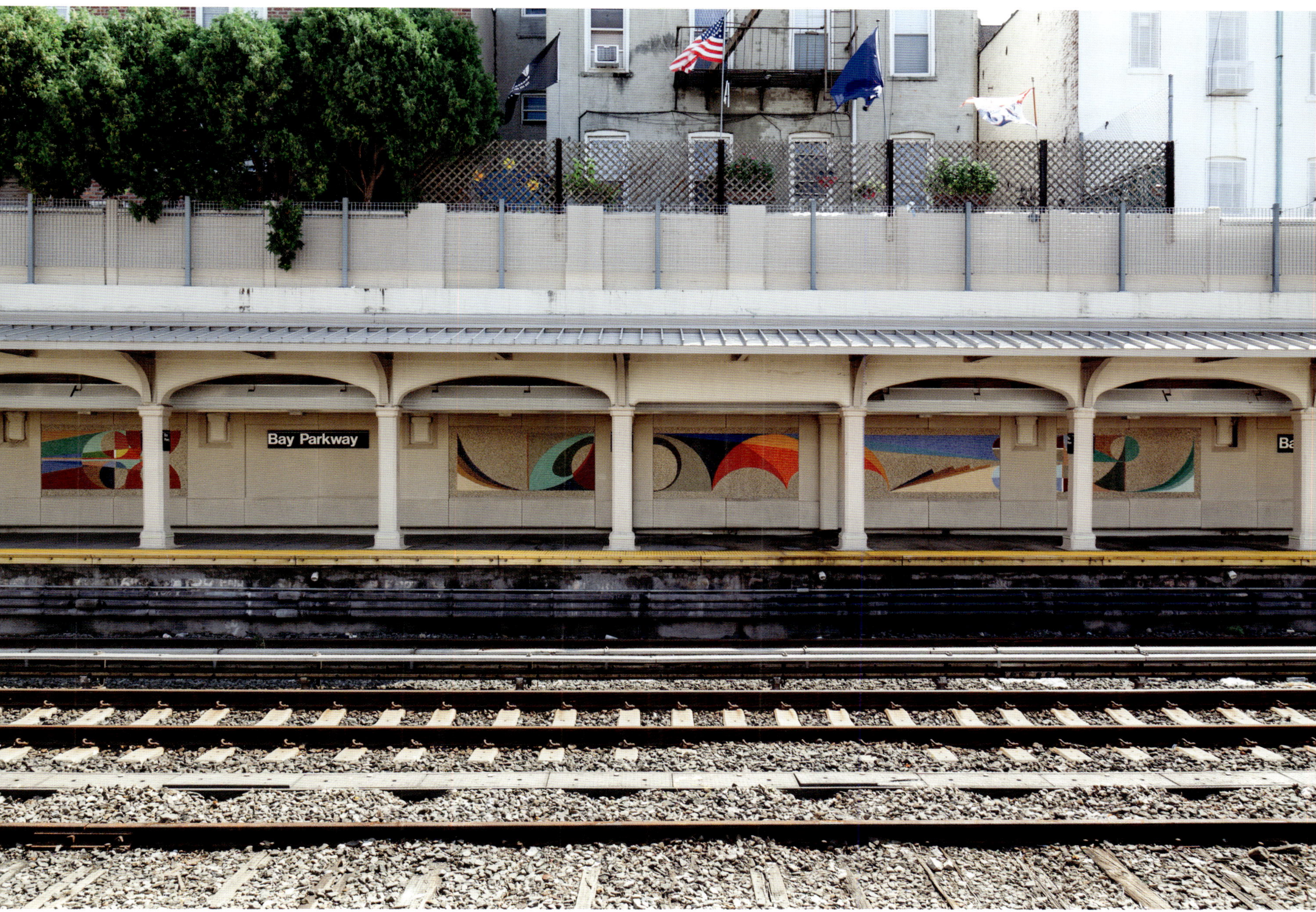

Photo by Peter Peirce

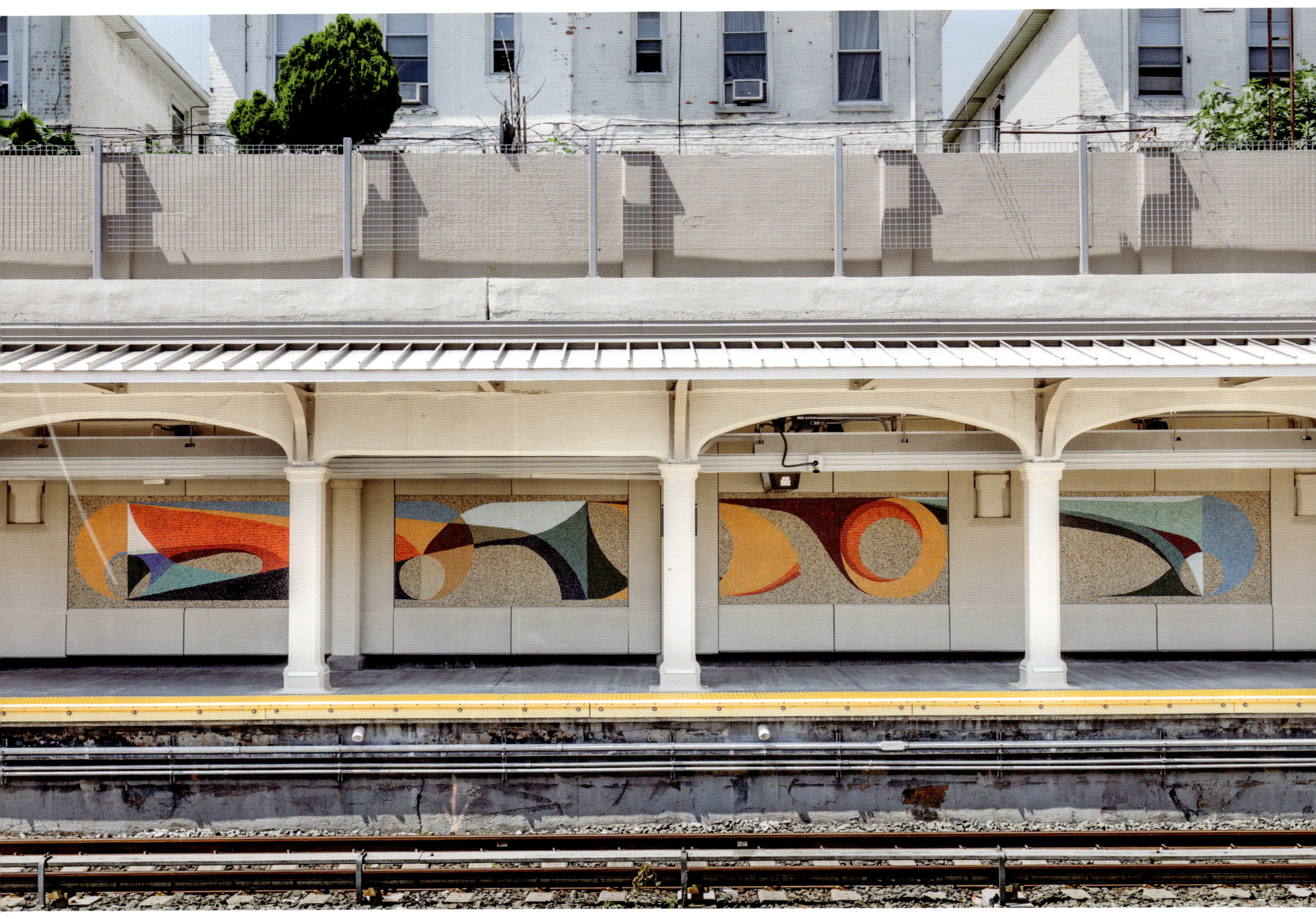

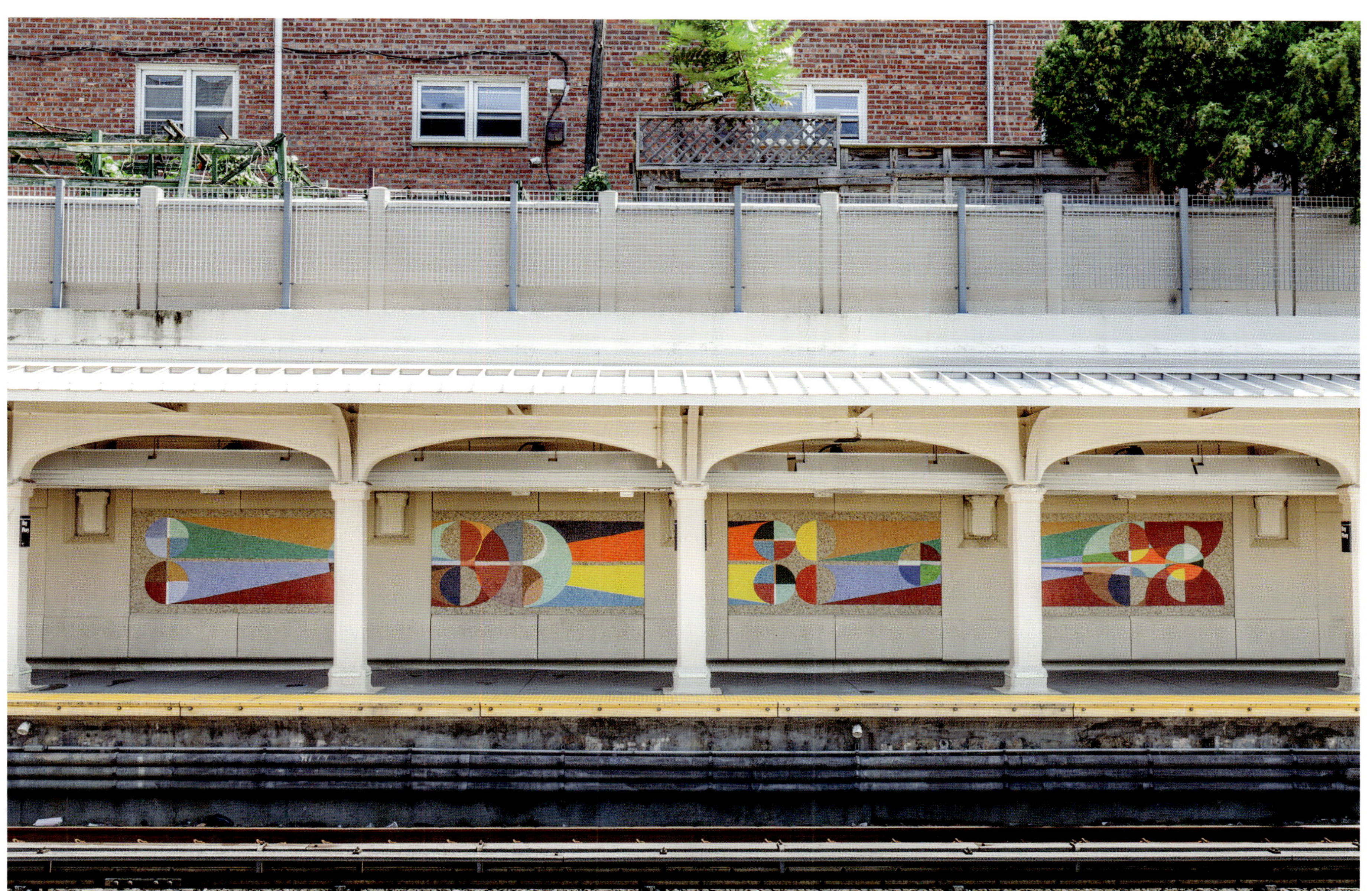

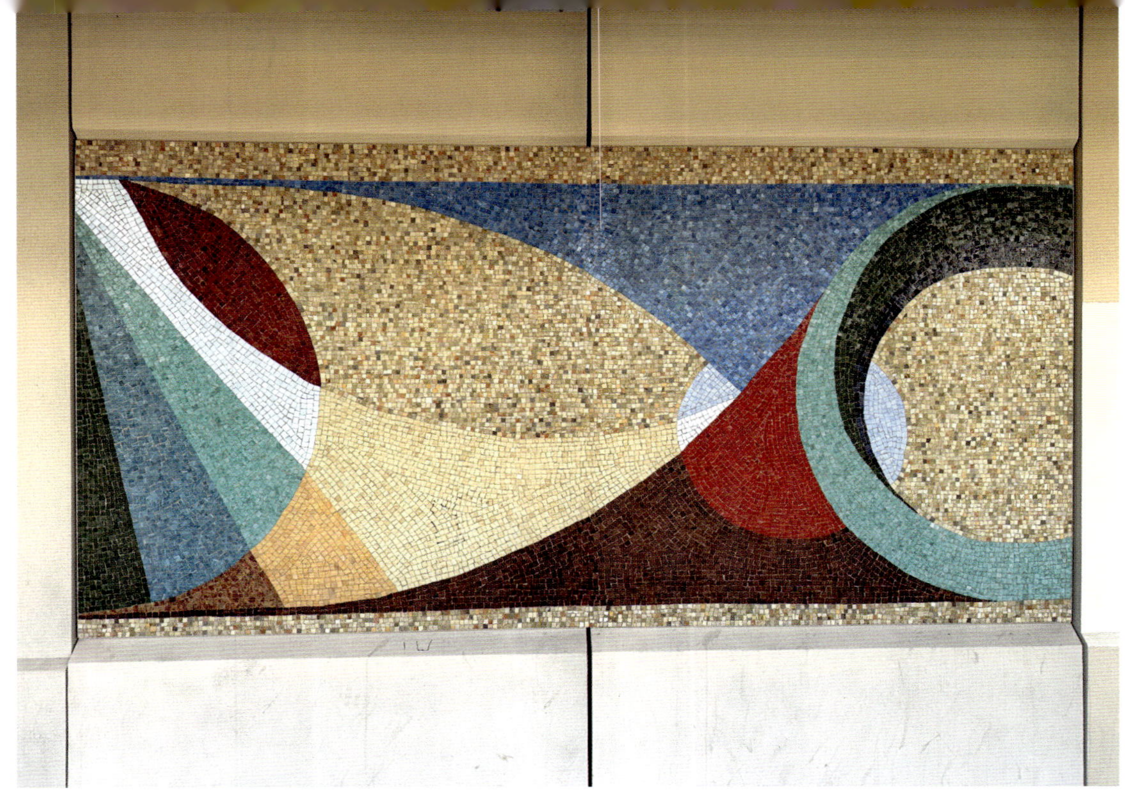

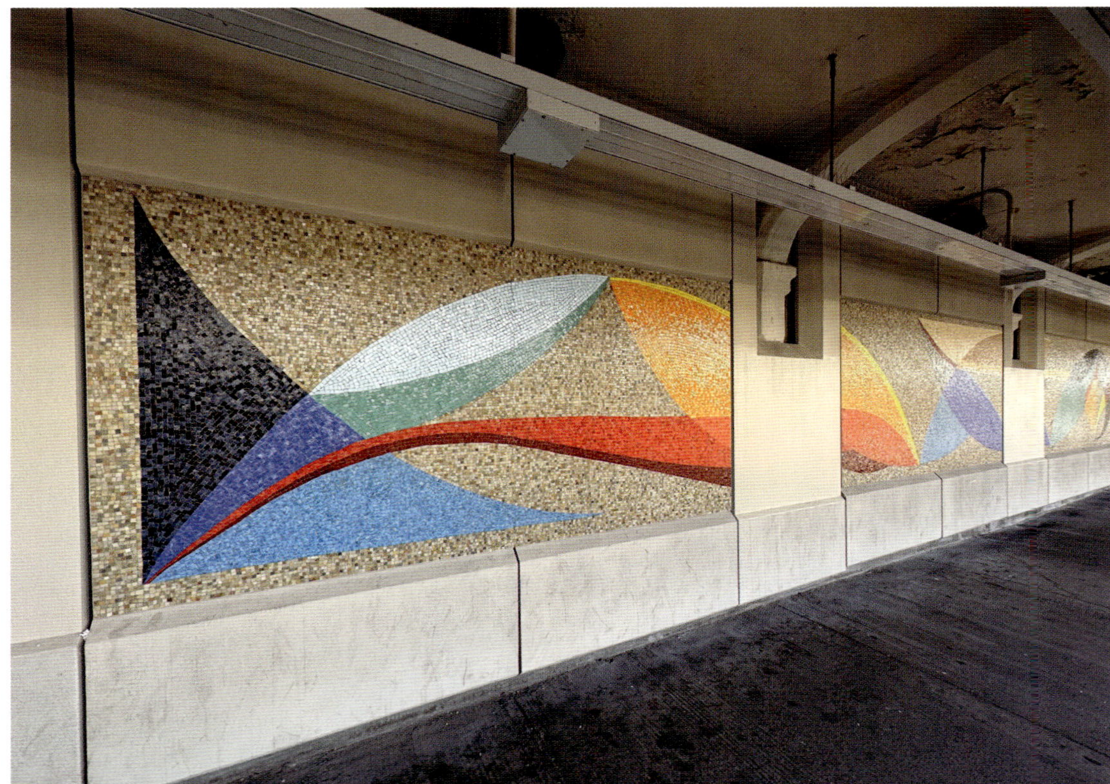

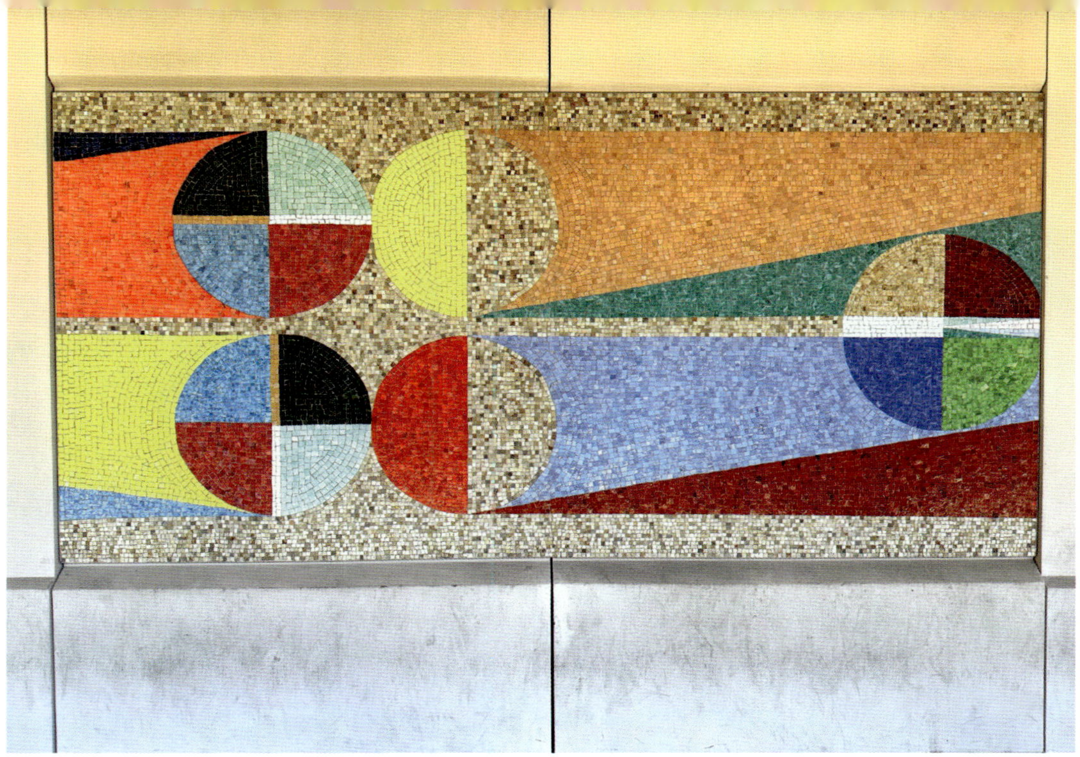

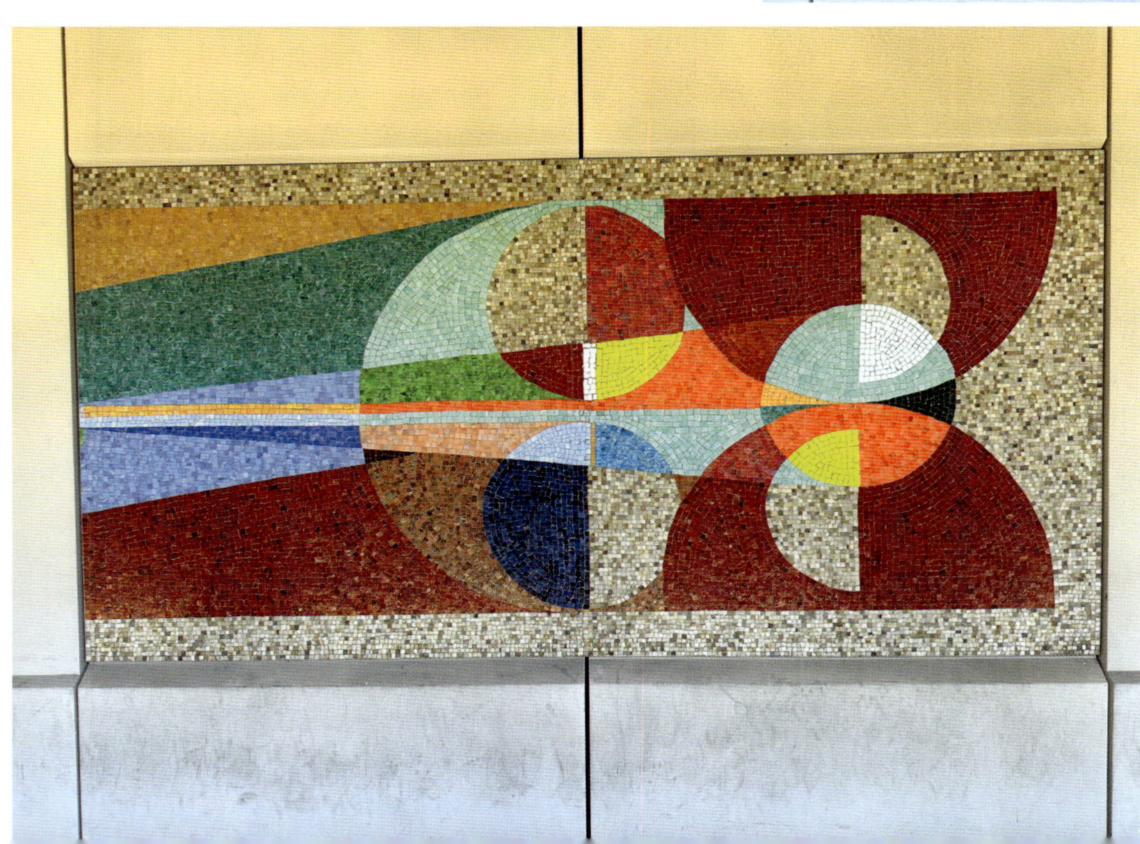

Ore-Giron draws from twentieth-century movements such as Italian futurism and neoconcretism that rejected figurative painting in favor of geometric forms and blocks of color, as well as from the symbology of Indigenous textiles, hieroglyphics, and architecture (which the aforementioned movements probably culled from). Coming from a mixed background (his father is Peruvian, his mother of Irish descent) and growing up in the culturally mixed state of Arizona, he is interested in exploring the visual traditions of ancient Indigenous civilizations, reimagining the iconography of the Old World (particularly of the Global South) for the modern world he inhabits. Ore-Giron is also a musician and DJ, and music plays a large role in his practice. The title of his MTA commission is a reference not only to the different "tribes" that reside in the neighborhood around Bay Parkway, but is a callback to A Tribe Called Quest's 1990 album *People's Instinctive Travels and the Paths of Rhythm*. Just as he samples and remixes his musical infuences onto the MTA project, in his work he remixes the imagery and symbols of Indigenous cultures with a modern sensibility, creating icons anew. In *Talking Shit with Inti* (2023), Ore-Giron references the Inca sun deity, who was traditionally depicted as a disk with rays and a human face; in his retelling, Inti bears the hallmarks of this ancient god (rays, human face) but with colorful geometric forms and abstracted cosmic landscapes. Gold, royal purple, and teal dominate on a work that suggests religiosity in the visual language of the twentieth century.

***Uptown Rocker*, 2016**
Flashe on linen
Courtesy of the artist and James Cohan Gallery

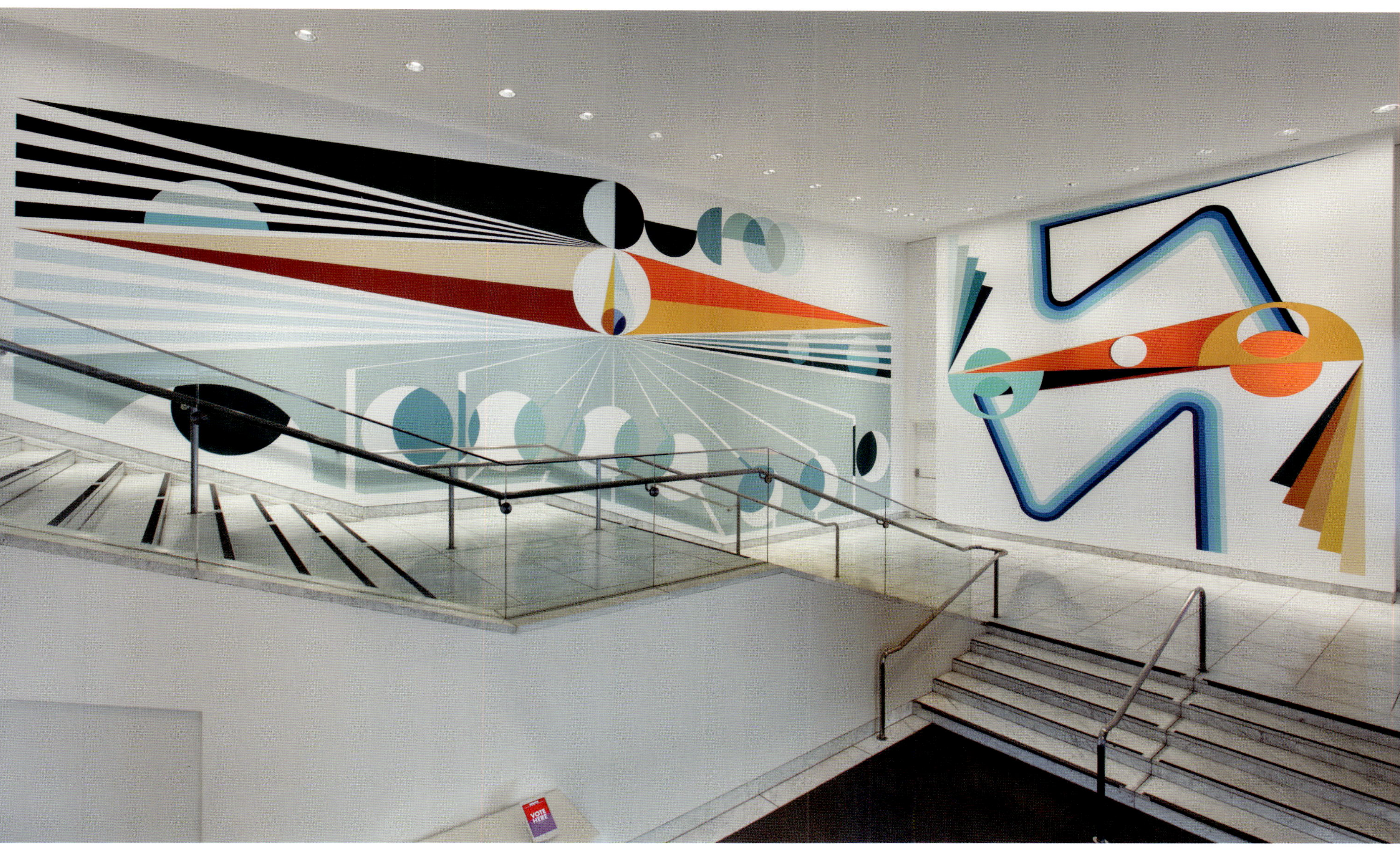

Installation for the exhibition *Made in L.A.*
Breaking A (left), 2018, and ***Angelitos Negros*** (right), 2018
Made in L.A., June 3–September 2, 2018, Hammer Museum, Los Angeles
Photo by Brian Forrest

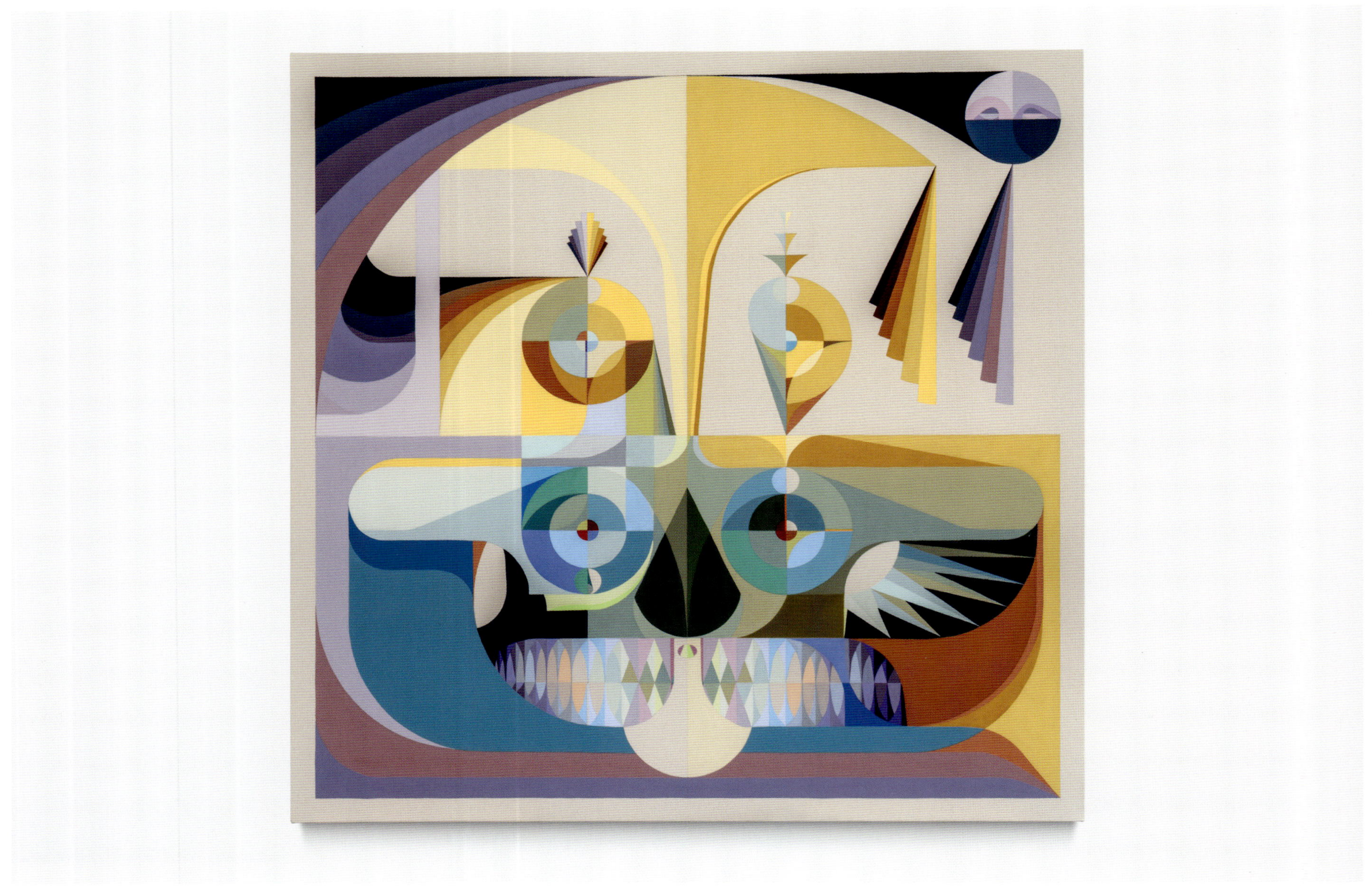

***Talking Shit with Inti*, 2023**
Mineral paint and flashe on linen
Courtesy of the artist and James Cohan Gallery

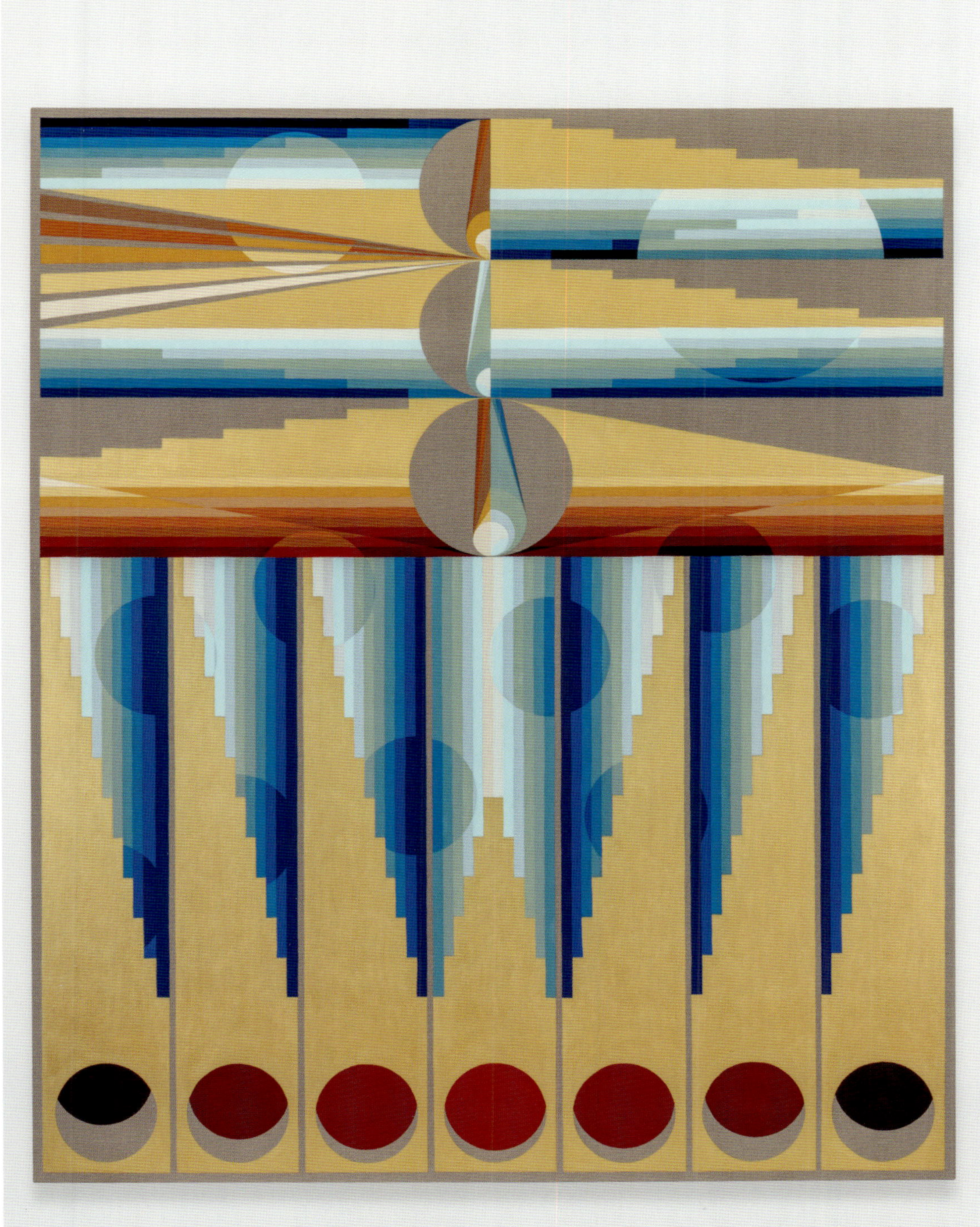

***Infinite Regress CL*, 2021**
Mineral paint and flashe on linen
Courtesy of the artist and James Cohan Gallery

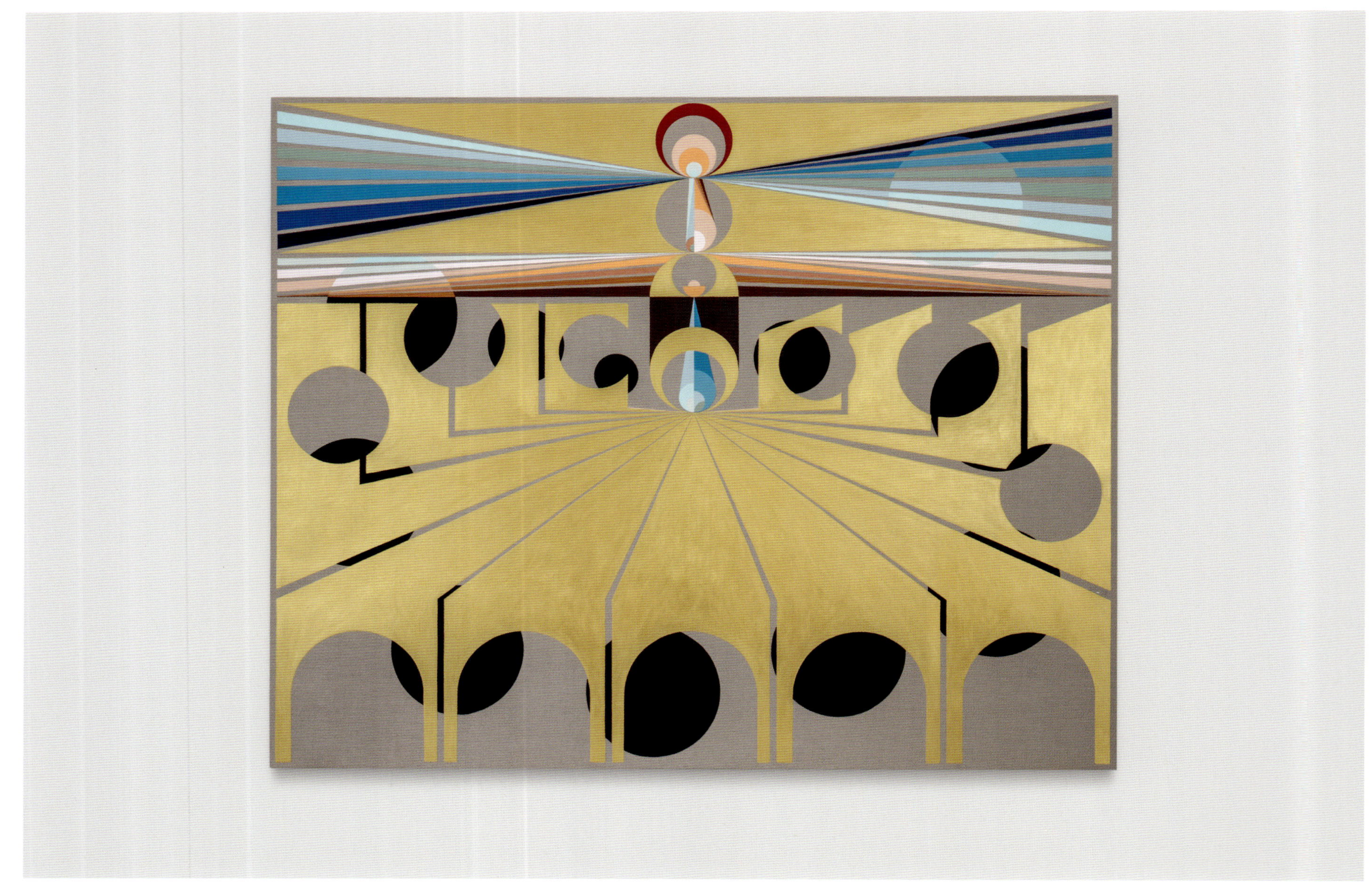

***Infinite Regress CXC*, 2022**
Mineral paint and flashe on linen
Courtesy of the artist and James Cohan Gallery

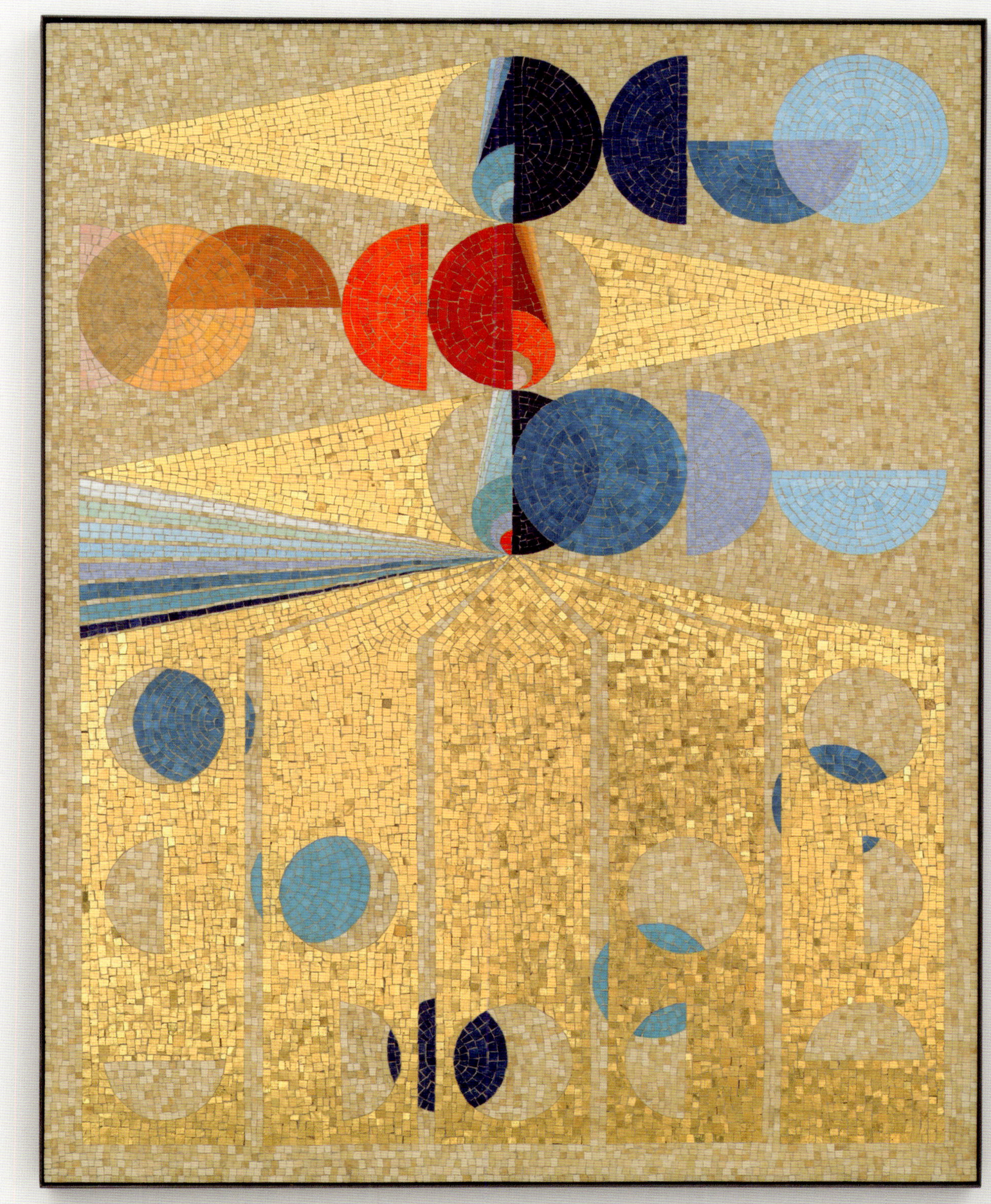

***Infinite Regress LIII (Variation 1)*, 2024**
Smalti hand-cut mosaic glass and 24-carat gold
Courtesy of the artist and James Cohan Gallery

Liliana Porter (b. 1941)

50th STREET (1 TRAIN)

***Alice: The Way Out*, 1994**

Rarely do works in the subway reference familiar iconography but in the case of the 50th Street station, Liliana Porter pulled from a tale that has had a deep impression in the cultural landscape for over a century. *Alice: The Way Out* features characters from *Alice's Adventures in Wonderland* frolicking through mosaic panels by the turnstiles; they are silhouetted, as if back lit from stage lights. This allusion to the Theater District in which this station resides is made more apparent in one panel in which Alice peeks through a curtain. As one of the earlier works in the MTA Arts for Transit, it is minimally composed with a monochromatic palette, save for a few red hearts. It is precisely because of this minimal approach that the artwork has a maximum impact. It takes only a few recognizable figures to recall this timeless tale and imagine oneself as Alice venturing underground for a journey, albeit one that is decidedly less fantastical than hers.

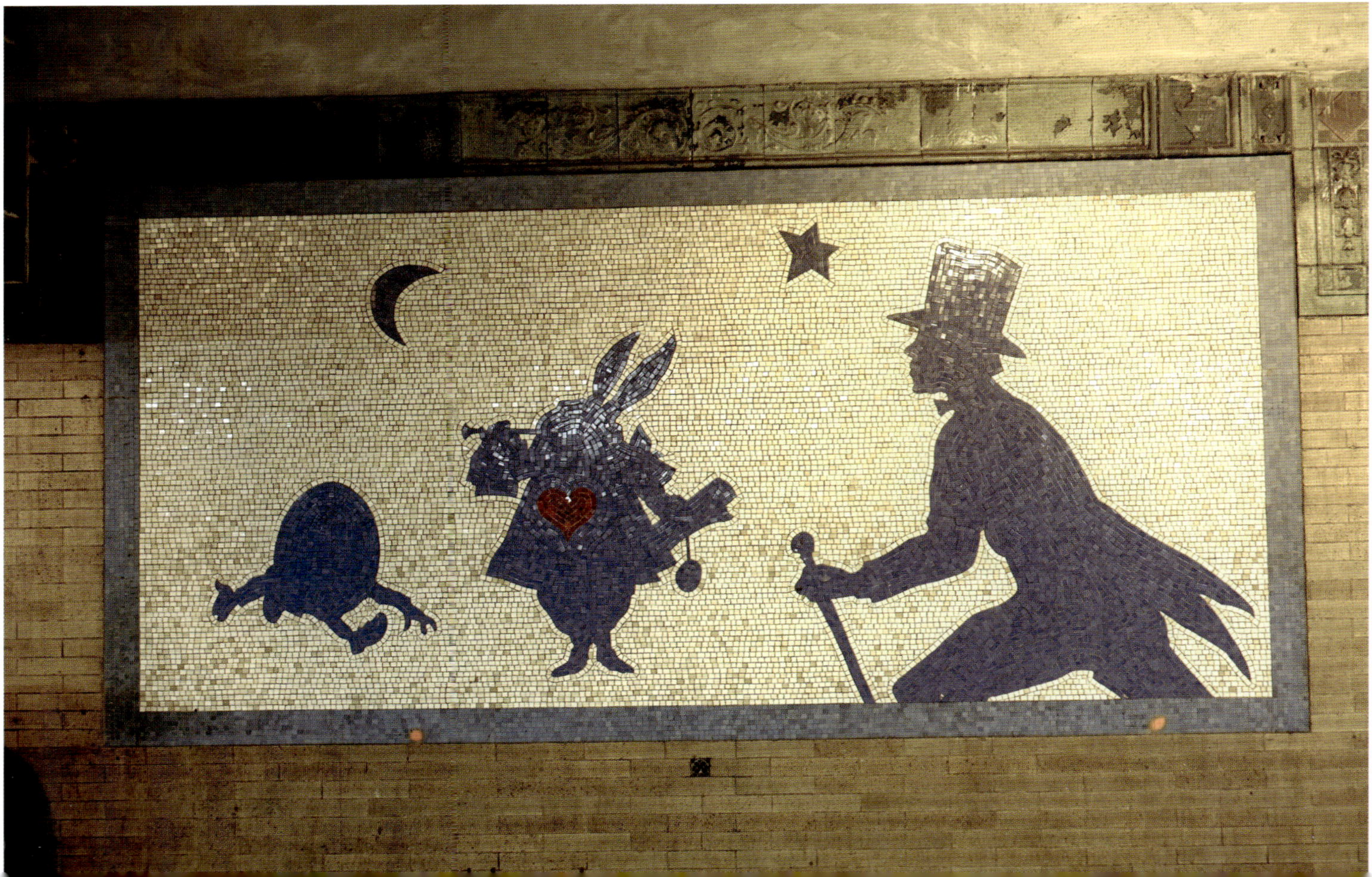

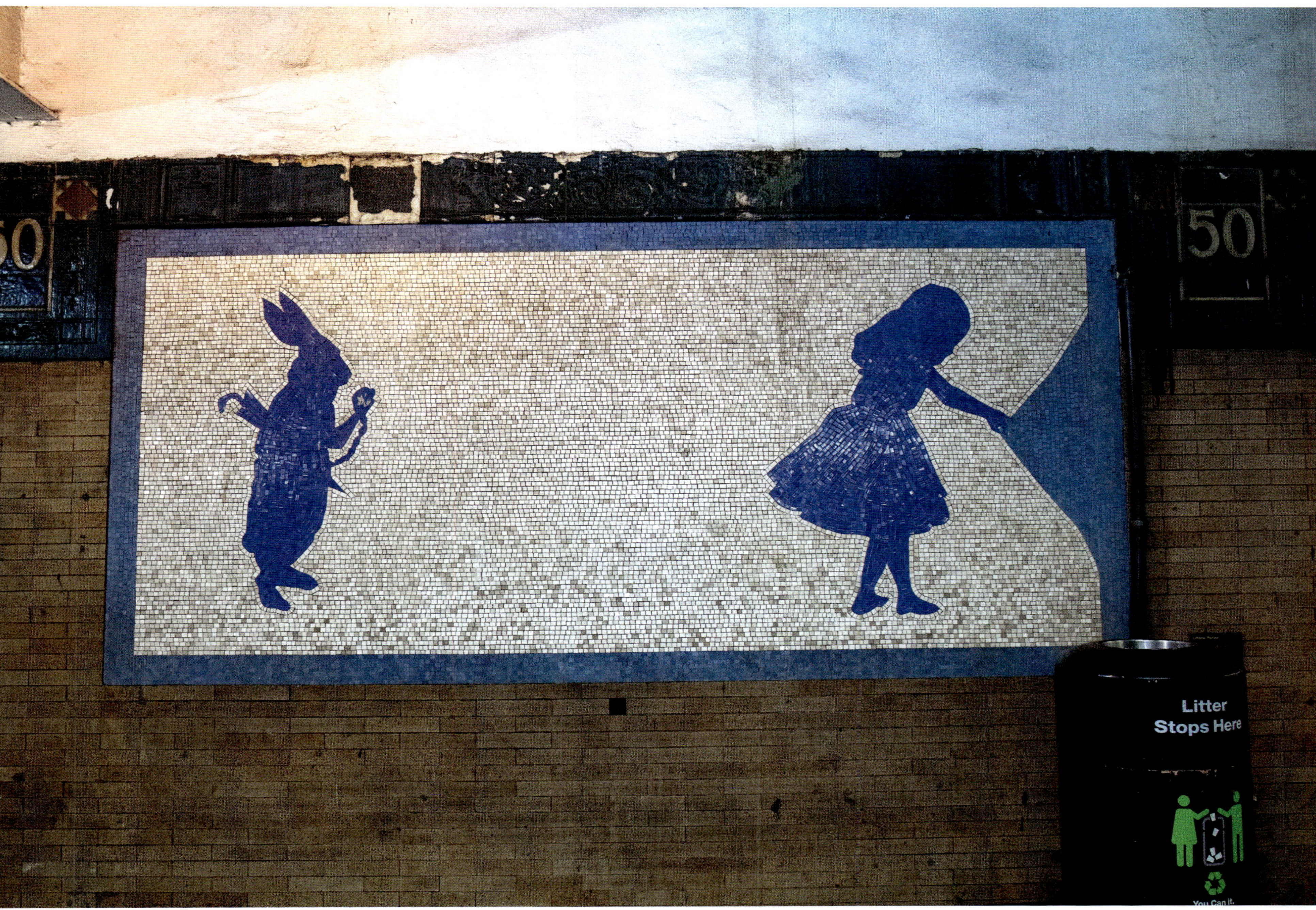
50
Litter
Stops Here

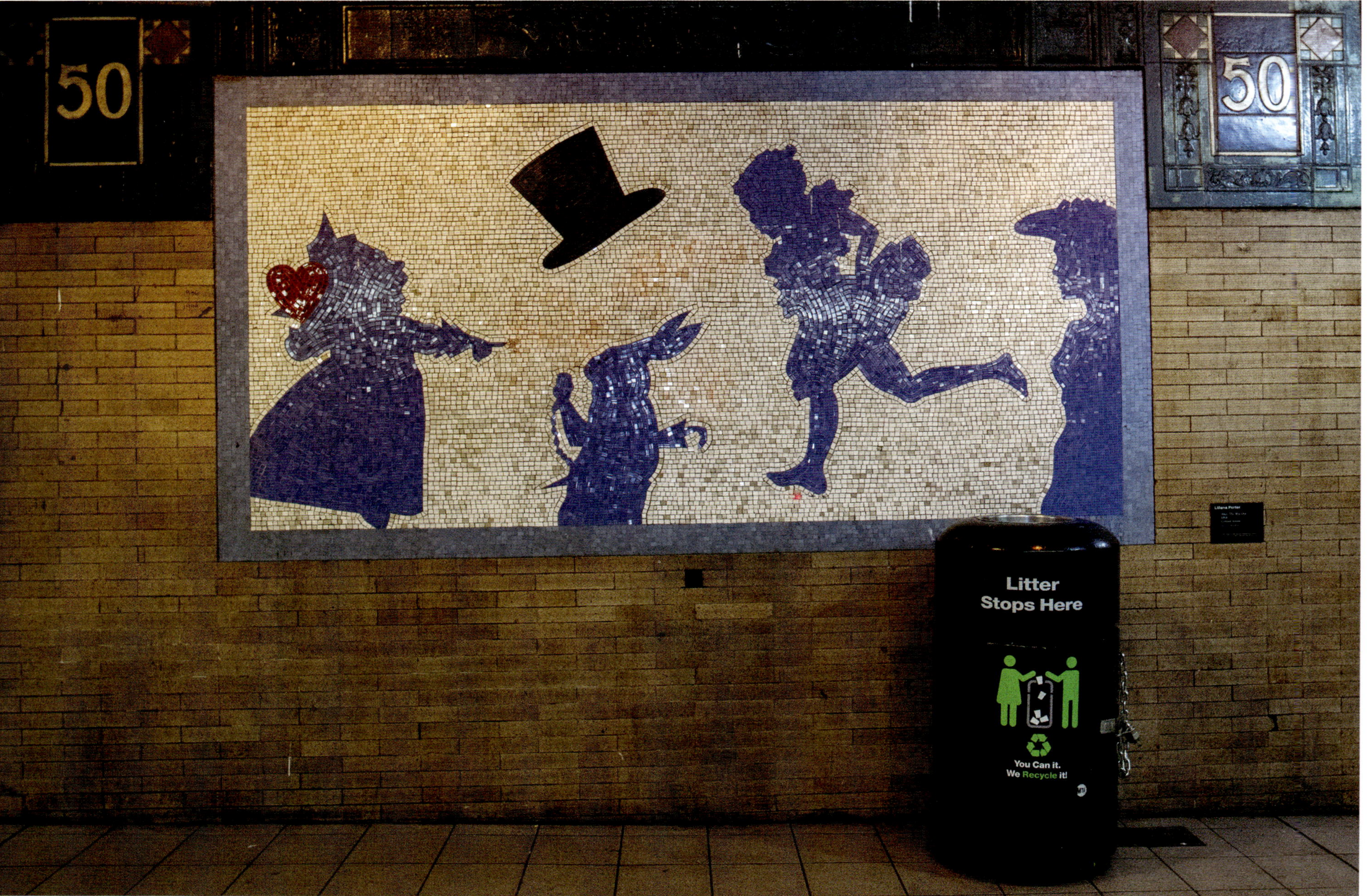
50
50
Litter
Stops Here
You Can it.
We Recycle it!

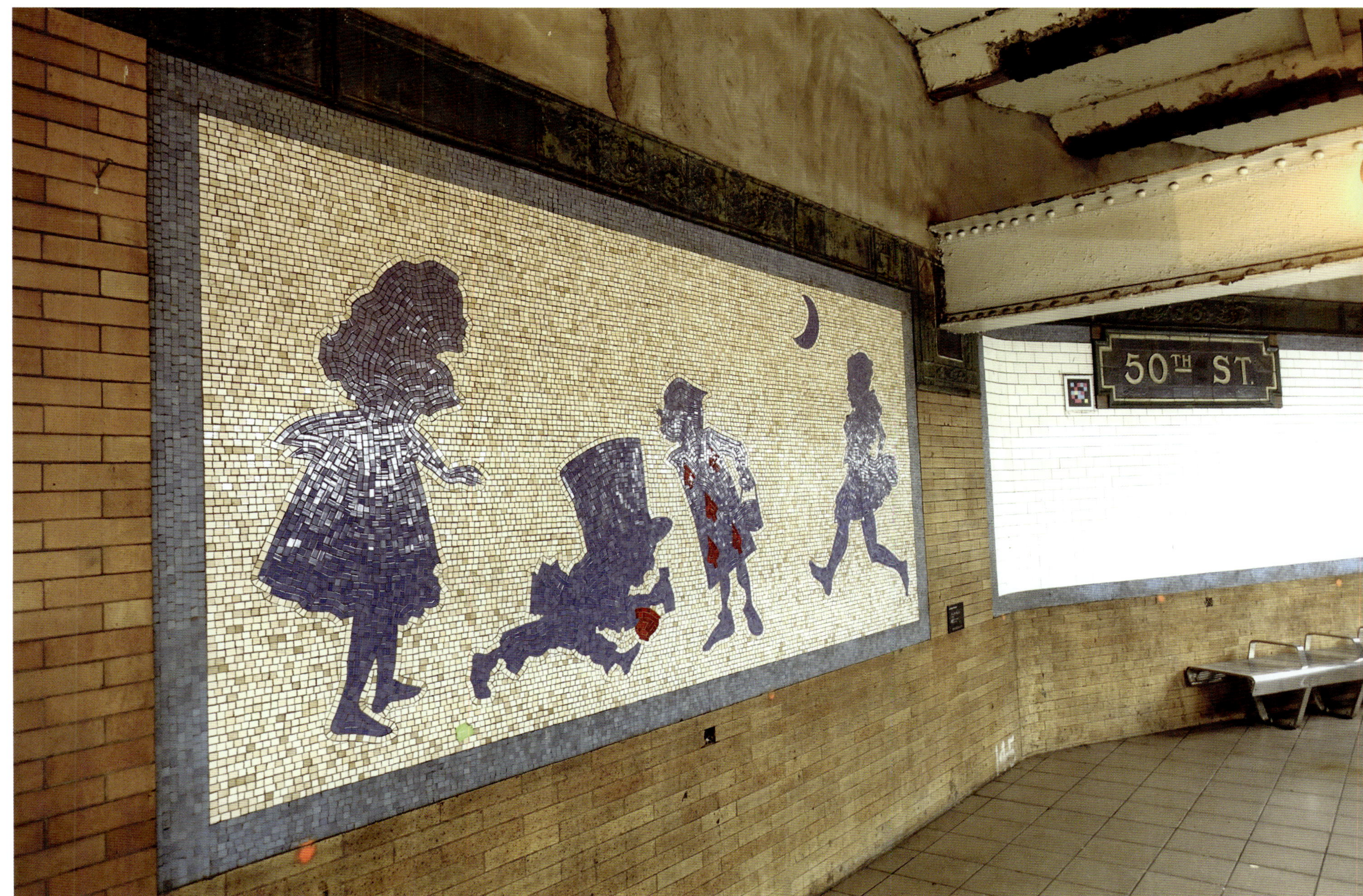
50TH ST.

Alice's tale is one in which her perception of time and place is consistently challenged and upended. Porter has spent her long career doing the same, challenging viewers from large-scale installations to intimate works on paper. Born in Argentina, Porter moved to New York in the 1960s and worked closely with Luis Camnitzer and Jose Guillermo Castillo, cofounding the New York Graphic Workshop. They began sending portable artworks through the mail: postcards drawn with prechosen shadows on it, inviting the receiver to complete the work by placing the prescribed object on the card—a water glass, an olive, a crumbled piece of paper. Porter continued to explore this extension of the medium with her series from the 1970s, conceptual works that blended photography, drawing, and performance. In *Untitled (Cube)*, she draws a plinth around a print of a cube, blurring the lines of drawing and photography. She further blurred those boundaries by extending the lines of the plinth onto the gallery walls when exhibiting the piece.

***Wrinkle*, 1968**
Photoetching
Courtesy of the artist

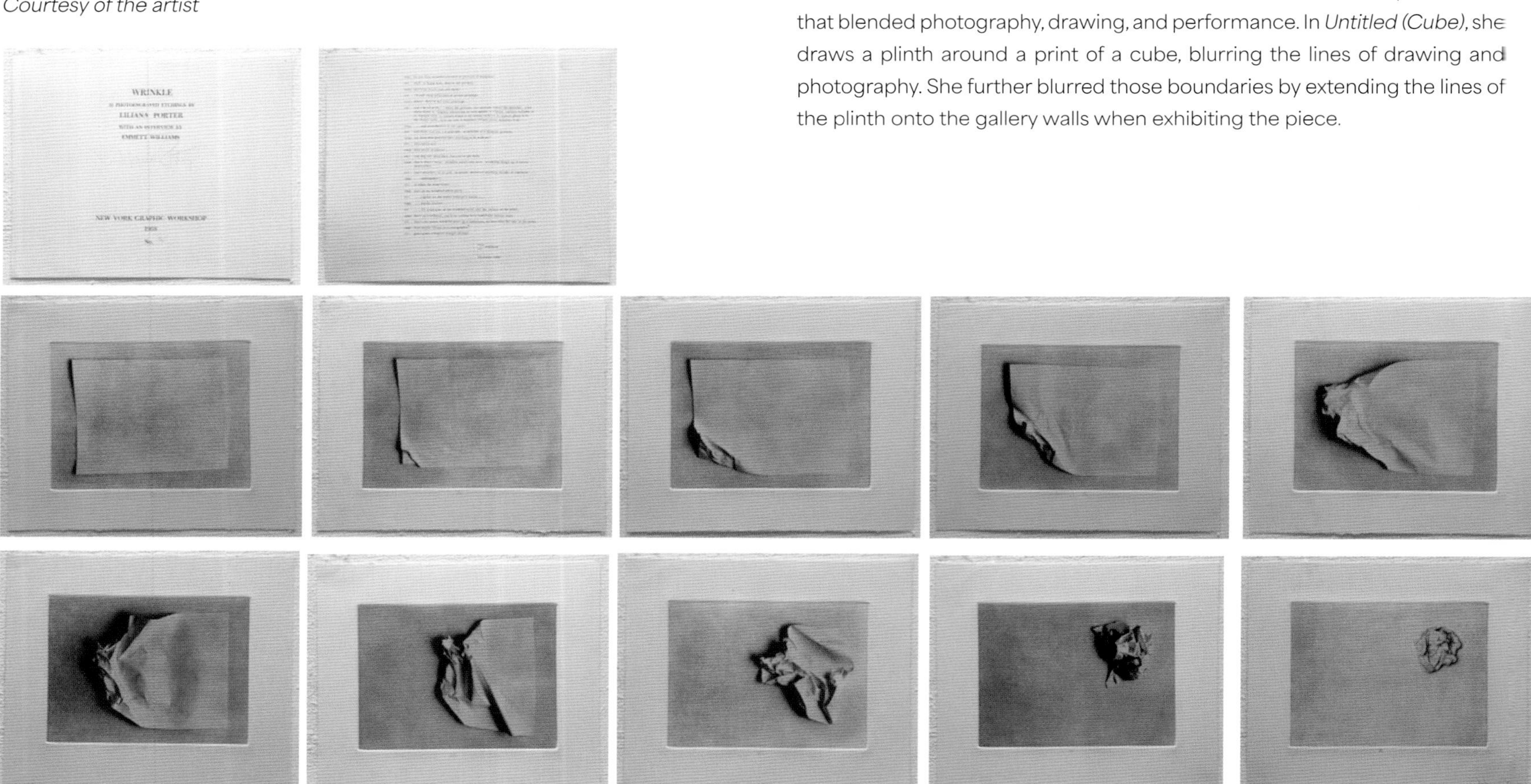

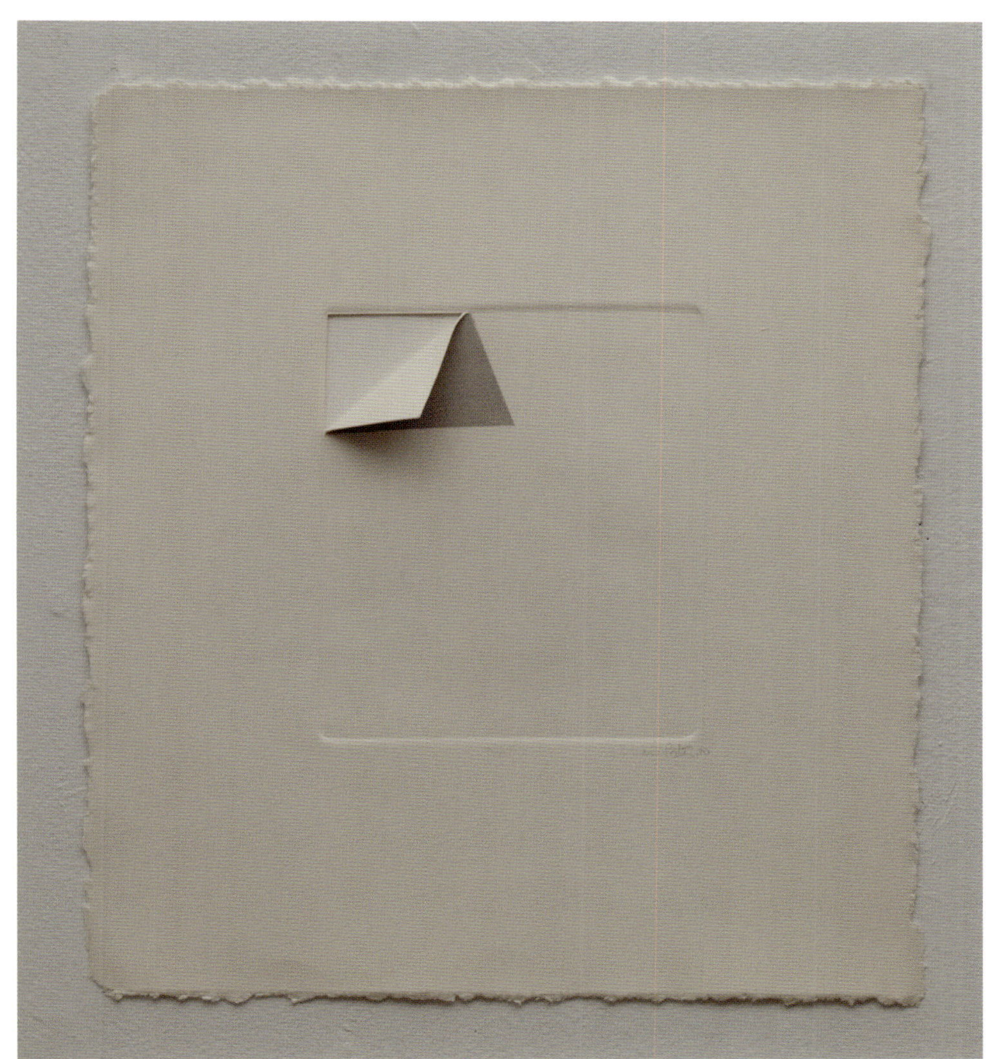

***Shadow*, 1970**
Etching
Courtesy of the artist

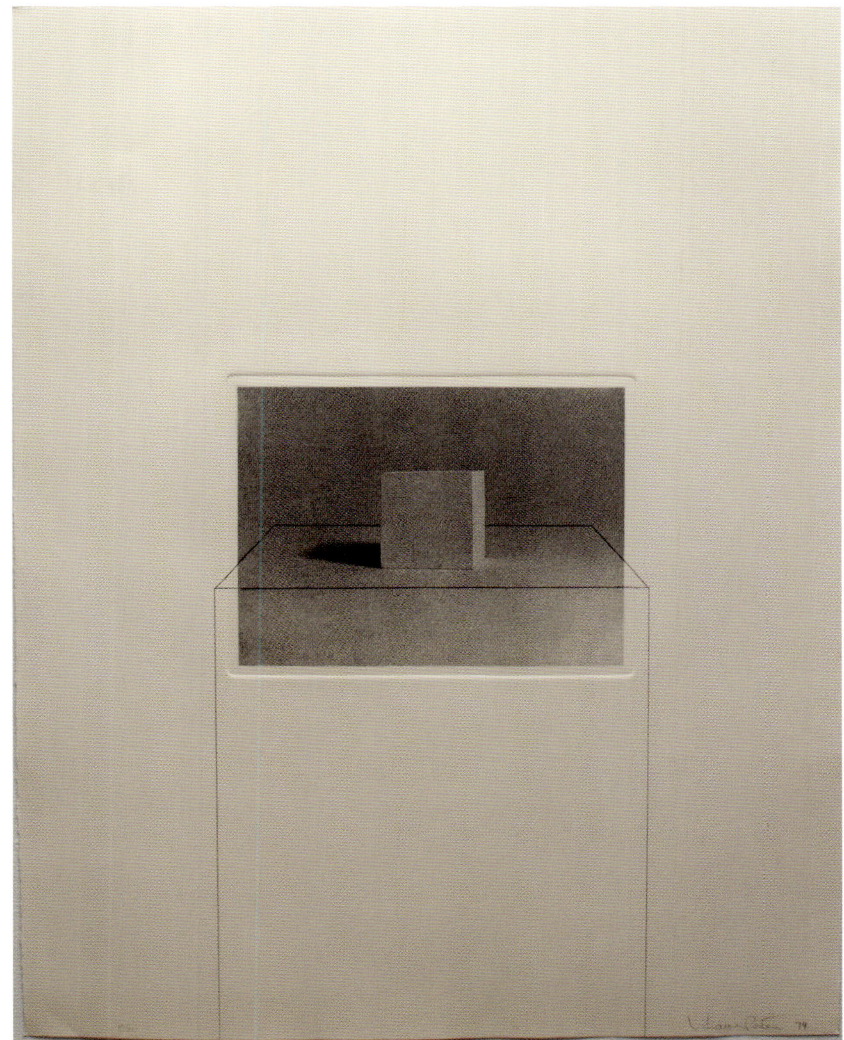

***Untitled (Cube)*, 1974**
Gelatin silver print and graphite
Courtesy of the artist

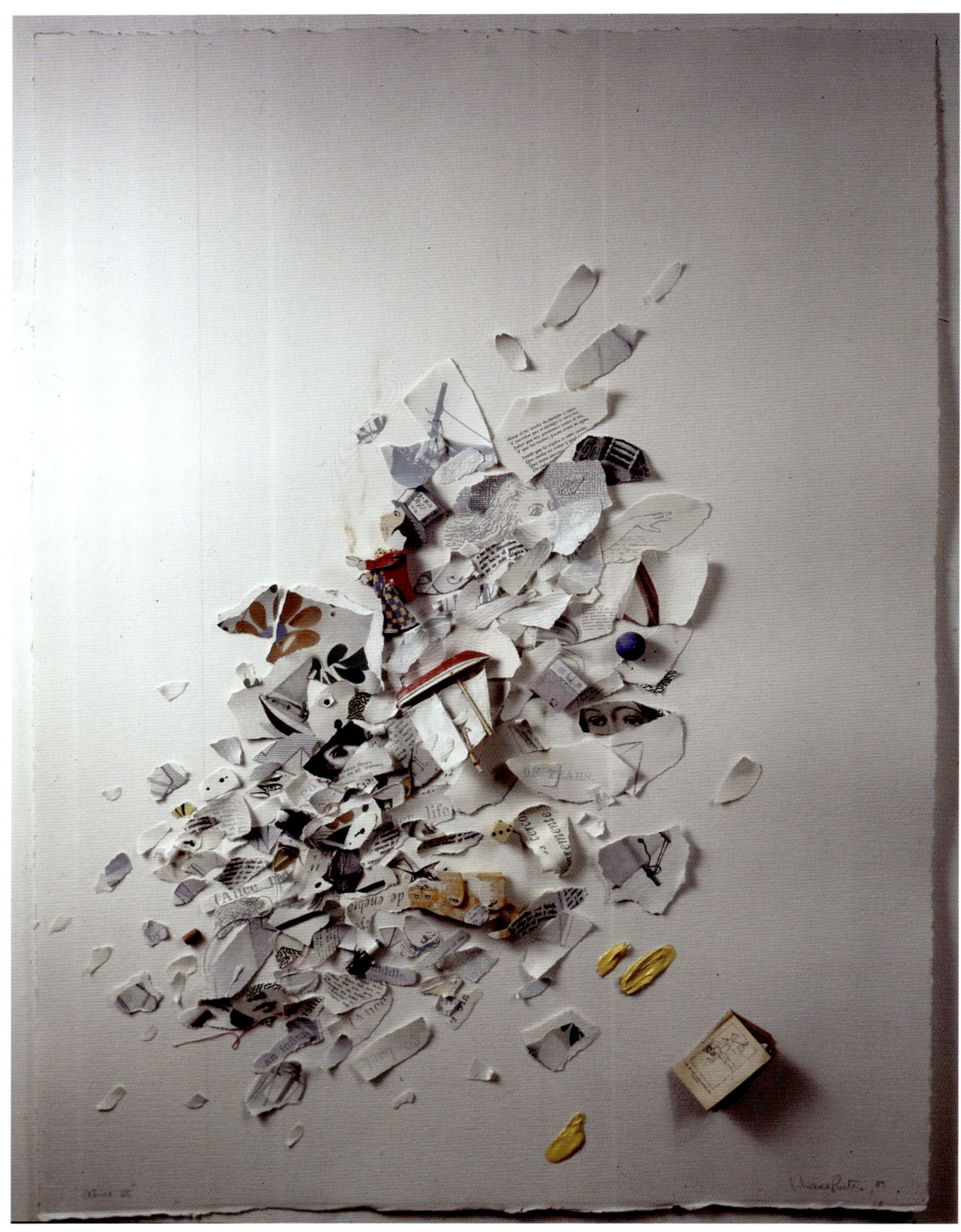

***Alice III*, 1989**
Collage on paper
Courtesy of the artist

While Porter's early conceptual works raised serious questions about traditional composition and means of exhibiting, they always had an impish edge to them. This mischievousness became more pronounced as she moved from purely performative works to photography and installation. Working with objects that she collects from markets around the world—porcelain collectibles, tiny dollhouse figurines, vintage toys—she creates tableaux that have a theatrical quality to them. Though they are devoid of people, Porter's studies are nonetheless full of life and drama and humor. Her works range from spare compositions—such as a tiny construction worker drilling a hole into the lined paper on which he's placed—to dense still lives packed with all manner of bric-a-brac. Scale is an important element, since her imaginary worlds are seemingly populated only by very small figures, the largest the size of an adult finger. This is used to great effect in her installations, such as in *Man with Axe,* produced for the 57th Venice Biennale in 2017. Here a tiny figurine of a man with an axe leaves behind a sprawling pile of porcelain debris, the objects increasing comically in size. Elsewhere, another figurine sits on the edge of a platform, knitting a giant cloud of gossamer fabric. Much like the world that Alice encounters through the looking glass, Porter's worlds are disorienting and puzzling, but the artist always keeps it playful, fabricating these worlds with a twinkle in her eye.

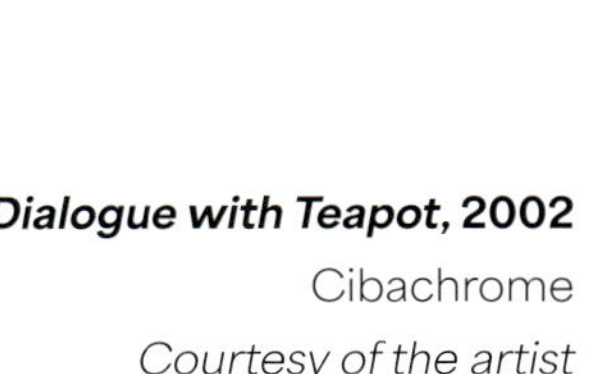

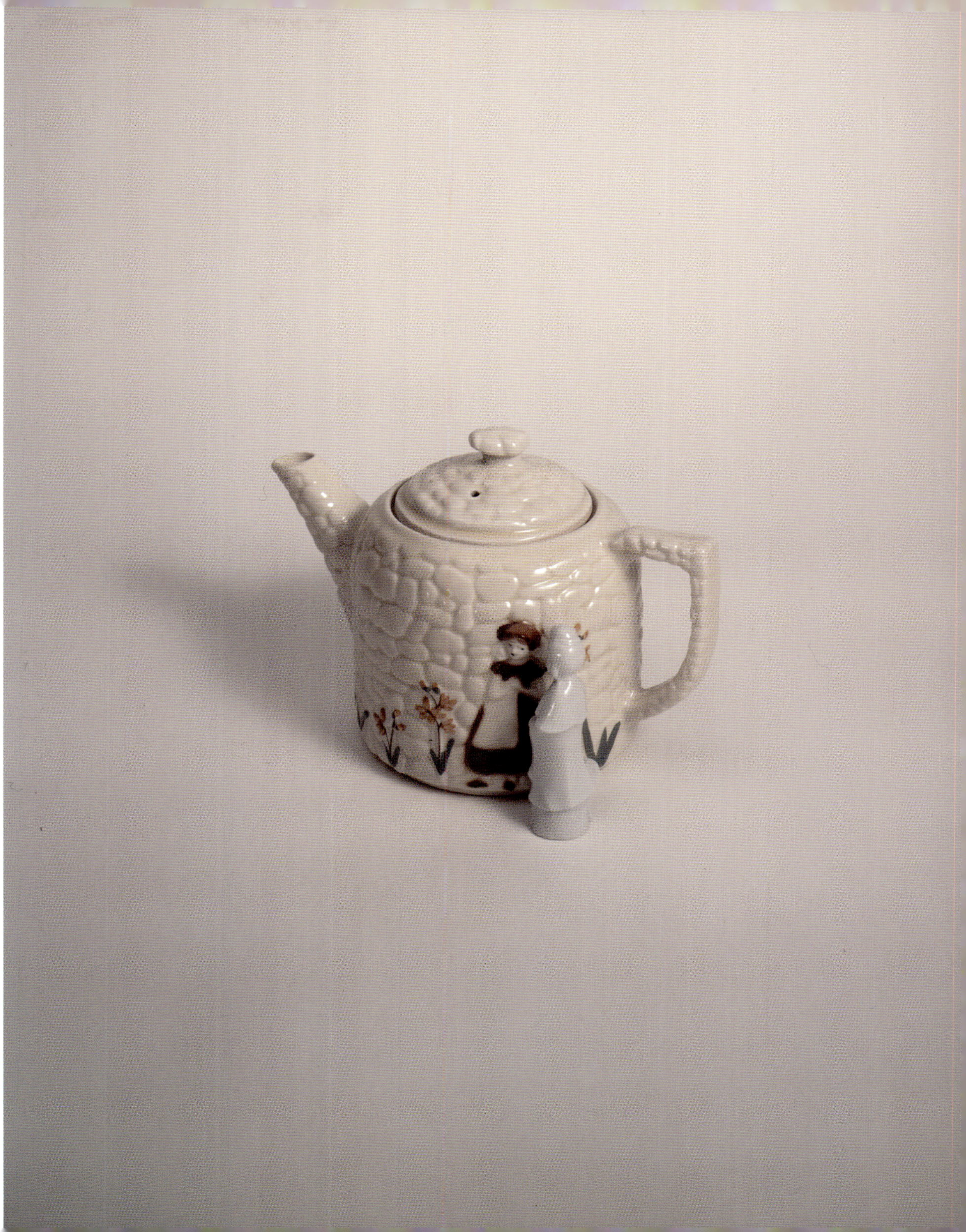

***Dialogue with Teapot*, 2002**
Cibachrome
Courtesy of the artist

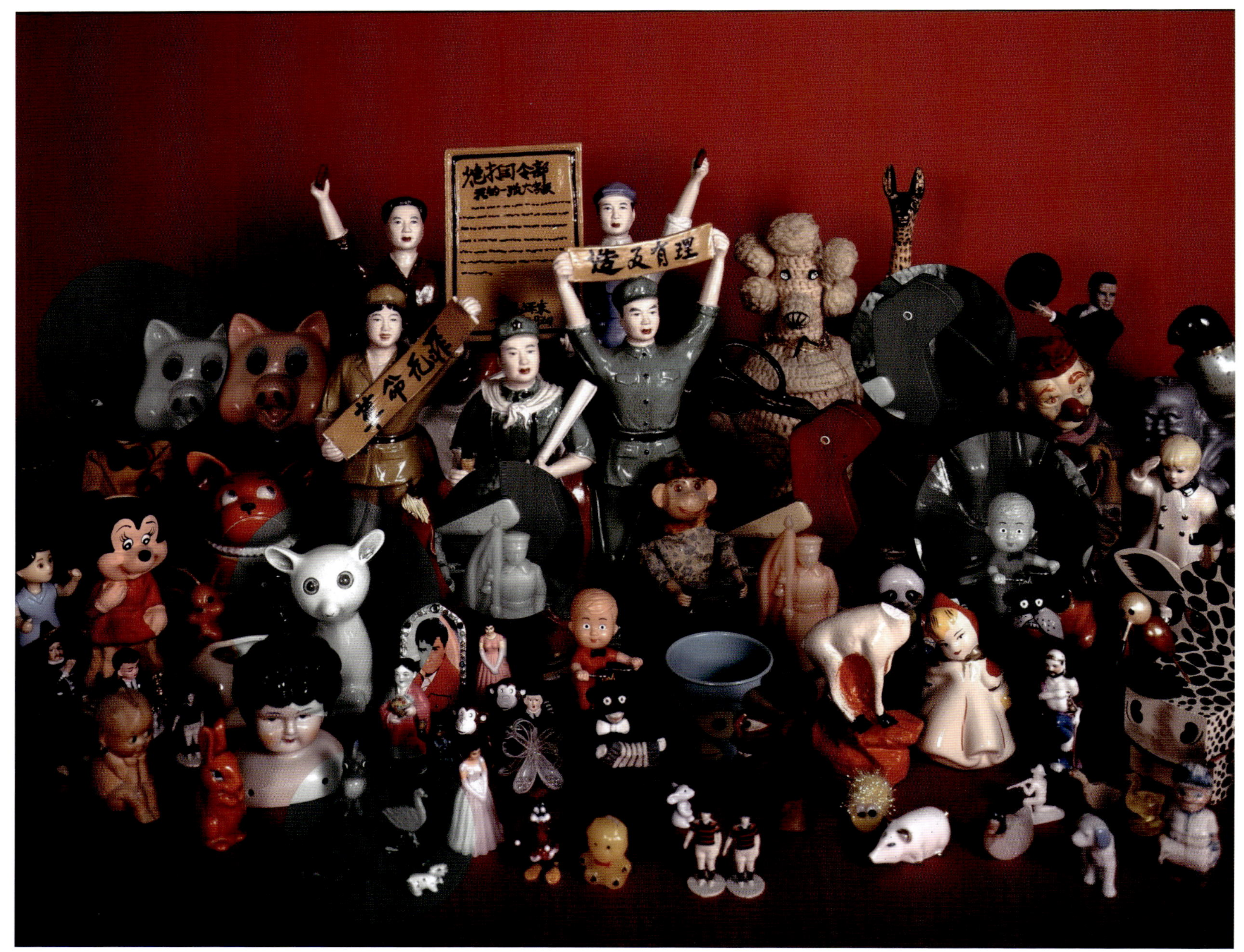

***Please Don't Move (with red background)*, 2002**

Cibachrome

Courtesy of the artist

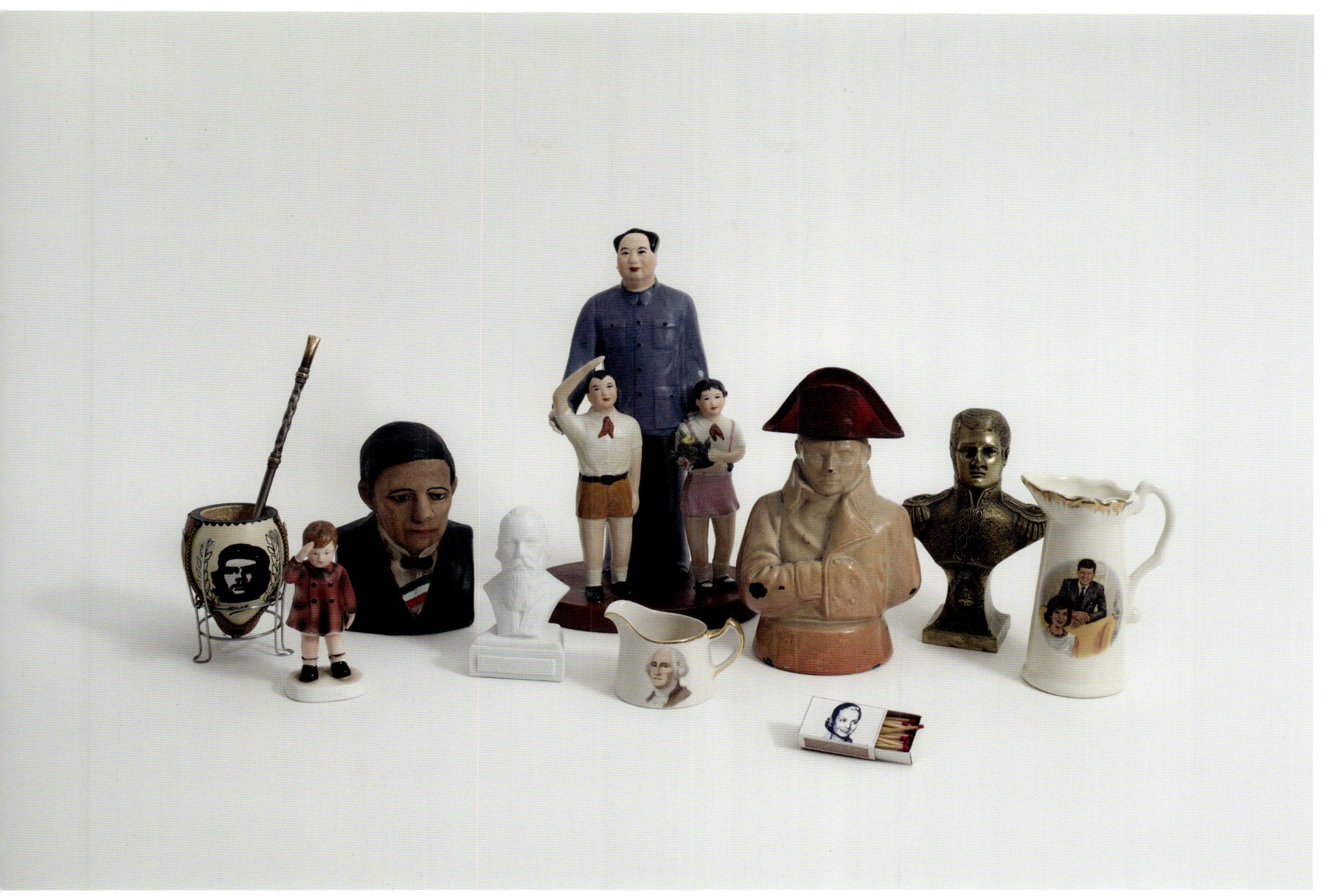

***Memorabilia*, 2016**
Fuji-flex c-print
Courtesy of the artist

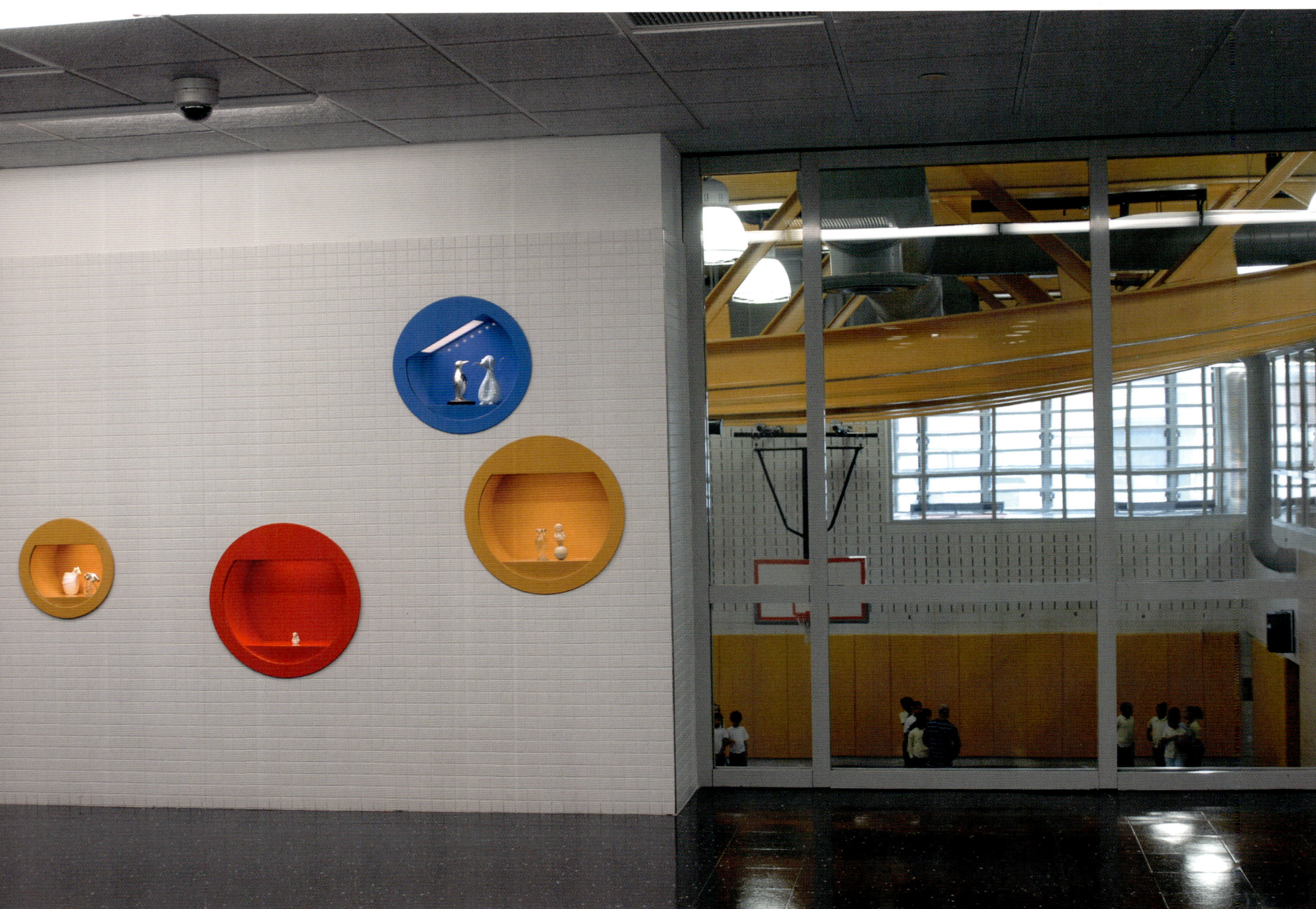

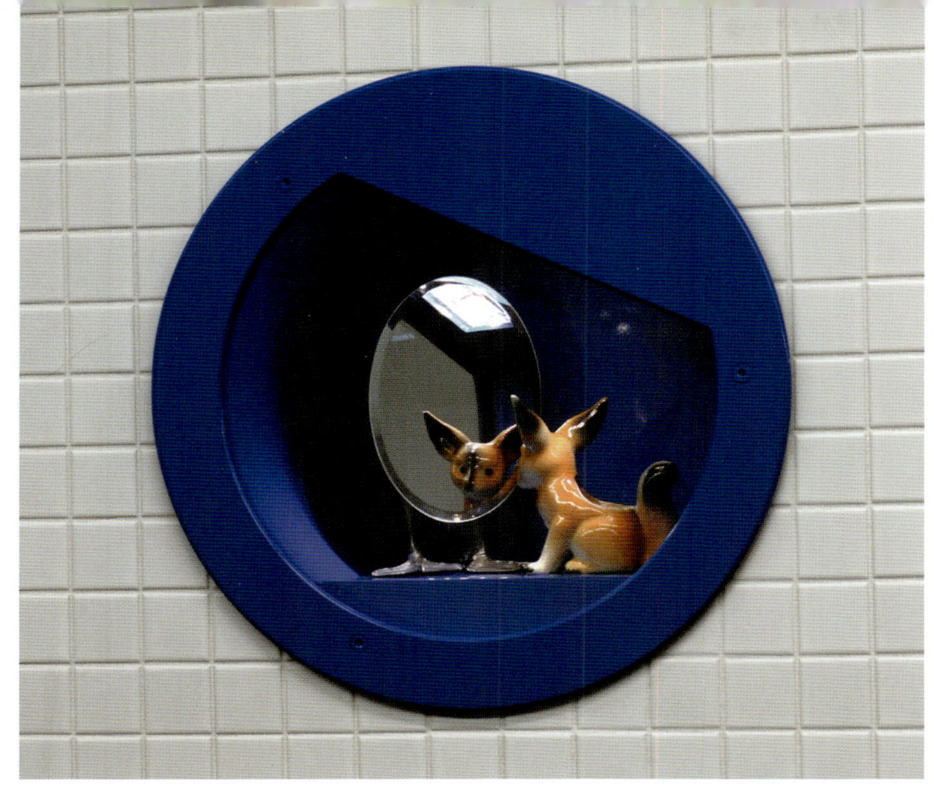

***Situations with Them*, 2007**
Detail

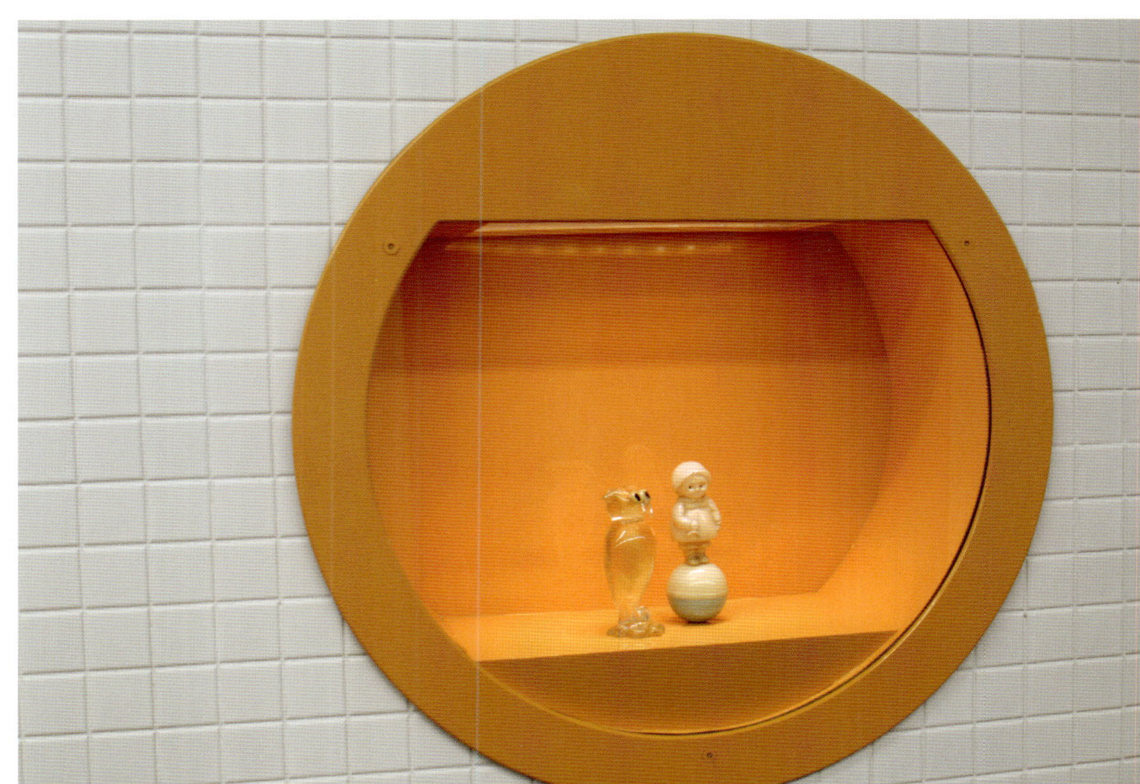

***Situations with Them*, 2007**
Wall installation of twelve enclosed dioramas at PS/IS 96 in New York City
Courtesy of the artist

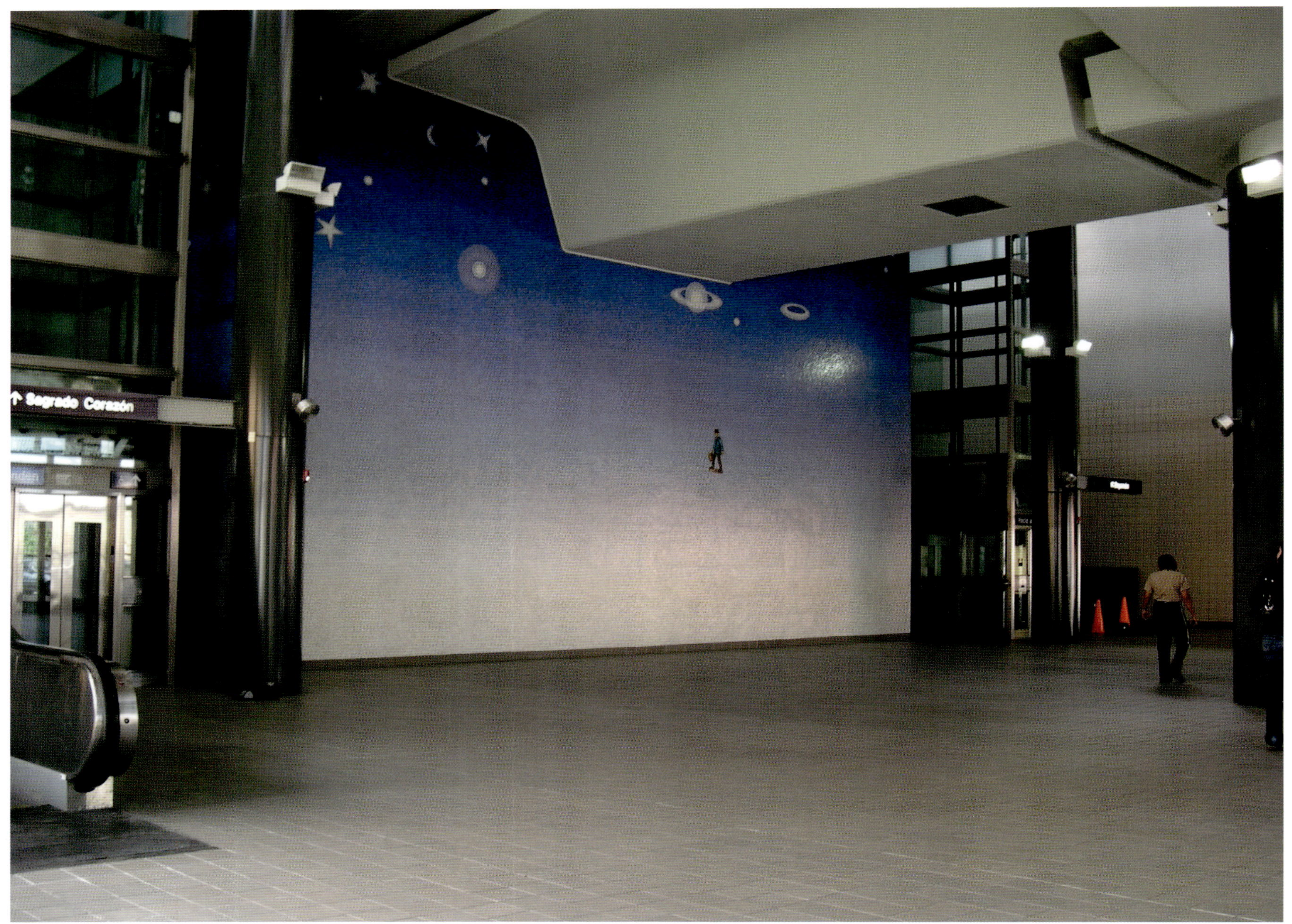

***El Viajero / The Traveler*, 2004**

Glass mosaic mural at the Domenech Station in San Juan, Puerto Rico

Courtesy of the artist

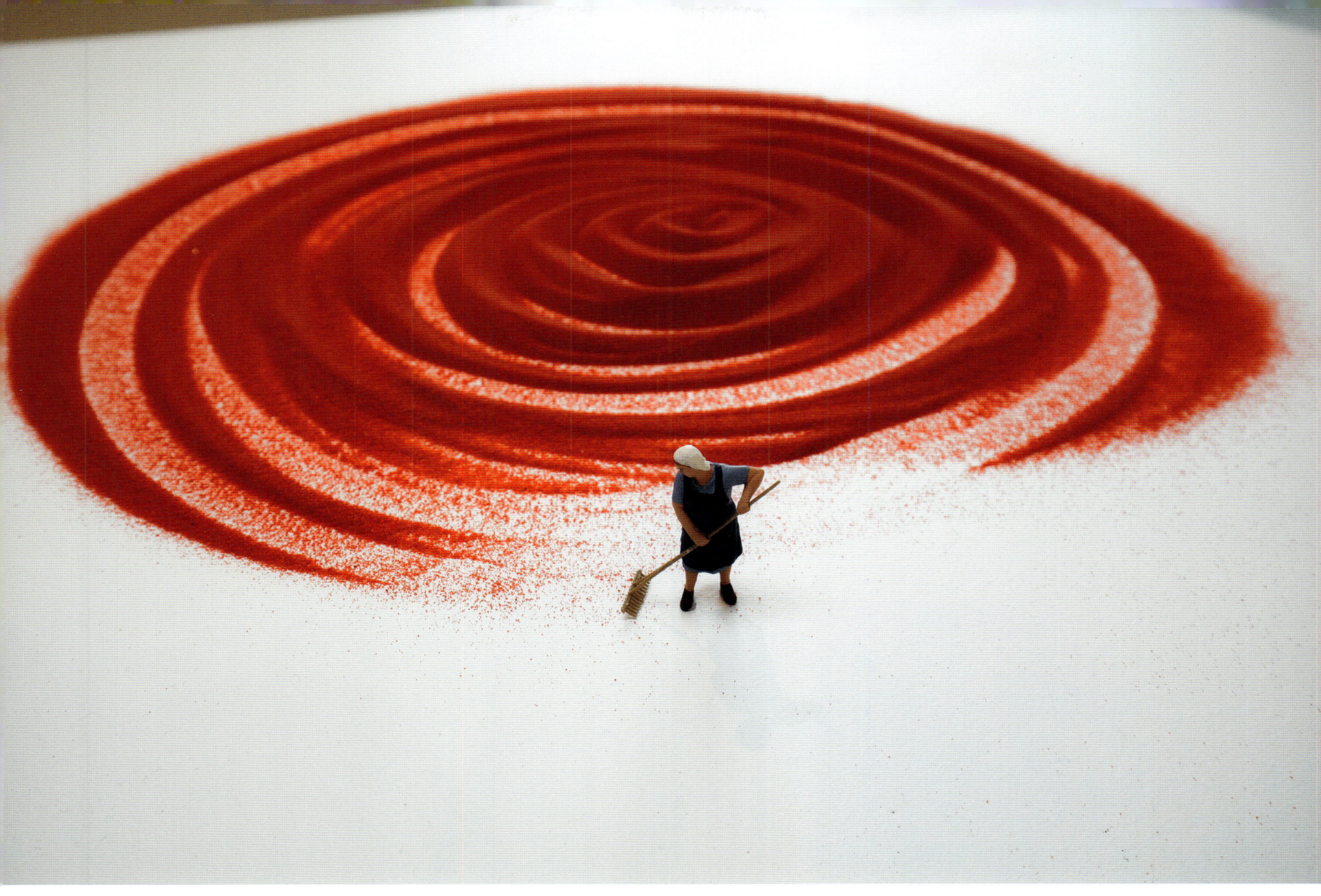

***Red Sand*, 2018**
Red sand, figurine. Site-specific installation at Art OMI in Ghent, New York.
Courtesy of the artist

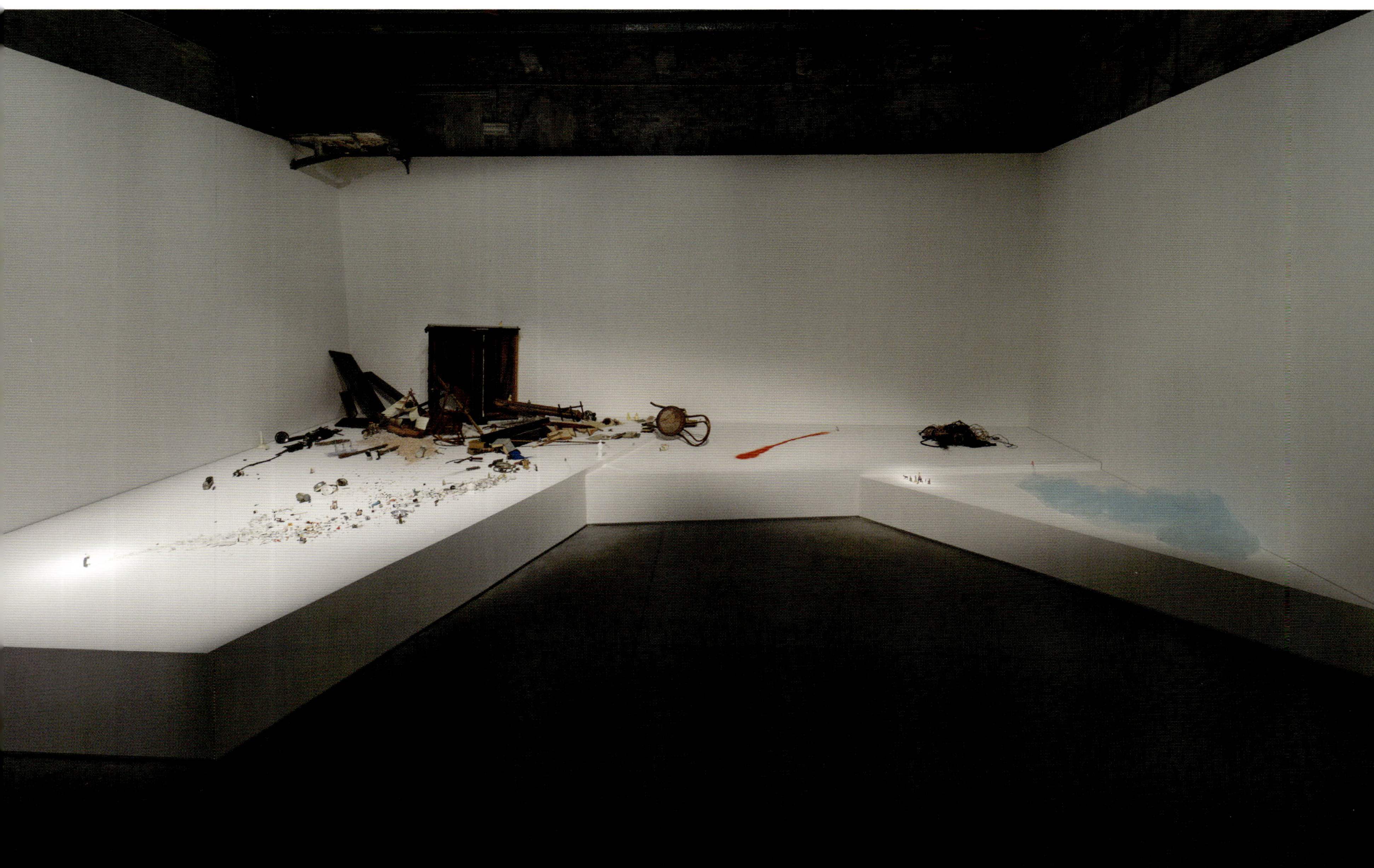

***Man with Axe*, 2017**
Site-specific installation for the 57th International Art Exhibition of La Biennale di Venezia, Venice, Italy
Courtesy of the artist

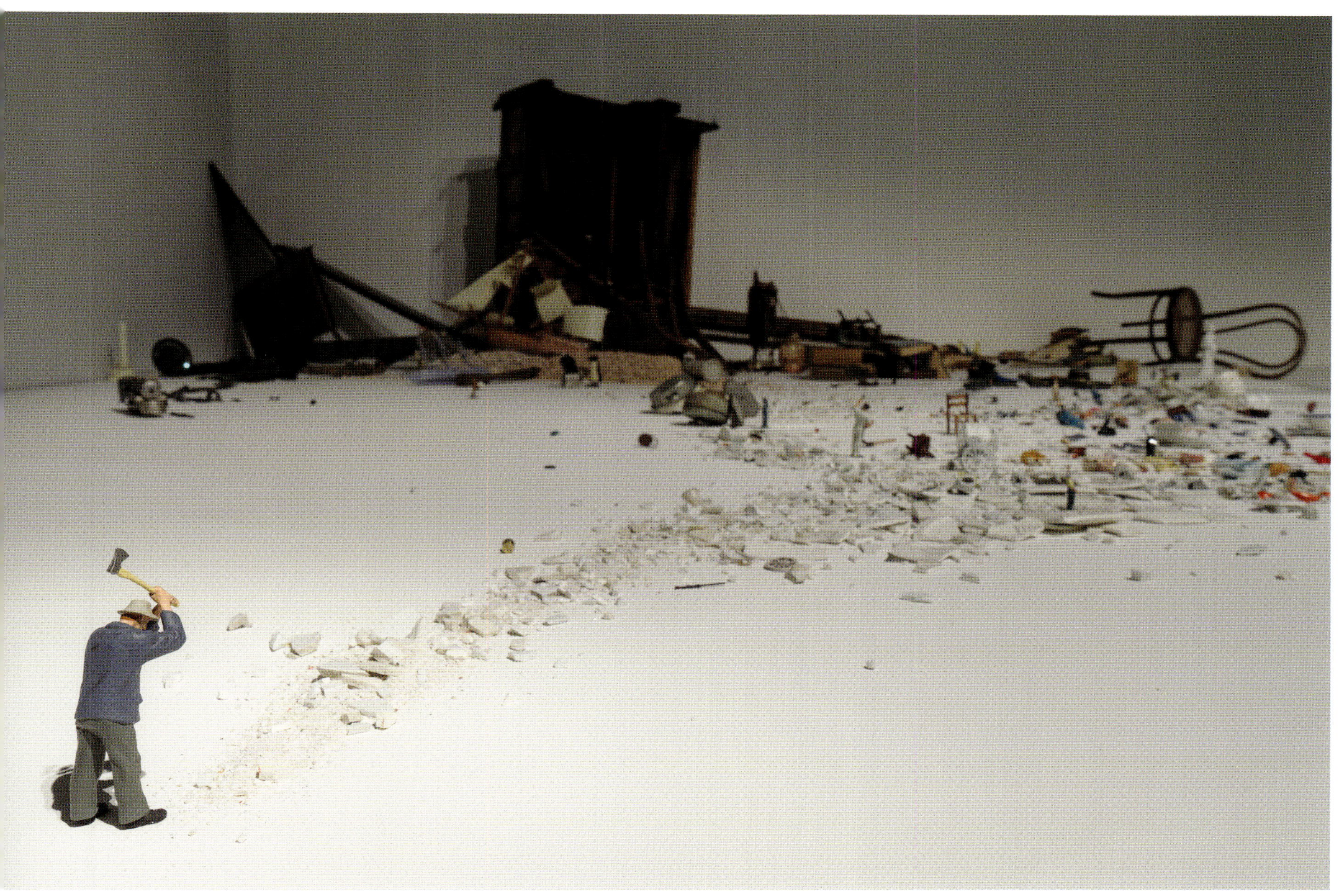

***Man with Axe*, 2017**
Detail

Jean Shin (b. 1971)

63rd ST./ LEXINGTON AVE. (F TRAIN)

***Elevated*, 2017**

When the 2nd Ave. subway extension in Manhattan was finally realized after decades of stalled planning, several artists were asked to create artwork for these gleaming new stations. Korean American artist Jean Shin has the first work that riders would experience at 63rd Street / Lexington Avenue. Unlike the other stops, Shin's work occupies an existing station that connects to the extension. Thus, *Elevated* became a gateway between these worlds, old and new. To honor this, Shin reached back in time to the destruction of the original elevated train from the early 1940s. Pulling from an archive of photographs taken in the area, she created mosaics of denizens of the neighborhood going about their business under the ghostly image of the elevated tracks. When this shift underground occured, those riders lost their view of the sky; Shin gives the sky back by creating a vast mosaic sky on which the black-and-white figures were placed. In another area, vintage photographs are printed on reflective glass. At the station entrance, she further recalls the former elevated station by reconstructing images of the beams being dismantled into a photo collage that was then transferred onto ceramic tile. Reaching back into the past was her way of reusing materials from that time—in this case, memory and documentation—and creating a visual time machine for current riders.

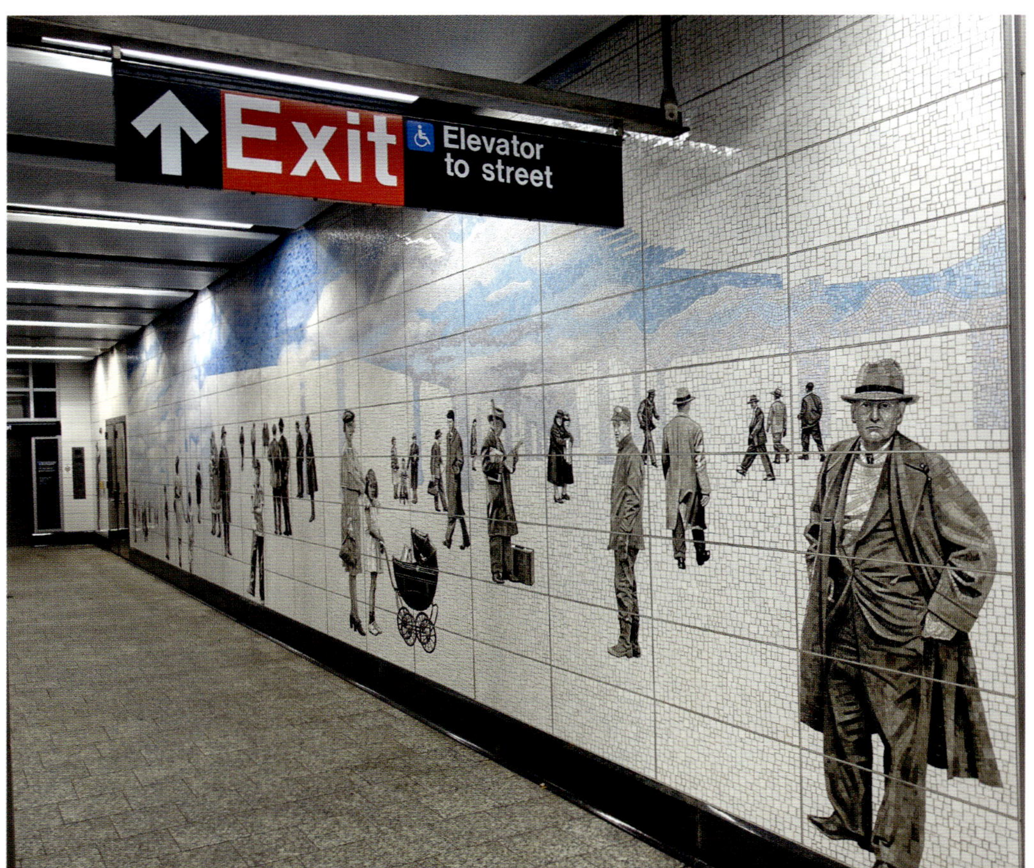

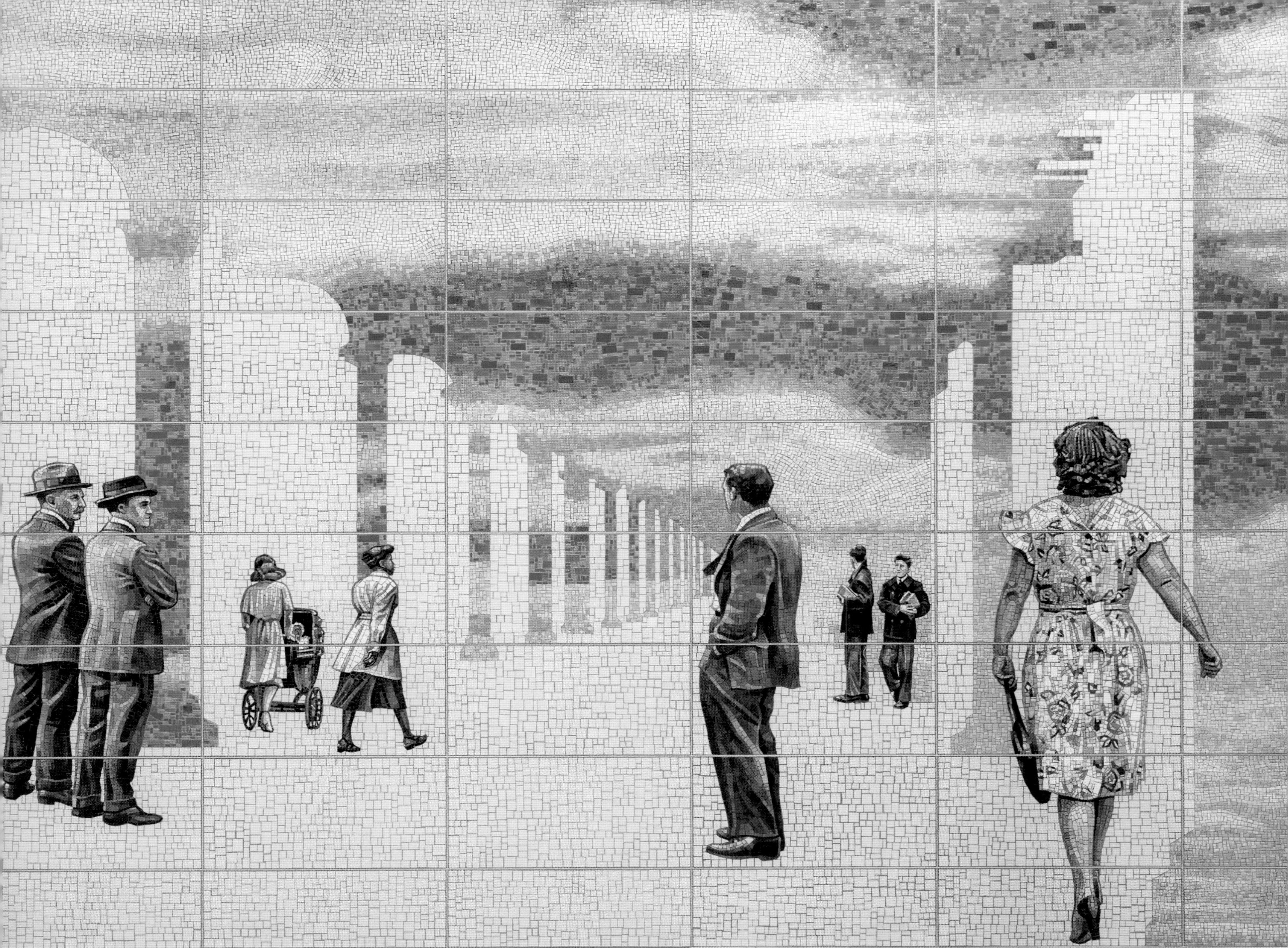

Photo by Etienne Frossard

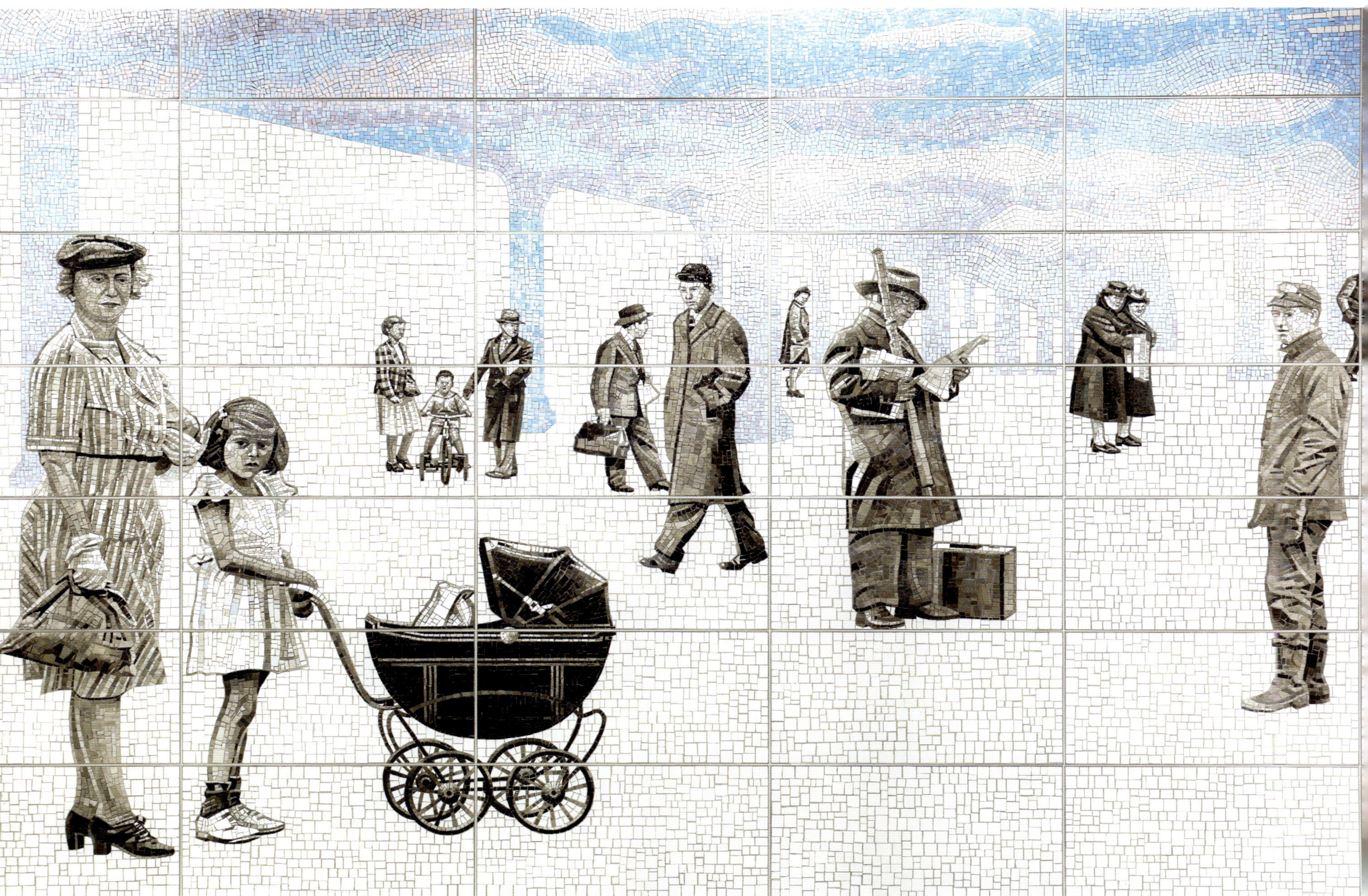

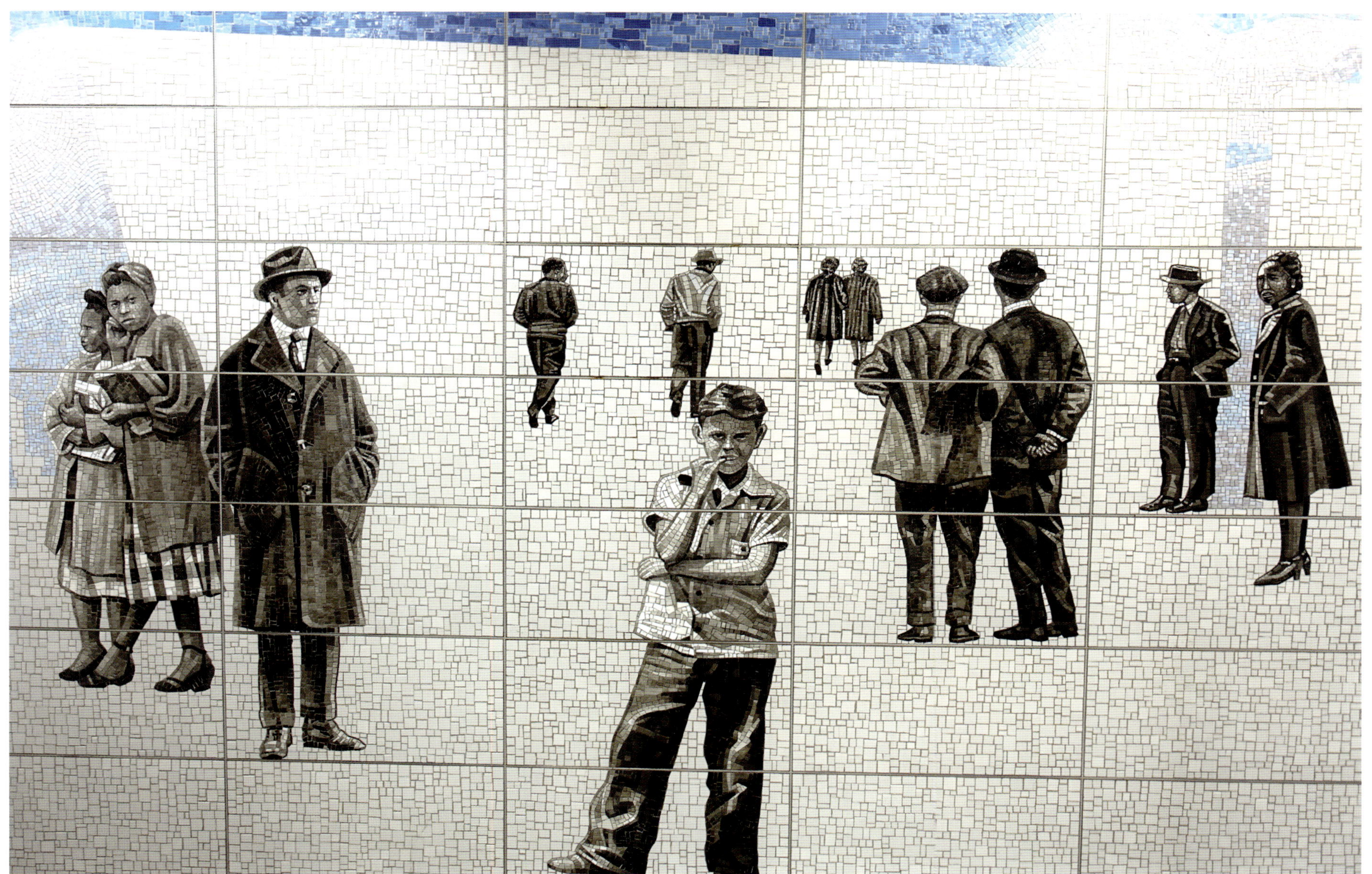

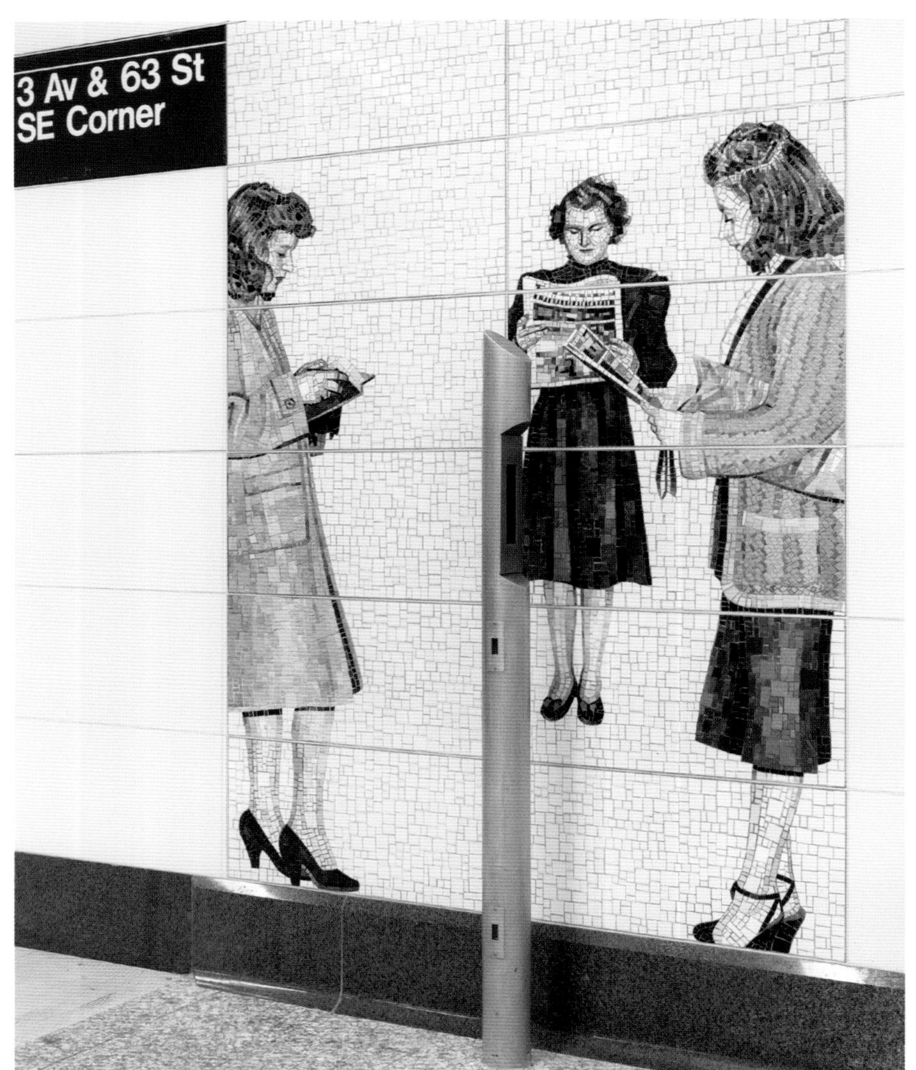
3 Av & 63 St
SE Corner

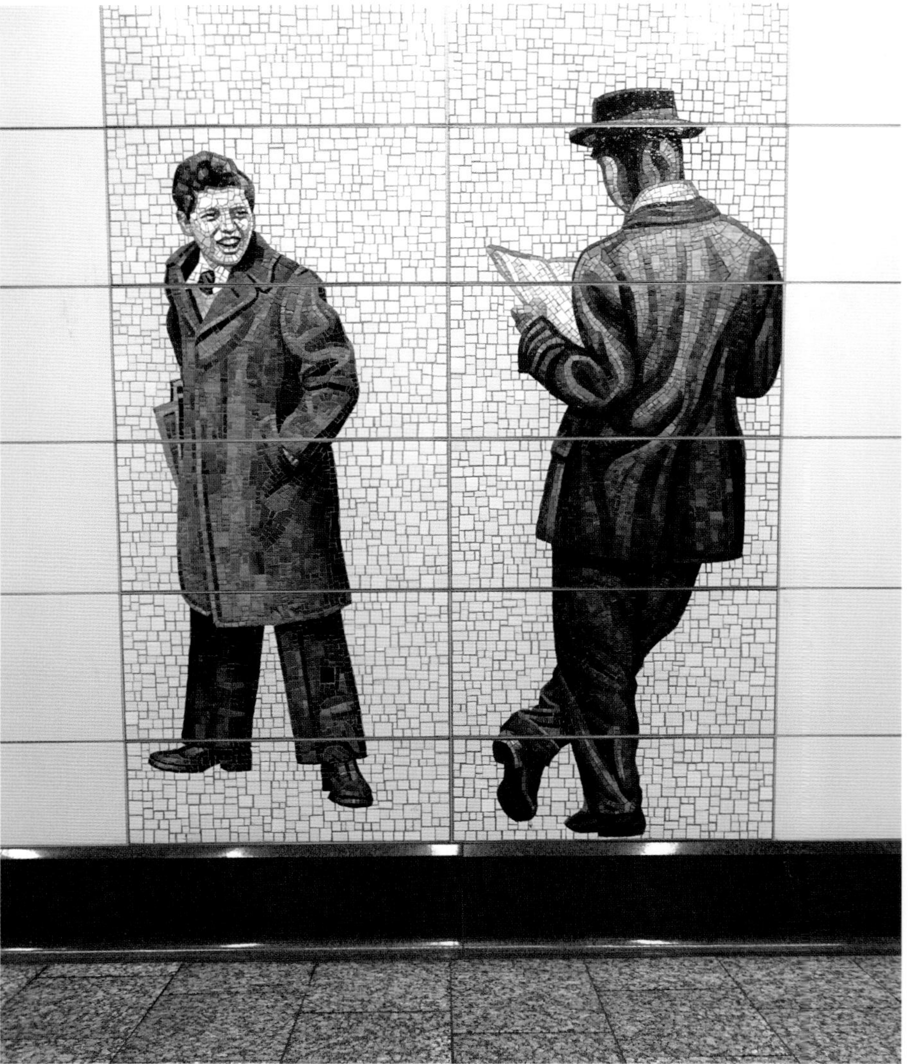

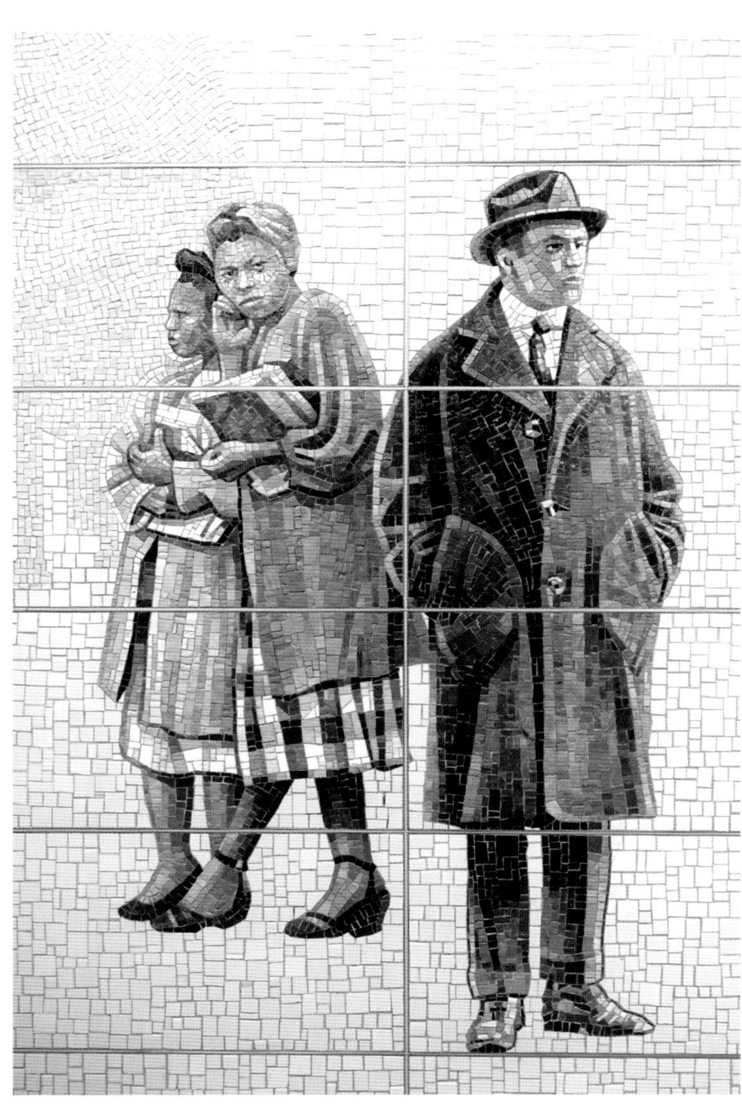

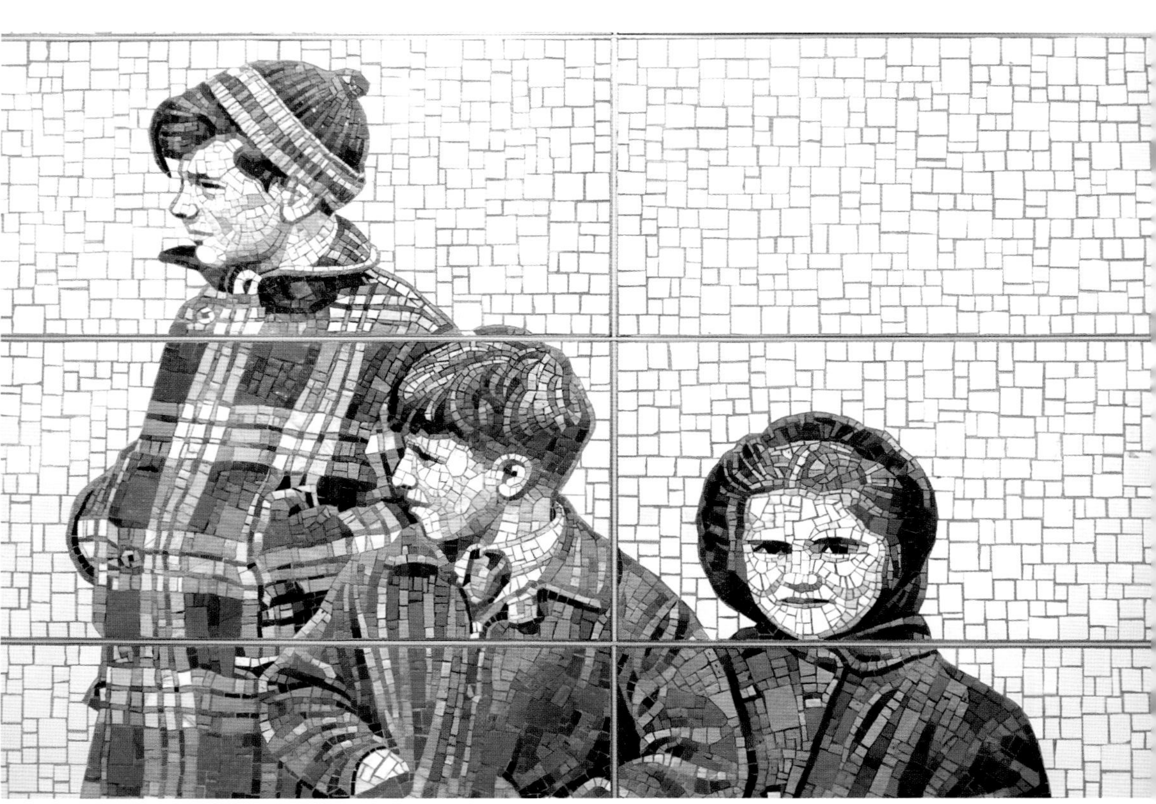

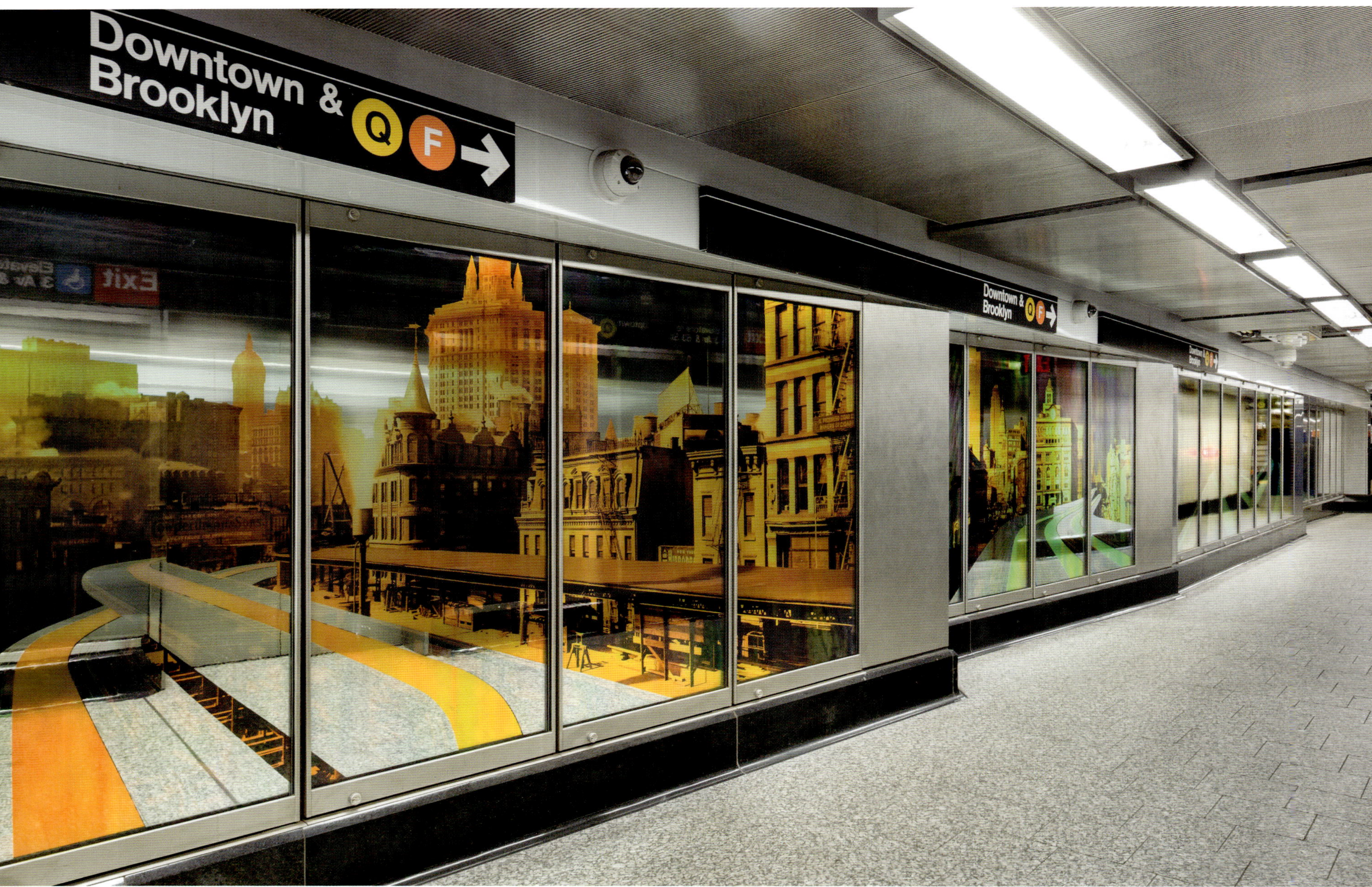
Downtown & Brooklyn
Q
F
Exit
Downtown & Brooklyn

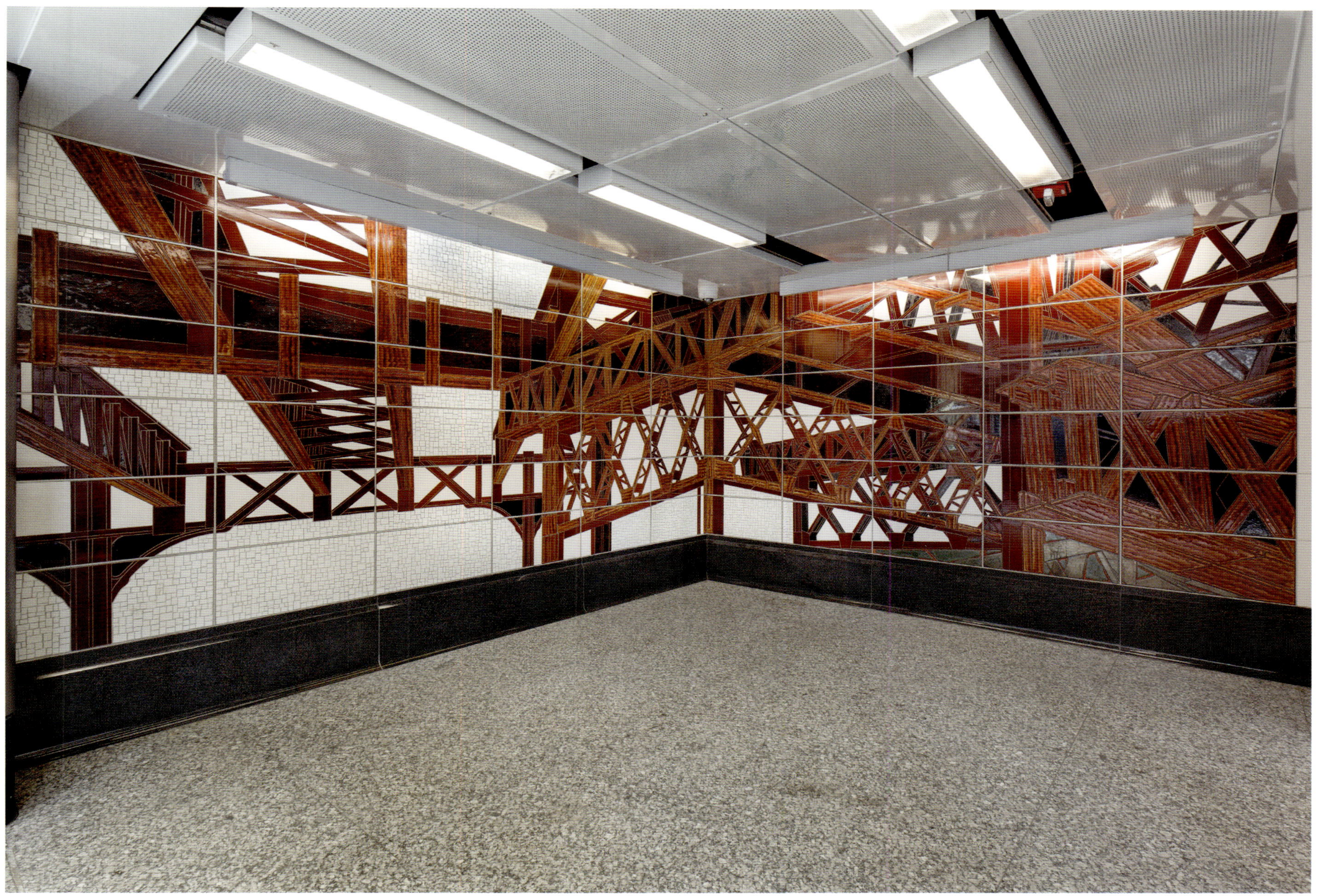

Jean Shin often explores the aesthetic possibilities of the detritus of modern life while interrogating our relationship and impact on the environment. Obsolete mobile phones, buttons, plastic bottles, old jeans—all these materials have passed through Shin's hands to produce large-scale installations and public artworks. Much of her work, no matter where it is, puts a focus on the surrounding community. In this way, Shin is an ideal artist for the MTA project, one who thoughtfully researches every site to thoroughly inform her work, as she has done in *Elevated*. Every aesthetic decision is born out of considerations from this research, giving viewers multiple lenses in which to engage with the work.

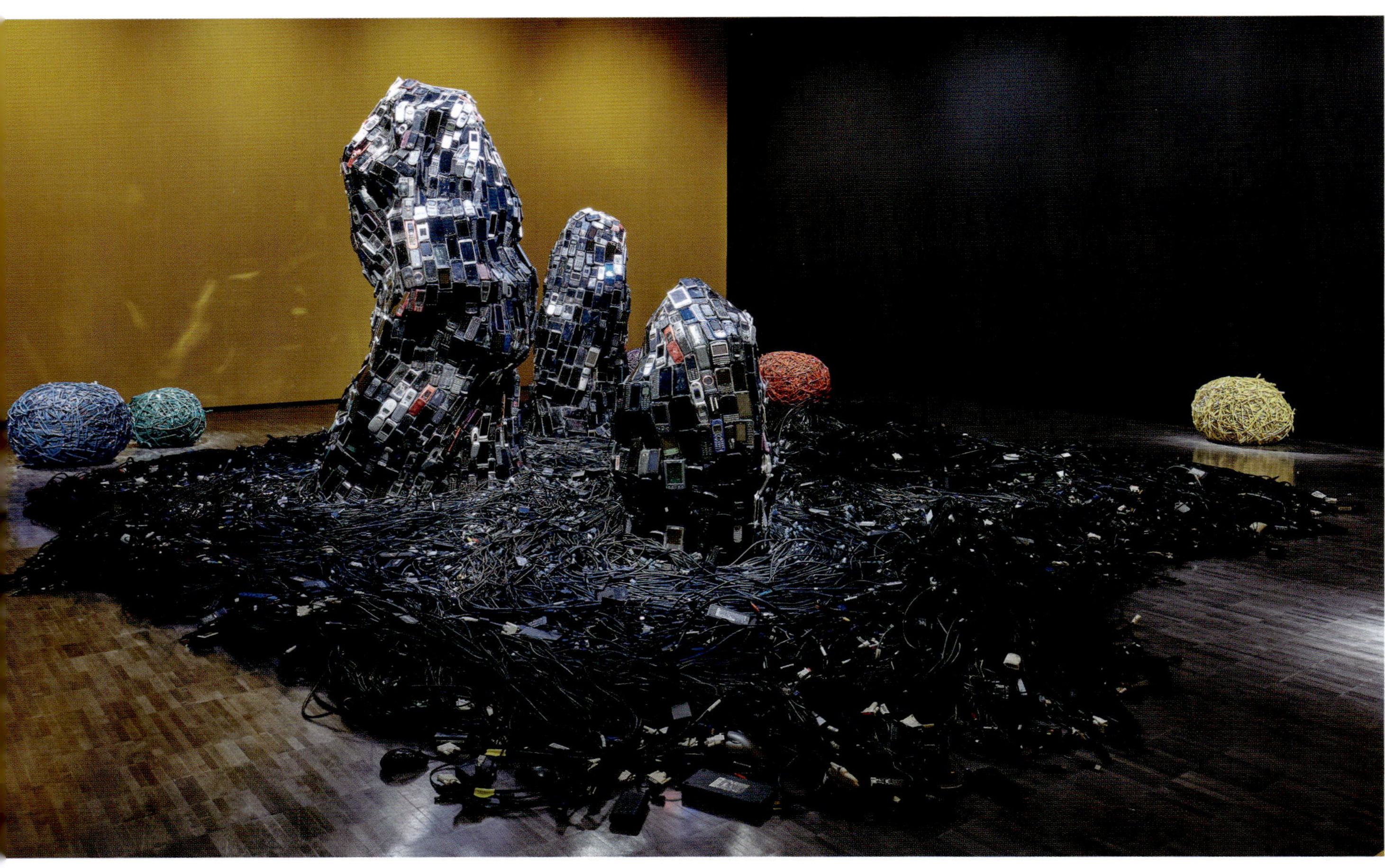

***Huddled Masses*, 2020**
Cell phones and computer cables
Installation at Asian Art Museum, San Francisco
Courtesy of Studio Jean Shin

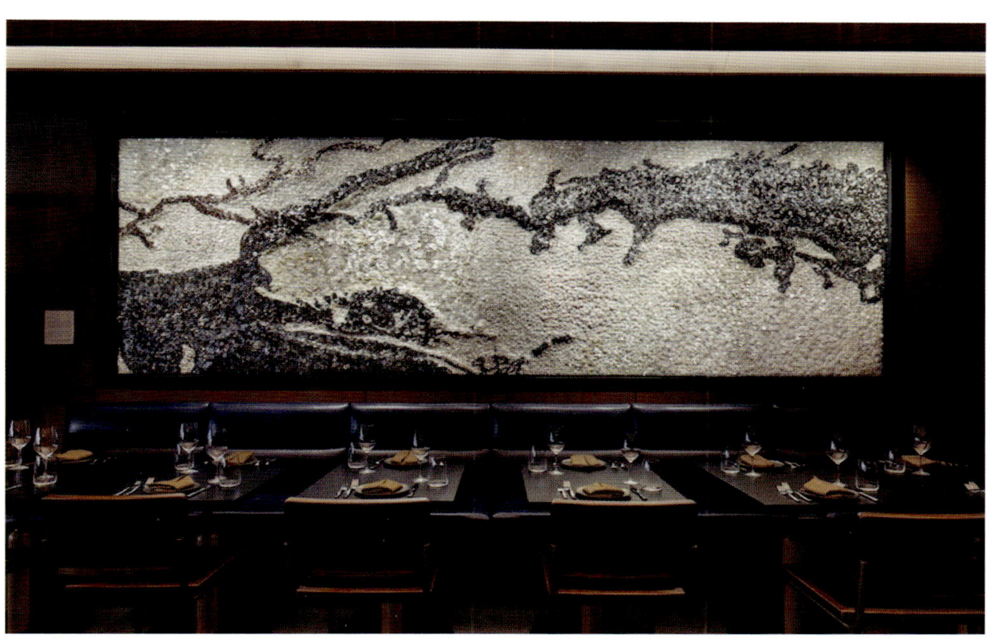

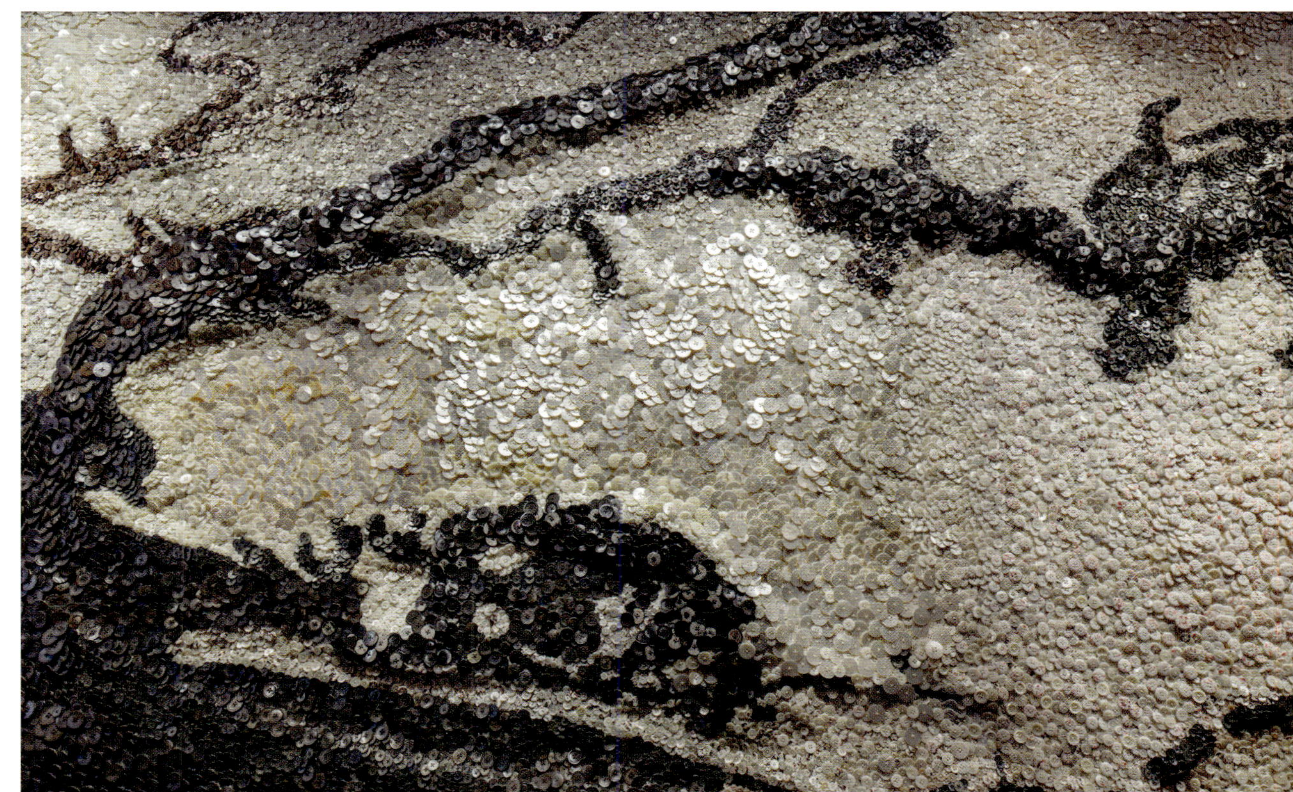

***Water's Echo*, 2023**

Mother-of-pearl shell buttons, thread, and canvas mounted on wood panel

Installation at Perelman Performing Arts Center

Courtesy of Studio Jean Shin

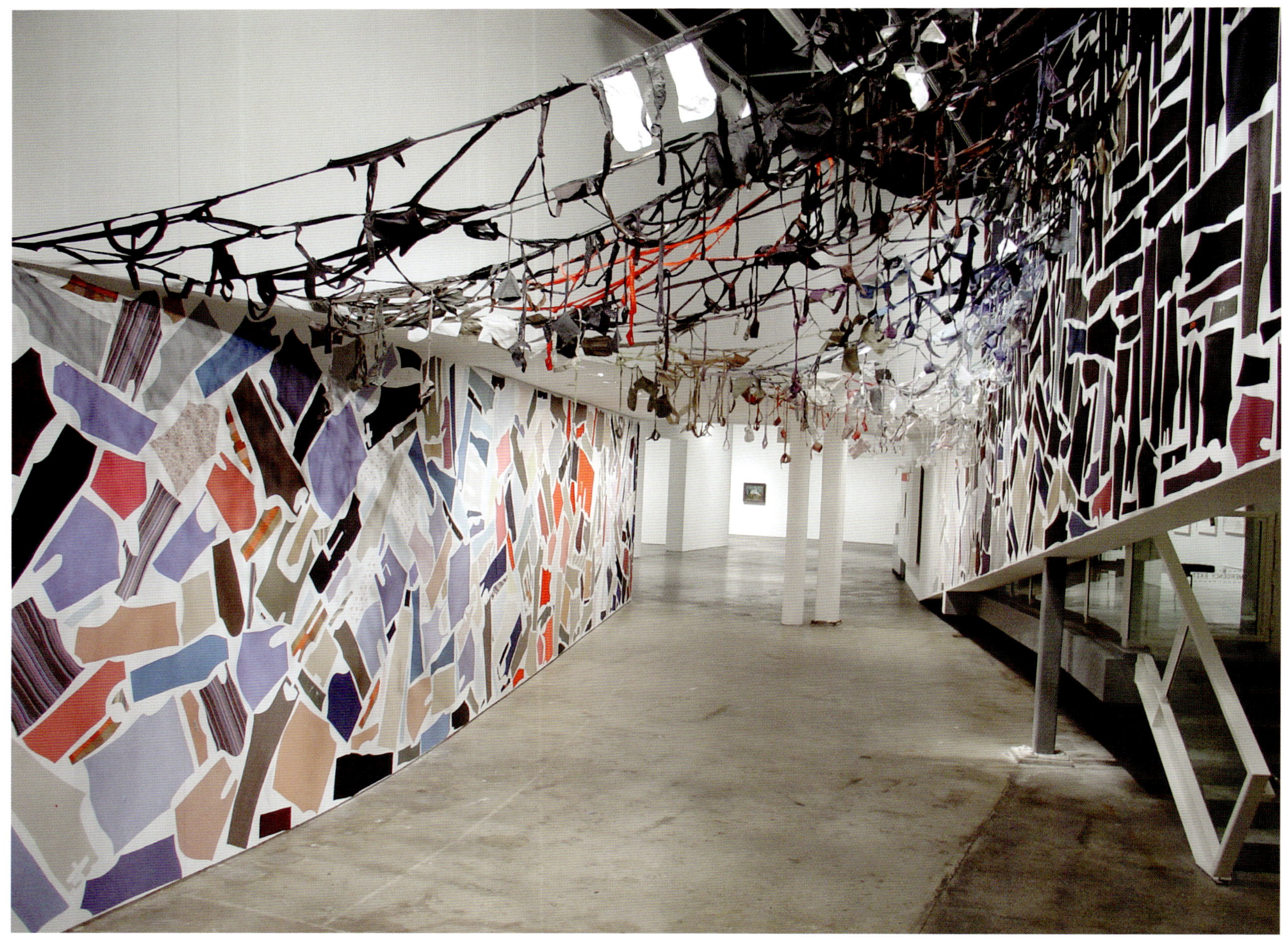

***Cut Outs and Suspended Seams*, 2004**
Cut fabric (clothes from MoMA museum employees), thread, starch
Installation at the Museum of Modern Art QNS (now MoMA PS1)
Courtesy of Studio Jean Shin

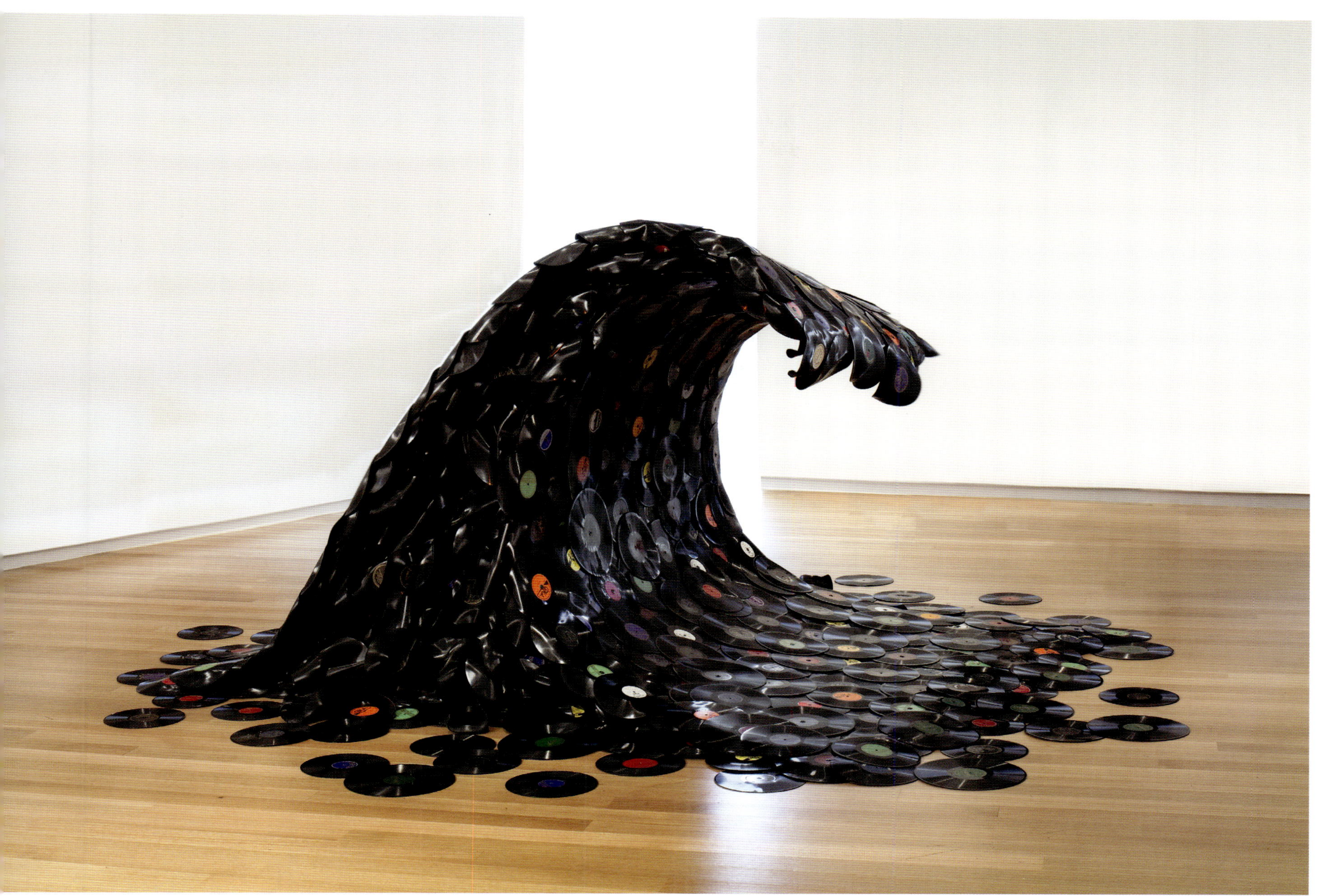

***Sound Wave*, 2007**
Melted records on wooden armature
Courtesy of Studio Jean Shin

In *MAiZE* (2017), Shin collaborated with 800 community members in Davenport, Iowa, to create a life-sized maze composed of thousands of plastic soda bottles, all in the unnatural shade of fluorescent green that is the distinguishing marker of the region's favorite soft drink. Iowa and the surrounding heartland of the country rely on industrial farming, particularly of corn, for their economic survival. A majority of this corn is turned into corn syrup, which ends up in sodas bottled in plastic. In much the same way that corn has transformed our landscape, with miles and miles of cornfields filling the landscapes of Middle America, plastic has also altered our environment, filling landfills, dumped by the tons into our oceans, and becoming an integral part of supermarket shelves. *MAiZE* asks the audience to consider this impact and the cyclical nature of these man-made things: industrial farming, plastic packaging, consumption of processed sugars. Though the installation follows the form of that wholesome signifier of plentiful harvest, the corn maze, the resulting work cannot escape the unnatural glow and unyielding rigidity of the material. Throughout her work, Shin is able to connect communities and the history of place, weaving multiple narratives to compelling conclusions. A maze holds a labyrinth of ideas, and an old train station becomes a conduit to the past.

***MAiZE*, 2017 (detail)**
Plastic soda bottles, adhesive, and vinyl tubing
Installed at Figge Art Museum, Davenport, Iowa
Courtesy of Studio Jean Shin

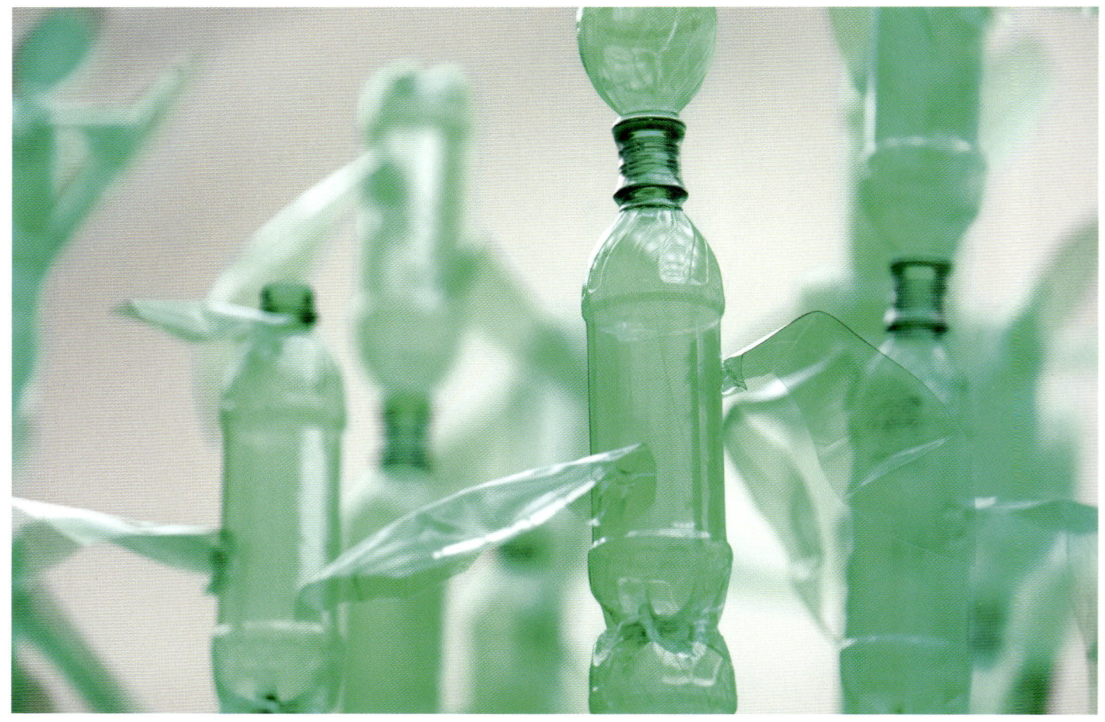

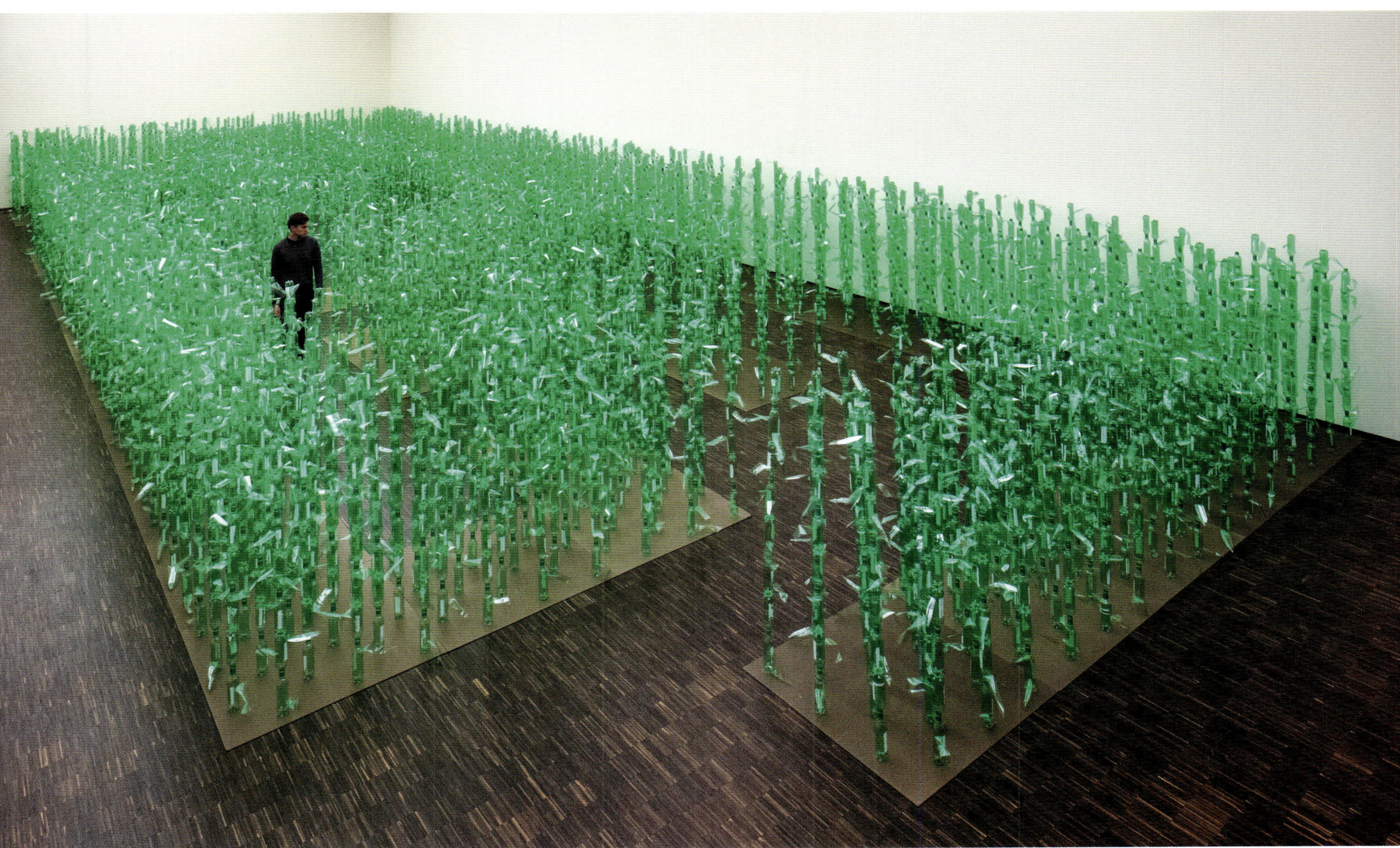

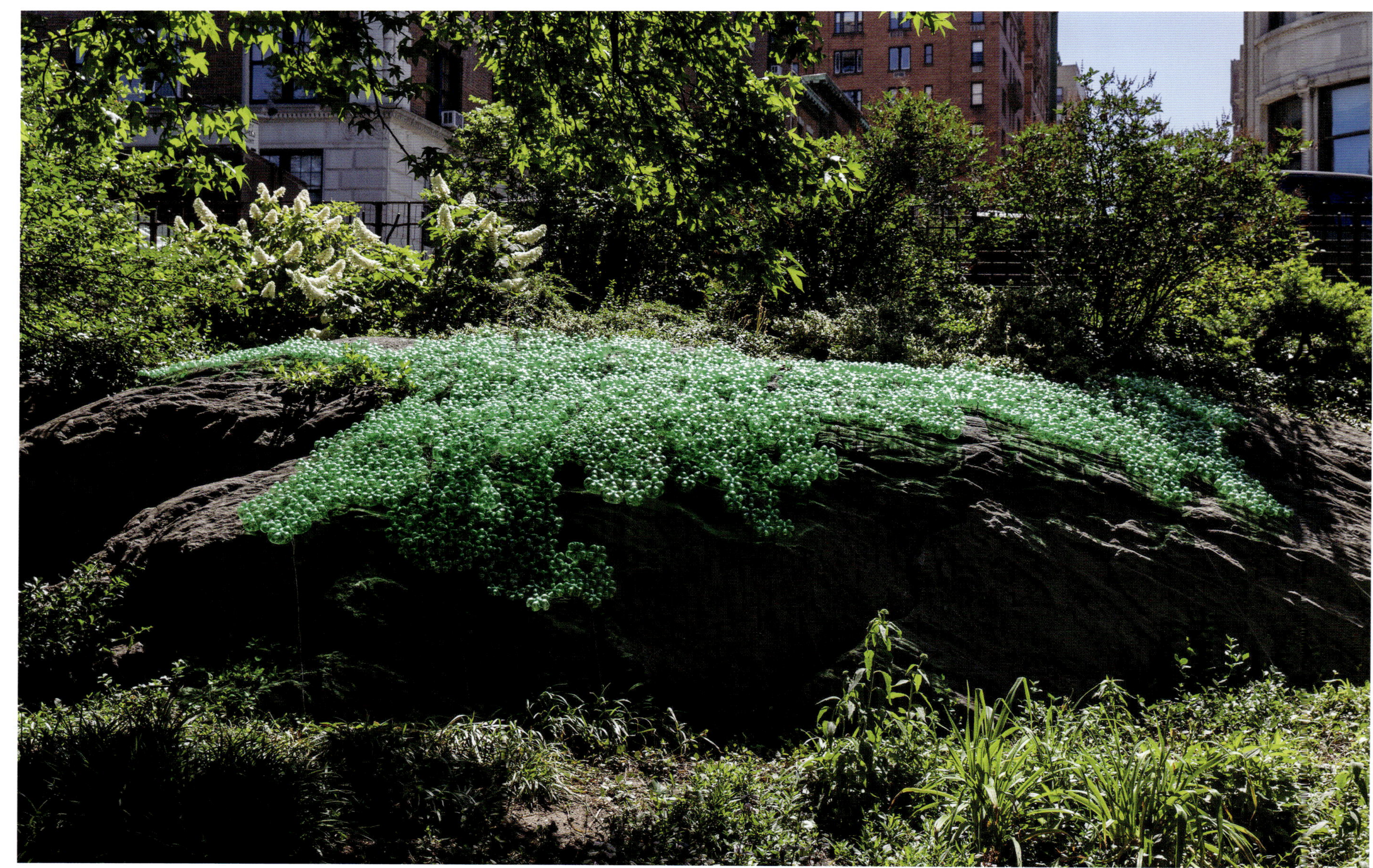

***Invasives*, 2020**
Mountain Dew soda bottles, rivets, cables
Outdoor installation at Riverside Park, NYC
Courtesy of Studio Jean Shin

***SOS*, 2021-2022**

Salvaged hemlock branches from Olana State Historic Site, leather remnants, upholstery tacks

Courtesy of Studio Jean Shin

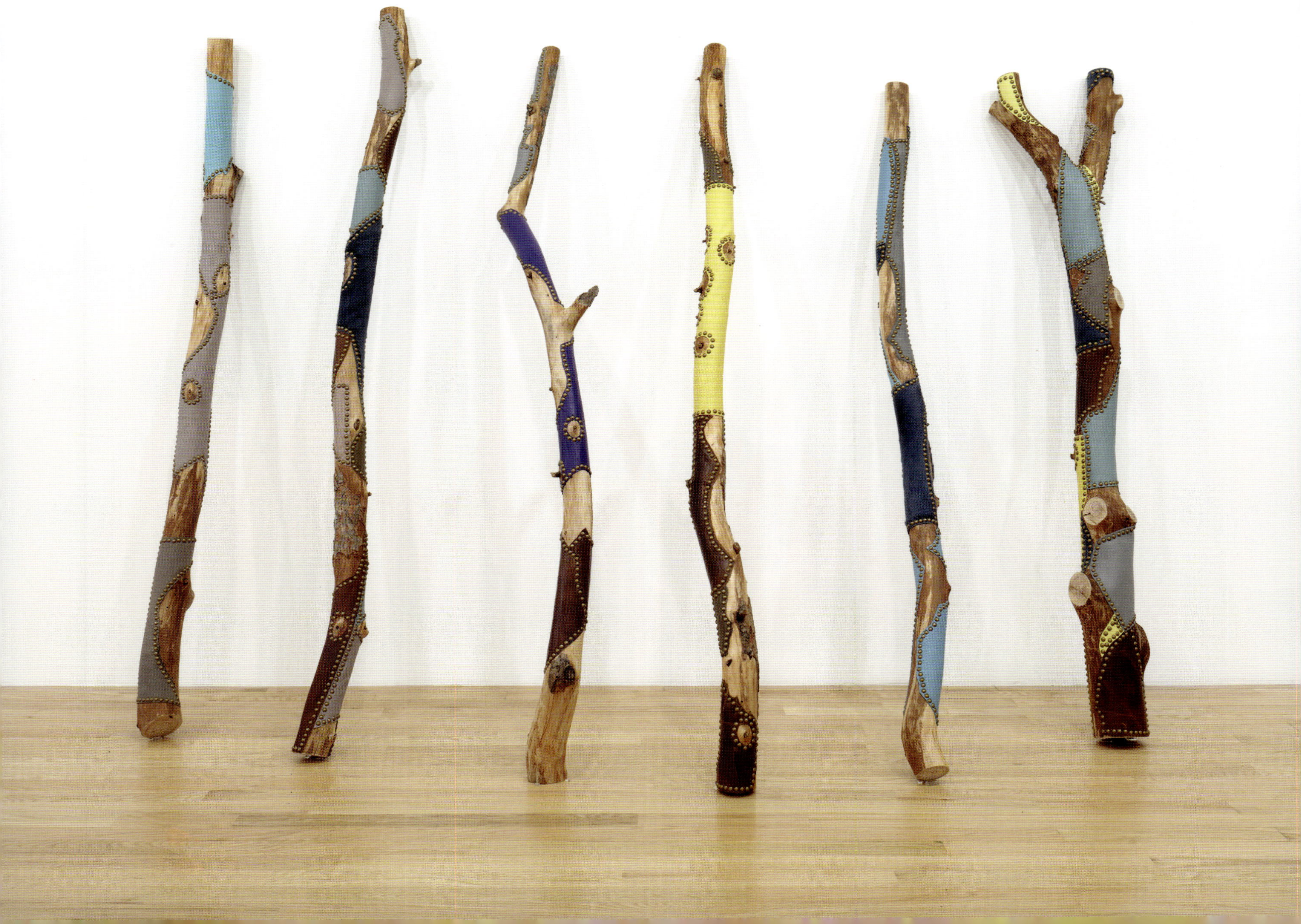

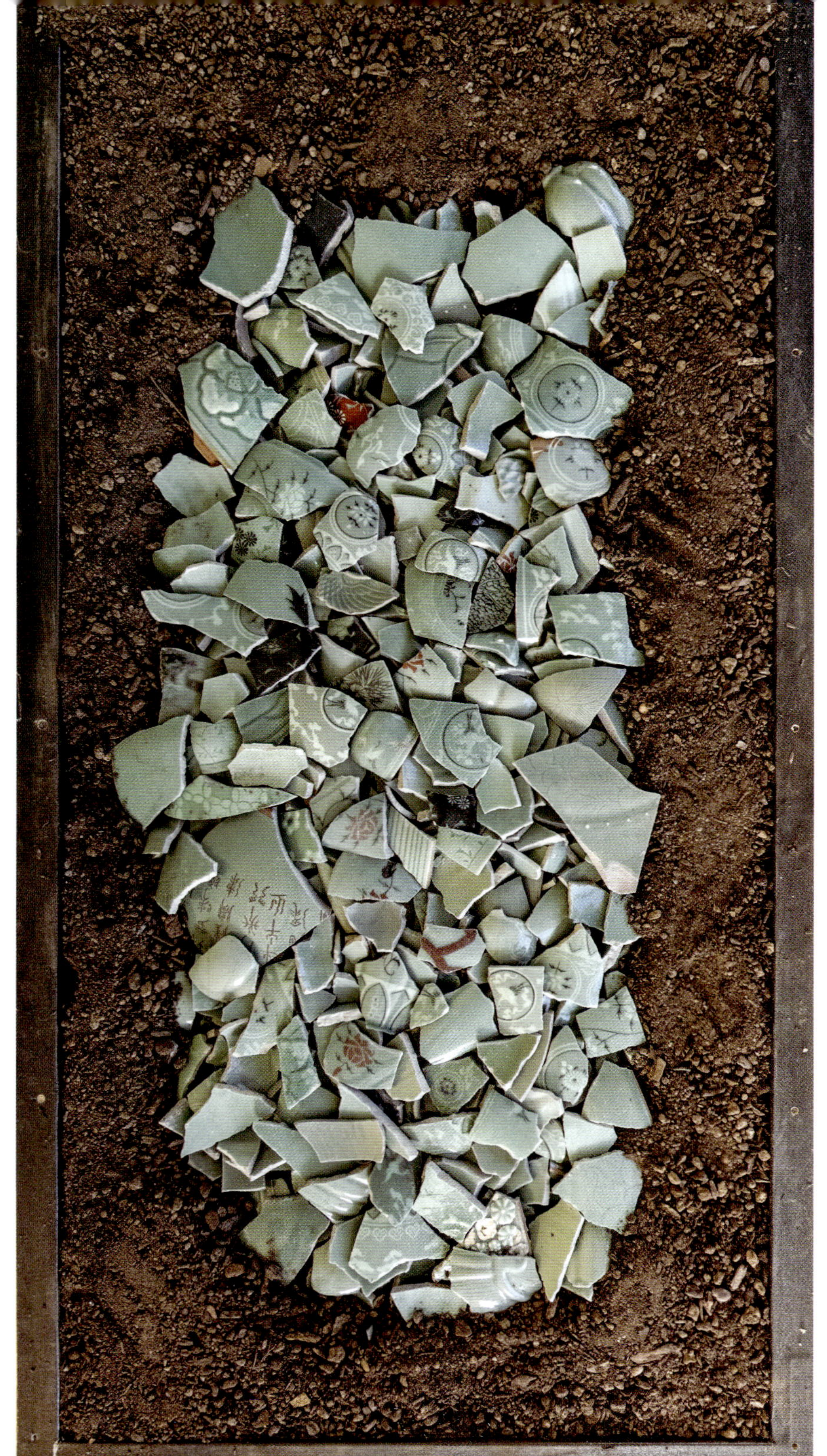

***Displaced: Crate #1*, 2023**

Dirt, Plexiglas, project remnants (Korean celadon pottery shards), studio debris, wooden crate

Courtesy of Studio Jean Shin

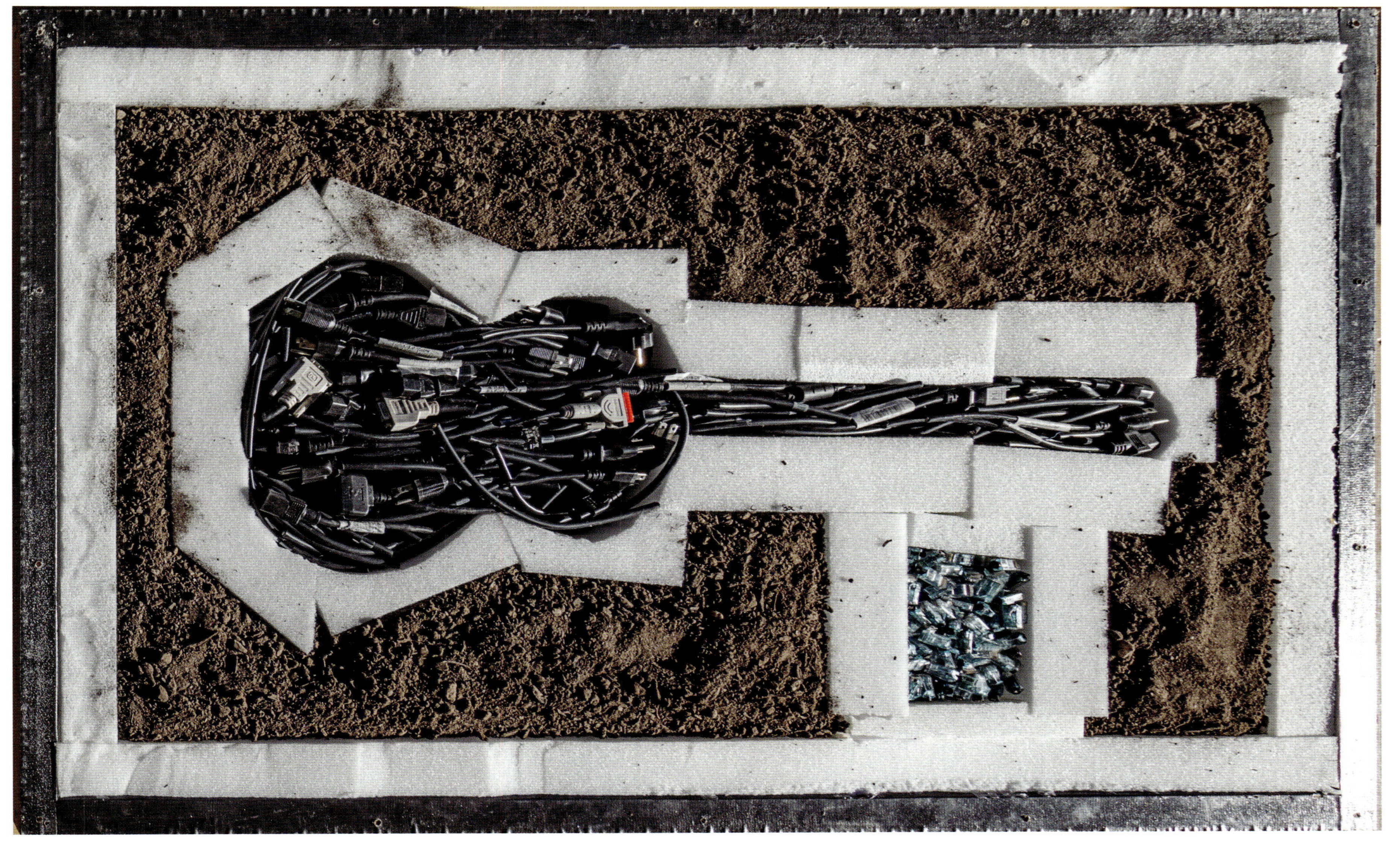

***Displaced: Crate #4*, 2023**
Dirt, Plexiglas, project remnants (salvaged cables, cords, and ethernet plugs), studio debris, wooden crate
Courtesy of Studio Jean Shin

A NOTE ON THE FABRICATORS

When talking with the artists for this book, many of them expressed gratitude for the fabricators that helped them achieve their vision for their project, and often credited them as collaborators and partners. MTA Arts & Design works with many fabricators—mosaic studios, glassmakers, metalworkers, ceramicists—to elevate the artists' work; some of these companies have worked on numerous commissions. Below is a list of some of these fabricators and the artists they collaborated with.

Mayer of Munich: Firelei Báez, Nick Cave, Marcel Dzama

Miotti Mosaics: Jane Dickson, Al Loving, Liliana Porter, Jean Shin

Tom Patti Designs: Jeffrey Gibson, Jean Shin

Mosaicos Venezianos de México: Eamon Ore-Giron

Frank Giorgini: Jean Shin

ACKNOWLEDGMENTS

This book would not have come together without the input and assistance of all the artists and their studios, and participating galleries. I would like to thank them all: Firelei Báez and Susan Grogan; Jeffrey Gibson and Hauser & Wirth Gallery, especially Christine McMonaghe and Emily Larson; Nick Cave, Bob Faust, and Jack Shainman Gallery, especially Brandon Foushee and Dylan Farley; Jane Dickson and Karma Gallery, especially Yvonne Zhou and Ella Wigram; Marcel Dzama and David Zwirner Gallery, especially Stephanie Stevens; The Estate of Al Loving, Magdalena Ramos Mullane, and Garth Greenan Gallery, especially Jem Stern; Portia Munson and P.P.O.W. Gallery, especially Eden Deering and Wendy Olsoff; Eamon Ore-Giron and James Cohan Gallery, especially Isabella St. Ivany, Emily Ruotolo, and Jayson Thompson; Liliana Porter; Jean Shin; and Tali Cherizli.

I would also like to thank those who have helped along the way with connections, support, and cheerleading: Michael Steinberg, Audree Anid, Julia Mechtler, Sarah Ilene Klein, Tszyu Sue Chen-Holmes, and especially David Chitayat, my biggest cheerleader.

ABOUT THE AUTHOR

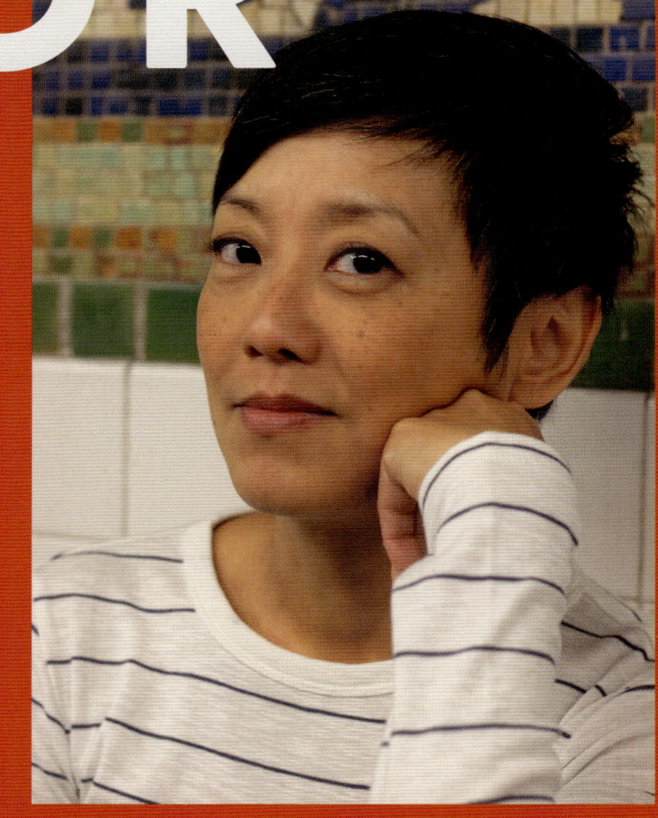

Photo by Abigail Ekue

Xhingyu Chen is an arts writer based in New York. She has been writing about contemporary art for two decades. A native New Yorker, she lived in Shanghai for over a decade, where she covered the local art scene for publications like the *New York Times*, *Art Asia Pacific*, *Sculpture Magazine*, *Yishu Journal*, and *Nukta Art*. Her first book, *Chinese Art: New Media 1990-2010*, was published in 2011. She continues to explore and write about art in the New York subway system on her Instagram, @ride_the_museum. She lives in Brooklyn with her husband and two art-loving kids.